Third Edition

SOCIAL WELFARE
Politics and Public Policy

Diana M. DiNitto
The University of Texas at Austin

PRENTICE HALL
Englewood Cliffs, New Jersey 07632

Library of Congress Cataloging-in-Publication Data

DiNitto, Diana M.
   Social welfare : politics and public policy / Diana M. DiNitto.—
3rd ed.

   Includes bibliographical references and indexes.
   ISBN 0-13-817065-7
   1. Public welfare—United States.   2. United States—Social
policy.   I. Title.
HV95.D56   1991
361.6'13'0973—dc20   90-46429

Editorial/production supervision: *Edith Riker/Bea Marcks*
Interior design: *Edith Riker*
Cover design: *Diane Conner*
Prepress buyer: *Debra Kesar*
Manufacturing buyer: *Mary Ann Gloriande*

For VINCENT, MARY, and DANIEL DiNITTO
From DIANA

© 1991, 1987, 1983 by Prentice-Hall, Inc.
A Division of Simon & Schuster
Englewood Cliffs, New Jersey 07632

Printed in the United States of America

10 9 8 7 6 5 4 3

ISBN   0-13-817065-7

Prentice-Hall International (UK) Limited, *London*
Prentice-Hall of Australia Pty. Limited, *Sydney*
Prentice-Hall Canada Inc., *Toronto*
Prentice-Hall Hispanoamericana, S.A., *Mexico*
Prentice-Hall of India Private Limited, *New Delhi*
Prentice-Hall of Japan, Inc., *Tokyo*
Simon & Schuster Asia Pte. Ltd., *Singapore*
Editora Prentice-Hall do Brasil, Ltda., *Rio de Janeiro*

CONTENTS

PREFACE

Social Welfare: Politics and Public Policy, Third Edition is intended to introduce students to the major social welfare policies and programs in the United States and to stimulate them to think about major conflicts in social welfare today. The book's focus is on *issues*, and it emphasizes that social welfare in America involves a series of *political* questions about what whould be done for groups such as the poor, the near-poor, and the nonpoor—or whether anything should be done at all.

Social Welfare: Politics and Public Policy describes the major social welfare programs—their histories, trends, and current problems and prospects. But more important, it tackles the difficult conflicts and controversies which surround these programs. Social welfare policy is *not* presented as a series of solutions to social problems. Instead, social policy is portrayed as public conflict over the nature and causes of social welfare problems; over what, if anything, should be done about them; over who should do it; and over who should decide about it.

The major programs—covered in this book include:

Social Security	Job Training Partnership Act
Unemployment Compensation	Mental Health
Supplemental Security Income	Care of the Elderly
Aid to Families with Dependent Children	Child Welfare Services
General Assistance	Legal Services
Food Stamps	Vocational Rehabilitation
School Lunches	Medicare
Community Action	Medicaid

All of them are described and analyzed, and alternative proposals and "reforms" are considered. Public policies that address gender inequality and the inequalities faced by members of various ethnic groups are also discussed.

This book is designed for undergraduate and beginning graduate courses in social welfare policy. It does not require prior knowledge of social welfare.

Many texts on social policy treat social insurance, public assistance, and social service programs *descriptively*; by so doing they tend to obscure important conflicts and issues. Other books treat these programs *prescriptively*; by so doing they imply that there is one "right" way to resolve social problems. *Social Welfare: Politics and Public Policy* views social policy as a *continuing political struggle* over the issues posed by poverty and other social welfare problems in society—different goals and objectives, competing definitions of problems, alternative approaches and strategies, multiple programs and policies, competing proposals for reform, and different ideas about how decisions should be made in social welfare policy.

Although Professor Thomas R. Dye no longer appears as a coauthor of the book, I wish to thank him for his comments on the third edition. Without him there would never have been a book at all. I also wish to acknowledge the anonymous reviewers who commented on this edition.

My visiting professorship at the University of Illinois at Urbana–Champaign was a great help in completing this edition, and I am always appreciative of the support given to me by my colleagues at the University of Texas at Austin. Thanks also go to Kate Daly, Jeannette Ingram, Kelly Larson, Rose Flandes, and Emma Dierkens for their assistance with word processing, and Bonnie Phillips-Barksdale and Andrew Guariguata for assistance with library research.

D. M. D.

1

POLITICS, RATIONALISM, AND SOCIAL WELFARE

POLITICS AND SOCIAL WELFARE POLICY

No one is really happy with the nation's welfare system—not the working taxpayers who must support it, not the social welfare professionals who must administer it, and certainly not the poor who must live under it. Since the passage of the Social Security Act of 1935, the federal government has tried to develop a rational social welfare system for the entire nation. Today, a wide variety of federal programs serves individuals who are aged, poor, disabled, sick, or have other social needs. *Income maintenance* (social insurance and public assistance) is the largest single item in the federal budget, easily surpassing national defense. The Department of Health and Human Services is the largest department of the federal government, and many additional welfare programs are administered by other departments. Yet even after fifty-five years of large-scale, direct federal involvement, social welfare policy remains a central issue in American politics.

Social welfare policy involves a series of *political* issues about what should be done about the poor, the near-poor, and the nonpoor—or whether anything should be done at all. The real problems in social welfare are not problems of organization, administration, or service delivery. Rather, they involve political conflicts over the nature and causes of poverty and inequality, the role of government in society, the burdens to be carried by taxpayers, the appropriate strategies for coping with social problems, the issues posed by specific social insurance and public assistance programs, the relative reliance to be placed on providing cash rather than services to the poor, the need for reform, and the nature of the decision-making process itself. In

1

short, social welfare is a continuing political struggle over the issues posed by poverty and inequality—and by other social problems in society.

Policy making is frequently portrayed as a *rational* process in which policy makers identify social problems, explore all of the alternative solutions, forecast all of the benefits and costs of each alternative solution, compare benefits to costs for each solution, and select the best ratio of benefits to costs. In examining social welfare policy, we shall explore the strengths and weaknesses of this rational model.

More important, we shall portray social welfare policy as a *political* process—as conflict over the nature and causes of poverty and other social problems and over what, if anything, should be done about them. Social welfare policy is political because of disagreements about the nature of the problems confronting society, about what should be considered *benefits* and *costs*, about how to estimate and compare benefits and costs, about the likely consequences of alternative policies, about the importance of one's own needs and aspirations in relation to those of others, and about the ability of government to do anything rationally. We shall see that the *political* barriers to *rational* policy making are indeed very great.

SCOPE OF SOCIAL WELFARE POLICY

Social welfare policy is anything government chooses to do, or not to do, that affects the quality of life of its people. Broadly conceived, social welfare policy includes nearly everything government does—from taxation, national defense, and energy conservation, to providing health care, housing, and public assistance. More elaborate definitions of social welfare policy are available;[1] most of these definitions refer to actions of government which have an "impact on the welfare of citizens by providing them with services or income."[2] Some scholars have insisted that government activities must have "a goal, objective, or purpose" in order to be labeled a "policy."[3] This definition implies a difference between governmental actions and an overall plan of action toward a specific goal. The problem, however, in insisting that government actions must have *goals* in order to be labeled as *policy* is that we can never be sure what the goal of a particular government action is. We generally assume that if a government chooses to do something, there must be a goal, objective, or purpose, but often we find that bureaucrats who helped write the law, lobbyists who pushed for its enactment, and members of Congress who voted for it all had different goals, objectives, and purposes in mind! The stated intentions of a law may also be quite different from what government agencies actually do. All we can really observe is what governments choose to do or not do.

Political scientists Heinz Eulau and Kenneth Prewitt supply still another definition of public policy. They write, "Policy is defined as 'standing decision' characterized by behavioral consistency and repetitiveness on the part of those who make it and those who abide by it."[4] Now certainly it would be a wonderful thing if government activities were characterized by "consistency and repetitiveness," but it is doubtful that we would ever find a public policy in government if we insisted on these criteria. As we shall see, much of what government does is *in*consistent and *non*repetitive. For practical purposes, we will limit much of our discussion to the policies of government which *directly* affect the income and services available to persons who are aged, poor, disabled, sick or otherwise vulnerable. We would discourage lengthy discussions of the definition of social welfare policy. These discussions are often futile, even exasperating, since few people can agree on a single definition of social policy. Moreover, these discussions divert attention away from the study of specific welfare policies.

Note that we are focusing not only on government action but also on government *inaction*—that is, what government chooses *not* to do. We contend that government inaction can have an impact on society that is just as important as government action.

The boundaries of social welfare policy are fuzzy. But clarifying our concerns and interests should be viewed as a challenge, not an obstacle. Specifically, we will be concerned with major government programs in

Income Maintenance
    Aid to Families with Dependent Children (AFDC)
    General Assistance (GA)
    Social Security
    Supplemental Security Income (SSI)
    Unemployment Compensation
    Workers' Compensation

Nutrition
    Food Stamps
    School Breakfasts
    School Lunches
    Special Supplemental Food Program for Women, Infants, and Children (WIC)
    Meals on Wheels

Health
    Medicaid
    Medicare
    Public Health

Social Services
    Community Action programs
    Community mental health
    Job Training Partnership Act (JTPA)
    Legal services
    Social services for children and families
    Social services for older Americans
    Vocational Rehabilitation

Some of these programs are called *public assistance* because people must be poor (according to legal standards) in order to receive benefits, benefits which are paid out of general revenue funds. Public assistance programs include AFDC, Food Stamps, Medicaid, SSI, School Lunches, and General Assistance. Other programs are called *social insurance* because they are designed to prevent poverty. People pay into these programs during their working years and are entitled to benefits whether poor or not. Social insurance programs include Social Security, Medicare, Unemployment Compensation, and Workers' Compensation. Still other programs are labeled *social service* programs because they provide care, counseling, training, or other forms of assistance to children, the elderly, disabled persons, and others. Child and family services, care for the elderly, community action, JTPA, legal services, mental health care, public health, and vocational rehabilitation are all examples of social services.

We shall endeavor, first of all, to *describe* these programs. But we shall also be concerned with the *causes* of social welfare policy—why policy is what it is. We want to learn about some of the social, economic, and political forces that shape social welfare policy in America. We shall be concerned with how social policies have developed and changed over time. We shall also be concerned with the *consequences* of welfare policies—their effects on target groups and on society in general. We shall consider some alternative policies, such as possible changes, reforms, improvements, or phaseouts. Finally, we shall be concerned with *political conflict* over the nature and causes of poverty and other social problems—and conflict over what, if anything, should be done about them.

SOCIAL WELFARE POLICY: A RATIONAL APPROACH

Ideally, social welfare policy ought to be rational. A policy is rational if the ratio between the values it achieves and the values it sacrifices is positive and higher than any other policy alternative. Of course, we should not measure benefits and costs in a narrow dollar-and-cents framework, while ignoring basic social values. The idea of rationalism involves the calculation of *all* social, political, and economic values sacrificed or achieved by a public policy, not just those that can be measured in dollars.

Rationalism has been proposed as an *ideal* approach to both studying and making public policy.* Indeed, it has been argued that rationalism provides a single *model of choice* that can be applied to all kinds of problems, large and small, public and private.[5] We do *not* contend that government policies are in fact rational, for they are not. Even so, the model remains important because it helps us to identify barriers to rationality. It assists us in posing the question: Why is policy making not a more rational process?

Let us examine the conditions for rational policy making more closely:

1. Society must be able to identify and define social problems and agree that there is a need to resolve these problems.
2. All of the values of society must be known and weighed.
3. All possible alternative policies must be known and considered.
4. The consequences of each policy alternative must be fully understood in terms of both costs and benefits, for the present and for the future, and for target groups and the rest of society.
5. Policy makers must calculate the ratio of benefits to costs for each policy alternative.
6. Policy makers must choose the policy alternative that maximizes *net* values—that is, the policy alternative that achieves the greatest benefit at the lowest cost.

---

* Other major theoretical approaches to the study of public policy include institutionalism, elite theory, group theory, systems theory, and incrementalism. For an introduction to these approaches, see Thomas R. Dye, *Understanding Public Policy,* 6th ed. (Englewood Cliffs, NJ: Prentice-Hall, 1987), especially Chapter 2.

Because this notion of rationality assumes that the values of *society as a whole* can be known and weighed, it is not enough to know the values of some groups and not others. There must be a common understanding of societal values. Rational policy making also requires *information* about alternative policies and the *predictive capacity* to foresee accurately the consequences of each alternative. Rationality requires the *intelligence* to calculate correctly the ratio of costs to benefits for each policy alternative. This means calculation of all present and future benefits and costs to both the target groups and nontarget groups in society. Finally, rationalism requires a *policy-making system* that facilitates rationality in policy formation. The Israeli political scientist Yehezkel Dror provides a diagram of such a system in Figure 1–1.

Identifying *target groups* means defining the segment of the population for whom the policy is intended—aged, poor, sick, or disabled individuals, abused children, or others in need. Then the desired effect of the program on the target groups must be determined. Is it to change their physical or economic condition—for example, to increase the cash income of the poor, to improve the housing conditions of ghetto residents, to improve the treatment of children, or to improve the health of the elderly? Or is the program designed to change their knowledge, attitudes, or behavior—for example, to provide job skills, to improve literacy, or to increase awareness of legal rights? If several different effects are desired, what are the priorities among them? What are the possible *unintended consequences* on target groups—for example, does public housing improve the physical environment for many blacks at the cost of increasing housing segregation between blacks and whites? What is the impact of a policy on the target group in proportion to that group's total need? A program that promises to meet a recognized national need—for example, to eradicate poverty—but actually meets only a small percentage of that need may generate great praise at first but bitterness and frustration later when it becomes known how insufficient the impact really is, relative to the need.

Policies are likely to have different effects on various segments of the population. Identifying important *nontarget groups* for a policy is an important but difficult process. For example, what is the impact of welfare reform proposals, such as a guaranteed annual income, on groups other than the poor—that is, on working-class families, government bureaucrats, social workers, and taxpayers? Rational policy making requires consideration of *spillover effects*. These nontarget effects may involve benefits as well as costs—for example, the benefits to the construction industry from public-housing projects or the benefits to farmers, food manufacturers, and grocery store owners from the Food Stamp program.

When will the benefits or costs be felt? Is the policy designed for short-term emergency situations or is it a long-term developmental effort? If it is short term, what will prevent bureaucrats from turning it into a long-term program, even after immediate needs are met? Many studies have shown that new or innovative programs have short-term positive effects—for example, Head Start and other education and job-training programs. However, the positive effects sometimes disappear as the novelty of and enthusiasm for new programs wear off. Other programs experience difficulties at first (for example, physicians and hospitals were initially reluctant to accept Medicare and Medicaid patients) but turn out to have *sleeper* effects (today, Medicare and Medicaid have achieved widespread acceptance).

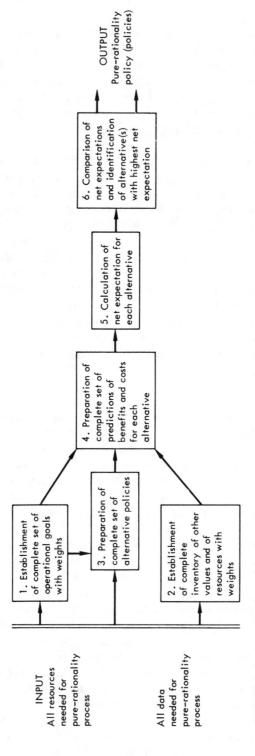

FIGURE 1-1 A rational model of a decision system. (Reprinted from Thomas R. Dye, *Understanding Public Policy*, 6th ed., Englewood Cliffs, N.J.: Prentice Hall, 1987, p. 33.)

Rational policy makers must measure benefits and costs in terms of general social well-being. Government agencies have developed various forms of cost-benefit analysis to identify the direct costs (usually, but not always, in dollars) of providing aid and assistance to the *average* family, worker, or job trainee. It is more difficult to identify and measure general units of social well-being. We need to know, for example, how to measure improved health, improved job skills, better nutrition, and greater employment opportunities. We are still struggling with better ways to measure many of these social values.

Actually, *comprehensive* rationality in public policy making may not really be rational. This apparent contradiction was noted many years ago by Herbert A. Simon, a Nobel Prize winner for his studies of the decision-making process in large organizations. It is so costly and time consuming to learn about *all* of the policy alternatives available to decision makers, to investigate *all* of the possible consequences of each alternative, and to calculate the cost-benefit ratio of *each* alternative that the improvement in the policy selected is not worth the extra effort required to make a comprehensive rational selection. Simon developed a theory of *bounded rationality*, which recognizes the practical limits to complete rationality. He wrote, "It is impossible for the behavior of a single isolated individual to reach *any high degree of rationality*. The number of alternatives to be explored is so great and the information to evaluate them so vast that even an approximation of objective rationality is hard to conceive."[6]

In contrast to completely rational decision making, the notion of bounded rationality means that policy makers consider a limited number of alternatives, estimate the consequences of these alternatives using the best available means, and select the alternative that appears to achieve the most important values without incurring unacceptable costs. Instead of maximizing the ratio of benefits to costs, policy makers search for a *satisfying* choice—a policy alternative that is good enough to produce the desired benefits at a reasonable cost. This means that policy makers do not try to create the best of all possible worlds but rather seek to get by, to come out all right, to avoid trouble, to compromise.

Rationalism, then, presents an ideal model of policy making—in social welfare and in other policy fields. But policy making in the real world is not usually a rational process. Policy making occurs in a political context which places severe limits on rationality.

SOCIAL WELFARE POLICY: A POLITICAL APPROACH

Social welfare policy is *political*. By political, we mean that social welfare policy arises out of the conflict over the nature of the problems confronting society and over what, if anything, should be done about them.

Politics has been described as the process which determines "who gets what, when, and how."[7] It is an activity through which people try to get more of whatever there is to get—money, jobs, prestige, prosperity, respect, and power itself. Politics, then, is conflict over the allocation of values in society, and this conflict is central to politics and policy making. "Politics arises out of conflicts, and it consists of the activities—for example, reasonable discussion, impassioned oratory, balloting, and street fighting—by which conflict is carried on."[8]

Why do we expect conflict in society over who gets what? Why can't we agree on *a theory of justice* according to which everyone would agree on what is fair for all members of society, particularly the poor, the aged, and the sick?[9] Why can't we have a harmonious, loving, caring, sharing, society of equals? Philosophers have pondered these questions for centuries. James Madison, perhaps the first American to write seriously about politics, believed that the causes of *faction* (conflict) are found in human diversity—"a zeal for different opinions concerning religion, concerning government, and many other points...[and] an attachment to different leaders ambitiously contending for preeminence and power." More importantly, according to Madison, "[t]he most common and durable source of faction has been the various and unequal distribution of property. Those who hold and those who are without property have ever formed distinct interests in society."[10] In short, differences among people, particularly in the sources and amount of their wealth, are the root cause of social conflict.

It is the task of government to regulate conflict. It does so

1. by establishing and enforcing general rules by which conflict is carried on,
2. by arranging compromises and balancing interests in public policy, and
3. by imposing settlements which the parties to a dispute must accept.

Governments must arrange settlements in the form of public policy—settlements that allocate values in such a way that they will be accepted by both *winners* and *losers,* at least temporarily. Finally, governments must impose these settlements by enforcing public policy and by promising rewards or threatening punishments.

From a political perspective, public policy is the outcome of conflicts in government over who gets what—and when and how they get it. A policy may be considered *politically* rational when it succeeds in winning enough support to be enacted into law, implemented by executive agencies, and enforced by the courts. Or it may be considered *politically* rational if it is supported by influential groups and believed to be popular among the voters. But this is not the same type of rationality that we described earlier in the rational model.

Indeed, the political approach raises serious questions about rationality in policy making. It suggests that:

1. There are *no social values* that are generally agreed upon, but only the values of specific groups and individuals, many of which are conflicting.
2. Problems cannot be defined because people do not agree on what the problems are. What is a problem to one group may be a benefit to another group.
3. Many conflicting costs and values cannot be compared or weighed. For example, how can we compare the value of individual dignity with the cost of a general tax increase?
4. Policy makers, even with the most advanced computerized analytic techniques, cannot predict the consequences of various policy alternatives or calculate their cost-benefit ratios when many diverse social, economic, and political values are involved.

5. The environment of policy makers, particularly the political system of power and influence, makes it virtually impossible to forecast the consequences of public policy or accurately weigh many social values, particularly those that do not have active or powerful proponents in or near government. The poor and the sick may have little access to governmental representation.

6. Policy makers are not necessarily motivated to make decisions on the basis of social values. Instead, they often seek to maximize their own rewards—power, status, reelection, wealth, and so on. Policy makers have their own needs, ambitions, and inadequacies, all of which can prevent them from performing in a highly rational manner.

7. Large, segmented government bureaucracies create barriers to coordinated policy making. It is difficult to bring all of the interested individuals, groups, and experts together at the point of decision. Governmental decision making is *disjointed.*

How can we bridge the differences between the ideal model of *rational* policy making and the realization that policy making is a *political* activity? Political scientist Charles E. Lindblom first presented an *incremental* model of policy making as a critique of the rational model.[11] Lindblom observed that government policy makers do *not* annually review the entire range of existing and proposed policies, or identify all of society's goals, or research the benefits and costs of all alternative policies to achieve these goals. They, therefore, do not make their selections on the basis of all relevant information. Limits of time, knowledge, and costs pose innumerable obstacles in identifying the full range of policy alternatives and in predicting their consequences. Political limitations prevent the establishment of clear-cut societal goals and the accurate calculation of cost-benefit ratios. The incremental model recognizes the impracticality of comprehensive rational policy making and describes a more *conservative* process of public decision making.

Incremental policy making considers existing policies, programs, and expenditures as a base. It concentrates attention on newly proposed policies and programs, on budgetary increases or decreases, and on other modifications to existing programs. Incrementalism is conservative in that policy makers generally accept the legitimacy of established policies and programs. The focus of attention is on proposed *changes* in those policies and programs. This narrows the attention of policy makers to a limited number of new initiatives and increases or decreases in the budget.

There are important political advantages to incrementalism in policy making. Conflict is reduced if the dispute can be confined to the question of increasing or decreasing existing budgets or to the question of modifying existing programs. Conflict would be greater if policy making focused on major policy shifts involving great gains or losses for various groups in society or on *all-or-nothing, yes-or-no* policy decisions. To have existing policies reconsidered every year would generate a great deal of conflict; it is easier politically to continue previously accepted policies.

Policy makers may also continue existing policies because of uncertainty about the consequences of completely new or different policies. Forecasting is never perfect. It is safer to stick with known programs when the consequences of new programs cannot be accurately predicted. Under conditions of uncertainty, policy makers continue past policies or programs whether they have proven effective or not. Only in a crisis do political decision makers begin to consider new and untried policies as preferable to existing ones. Thus, groups and individuals who seek more than incremental change in public policy usually try to generate a crisis atmosphere.

Policy makers also realize that individuals and organizations—executive agencies, congressional committees, and interest groups—accumulate commitments to existing policies and programs. For example, it is accepted wisdom in Washington that bureaucracies persist over time regardless of their utility, that they develop routines that are difficult to alter, and that individuals develop a personal stake in the continuation of organizations and programs. These commitments are serious obstacles to major change. It is easier politically for policy makers to search for alternatives which involve only a minimum of budgetary, organizational, or administrative change.

Finally, in the absence of generally agreed-upon social goals or values, it is politically expedient for governments to pursue a variety of different programs and policies simultaneously, even if some of them are overlapping or even conflicting. In this way, a wider variety of individuals and groups in society are *satisfied*. Comprehensive policy planning for specific social goals may maximize some people's values, but it may also generate extreme opposition from others. A government that pursues multiple policies may be politically more suitable to a pluralistic society comprising individuals with varying values.

THE POLICY-MAKING PROCESS

Policy making involves a combination of processes. These processes are not always clear-cut and distinguishable in the complex world of policy making, but we can identify them for purposes of analysis. They include:

1. *Identifying Policy Problems.* Publicized demands for government action can lead to the identification of policy problems.
2. *Formulating Policy Alternatives.* Policy proposals can be formulated through political channels by policy-planning organizations, interest groups, government bureaucracies, and the president and Congress.
3. *Legitimizing Public Policy.* Public policy is legitimized as a result of the public statements or actions of the president, Congress, or courts; this includes executive orders and budgets, laws and appropriations, rules and regulations, and decisions and interpretations, all of which have the effect of setting policy directions.
4. *Implementing Public Policy.* Public policy is implemented through the activities of public bureaucracies and the expenditure of public funds.
5. *Evaluating Policy.* Policies are evaluated formally and informally by government agencies, by outside consultants, by interest groups, by the mass media, and by the public.

This is a formal breakdown of the policy-making process used by many students of public policy.[12] What it says is that some groups succeed, usually through the help of the mass media, in capturing public attention for their own definition of a problem. Various government bureaucracies, private organizations, and influential individuals, then, propose solutions in terms of new laws or programs, new government agencies, or new public expenditures. These proposals twist their way through the labyrinths of government and eventually emerge (generally after many alterations and amendments) as laws and appropriations. Government bureaucracies are created to carry out these laws and spend these funds. Eventually, either through formal evaluation studies or informal feedback, the successes and failures of these laws, bureaucracies, and expenditures are examined.

All of this activity involves both rational problem solving and political conflict. This is true whether we are describing Social Security or the Food Stamp program, employment training or mental health care, child protective services or legal services. Both rational and political considerations enter into each stage of the policy-making process.

Agenda Setting

Deciding what is to be decided is the most important stage of the policy-making process. We might refer to this stage as *agenda setting*. Societal conditions not defined as problems never become policy issues. These conditions never get on the *agenda* of policy makers. Government does nothing, and conditions improve, remain the same, or worsen. On the other hand, if conditions in society are defined as problems, then they become policy issues, and government is forced to decide what to do.

Policy issues do not just happen. Creating an issue, dramatizing it, calling attention to it, and pressuring government to do something about it are important political tactics. These tactics are employed by influential individuals, organized interest groups, policy-planning organizations, political candidates and office holders, and perhaps most important, the mass media. These are the tactics of agenda setting.

Nondecisions

Preventing certain conditions in society from becoming policy issues is also an important political tactic. *Non-decision making* occurs when influential individuals or groups act to prevent the emergence of challenges to their own interests in society. According to political scientists Peter Bachrach and Morton Baratz:

> Nondecision-making is a means by which demands for change in the existing allocation of benefits and privileges in the community can be suffocated before they are even voiced; or kept covert; or killed before they gain access to the relevant decision-making arena; or failing all these things, maimed or destroyed in the decision-implementing stage of the policy process.[13]

Non-decision making occurs when powerful individuals, groups, or organizations act to suppress an issue because they fear that if public attention is focused on it, something which may not be in their best interest will be done. Non-decision making also occurs when political candidates, office holders, or administrative officials anticipate that powerful individuals or groups will not favor a particular idea and therefore do not pursue it. They do not want to rock the boat.

The Mass Media

The power of the mass media is its ability to set the agenda for decision making—to decide what problems will be given attention and what problems will be ignored.[14] Deciding what is *news* and who is *newsworthy* is a powerful political weapon. Television executives and producers, as well as newspaper and magazine editors, must decide what people, organizations, and events will be given public attention. Without media coverage, the general public would not know about many of the conditions or government programs affecting the poor or about alternative policies or programs. Without media coverage, these topics would not likely become objects of political discussion, nor would they likely be considered important by government officials even if they knew about them. Media attention can create issues and personalities. Media inattention can doom issues and personalities to obscurity.

The Budget

The budget is the single most important policy statement of any government. The expenditure side of the budget tells us who gets what in public money, and the revenue side of the budget tells us who pays the cost. There are few government activities or programs that do not require an expenditure of funds, and no public funds may be spent without legislative authority. The budgetary process provides a mechanism for reviewing government programs, assessing their costs, relating them to financial resources, and making choices among alternative expenditures. Budgets determine which policies and programs will be increased, decreased, allowed to lapse, initiated or renewed. The budget lies at the heart of all public policies.

In the federal government, the Office of Management and Budget (OMB), located in the Executive Office of the President, has the key responsibility for the preparation of the budget. The OMB begins preparation of a federal budget more than a year before the beginning of the fiscal year for which it is intended. (For example, work began in January 1989 on the budget for the fiscal year beginning October 1, 1990, and ending September 30, 1991.) Budget materials and general instructions go out from the OMB to departments and agencies, which are required to submit their budget requests for increases or decreases in existing programs and for new programs. With requests for spending from departments and agencies in hand, OMB begins its own budget review. Hearings are held for each agency. Top agency officials support their requests as convincingly as possible. On rare occasions, a dissatisfied department head may ask the OMB director to present the department's case directly to the president. As each January approaches, the president and the OMB director devote a great deal of time to the budget document, which is by then approaching its final stages of assembly. Finally, in January, the president sends *The Budget of the United States Government* to Congress. This will be the budget for the fiscal year beginning October 1 and ending September 30 of the following year. After the budget is in legislative hands, the president may recommend further amendments as needs dictate.

Congress has established separate House and Senate budget committees and a joint Congressional Budget Office to review the president's budget after its submission to Congress. These committees initially draft a concurrent resolution setting target totals to guide congressional actions on appropriations and revenue bills considered throughout the year. Thus, congressional committees considering specific budget appropriations have not only the president's recommendations to guide them but also the guidelines established by the budget committees. If an appropriations bill exceeds the target set by the earlier resolution, it is sent back to the budget committees for reconciliation.

Consideration of specific appropriations is a function of the appropriations committees in both houses. Each of these important committees has about ten fairly independent subcommittees which review the budget requests of particular agencies or groups with related functions. These subcommittees hold hearings in which department and agency officials, interest groups, and other witnesses testify about new and existing programs and proposed increases or decreases in spending. The appropriations subcommittees are very important, because neither the full committees nor Congress has the time or expertise to conduct in-depth reviews of programs and funding. Although the work of the subcommittees is reviewed by the full committee and the appropriations acts must be passed by the full Congress, in practice most subcommittee decisions are routinely accepted.

In overall programs and expenditures, however, it is rare that Congress ever makes more than a 5 percent change in the budget originally recommended by the president. Most appropriations are determined by executive agencies interacting with the OMB, and Congress usually makes only minor adjustments in the president's budget.

This description of the federal government's budget process may make it sound like it is the most rational aspect of policy making, but it is no less political than any of the other aspects. Methods such as "planning, programming and budgeting systems" and "zero based budgeting" have been introduced in attempts to make budgeting a more rational process, but in the long run

> If politics is regarded in part as conflict over whose preferences shall prevail in the determination of national policy, then the budget records the outcomes of this struggle. . . . Presidents, political parties, administrators, Congressmen, interest groups, and interested citizens vie with one another to have their preferences recorded in the budget. The victories and defeats, the compromises and the bargains, the realms of agreement and the spheres of conflict in regard to the role of the national government in our society all appear in the budget. In the most integral sense the budget lies at the heart of the political process.[15]

Implementation

Policy implementation includes all of the activities which result from the official adoption of a policy. Policy implementation is what happens after a law is passed. We should never assume that the passage of a law is the end of the policy-making process. Sometimes laws are passed and nothing happens! Sometimes laws are passed and executive agencies, presuming to act under these laws, do a great deal more than Congress ever intended. Political scientist Robert Lineberry writes:

The implementation process is not the end of policy-making, but a *continuation of policy-making by other means*. When policy is pronounced, the implementation process begins. What happens in it may, over the long run, have more impact on the ultimate distribution of policy than the intentions of the policy's framers.[16]

Specifically, policy implementation involves:

1. The creation, organization, and staffing of new agencies to carry out the new policy, or the assignment of new responsibilities to existing agencies and staff;
2. The development of specific directives, rules, regulations, or guidelines to translate new policies into courses of action; and
3. The direction and coordination of personnel and expenditures toward the achievement of policy objectives.

The best laid plans of policy makers often do not work. Before a policy can have any impact, it must be implemented. And what governments *say* they are going to do is not always what they end up doing.

Traditionally, the implementation of public policy was the subject matter of public administration. And traditionally, administration was supposed to be free of politics. Indeed, the separation of *politics* from *administration* was once thought to be the cornerstone of a scientific approach to administration. But today it is clear that politics and administration cannot be separated. Opponents of policies do not end their opposition after a law is passed. They continue their opposition in the implementation phase of the policy process by opposing attempts to organize, fund, staff, regulate, direct, and coordinate the program. If opponents are unsuccessful in delaying or halting programs in implementation, they may seek to delay or halt them in endless court battles. In short, conflict is a continuing activity in policy implementation.

The federal bureaucracy makes major decisions about the implementation of public policy. There are over two million civilian employees of the federal government. This huge bureaucracy has become a major base of power in America—independent of Congress, the president, the courts, or the people. The bureaucracy does more than simply fill in the details of congressional policies, although this is one power of bureaucratic authority. Bureaucracies also make important policies on their own by (1) proposing legislation for Congress to pass; (2) writing rules, regulations, and guidelines to implement laws passed by Congress; and (3) deciding specific cases in the application of laws or rules.

In the course of implementing public policy, federal bureaucracies have decided such important questions as the safety of nuclear power plants, the extent to which women and members of ethnic minority groups will benefit from affirmative-action programs in education and employment, whether opposition political parties or candidates will be allowed on television to challenge a presidential speech or press conference, and whether welfare agencies will search Social Security Administration files to locate nonsupporting parents.

The decisions of bureaucracies can be overturned by Congress or the courts if sufficient opposition develops. But most bureaucratic decisions go unchallenged.

ILLUSTRATION: THE PUBLIC'S AGENDA FOR GOVERNMENT SPENDING

Americans are not hesitant to voice their opinion on government spending. They are understandably concerned about where their tax dollars go, and they express concern about the country's large annual budget deficits. These deficits (about $220 billion in 1990) mean that the federal government is spending far more than the revenues it collects each year. The problem is analogous to what happens when you continually spend more than your income each month. The amount you owe accumulates, and your debt grows larger and larger. In spite of President Reagan's desire to rein in the federal budget, the national debt grew much faster during his presidency than during any other administration. Annual deficits have accumulated into a national debt that now stands at about $3 trillion!

Congress made a vigorous attempt to prevent the federal government from continuing to operate in the red by passing the Balanced Budget and Emergency Deficit Reduction Act of 1985. This measure, known as Gramm-Rudman-Hollings, was named for its sponsors, Senators Phil Gramm (R-Texas), Warren Rudman (R-New Hampshire), and Ernest Hollings (D-South Carolina). The act calls for across-the-board cuts in defense and many domestic programs if Congress fails to meet specific deficit reduction goals. More stringent deficit cutting measures were enacted in 1990.

In 1981, a Gallup poll based on a scientifically selected sample of Americans showed that 51 percent of Americans thought defense spending was inadequate, while 22 percent thought it was about right, and 15 percent thought it was excessive.[a] But since that time, public opinion has changed. A 1988 Gallup poll showed that 42 percent thought that defense spending should be kept the same, 35 percent believed it should be reduced, and 17 percent supported an increase.

Social welfare expenditures are an especially critical part of the federal budget because these costs make up the largest portion of the budget. The following Gallup poll question and accompanying table (see page 16) compares public opinion on spending for defense, education, and some social welfare programs.

Two-thirds of those surveyed say they are supportive of increased spending for medical and health care and for public education. There is also considerable support for more money for food programs. Far fewer people advocate increased spending for defense. Even within subgroups of the population, this distribution of opinions is relatively consistent. For example, on the question of health-care spending, 70 percent of women and 64 percent of men support an increase. In general, the viewpoints of women and men do not differ much on this issue. Interestingly, people sixty-five years of age and older were slightly *less* likely to favor an increase in health-care spending than younger people. Sixty-one percent of older Americans compared to 67–69 percent of those in younger age groups favored an increase. Blacks and whites differed by a greater margin—84 percent of blacks compared to 64 percent of whites favored an increase. Those with less than a high school education favored increases more than those with higher levels of education—for example, 74 percent of high school graduates compared with 62 percent of college graduates. Democrats were more likely to favor an increase than Independents and Republicans. Seventy-five percent of Democrats, 67 percent of Independents, and 59 percent of Republicans favored an increase. Of those in the lowest income group (earning under $15,000 a year), 71 percent supported increases compared to 61 percent of those in the highest income group (earning $50,000 and over a year).

a. *The Gallup Report,* Report No. 274 (July 1988), p. 4–9.

Now I am going to ask you a question about government spending. In answering, please bear in mind that sooner or later all government spending has to be taken care of from the money you and other Americans pay in taxes. As I read each program, tell me if the amount of money now spent on that purpose should be increased, kept at the present level, reduced, or ended altogether:

	INCREASED	KEPT SAME	REDUCED	ELIMINATED	NO OPINION
Improving medical and health care for Americans generally	67%	24	3	1	5
Federal money to improve the quality of public education	66	22	6	1	5
Providing food programs for low-income families	44	35	13	2	6
Total spending for defense and military purposes	17	42	34	1	6

Fewer Americans favor increases in food programs for low-income families. Women again approved of increases somewhat more frequently than men, 47 and 40 percent, respectively, while 32 percent of women and 38 percent of men felt spending should be kept the same. Younger people were also somewhat more receptive to increases than older people. Fifty-one percent of those aged eighteen to twenty-nine favored increases as compared to 42 percent of those fifty and older. Blacks were again more receptive to increased spending for food programs than whites, 65 and 41 percent, respectively, and those with less than a high school education were more supportive than college graduates (53 versus 36 percent). Republicans (32 percent) were least likely to support increases. Those with annual incomes of less than $15,000 also favored increases more than those with incomes over $50,000 (52 versus 30 percent). Within each of these subgroups, respondents were more likely to favor maintaining current spending levels than reducing or eliminating spending. Despite what people may think about large disparities between Democrats and Republicans and other subgroups such as the rich and the poor, there is a considerable agreement on how Americans feel about government spending.

As with health-care spending, there is a great deal of agreement that spending for education should also be increased. There is far less support for increased defense and military spending. The greatest support among all groups is for keeping defense spending at its current level. Nineteen percent of men and 15 percent of women support increases in this category, while 36 percent of men and 32 percent of women want spending kept the same. Twenty percent of those in the thirty-to-forty-nine-year-old age bracket favored increases compared with 17 percent of younger people and 14 percent of older people. Seventeen percent of both blacks and whites want increases, while 43 and 41 percent respectively want to keep defense spending at current levels. Twenty-two percent of high school graduates favored increases compared with 19 percent of those with less education and 12 percent of college graduates. Twenty-one percent of Republicans favored increases compared with 15 percent of both Democrats and Independents.

The results of public opinion polls which generally take only a few minutes of the respondents' time are interesting and supposedly quite accurate in reflecting the nation's opinions, but they do not tell us much about *why* people answer the way they do. Some researchers have used more in-depth methods to study public opinion on social welfare issues. For example, one 1988 study used three-hour sessions in which participants who were representative of the population, both in terms of their personal characteristics and their geographical location, viewed video tapes about social welfare programs and possible reforms and then participated in discussion groups.[b]

The participants were then asked a number of questions about social welfare programs. There was clearly dissatisfaction with the current AFDC program for poor families. Only 35 percent thought the program was good. Sixty-four percent thought payments went to people who should not get them, and 74 percent said AFDC perpetuates poverty. The participants seemed to feel negatively about AFDC because it does not do enough to require recipients to work and because it gives cash to poor people. Reform proposals that stressed work and

b. Jon Doble and Keith Melville, "The Public's Social Welfare Mandate," *Public Opinion* (January/February 1989), pp. 45–49, 59.

economic independence were favored by most participants, especially by the near-poor (those who earned $10,000 to $20,000). While the more conservative study subjects supported work measures in order to get tough with the lazy, liberals supported them because of the additional services that would be provided to the poor. Participants were divided on their willingness to pay more taxes to see AFDC improved; about half said they would pay an extra $25 a year while the other half said they would not support increased costs.

Respondents were less familiar with early childhood intervention programs addressed in the study (these included WIC, a nutrition program for young children, and Head Start, an educational program), but there was a high level of support for these programs among those who did know of them. There was considerable willingness to pay more taxes to support Head Start. More than 25 percent of the respondents said they would pay another $50 in taxes a year for this purpose. The response to increased taxes for WIC was positive but not as enthusiastic, primarily because a considerable number of respondents worried that it may encourage more pregnancies.

When it came to helping the working poor, there was stronger support for increasing the minimum wage than offering welfare. While there were considerable differences in opinion about *how* to help the working poor, a consensus did emerge about providing health care. Eighty-one percent of the participants believe that health care should be a right, regardless of income. Fifty-five percent said they would pay $25 a year more in taxes to see the government provide health care for the working poor, but this is a relatively small sum considering the high costs of health care.

Respondents were very concerned about long-term health care for the elderly and disabled, because most recognized that a serious disabling condition could send many of us into bankruptcy. The growing consensus among Americans is that this type of care should be a top priority for government intervention; however, only 11 percent of those in this study were willing to pay $125 more a year in taxes for this purpose. Reluctance to pay more was attributed to the high costs of health care. Instead, participants favored some cooperative form of assistance, with the individual and the government sharing the responsibility.

As public opinion polls on social welfare generally indicate, Americans voice support for an expanded social welfare agenda for the country, but they are not willing to pay much more for it. This contradiction is borne out everyday in the political struggles over welfare reform. And while public opinion is important, it frequently does not determine the social welfare agenda, even in a democracy. In the following chapters we look more closely at politics and social welfare programs.

SUMMARY

Although there are elements of rationalism in policy making, the policy process is largely political. Our abilities to develop policies rationally are limited because we cannot agree on what constitutes social problems and on what, if anything, should be done to alleviate these problems. We also hesitate to take bold, new steps in our current welfare system because we fear making large, costly errors that may be difficult to reverse.

Reducing the national debt, which now stands at about $3 trillion, is a major concern of government, but raising taxes is usually not a popular solution to such problems. And while there is public support for increasing spending for health care, public education, and nutrition programs, Americans are still not willing to pay much more in taxes to see these goals met. These inconsistencies also contribute to a system in which public policy is made incrementally. The wheels of progress move slowly when it comes to social welfare policy making.

Social welfare policy development and implementation are much more a political "art and craft"[17] than a rational science. It is not enough for human-service professionals to know the needs of people and to want to provide services to help them. Policy advocates must both understand the political process and be adept at working within it if they are to have a voice in shaping social policy.

NOTES

1. See, for example, David G. Gil, "A Systematic Approach to Social Policy Analysis," *Social Service Review* 44 (December 1970), 411–26.
2. T.H. Marshall, *Social Policy* (London: Hutchinson University Library, 1955), p. 7; also cited in Neil Gilbert and Harry Specht, *Dimensions of Social Welfare Policy,* 2d ed. (Englewood Cliffs, NJ: Prentice-Hall, 1986), pp. 2 and 4. The distinction between *social policy* and *social welfare policy* is discussed in George Rohrlich, "Social Policy and Income Distribution," in Robert Morris, ed., *Encyclopedia of Social Work,* 16th ed. (New York: National Association of Social Workers, 1971), pp. 1385–86.
3. See Carl T. Friedrich, *Man and His Government* (New York: McGraw-Hill, 1963), p. 70; Harold Lasswell and Abraham Kaplan, *Power and Society* (New Haven, Conn.: Yale University Press, 1970), p. 71.

4. Heinz Eulau and Kenneth Prewitt, *Labyrinths of Democracy* (Indianapolis: Bobbs Merrill, 1973), p. 465.
5. Edith Stokey and Richard Zeckhauser, A Primer of Policy Analysis (New York: W.W. Norton, 1978).
6. Herbert A. Simon, *Administrative Behavior* (New York: Macmillan, 1945), p. 79. See also his *Models of Man* (New York: John Wiley, 1957), and *The Sciences of the Artificial* (New York: John Wiley, 1970). Simon was trained as a political scientist; he won the Nobel Prize in economics in 1978.
7. Harold D. Lasswell, *Politics: Who Gets What, When, How* (New York: Free Press, 1936).
8. Edward C. Banfield and James Q. Wilson, *City Politics* (Cambridge: Harvard University Press, 1963), p. 7.
9. John Rawls, *A Theory of Justice* (Cambridge: Harvard University Press, 1972).
10. James Madison, *The Federalist, No. X* (November 23, 1787). Reprinted in *The Federalist of the New Constitution* (London: J. M. Dent & Sons, 1911), pp. 41–48.
11. Charles E. Lindblom, "The Science of 'Muddling Through,'" *Public Administration Review* 19 (Spring 1959), pp. 79–88.
12. See Charles O. Jones, *An Introduction to the Study of Public Policy*, 2nd ed. (Boston: Duxbury Press, 1978); Thomas R. Dye, *Understanding Public Policy*, 6th ed. (Englewood Cliffs, N.J.: Prentice-Hall, 1987).
13. Peter Bachrach and Morton S. Baratz, *Power and Poverty: Theory and Practice* (New York: Oxford University Press, 1970), p. 44.
14. Thomas R. Dye and Harmon Zeigler, *American Politics in the Media Age*, 2nd ed. (Monterey, Cal.: Brooks/Cole Publishing Co., 1986), especially Chapter 5.
15. Aaron B. Wildavsky, *The Politics of the Budgetary Process*, 3rd ed. (Boston: Little, Brown, 1979), pp. 4–5.
16. Robert L. Lineberry, *American Public Policy* (New York: Harper & Row, 1977), p. 71.
17. Aaron Wildavsky, *The Art and Craft of Policy Analysis* (Boston: Little, Brown, 1979).

2

GOVERNMENT
AND
SOCIAL WELFARE

HISTORICAL PERSPECTIVES ON SOCIAL WELFARE

Social welfare policy as we know it today dates back to the beginning of the seventeenth century in Elizabethan England. Colonists who settled in the New World brought with them many of the English welfare traditions. In the colonies as in England, the earliest sources of welfare aid for the destitute were families, friends, and churches.[1] Eventually local and then state governments intervened as a last resort. However, the twentieth century brought an increased number of social welfare problems for Americans. The magnitude of these problems caused the federal government to enact its own welfare legislation during the New Deal era of the 1930s. With the Great Society programs of the 1960s—another large-scale attempt on the part of the federal government to alleviate poverty and suffering—the federal government's role in social welfare continued to grow.

During the 1980s, however, a different response to hardship in America emerged. Concerned with growing costs and disillusioned with the perceived failure of many welfare programs, President Reagan's administration attempted to limit the federal government's role in social welfare, by shifting more of the responsibilities for these services back on state governments and the private sector.

In the following pages, we briefly review some major events in the history of social welfare, discuss factors which have contributed to the growth of welfare programs in the United States, and consider initiatives under the Reagan and Bush administrations to address social welfare problems.

Elizabethan Poor Law

In the Old World, the first sources of welfare assistance—family, friends, the community—provided mutual aid. Aid was mutual because people relied on one another. If a family's food crop failed or the breadwinner became ill and was unable to work, brothers, sisters, or neighbors pitched in, knowing that they would receive the same assistance if they should need it one day. Later, it became the duty of the church and of wealthy feudal lords to help the needy.[2] During much of the Middle Ages, emphasis was placed on doing charitable works as a religious duty.[3] Attitudes toward the poor were benevolent. Those destitute through no fault of their own were treated with dignity and respect and were helped through the hard times.[4]

These early systems of aid were informal systems. There were no formal eligibility requirements, no application forms to complete, and no background investigations. But as the structure of society became more complex, so did the system of providing welfare assistance.

The first laws designed to curb poverty were passed in England during the fourteenth and fifteenth centuries. In 1349 the Black Death (bubonic plague) drastically reduced the population of the country. King Edward III responded with the Statute of Laborers to discourage vagrancy and begging; all able-bodied persons were ordered to work, and the giving of alms was forbidden.[5]

Changes in the structure of society eventually forced the Elizabethan government to intervene in providing welfare. The Industrial Revolution that occurred in England meant a shift from an agrarian-based economy to an economy based on the wool industry. People left their home communities to seek industrial employment in the cities. The feudal system of life fell apart as the shift away from agriculture and toward industry was completed. Government was becoming more centralized and played a stronger role in many aspects of society, including social welfare. At the same time, the role of the church in welfare was diminishing.[6]

The interplay of new social forces—the breakdown of the feudal system, the Industrial Revolution, and the reduction of the labor force—brought about the Elizabethan Poor Law of 1601,[7] the first major event in the Elizabethan government's role in providing social welfare benefits. The law was passed mostly as a means of *controlling* those poor who were unable to locate employment in the new industrial economy and who might cause disruption.[8] Taxes were levied to finance the new welfare system. Rules were harsh. Children whose parents were unable to support them faced apprenticeship. Able-bodied men dared not consider remaining idle.

Distinguishing the *deserving* from the *nondeserving* poor was an important part of the Elizabethan Poor Law. Affluent members of society did not want to be burdened with assisting any but the most needy. The deserving poor were orphaned children, those who were lame or blind, and workers unemployed through no fault of their own. The nondeserving poor were vagrants or drunkards—those considered lazy, shiftless, and unwilling to work. *Outdoor* relief was help provided to some deserving poor in their own homes. *Indoor* relief was also provided to those unable to care for themselves, usually in almshouses, which were institutions that housed the poor. The nondeserving poor were sent to workhouses, where they were forced to do menial work in return for only the barest of life's necessities.[9]

Stringent residency requirements had to be met by all recipients. Welfare aid was administered by local units of government called parishes. Parishes were specifically instructed to provide aid only to persons from their own jurisdictions. There was little sympathy for transients.

Early Relief in the United States

Many aspects of the Elizabethan welfare system were adopted by American colonists. For example, residency requirements were strictly enforced through the policies of *warning out* and *passing on*.[10] Warning out meant that newcomers were urged to move on to other towns if it appeared that they were not financially responsible. More often, passing on was used to escort the transient poor back to their home communities. These practices continued well into the nineteenth century. In one year alone, eighteen hundred people were transported from one New York community to another as a result of these policies.

Life was austere for the colonists. The business of making America livable was a tough job, and the colonists were by no means well-off. "Many of them were paupers, vagrants, or convicts shipped out by the English government as indentured servants."[11] Life in the colonies, while better for many, still brought periods when sickness or other misfortune might place a person in need.

The colonists used four methods to assist the needy. *Auctioning* the poor to the family that was willing to care for them at the lowest cost was the least popular method. A second method was to put the poor and sick under the supervision of a couple who was willing to care for them for the least cost possible. The third method, *outdoor relief,* was provided to most of the needy. And the fourth method was the use of almshouses. Many claimed almshouses were the best method of aid because of the quality of medical care they provided to the sick and elderly. Almshouses in the cities provided a much higher level of care than rural almshouses, which were often in deplorable condition and little more than rundown houses operated by a farm family. Politicians, almshouse administrators, and doctors seemed pleased with the progress they had made in assisting the needy during the eighteenth and nineteenth centuries.

The Great Depression and the New Deal

From 1870 to 1920, America experienced a period of rapid industrialization and heavy immigration. Private charities, churches, and big city political machines and bosses assisted the needy during this period. The political machine operated by trading baskets of food, bushels of coal, and favors for the votes of the poor. To finance this primitive welfare system, the machine offered city contracts, protection, and privileges to business interests, which in return paid off in cash. Aid was provided in a personal fashion without red tape or delays. Recipients did not feel embarrassed or ashamed, for after all, "they were trading something valuable—their votes—for the assistance they received."[12]

As social problems mounted, leading to increased crowding, unemployment, and poverty in the cities, the states began to take a more active role in welfare. *Mothers' aid* and *mothers' pension* laws were passed by state governments to assist children in families where the father was deceased or absent. Other pension programs were established to assist the poor, aged, blind, and disabled. Federal government involvement in welfare was not far away.

The Great Depression, one of the bleakest periods in American history, followed the stock market crash of October 1929. Prices dropped dramatically, and unemployment was rampant. By 1932, one out of every four individuals was without a job, and one out of every six was on welfare. Americans who had always worked lost their jobs and depleted their savings or lost them when banks folded. Many were forced to give up their homes and farms because they could not continue to meet the mortgage payments. Economic catastrophe struck deep into the ranks of the middle classes. Many of the unemployed and homeless were found sleeping on steps and park benches because they had nowhere else to go.[13]

The events of the Great Depression dramatically changed American thought. The realization that poverty could strike so many forced Americans to consider large-scale economic reform. President Franklin Delano Roosevelt began to elaborate the philosophy of the New Deal that would permit government to devote more attention to the public welfare than did the philosophy of *rugged individualism* so popular in the earlier days of the country. The New Deal was not a consistent or unifying plan; instead it was a series of improvisations which were often adopted suddenly, and some of them were even contradictory. Roosevelt believed that the government should act humanely and compassionately toward those suffering from the depression. The objectives of the New Deal were "relief, recovery, and reform" and Roosevelt called for "full persistent experimentation. If it fails, admit it frankly and try something else. But above all try something. The millions who are in want will not stand by silently forever while the things to satisfy their needs are in easy reach."[14] Americans came to accept the principle that the entire community has a responsibility for welfare.

Included in the New Deal were a number of social welfare provisions. The Social Security Act of 1935, the cornerstone of social welfare legislation today, authorized a Social Security retirement benefits program which was administered by the federal government. Work programs established through projects such as the Works Progress Administration (WPA) and the Civilian Conservation Corps (CCC) provided jobs for many Americans. Federal grants-in-aid programs to states and communities were initiated to provide financial assistance to some of the poor. These groups were dependent children, the elderly, and those who were blind. Other programs included unemployment compensation, employment services, child welfare, public housing, urban renewal, and vocational education and rehabilitation.

The War on Poverty

From 1935 through the 1950s, welfare programs did not change very much. Eligibility requirements were loosened, payments were increased, a few new categories of recipients were added, and some medical care was provided to welfare recipients, but there were few major changes in the system of providing social welfare benefits. But the 1960s brought unusual times for Americans. The beginning of this decade was a period of prosperity for most, but this made the dichotomy between the "haves" and "have nots" more apparent. As a result, civil rights issues and the depressed condition of minorities came to the foreground. While most Americans were relatively well-off, twenty-five million remained poor. Influenced by the writings of economist John Kenneth Galbraith, who had directed attention to the existence of poverty in the midst of this affluent culture, President John F. Kennedy began to address the problem of poverty.

After Kennedy's assassination in 1963, President Lyndon Baines Johnson followed in the tradition of his predecessor by "declaring war on poverty" in March 1964. The war on poverty comprised many social programs designed to *cure* poverty in America. The goals of the war were to allow ghetto and poor communities to develop their own programs which would arrest poverty and root out inequality in the lives of Americans. Model-cities programs, community-action agencies, and other devices were tried, but many of these strategies proved unsatisfactory. As the 1970s approached, the new presidential administration of Richard Nixon began dismantling the agencies of the war on poverty. The welfare rights movement had come and gone.

President Nixon, determined to clean up what had been labeled the "welfare mess," attempted another type of reform in 1970—a guaranteed annual income for all those who were poor. Parts of the plan were adopted, notably the Supplemental Security Income (SSI) program in 1972. But for the most part, the concept of a guaranteed annual income was rejected by Congress. Some members of Congress were concerned that Nixon's proposal was too much welfare, and others were concerned that it was too little welfare.

Meanwhile, another type of welfare movement had arisen as social services designed to address problems other than poverty grew increasingly popular in the 1960s and 1970s. Consequently, legislation was passed to assist abused children, to provide community mental health services, and to develop social services programs for the elderly.

"The Revolution No One Noticed"

While Americans were preoccupied with the turmoil of the 1960s—the civil rights movement and the war in Vietnam—a revolution no one noticed was taking place.[15] For many years, the argument on behalf of social welfare in America had followed clear lines: The United States was spending the largest portion of its budget for defense; programs for the poor, the sick, the aged, and minorities were underfinanced. It was argued in the 1960s that in order to be more responsive to the needs of its citizens, the nation should *change its priorities;* it should spend more on social programs to reduce poverty and less on wars like Vietnam. The argument ended with a call for a revolution in national priorities.

In a single decade, America's national priorities were reversed (see the illustration entitled "Welfare and Warfare"). In 1965, national defense expenditures accounted for 42 percent of the federal government's budget, while social welfare expenditures (social insurance, health, and public assistance) accounted for less than

25 percent. While the mass media focused on the war in Vietnam and on Watergate, a revolution in national policy making was occurring. By 1975, defense accounted for only 25 percent of the federal budget, and social welfare expenditures had grown to 43 percent of the budget (see Figure 2–1).

Social welfare is now the major function and major expenditure of the federal government. This reversal of national priorities occurred during both Democratic and Republican administrations and during the nation's longest war. "The mid-to-late 1960s were quite prosperous years. The unemployment rate fell under 4 percent, real income rose briskly. In the flush of affluence, new programs could be introduced with minimal fiscal strain, even as the Vietnam War expenditures were swelling."[16] In short, ideas that welfare expenditures are not likely to increase during Republican administrations or during times of war turned out to be wrong. America's commitment to social welfare was growing.

But not everyone was comfortable with this revolution in public spending. There was fear that the nation was sacrificing national defense in order to spend money on social welfare programs which might not work. As the 1970s ended and the 1980s emerged, a more cautious attitude toward social welfare spending had developed.

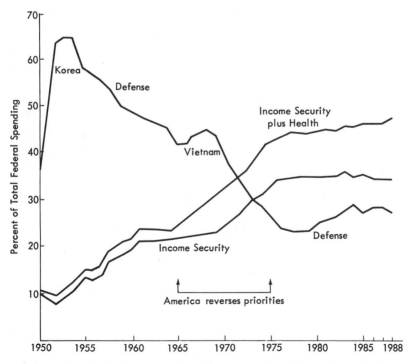

FIGURE 2–1   Welfare and defense priorities (percentage of total federal spending).

ILLUSTRATION: WELFARE AND WARFARE

Today, federal expenditures for social welfare far exceed federal expenditures for national defense. In the 1991 federal budget, direct benefit payments to individuals accounted for 43 percent of the federal budget. These direct payments include social insurance payments (like Social Security and Medicare) and public assistance payments (like Food Stamps, Supplemental Security Income, and the federal portion of AFDC and Medicaid). Health programs, primarily Medicaid and Medicare, alone comprise nearly 15 percent of the total budget. Only 25 percent of the 1991 budget was devoted to national defense.

Not so long ago, the relationship between federal spending for "welfare" and "warfare" (or "guns and butter" as it was once called) was reversed; before 1973 the federal government spent more on national defense than it did on social welfare. Figure 2–1 shows the changing trends in spending for welfare and defense. Note that defense spending jumped up at the beginnings of the Korean War (1950–52) and the Vietnam War (1964–68) and again during the military buildup begun under President Carter and continued under President Reagan. In contrast, social welfare spending rose slowly for many years and then exploded in the 1970s after the Great Society programs were in place. Social welfare and health spending remained at high levels despite a significant increase in defense spending during this period.

The portion of the total federal budget devoted to social welfare is likely to grow even further. Medical costs have escalated rapidly. A significant development in international relations has occurred that may also affect the composition of the budget. President Bush has announced a reduction in military spending as a result of amazing political changes in various parts of the world, most notably the moves toward greater democratization in Russia and the other Communist bloc countries, and in East and West Germany where the Berlin Wall has finally come down.

THE EXPANSION OF SOCIAL WELFARE

Since the early 1900s, many factors have contributed to the increase in the number of social welfare programs, the number of people receiving assistance, and the amount spent on welfare programs. Among them are (1) the rural-to-urban migration, (2) the elimination of residency requirements, (3) the welfare rights movement, (4) cost-of-living increases, (5) the aging of America, and (6) increases in single-parent families.

The Rural-to-Urban Migration

As the Industrial Revolution reached its peak during the late 1800s and early 1900s, America experienced some of its sharpest growing pains. America changed from a rural, agrarian society to an urban, industrial society. People migrated from poor rural farming communities hoping to find jobs and brighter futures in the cities. In addition, foreigners were also emigrating to American cities, seeking an improved standard of living. The dreams of many individuals were shattered. Those who found jobs were often forced to work long hours for low pay under poor working conditions. Housing was often crowded; sanitation and health problems were common. Those who had come to the cities to make good were often far from their families who could have provided them with financial and psychological support. Social welfare became a growing problem for governments. As the Great Depression unfolded, the cities and states were no longer able to cope with worsening social conditions. The response to this major economic crisis was the Social Security Act of 1935, by which the federal government assumed its role as the major financier of social welfare programs.

Residency Requirements Eliminated

One method traditionally used to restrict the number of people who were eligible for welfare assistance was residency requirements. During Elizabethan and colonial times, people believed that residency requirements were needed because the poor and needy should be provided for by their home parishes. The financially dependent were not welcome in new communities. However, as society became more mobile and people moved more frequently to seek jobs and other opportunities, the argument for residency requirements no longer seemed to hold up. But states and communities continued to impose these restrictions to limit the number of people dependent on welfare. Requiring that potential recipients had to reside in the city or state for six months or a year or even requiring that they intended to reside in the city or state were ways of keeping welfare caseloads small. Following a number of court challenges, the Supreme Court in 1969 declared residency requirements in federally supported welfare programs unconstitutional.[17] As a result, it became easier to qualify for assistance, and welfare caseloads grew, especially during the 1970s.

Welfare Rights

In the 1960s, black and other poor Americans showed their discontent with the welfare system through the *welfare rights movement.* It arose in the wake of the civil rights movements, as the poor expressed their dissatisfaction with a political system that had denied them the standard of living that other Americans were enjoying. These movements were a stormy time in American domestic history, especially from 1964 to 1968, when major cities experienced a series of riots. As the number of disturbances increased, so did the number of people *applying* for welfare. In addition, a greater percentage of welfare applications were being *approved* than ever before. The welfare rights movement brought changes in the behavior and attitudes of welfare recipients.[18] Frances Fox Piven and Richard Cloward wrote that "[t]he mood of applicants in welfare waiting rooms had changed. They were no longer as humble, as self-effacing, as pleading; they were more indignant, angrier, more demanding."[19] The mood of welfare administrators and caseworkers had also changed. Many of the practices that had been part of lengthy background investigations ceased. The process of obtaining aid was speeded up and welfare agencies were not so quick to terminate benefits when recipients did not comply with the rules. "For all practical purposes, welfare operating procedures collapsed; regulations were simply ignored in order to process the hundreds of thousands of families who jammed the welfare waiting rooms."[20] By 1968, the welfare rights movement was coming to a close. Riots were ceasing, but despite the demise of the movement and the National Welfare Rights Organization, which had been formed to improve the plight of the poor, record numbers of applicants were being certified for welfare benefits.

Cost-of-Living Adjustments

Some of the welfare spending increases since the 1970s are due to congressional approval of cost-of-living adjustments, known as COLAs, which are designed to keep welfare benefits in line with inflation. Political scientist Aaron Wildavsky tells us that in the past, Congress had increased Social Security payments by taking a special vote each time an increase was considered. But later, Congress decided to make automatic cost-of-living adjustments in the Social Security, Food Stamp, and SSI programs.[21] This practice is also called indexing. Annually or biannually, social welfare payments are adjusted to account for the increased cost of living. Commenting on the purpose of automatic cost-of-living adjustments, Wildavsky writes:

> Such action was not intended to provide greater benefits to recipients, but only to automatically assure them of constant purchasing power. The index makes changes non-discretionary...Legislators may see such automatic increases as either favorable or unfavorable. Some may miss the almost yearly opportunity to show their constituents how much they have contributed to the nation's welfare. Others may be happy to continue constant benefits without being seen as wasteful spenders.[22]

By the early 1980s the rationale for COLAs had come under attack. While social welfare payments were being adjusted according to the increased cost of living, the wages of many workers in the sluggish economy had not kept pace with inflation. Some modifications have been made to control COLAs (see, for example, Chapter 4 on the Social Security program), but COLAs continue to be an important concept in federal social welfare programs.

The Aging of America

The growing number of elderly persons in the United States has put an increasing strain on the social welfare system. Today, those over the age of sixty-five comprise more than 11 percent of the population, compared to 4 percent at the turn of the century. By the year 2000, the figure will be near 12 percent.[23] Improved living conditions and advances in medicine have helped Americans look forward to longer lives than ever before. But as people grow older, they may become increasingly vulnerable and are sometimes unable to meet their own needs. There is widespread agreement in the United States that the elderly deserve publicly supported care. The tripling of the size of the elderly population during this century has increased the need for greater planning and additional services to insure that older Americans receive proper treatment. The largest programs for this segment of the population, Social Security retirement benefits and Medicare, are discussed at length in Chapters 4 and 10.

Increase in Single-Parent Families

The changing patterns of American family life are another factor that explains increases in welfare expenditures. Divorce, although slowing some, is rampant. The number of adults who bear children but never marry has grown. The pregnancy rate among teenagers who are unmarried and ill-equipped to care for children has caused national alarm. As a result of these new patterns, the number of single-parent families, especially those headed by women, has grown considerably. From 1950 to 1975, the number of female-headed households doubled to over seven million, and 70 percent included children.[24] In 1988, 6.9 million families were below the poverty line; 2.9 million were headed by two parents. Of the remaining 4 million families headed by a single parent, 92 percent were headed by women. These female-headed families had a whopping poverty rate of 33 percent—nearly three times higher than male-headed families.[25] It would seem that the women's rights movement increased opportunities for education and job advancement that would have raised many female-headed households out of poverty during the last two decades, but the bleak picture for women and their children remains. As a result, welfare programs such as Aid to Families with Dependent Children, Medicaid, and Food Stamps continue to be critical resources for those who are poor.

FINANCES IN THE WELFARE STATE

Prior to the Great Depression, local and state governments shouldered the major responsibility for social welfare programs; the federal government was virtually uninvolved. But today the picture is quite different. Since 1935, there have been important changes in the way almost all social welfare programs are financed. While federal, state, and local expenditures for social welfare have all increased, the federal government is clearly the largest spender, providing three-quarters of all funds for public assistance and social insurance.[26]

But how does the federal government acquire the funds to pay for its activities—from defense to social welfare programs? The answer, of course, is through the taxes that are paid by individual citizens and corporations. As shown in Figure 2–2, individual income taxes are the largest source of federal government revenues (budget receipts). Individual income taxes account for 43 percent of budget receipts. These taxes are channeled to the federal government's general revenue fund, which is used to pay for most of its activities, among them the financing of public assistance programs. The second major source of budget revenue is the Social Security tax. This is a special tax levied against an individual's income which is used to finance the social insurance programs. Social insurance receipts account for 34 percent of the federal budget. The federal government also collects revenues through corporation income taxes, excise taxes (taxes on products), and other sources, but individual income taxes and Social Security taxes combined constitute more than three-fourths (77 percent) of the total budget. Corporation income taxes account for only 11 percent. There is an important source of government funding that does not appear in Figure 2–2. Current federal

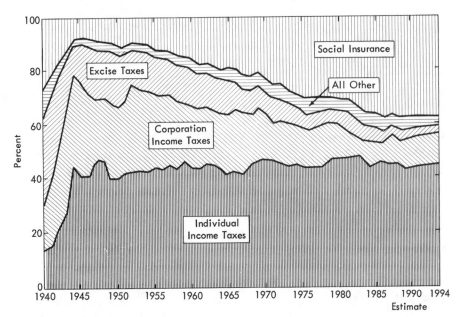

FIGURE 2–2   Percent composition of United States government receipts. (Historical Tables, *Budget of the United States Government*, Fiscal Year 1990.)

budget deficits are now so large that the government must borrow a considerable amount to meet its budget commitments.

The states collect taxes in several ways. Like the federal government, most states levy a personal income tax, although state income taxes are much lower than federal income taxes. Only a handful of states have not adopted an income tax. The sales tax is another mechanism used by states to generate revenue. A portion of these taxes is used to provide social welfare services. At the local level, the property tax, principally used to fund education, is the major source of revenue. Local governments (counties, cities, and municipalities) provide the smallest share of welfare services. These governments are mainly concerned with providing other types of services, such as police and fire protection, to citizens.

Taxes, then, are the essential elements in the federal, state, and local governments' abilities to generate revenues to support their activities, and there is always concern about the types of taxes that should be used to generate revenues, who should pay those taxes, and who should benefit from tax revenues. Some taxes are regressive (they tax the poor at a higher rate than the rich) and others are progressive (they tax the rich at higher rates than the poor). The Social Security tax and sales taxes are considered regressive while the federal and state income taxes are supposed to be progressive, although they are less progressive than many people think they should be.

It has been argued that "everyone is on welfare" because the government helps all people, some directly through social welfare programs, others through tax incentives.[27] Government sponsored welfare programs (public assistance and social insurance) comprise the bulk of help to the poorest citizens. Low income workers may also benefit from the *Earned Income Tax Credit* (EITC). The EITC is a special tax rebate that is paid to low income workers with children through the Internal Revenue Service (IRS). Although the amounts are quite modest, this type of tax credit is designed to redistribute income to poorer citizens.

Compared to lower- and upper-income groups, the middle-classes pay most of the federal income taxes in the country. Much of the social welfare assistance to the middle-classes comes in the form of fringe benefit programs (such as health care and pension plans) offered by employers. Workers can claim federal income tax deductions from their gross personal income for these fringe benefits. Workers also benefit from provisions like the *dependent-care tax credit*. The primary example is a deduction for working families who pay for child care. This credit is available to those of all income levels. It has been used less frequently by low income workers, however, because the costs of child care are usually beyond their reach. Some have called for eliminating this credit for upper-income workers in order to increase tax revenue or to concentrate more resources on poorer families. There have also been suggestions for expansion of the dependent-care credit to offer more incentives for family members to care for aged and disabled members rather than rely on public programs such as Medicaid that pays for custodial nursing home care for the poor.

Many businesses also get government assistance such as federal contracts, farm subsidies, and various tax deductions. These provisions have been called "corporate welfare." In addition to helping the more affluent who own businesses, this type of government assistance helps to offset the cost of the fringe benefits that employers pay to workers.

The rich get most of their help directly from the tax system through various loopholes, deductions, and credits (called *tax expenditures*) that favor the more affluent over the less affluent. Some of these deductions are for the mortgage interest paid on first and second homes and for property taxes and charitable contributions. These deductions are also taken by middle-class families although the amount of their deductions is generally smaller.

Considered in this perspective, all groups benefit from government assistance, and it has been argued that redistribution of income that results from public policy favors the rich rather than the less affluent. In the following sections of this chapter that address the Reagan and Bush presidential administrations, we will continue to explore provisions for financing the federal government's activities.

THE LEGACY OF REAGANOMICS

In some ways, social welfare in the United States has come a long way. The number of people served by the various welfare programs and the amount of money spent on these programs are impressive. But in other ways, the social welfare programs of today are not so different from those of Elizabethan and colonial times. Payments to recipients are often low, and the conditions under which services are rendered can still be demeaning. There are many other problematic aspects of social welfare. While helping many, the expansion of social welfare has also resulted in a mixture of public policies and programs which are often inconsistent, conflicting, and overlapping. A number of critics believe that welfare programs encourage dependency and that by doing so, they have led to an increase rather than a decrease in the numbers of people receiving assistance.

During the 1980s these concerns resulted in disillusionment with the welfare system and eroded many of the liberal ideas and hopes of the two preceding decades. As a result, with the support of the Reagan administration, more conservative philosophies about welfare gained popularity. These philosophies suggested that (1) government spending for welfare should be kept to a minimum; (2) government, especially the federal government, should minimize its role in welfare policy and programs; (3) only those in extreme circumstances—the "truly needy"—should receive welfare assistance; and (4) welfare should be provided on a short-term rather than long-term basis whenever possible. As Reagan assumed the presidency, changes at the federal level soon began to reflect these ideas.

Reaganomics and the Supply Side

The economic ideas which have been labeled "Reaganomics," ideas which represent important political forces, have certainly affected social welfare policy in the last decade. Whether or not one agrees with the ideas, they are essential to understanding current approaches to welfare and the economy. Any brief description of Reaganomics risks oversimplification of many complex issues—inflation, economic growth, *supply-side* economics, capital investment, and money supply. However, we can briefly describe some of the central ideas that guided the Reagan administration through its two terms.

An important component of Reaganomics is the belief that past Keynesian policies to reduce unemployment and hold down inflation had failed. (Keynesian economics is based on the notion that government can boost employment or cut inflation by manipulating the *demand side* of the economy—increasing government spending and expanding the money supply to boost employment, and doing just the opposite to hold down inflation.) When Reagan entered office, he viewed the most important causes of the nation's economic problems—unemployment, inflation, low productivity, and low investment—as being the government itself. According to Reagan, "The federal government through taxes, spending, regulatory, and monetary policies, [had] sacrificed long-term growth and price stability for ephemeral, short-term goals."[28]

According to Keynesian economic ideas, unemployment and inflation should not occur together. (Unemployment should reduce income, which in turn would force down prices.) But according to government figures, *both* unemployment and inflation remained high during the 1970s. Government efforts to reduce unemployment simply added to inflation, and government efforts to cut inflation simply added to unemployment. Reagan decided to combine the unemployment rate with the inflation rate and to call it the *misery index*. In 1960, the misery index was 7.3, but by 1980 it had mushroomed to 17.2.[29] During the Reagan presidency, the misery index dropped due to improvements in the economy. It is difficult to say how much of this reduction could be directly attributed to the Reagan reforms, but economic upturns probably accounted for much of the president's unprecedented popularity during both his terms in office.

President Reagan pursued a package of four sweeping policy directives designed to achieve economic recovery. They were:

1. Budget reform to cut the rate of growth in federal spending.
2. Tax reductions of 25 percent over three years on personal income, and additional tax reductions on business investment.
3. Relief from federal regulations that cost industry large amounts of money for small increases in safety.
4. Slower growth of the money supply, to be delivered with the cooperation of the Federal Reserve Board.

Reagan was especially successful in reducing taxes during both his terms. The federal individual income tax used to begin at 12 percent of the *first* $1,000 of *taxable* income. (Generally the first $6,000 of income for a family of four was *nontaxable*.) There were fifteen tax brackets. At each bracket the tax rate increased. For example, a tax of 50 percent was levied on taxable income over $38,000, and a rate of 70 percent was levied on taxable income over $200,000.

In the 1970s, inflation pushed Americans into higher tax brackets even though their buying power had not increased. This meant that Americans were paying an increasing amount of their incomes to the federal government as inflation pushed up their salaries, even though their salary increases did not enable them to live a better life. These automatic tax increases caused by inflation were labeled *bracket creep*.[30]

Tax Cuts

In 1981, the Reagan administration persuaded Congress to cut personal income taxes for all income groups by 25 percent. Reagan also persuaded Congress to *index* tax rates in the future to eliminate bracket creep. If inflation carries taxpayers into higher brackets, their taxes will be *adjusted*, or indexed, so that they will *not* carry a heavier burden.

During Reagan's second term, he again successfully urged Congress to reform the tax system. The reforms were intended to reduce tax rates while eliminating tax breaks, called *loopholes*. The number of individual tax brackets was reduced to two primary categories—a 15 percent and a 28 percent bracket. (Although some upper-middle-income earners have been paying a 33 percent marginal tax rate). The number of corporate tax brackets was also reduced. Some other reforms included increasing the personal income tax exemption, eliminating some real estate tax shelters used primarily by the wealthy, and taxing capital gains as ordinary income instead of using lower rates. Reagan called it "the best antipoverty bill, the best pro-family measure, and the best job-creation program ever to come out of the Congress."[31]

According to Reaganomics, large tax cuts would not necessarily reduce government income or create large government deficits, at least in the long run. Taxes discourage work, productivity, investment, and economic growth. Reduce taxes, and the paradoxical result will be an *increase* in government revenue, because more people will work harder and start businesses knowing they can keep a larger share of their earnings. Tax cuts will stimulate increased economic activity, and although tax rates are lower, this increased activity will eventually produce more government revenue.

Reagan's policies were designed to provide incentives for Americans to work, save, and invest. Theoretically, the economy will grow more rapidly because Americans can keep more of what they earn and purchase more goods with their earnings. Inflation will be brought under control by producing more goods rather than by limiting demand. Americans will also be encouraged to save a greater proportion of their incomes, and businesses will be encouraged to build new plants and provide more jobs.

Economist Arthur Laffer developed the diagram shown in Figure 2–3. If the government imposed no taxes (a zero tax rate), the government would receive no revenue (point A). Initially, government revenues rise with increases in the tax rate. However, when tax rates become too high (beyond point C), they discourage workers and businesses from producing and investing. When this discouragement occurs, the economy declines and government revenues fall. Indeed, if the government imposed a 100 percent tax rate and confiscated everything that workers or business produced, then everyone would quit working, and the government would receive *no* revenues (point B).

According to the *Laffer curve,* modest increases in tax rates will result in increased government revenues, up to an optimum point (point C) after which further increases will discourage work and investment. Laffer does not claim to know exactly what the optimum rate of taxation should be. But Laffer and the Reagan administration believed that the United States was in the *prohibitive range.* Tax reductions, they concluded, would actually increase government revenues.

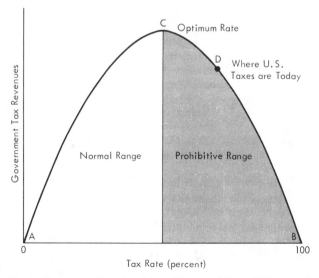

FIGURE 2–3   The Laffer curve. (Reprinted from Thomas R Dye. *Understanding Public Policy,* 6th ed. Englewood Cliffs, N.J.: Prentice Hall, 1987, p. 269.)

Critics of the new supply-side economics argued that it was really a return to an old and discredited *trickle-down* approach to the economy. Taxes and regulations on businesses and affluent Americans are reduced in the hope that they will reinvest their profits and expand job opportunities for the poor and working classes. In other words, incentives are provided for the wealthy in the hope that benefits will trickle down to the poor.[32] Not everyone, of course, agreed with this plan.

Social Welfare Cuts

When Reagan assumed the presidency, he asserted that his administration would protect the "truly needy" by not making significant cuts in many of the income security programs. Reagan referred to this as preserving the "social safety net," but many of the programs he referred to were social insurance programs to which beneficiaries are entitled regardless of their incomes, such as Social Security and Medicare. Many programs for the *poor,* such as Aid to Families with Dependent Children and Food Stamps, were not in the safety net; they were targeted for cuts. Federal spending was reduced, and significant numbers of recipients were removed from the rolls. The devolution of social welfare was one of the most serious criticisms of the Reagan administration.

One of Reagan's major goals was to restructure federal-state relations— specifically, to turn over to the states many of the domestic programs of the national government. For example, the president suggested a swap in which the federal government would assume full responsibility for the Medicaid program, and the states would in return take over the Food Stamp program and the federal portion of the AFDC program. (Chapter 10 describes Medicaid, Chapter 8 describes Food Stamps, and Chapter 6 describes AFDC.) The swap was intended to "end cumbersome administration" and make the programs "more responsive to both the people they are meant to help and the people who pay for them."[33] Critics of the proposal contended that the swap would be a step backward in social welfare policy. Many social welfare functions were assumed by the federal government *because* the states failed to respond to the needs of the poor. Even if state governments were well motivated to care for their poor, differences in the economic resources of the states would result in unequal treatment from state to state.

These swaps never occurred, but the Reagan administration was successful in using block grants as a means of establishing a New Federalism. *Block grants* are federal payments to state or local governments for general functions, such as health, welfare, education, law enforcement, and community development. The money must be spent for the function specified in the block grant, but states and communities are free to decide specific uses for the funds. In Reagan's view, block grants were to be used to reduce the power of "the Washington bureaucrats," to return decision making to state and local governments, and to make federal money available for various purposes with "no strings attached." The Reagan administration considered block grants preferable to *categorical grants,* which are made after federal departments and agencies review specific applications of state or local governments on a project-by-project basis. The concept of block grants was developed as a reaction to centralization of power in the Washington bureaucracy. The first major block grants came in the field of law enforcement (the Crime Control and Safe Streets Act of 1968) and later in housing and urban affairs (the Housing and Community Development Act of 1974).

By consolidating many social welfare programs into state block grants, Reagan was able to reduce social welfare spending because the amount allocated to the block grants was less than the sum of money previously spent on the individual social welfare programs. Block grants also shifted decision making about specific uses of federal social welfare dollars to state political arenas, where support for social welfare programs is not always as great as it is in Washington. As decision making was shifted to the states, much of the politicking and much of the competition for funds were also shifted from Washington to state and local levels. For example, many health interests must now compete with each other to obtain scarce federal dollars, which are distributed through state welfare agencies.

Federal revenue sharing, another method of funding social welfare programs, was completely eliminated under the Reagan administration in 1987.[34] Revenue sharing for specific purposes, such as health needs, housing, and nutrition, began in the 1960s and was targeted for poor communities. In 1972, President Nixon initiated general revenue sharing. However, most cities eventually became eligible for the funds, and many began using them for services originally paid for by local governments, such as police and fire protection. The arguments against federal revenue sharing were that the federal government has a huge budget deficit and can no longer afford revenue sharing, especially when some state governments actually have budget surpluses and are better able to afford to pay for these services themselves.

The Close of the Reagan Years

Unfortunately, the good news that results from the affects of changes in public policy is often accompanied by bad news. After eight years of the Reagan presidency, this was certainly the case. The good news was that poverty rates, unemployment rates, and inflation rates had once again abated. The bad news came on two major fronts. Although overall poverty and unemployment were down, the country's budget deficit had grown at an incredible rate, and the Reagan budget knife had hurt many of the poorest Americans who are not part of the economic mainstream. Among the many changes in social welfare were: additional restrictions on the eligibility requirements for families receiving AFDC that resulted in many being removed from the program; cuts in Medicaid funds to states which failed to reduce error rates sufficiently; delays in cost of living adjustments in the Food Stamp program, restricted eligibility for the program, and additional penalties assessed for state error rates; increases in the share of rent paid by public housing tenants and elimination of most federal housing construction subsidies; cuts in funding for day care, foster care, and family planning services of approximately 22 percent; cuts in community action programs for low-income neighborhoods that amounted to about 39 percent of funding.[35]

Hopes that reductions in the tax rate and increases in economic productivity would begin to chip away at the budget deficit have not materialized. The estimated budget deficit for 1991 will be $169 billion or $231 billion if the bailout of the failed savings and loan industry, a result of deregulation, is included. By 1993 the national debt is projected to be $4 trillion (this is nearly $15,000 for every person in the United States).[36]

BUSH'S KINDER, GENTLER AMERICA

As President Reagan's second term was drawing to an end and the 1988 presidential campaign began, the men from both parties who comprised the group of serious contenders for the presidency were considered to be mostly unimpressive and were soon dubbed "The Seven Dwarfs." Not surprisingly, Vice President George Bush emerged as the Republican nominee after he was finally endorsed by President Reagan. Michael Dukakis, governor of Massachusetts, became the Democrats' choice. Dukakis had been a leader in social welfare reform in Massachusetts and had appeared on Boston public television many times as host of "The Advocates," a panel discussion program dedicated to the political issues of the day.

During the campaign, the candidates' personalities received considerable media attention. Bush was portrayed as a "wimp" who had trouble closing the gender gap, and he suffered from the image of most vice presidents—that of a ceremonial figurehead without serious assignments. Dukakis was portrayed as a rather humorless and undemonstrative individual, but he had appointed many women to high-level positions and received stronger backing from female voters. Dukakis was also said to have suffered from the *L word; L*, which stands for liberal, has come to represent wasteful spending and the image of a "bleeding heart" on social welfare matters. Dukakis's state is sometimes called "Taxachusetts" because of its high state income tax and generous welfare programs.

Bush selected Dan Quayle as his running mate, a young United States senator from Indiana who was not known nationally and who proved to be an extremely weak partner on the ticket, if not a liability, because of his unimpressive record. Dukakis, on the other hand, picked Lloyd Bentsen, a United States senator from Texas, to round out the ticket. Bentsen was a highly respected individual with years of political experience. With Reagan's backing, Bush emerged as the victor.

No New Taxes?

The new president immediately called for a "kinder, gentler America," but a number of the Reagan philosophies are evident in the Bush administration. Bush took office using a favorite refrain of his, "Read my lips—no new taxes." Following in his predecessor's footsteps, Bush pressed for a reduction in capital gains taxes (taxes paid on profits from the sale of assets such as real estate and stocks) which are now taxed like earned income and which are more likely to be sources of income for the affluent. Prior to tax reform, capital gains were taxed at lower rates. A reduction in capital gains taxes has been opposed on the grounds that it would further intensify the upper-income tilt of the Reagan tax reforms. During the past decade, evidence that the rich are getting richer and the poor are getting poorer mounted. The nonpartisan

Congressional Budget Office estimated that the lower-and middle-classes would pay a higher net federal tax rate for 1990 than they paid in 1980 *prior* to tax reform.[37] And while the poorest Americans have seen their income drop in the last decade, their federal tax rate has increased by 16 percent. This occurred at the same time that the richest Americans have enjoyed substantial increases in income and their income tax rates have been reduced by 5.5 percent. Rather than tax increases, Bush has supported tax breaks such as tax credits for child care and for adoption, tax incentives for Americans who contribute to personal savings accounts, and tax-free enterprise zones to stimulate economic growth in depressed urban areas.

The growing budget deficit and the inability of Congress to balance the budget caused President Bush to eat his words and consider new taxes. The bitter budget battle that ensued resulted in a series of new measures enacted late in 1990 that were primarily supported by Democrats in both the House and Senate. The "sin taxes"— those on alcohol and gasoline—which Bush was most amendable to raising, were increased as were the "luxury" taxes on items such as expensive cars and boats. The highest personal income tax rate was raised to 31 percent for individuals with annual income of more than $125,000 and couples with income more than $200,000, while the 33 percent rate being paid by upper-middle-income earners was reduced to 31 percent. Bush did not get the substantial capital gains tax cut he wanted, but the highest rate will noe be 28 (rather than 33) percent. The value of some deductions itemized in computing personal income taxes will be reduced, as will the value of the personal income tax exemption (now $2,050 for the taxpayer and each dependent) for high income individuals. Taxes on wages to support health care for the aged will be increased for many workers. The Earned Income Tax Credit for low-income working families was increased and new credits for health care and new parents were included. New measures were also enacted to strengthen Gramm-Rudman-Hollings by imposing spending ceilings to bring the budget into balance and cut the deficit.

The States as Laboratories

President Bush has continued to promote state responsibility for social welfare by speaking of the "states as laboratories." In the words of Justice Louis C. Brandeis, written in 1932, "It is one of the happy incidents of the federal system that a single courageous state may, if its citizens choose, serve as a laboratory; and try novel social and economic experiments without risk to the rest of the country."[38] The states have long been social welfare labs.[39] The forerunners of the federal-state AFDC program were state and locally supported mothers' aid and mothers' pension laws that first emerged in the early 1900s. State and local programs for the poor, aged, and disabled also predated federal intervention for these groups. But states were not consistent in their approaches. According to President Bush:

Until quite recently a case could be made in many areas of government policy and action that a national approach, with national rules and standards, was warranted. This was so because some states departed widely from national norms in such areas as racial segregation, and some were too poor to accomplish as much as may have been judged appropriate. A lot has changed in the past quarter century.[40]

The president proposes to continue to encourage state experimentation by (1) providing federal funds to help support state demonstration projects and by (2) granting waivers that allow states to deviate from federal rules that may prohibit or inhibit experimentation.[41] For example, waivers have allowed states to try alternatives to institutional care for mentally handicapped citizens that would not have been possible under existing rules. State initiatives have also been used to test out ideas that may be too controversial to gain nationwide support. For example, under Wisconsin's *Learnfare* program, "a welfare family with teenage children has its AFDC benefits reduced if the child drops out of school, [which is] defined as missing three days of school in a month without a valid excuse."[42] According to the president, "Some of these experiments are controversial, some may not work, others may prove to cost too much for the benefits produced. That is the nature of 'states as laboratories.' As any scientist knows, the road to success is marked by numerous laboratory failures."[43]

Privatization

Another important theme emphasized during the Reagan administration and now the Bush administration is *privatization*. Privatization can mean many things, but it largely involves federal, state, and local governments giving more responsibility to private organizations to deliver services—from space exploration and prisons to mass transportation and social welfare. The 1990 federal budget contained the following description of the concept.

> Generally, privatization can be defined as the transfer of government services, assets, and/ or enterprises to private sector owners and suppliers, when [they] have the capability of providing better services at lower costs. Privatization replaces monopolies with competition...to encourage efficiency, quality, and innovation in the delivery of goods and services.
> Privatization does not imply the abrogation of government responsibility for any of these services. Rather, it merely recognizes that what matters most is the service provided, not who provides it.[44]

Many social welfare services are already provided by the *private* sector (see also Chapter 7). For example, child care is a social service provided almost exclusively through the private-for-profit and private-not-for-profit sectors. Perhaps the best example is health care because it represents such a large part of private (as well as public) expenditures. The term "occupational welfare" has been used to describe health care and other "fringe" benefits offered to workers through their employers. In fact, the term fringe may no longer be a good word to describe them, because in many work settings, these privately sponsored benefits can easily amount to an additional 25 percent of the employee's salary or wages.

There has been a *blurring* of what constitutes the private and public sectors.[45] Many so-called private enterprises rely heavily on government funds. The housing industry, for example, has benefited from construction projects funded through the federal government's Department of Housing and Urban Development (HUD). Private contractors are able to sell many of their homes through the Federal Housing Administration home loan and mortgage guarantee programs. Many of the country's community mental health centers are actually not-for-profit corporations which have relied heavily on federal, state, and local governments for funding, but now they face greater pressure to accept clients who can pay for their own services. Many organizations today are really *quasi-public* or *semiprivate*.[46] The United States is truly a mixed economy, even in the social welfare domain.

The fear is that privatization will result in government "load shedding"[47] in which the government does abrogate responsibility for services, sometimes through deregulation. For example, it has been increasingly difficult to assess the impacts of services for the elderly[48] and of child care[49] because the government has reduced its efforts to collect data and monitor these programs. In some cases, privatization has occurred simultaneously with government reductions in the amount spent for services.[50] Load shedding can obviously result in a reduction of the amount of services that can be provided and the types of clients that can be served. For example, the Bush administration is trying to eliminate federal subsidies to the Amtrak railroad, but without federal help, Amtrak may find it difficult to offer customers rates competitive with other forms of transportation and to offer service to customers in remote areas. The trend toward privatization will continue.

One Thousand Points of Light

When President Bush called for "a kinder, gentler America," he also referred to the country's "1,000 points of light," a phrase which he used to describe the many Americans who volunteer to help those less fortunate than themselves—i.e., those who visit the elderly in nursing homes, tutor children from culturally disadvantaged environments, serve as foster parents, dish out meals in soup kitchens, act as buddies to persons with AIDS (PWAs), and perform many other services, all without much help from the government.

Americans are very generous. In fact, "1988 was a banner year for philanthropy in the United States, with charitable donations soaring to a record high of $104.37 billion."[51] Religious organizations were the greatest source of this voluntary aid.[52] According to a 1988 Gallup poll, 45 percent of adult Americans perform some type of volunteer work,[53] and these figures do not reflect much of the time, money, and energy that family and friends provide in assistance to each other.

Saying that the government cannot possibly meet all the country's social service needs, President Bush has tried to encourage even more volunteer efforts by supporting the idea of a national service program for young people. His proposal, called Youth Engaged in Service (YES), would be run by a foundation with substantial federal funding. Senators Ted Kennedy (D-Mass) and Sam Nunn (D-Ga) have also offered plans. The United States already has two longstanding voluntary-service agencies. The Peace Corps sends Americans to other countries to assist with community development efforts. ACTION operates the Volunteers in Service to America (VISTA) program, which places individuals in disadvantaged communities in the United States, and the Retired Senior Volunteer Program (RSVP), which encourages voluntarism among older Americans. The Peace Corps and VISTA are full-time assignments which provide volunteers a subsistence wage during their service.

Some plans for national service urge voluntary participation by youth; in return, they are to be given educational benefits to attend college. Others suggest that such service be required of all young people, similar to the military draft. Many individuals agree that the plans, especially if service is voluntary, have appeal. It has been suggested, however, that an entirely voluntary program would attract mostly poor young people,[54] even though they may be least able to afford this voluntary work, and this would further delay their obtaining a college or vocational education.[55] More affluent youth would not need to volunteer to earn education benefits. It is unlikely that large numbers of young people would join such a program voluntarily. Mandatory service for youth has not gotten a warm reception in some circles, because like the military draft, most people do not want to be told what to do.

Everyone appreciates the efforts of those who are willing to give their time or money to help others. It is difficult to imagine a society where such assistance is not available. Citizen involvement is also an important aspect of the provision of social services by public and private agencies. Volunteers do much to assist their communities by promoting better and increased social agency services, but volunteers only play a part in providing the services which clients need. Bishop John Ricard of the U.S. Catholic Conference commented on voluntary efforts to feed the hungry by saying, "Our efforts cannot and should not substitute for just public policies and effective programs to meet the needs of the hungry . . . [These efforts] should not be misread as a sign of success for voluntarism, but rather a desperate attempt to feed hungry people when others have abandoned their responsibility."[56] In addition, many clients need professional care, and volunteer services cannot make up for cuts in social service spending when professional services are needed. The challenge of a mixed economy of social services is to determine the best combination of public, private, professional, *and* voluntary efforts to help those in need.

POLITICS, THE WELFARE LOBBY, AND PACs

The poor are not represented in Washington in the same fashion as other groups in society.[57] The poor rarely write letters to members of Congress, and the poor are unlikely to make any significant campaign contributions. They are not usually found on a representative's home-state lecture circuit—service-club lunches, civic meetings, memorials, and dedications. The poor seldom come to Washington to visit their representative's office. Indeed, the poor do not turn out at the polls to vote as often as the nonpoor.

To the extent that the poor are represented at all in Washington, they are represented by *proxies*—groups that are not poor themselves but claim to represent the poor. Many of these groups have organized and reorganized themselves under various names over the years—the National Welfare Rights Organization (dissolved in the mid-1970s), the Children's Defense Fund, the National Anti-Hunger Coalition, the Low Income Housing Coalition, and the Food Research and Action Center.

Lobbyists for the poor can be divided roughly into three categories: (1) churches, civil rights groups, and liberal organizations, (2) organized labor, and (3) welfare-program administrators and lawyers. The churches (the National Conference of Catholic Bishops, the National Council of Churches, B'nai Brith, and others) often support programs for the poor out of a sense of moral obligation. Likewise, liberal activist groups (Common Cause, Americans for Democratic Action, and others) often support social programs out of an ideological commitment. Civil rights organizations (the National Urban League, the National Association for the Advancement of Colored People [NAACP], and others) support programs for the poor as a part of their general concern for the conditions affecting minorities.

The success of lobbying efforts on behalf of the poor often depends upon an alliance between organized labor, with its considerable political power, and the coalition which consists of churches, civil rights groups, and liberal activists. Organized labor—for example, the AFL-CIO—does all of the things that the poor find difficult to do in politics: political organizing, campaign financing, letter writing, and personal lobbying. Historically, organized labor has tended to support programs for the poor, even though union pay scales have moved a great distance from the poverty line. *Labor leaders* may be more likely to support social programs than the rank-and-file membership. Of course, the first concern of organized labor is labor legislation—labor relations, minimum wages, fair labor standards, and so on. But when labor leaders join others in support of social programs, the result is a strong political coalition.

Welfare-program administrators and lawyers have a direct financial interest in supporting social welfare spending. These groups may take the lead in trying to organize the others into coalitions that support particular programs. Supporters of proposals to reduce spending for social programs complain, "Virtually all of the lobbying has come from people who are involved directly or indirectly in administering these programs."[58] The welfare bureaucracy is said to create a powerful *poverty lobby,* which consists of "people doing well by the government's doing good."

Prominent among the organizations representing social-program administrators and lawyers are the American Federation of State, County, and Municipal Employees (AFSCME) and the Legal Services Corporation. Affiliated with the AFL-CIO, AFSCME is a labor union that includes many public workers whose jobs are directly affected by cutbacks in social programs. As a labor union, it is funded primarily by the dues of its own members. But the Legal Service Corporation, whose five thousand attorneys across the nation provide legal assistance to the poor, is itself funded by the federal government. Because the Legal Service Corporation has lobbied on its own behalf, its critics have charged that it is misusing its funds. The same charge was leveled against the now defunct Community Services Administration, which was supposed to assist antipoverty programs throughout the country and was not supposed to lobby Congress. However, there are very few government bureaucracies—from the Defense Department, to the National Aeronautics and Space Administration (NASA), to the Department of Agriculture—which do not, directly or indirectly, lobby Congress for their own programs.

The *welfare lobby* is strongest when its separate groups—churches, civil rights organizations, liberal groups, organized labor, and social welfare administrators—are unified and coordinated in their efforts. Lobbying on behalf of vulnerable groups and supporting legislation that is favorable to these groups are the kinds of political activity that go on every day with members of Congress and state legislatures. Another important form of political activity is support of individual candidates. It is no surprise that those who are interested in seeing specific types of legislation passed or defeated support candidates who share their views. Support may come verbally through endorsements and financially through campaign contributions at election time. Many special interests today are supported through the use of political action committees (PACs). PACs are used by all types of interest groups—the American Medical Association (AMA) operates one of the wealthiest PACs. All forms of business and industry—real estate, building, agricultural, automobile, insurance, hospital—have PACs. The National Association of Social Workers, AFSCME, and other groups interested in social welfare issues also operate some form of PAC. The number of PACs grew from 608 in 1974 to 4,165 by 1987.[59] In 1988, PACs raised nearly $370 million.[60] Many PACs have a vested interest in social welfare spending. The American Medical Association, once opposed to programs like Medicare and Medicaid, is now a strong supporter and defender of these programs. It is interested in the health of the nation and also wants to protect the interests of its own physician members. Other groups that provide social welfare services also do not wish to see their own colleagues adversely affected by budget cuts and governments regulations, and they raise money to prevent this. Although *a few* politicians refuse to accept PAC money, support of candidates through PACs rather than through individual contributions has become increasingly popular. The fear, however, is that as elected officials have become even more beholden to special interests, it has become increasingly difficult to resolve public-policy issues.[61] President Bush and others have proposed legislation to limit the use of PAC funds to support individual candidates.

SUMMARY

The roots of the American welfare system can be traced back to Elizabethan times. English poor laws stressed local government responsibility for welfare and emphasized distinguishing the deserving poor from the nondeserving poor. Welfare in the United States today remains similar in many respects.

In the early days of the country, welfare was provided by families, friends, private charities, and churches. But by the late nineteenth and early twentieth centuries, social problems were mounting. The Industrial Revolution had taken its toll on the country. Overcrowding in the cities led to a variety of social problems, including poverty. State governments began to enact programs for dependent children, the elderly, and the disabled. When the Great Depression struck, state and local aid was no longer enough. In 1935, the federal government passed the Social Security Act as part of America's New Deal. But these social welfare programs were not sufficient to eliminate poverty and suffering. In the 1960s, President Johnson declared war on poverty by pouring millions of dollars into grassroots social welfare programs. The Medicaid and Medicare programs and the Food Stamp program were also born in the 1960s, but millions remained poor. The welfare rights movement sprang up and died, and Americans witnessed a change in national budget priorities, with welfare spending overtaking defense spending.

The expansion of welfare has occurred for many reasons. Initially, it was caused by the increased numbers of people who moved to urban cities around the turn of the century to find work and who had no families on whom to rely when bad times struck. Later, in 1969, residency requirements, which were used to restrict the number of people who received help were eliminated, making it easier to receive aid. Potential welfare recipients saw other changes during the *welfare rights movement* of the 1960s, changes which made it easier to apply and qualify for benefits that might legally be theirs. Payments in some of the largest social insurance and public assistance programs now automatically increase as the cost of living rises, and this also increases the cost of welfare. As the aged population grows, so does the demand for more health care and social services. Finally, the number of single-parent families has increased. They are generally headed by women whose risk of being in poverty and of requiring welfare assistance is high.

Americans became disillusioned as they spent more on welfare without achieving the results they had expected. In the 1980s, America's welfare policies continued to be the focus of political conflict, and a more conservative mood developed. President Reagan, who soundly won two presidential victories, was successful in tightening eligibility requirements in many welfare programs, in reducing spending, and in consolidating many federal welfare programs. He also introduced a number of other economic reforms. These reforms are based on certain economic theories about how the rate at which people are taxed affects their incentive to work. Reagan's program for economic recovery was intended to increase work incentives and to slow inflation by reducing taxes and by slowing down the growth of the money supply. Another important aspect of Reagan's plan was to return to the states much of the decision-making power over how welfare dollars should be spent. While he pledged to continue aid to the "truly needy" and to maintain a "social safety net," many critics claimed that he was attempting to "balance the budget on the backs of the poor." Although it is difficult to pinpoint the exact causes, the economy improved after Reagan took office. Inflation decreased, and more people went back to work. But the number of poor remained high, and the federal deficit grew tremendously.

Many influences of the Reagan administration can be seen in the Bush administration. Bush has called for "a kinder, gentler America" in which Americans place greater emphasis on voluntarism. He has called for measures that will further encourage states to develop innovative solutions to reducing social problems, including involvement of the private sector in social welfare services. Bush has also called for greater use of the tax system to encourage savings and to assist with social welfare concerns like child care, but his interest in cutting capital gains taxes has been labeled as another measure to help wealthier Americans while the problems of the poorest remain. New tax measures and more stringent provisions to reduce the budget deficit were enacted in 1990. The activity of lobbying groups, which represent the poor, and of political action committees with vested interests in social welfare have increased as social welfare programs account for an increased share of the federal budget.

NOTES

1. For more detailed descriptions of the history of social welfare in the United States, see June Axinn and Herman Levin, *Social Welfare: A History of the American Response to Need* (New York: Harper & Row, 1975); Ronald C. Federico, *The Social Welfare Institution: An Introduction*, 3rd ed. (Lexington, Mass.: D.C. Heath, 1980); Blanche D. Coll, *Perspectives in Public Welfare: A History* (Washington D.C.: Department of Health, Education and Welfare, 1973).
2. See Federico, *Social Welfare Institution*, p. 42; and Coll, *Perspectives in Public Welfare*, pp. 1–2, for an elaboration of the role of the church and feudal landholders in the provision of welfare benefits.
3. Coll, op. cit., p. 2.
4. Ibid., pp. 2–3.
5. Federico, *Social Welfare Institution*, p. 104; Coll, *Perspectives in Public Welfare*, p. 4.
6. See Federico, *Social Welfare Institution*, pp. 42–43 for further elaboration.
7. Ibid.
8. Philip Klein, *From Philanthropy to Social Welfare* (San Francisco: Jossey-Bass, 1968), p. 10, cited in Federico, *Social Welfare Institution*, p. 53.
9. See Federico, *Social Welfare Institution*, p. 53; and Coll, *Perspectives in Public Welfare*, pp. 5–6 for elaboration on Elizabethan welfare.
10. This section relies on Coll, *Perspectives in Public Welfare*, pp. 17, 20, 21–22, 27–28.
11. Ibid., p. 17.
12. This paragraph relies on Thomas R. Dye, *Understanding Public Policy*, 4th ed. (Englewood Cliffs, N.J.: Prentice-Hall, 1981), pp. 116–17.
13. Paragraphs describing the Great Depression rely on Thomas R. Dye and L. Harmon Zeigler, *The Irony of Democracy*, 5th ed. (Monterey, Cal.: Duxbury Press, 1981), pp. 100–101.
14. Cited in Richard Hofstadter, *The American Political Tradition* (New York: Knopf, 1948), p. 316.
15. See Aaron Wildavsky, *Speaking Truth to Power: The Art and Craft of Policy Analysis* (Boston: Little, Brown, 1979), especially pp. 86–89, for an elaboration on this discussion of "the revolution no one noticed."
16. Robert D. Plotnick, "Social Welfare Expenditures: How Much Help for the Poor?" *Policy Analysis* 5, no. 2 (1979), 278.
17. *Shapiro v. Thompson*, 394 U.S. 618; and see Frances Fox Piven and Richard A. Cloward, *Regulating the Poor: The Functions of Public Welfare* (New York: Random House, 1971) for an elaboration on residency requirements, especially pp. 306–308.
18. See Frances Fox Piven and Richard A. Cloward, *Poor People's Movements: Why They Succeed, How They Fail* (New York: Vintage Books, 1977).
19. Ibid., p. 275.
20. Ibid.
21. Wildavsky, *Speaking Truth to Power*, p. 98.
22. Ibid.
23. Robert M. Moroney, *Families, Social Services and Social Policy: The Issue of Shared Responsibility* (Washington D.C.: Department of Health and Human Services, 1980), p. 58. DHHS publication no. (ADM) 80–846.
24. Ibid., p. 43.
25. U.S. Bureau of the Census, *Money Income and Poverty Status in the United States: 1988* (Washington D.C., 1989), p. 62.
26. U.S. Bureau of the Census, *Statistical Abstract of the United States, 1989* (Washington D.C., 1989), p. 346.
27. Mimi Abramovitz, "Everyone is in on Welfare: 'The Role of Redistribution in Social Policy' Revisited," *Social Work*, November-December, 1983, pp. 440-445; Richard M. Titmuss, The Role of Redistribution in Social Policy, *Social Security Bulletin, 28*, 6, June 1965, pp. 14–20.
28. President of the United States, *A Program for Economic Recovery*, February 18, 1981 (Washington: U.S. Government Printing Office, 1981).
29. Ibid.
30. Ibid., p. 6.
31. Eileen Shanahan, "President Signs Sweeping Overhaul of Tax Law," *Congressional Quarterly* (October 25, 1986), p. 2668.

32. See William Greider, "The Education of David Stockman," *Atlantic Monthly* (December 1981), pp. 27–54.
33. President Ronald Reagan, State of the Union Address, January 26, 1982.
34. See "The Drive to Kill Revenue Sharing," *Time* (March 11, 1985), pp. 30–31.
35. Editorial Research Reports 1, no. 10, *Congressional Quarterly*, March 9, 1984.
36. R.A. Zalvidar, "Debt ceiling goes through roof," *Austin American-Statesman*, July 12, 1990, p. A7.
37. "Study: Poor get poorer as rich find wealth less taxing," *Champaign-Urbana News Gazette*, February 17, 1990, p. 5.
38. Justice Louis D. Brandeis, dissenting in *New State Ice Co. v. Liebmann*, 1932, cited in *Budget of the United States Government, Fiscal Year 1991*, p. 171.
39. For further discussion and illustration of this concept, see David Osborne, *Laboratories of Democracy* (Boston: Harvard Business School Press, 1988).
40. *Budget of the United States Government, Fiscal Year 1991* (Washington: U.S. Government Printing Office), p. 171.
41. Ibid., Section IV.
42. Ibid., p. 176.
43. Ibid.
44. *Management of the United States Government, Fiscal Year 1990* (Washington: U.S. Government Printing Office), p. 3–105.
45. Martin Rein, "The Social Structure of Institutions: Neither Public nor Private," in Sheila B. Kamerman and Alfred J. Kahn, eds., *Privatization and the Welfare State* (Princeton, N.J.: Princeton University Press, 1989), pp. 49–71.
46. Ibid.
47. Marc Bendick, Jr., "Privatizing the Delivery of Social Welfare Services: An Idea to Be Taken Seriously," in Kamerman and Kahn, *Privatization and the Welfare State*, pp. 97–120.
48. Andrew W. Dobelstein with Ann B. Johnson, *Serving Older Adults: Policy, Programs, and Professional Activities* (Englewood Cliffs, N.J.: Prentice-Hall, 1985), pp. 125–128.
49. Kamerman and Kahn, *Privatization and the Welfare State*, p. 10.
50. Bendick, "Privatizing the Delivery of Social Welfare Services."
51. Janet Wilson, "Nationally, at Least, 1988 Was a Very Good Year for Philanthropy," *Austin American-Statesman* (December 17, 1989), p. H1.
52. Alfred Azula, "Churches No. 1 in Charity Funds, Study Says," *Austin American-Statesman* (December 8, 1988), p. A15.
53. Cited in *Statistical Abstract of the United States, 1989*, p. 371.
54. Jacob V. Lamar, "Enlisting with Uncle Sam," *Time* (February 23, 1987), p. 30.
55. William Raspberry, "National Service Plan Going Nowhere," *Austin American-Statesman* (April 28, 1989), p. A14.
56. Bishop John Ricard cited in the *Los Angeles Times*, quote reprinted in *Hunger Action Forum 2*, no. 3 (March 1989).
57. This discussion relies in part on "Special Treatment No Longer Given Advocates for the Poor," *Congressional Quarterly Weekly Report* (April 18, 1981), pp. 659–65.
58. Rep. Phil Gramm (D-Texas), quoted in *Congressional Quarterly (April 18, 1981)*, p. 662.
59. *Statistical Abstract of the United States, 1989*, p. 262.
60. Bernard Weinraub, "Bush to Urge Ban on Most PAC Donations to Candidates," *Austin American-Statesman* (June 10, 1989), p. 2B.
61. Brooks Jackson, "PAC Money Talks Louder Now," *The Wall Street Journal* (December 24, 1984), p. 26.

3

DEFINING POVERTY:
WHERE TO BEGIN?

DEFINING POVERTY

The very first obstacle to a rational approach to reducing poverty in America lies in conflict over the definition of the problem. Defining poverty is a *political* activity. Proponents of increased governmental support for social welfare programs frequently make high estimates of the number and percentage of the population that is poor. They view the problem of poverty as a persistent one, even in a generally affluent society. They argue that many millions of Americans suffer from hunger, inadequate housing, remedial illness, hopelessness, and despair. Their definition of the problem practically mandates the continuation and expansion of a wide variety of public welfare programs.

In contrast, others minimize the number of poor in America. They see poverty as diminishing over time. They view the poor in America today as considerably better off than the middle class of fifty years ago and even wealthy by the standards of most societies in the world. They deny that anyone needs to suffer from hunger, or remedial illness, if they make use of the public services already available to them. They believe that there are many opportunities for upward mobility in America and that none should suffer from hopelessness or despair. This definition of the problem minimizes the need for public welfare programs and encourages policy makers to limit the number and size of these programs.

Political conflict over poverty, then, begins with contending definitions of the problem of poverty. In an attempt to influence policy making, various political interests try to win acceptance for their own definitions of the problem. Political scientist E.E. Schattschneider explained:

Political conflict is not like an intercollegiate debate in which the opponents agree in advance on a definition of the issues. As a matter of fact, *the definition of the alternatives is the supreme instrument of power;* the antagonists can rarely agree on what the issues are because power is involved in the definition.[1]

Poverty has always been a concern during periods of economic depressions, but poverty has been a *political* issue only for the last thirty years. Prior to the 1960s, the problems of the poor were almost always segmented into areas—those who were elderly, disabled, widowed, orphaned, unemployed, medically indigent, delinquent, living in slum housing, and illiterate. According to one observer, it was not until the Kennedy and Johnson administrations that the nation began to see that these problems were tied together in a single bedrock problem—poverty:

The measures enacted, and those proposed, were dealing separately with such problems as slum housing, juvenile delinquency, dependency, unemployment, illiteracy, but they were separately inadequate because they were strikingly at surface aspects of what seemed to be some kind of bedrock problem, and it was the bedrock problem that had to be identified so that it could be attacked in a concerted, unified, and innovative way...The bedrock problem, in a word, was "poverty." Words and concepts determine programs; once a target was reduced to a single word, the timing became right for a unified program.[2]

But even political consensus that poverty is a problem does not necessarily mean that everyone defines poverty in the same fashion.

Poverty as Deprivation

One way to define poverty is as *deprivation*—insufficiency in food, housing, clothing, medical care, and other items required to maintain a decent standard of living. This definition assumes that there is a standard of living below which individuals and families can be considered *deprived*. This standard is admittedly arbitrary; no one knows for certain what level of material well-being is necessary to avoid deprivation.

Each year, the U.S. Social Security Administration (SSA) estimates the cash income needed by individuals and families to satisfy minimum food, housing, clothing, and medical-care needs. These figures are known as the *poverty level* and are sometimes called the poverty line, poverty index, or poverty threshold. This official calculation was first used in 1964. Each year, the SSA updates poverty level figures according to the Consumer Price Index. Some revisions have been made in the calculations. For example, different formulas are no longer used to calculate poverty rates for male and female households or for farm and nonfarm families. The poverty level is a crude measure of poverty. It is calculated by making an estimate of the costs of food for a household (determined according to the Thrifty Food Plan of the U.S. Department of Agriculture) and multiplying this figure by three, since it is assumed that about one-third of an average household budget is, or should be, spent on food. In 1990, the guideline for determining whether a family of four was in poverty was $12,700, up from poverty levels of $8,414 in 1980, $3,968 in 1970, and $2,973 in 1959 (see table 3–1). The poverty level is an *absolute* measure of poverty because it provides one figure for the number of poor in the country, and individuals and families fall either above or below it. According to this official definition, there were approximately 31.9 million poor people in the United States in 1988. This is a poverty rate of 13.1 percent of the population.

Even if we were to agree that poverty should be defined as deprivation, there would still be many problems in establishing an official poverty level based on money income as described above. First of all, the Social Security Administration's definition of poverty includes only cash income (before taxes) and excludes free medical care, food stamps, free school lunches, and public housing.[3] If these benefits were *costed out,* i.e., calculated as cash income, there would be *fewer* poor people in America than shown in official statistics. It is also thought that many individuals (poor and nonpoor) report their incomes at *lower* figures than they really are. Taking this into account might further reduce the number of persons counted as poor.[4]

There are other problems in this definition of poverty. It does not take into account regional differences in the cost of living, climate, or styles of living. (It is unlikely that a family of four can live on $12,700 in New York City, even if it might be possible in Hattiesburg, Mississippi.) It does not account for family assets. (An older family that has paid off its mortgage does not usually devote as much to housing as a young family that rents or has recently purchased a home.) It does not recognize differences in the status of families—for example, whether family members are students or retirees. Some of these people may not consider themselves poor, although they are counted as poor in official government statistics. This definition does not recognize the needs of families that may have income above the poverty line but have special problems or hardships that drain away income—chronic illnesses, large debts, or other problems. Finally, the estimate that one-third of family income is spent on food is outdated. The high costs of housing and utilities have changed the composition of the family budget. The poorest families in America now spend slightly more than one-fourth of their disposable income on food. (Higher income families spend considerably less. The national average is 12 percent.[5]) If the family food budget were multiplied by four, this would yield a higher poverty level.[6]

TABLE 3-1   Poverty Levels Based on Money Income and Size of Family

FAMILY SIZE	INCOME IN DOLLARS					
	1959	1970	1975	1980	1985	1990
1 Person	$1,503	$1,954	$2,724	$ 4,190	$ 5,250	$ 6,280
2 Persons	1,952	2,525	3,506	5,363	7,050	8,420
3 Persons	2,324	3,099	4,293	6,565	8,850	10,560
4 Persons	2,973	3,968	5,500	8,414	10,650	12,700
5 Persons	3,506	4,680	6,499	9,966	12,450	14,840
6 Persons	3,944	5,260	7,316	11,269	14,250	16,980
7 Persons	4,849	6,468	9,022	13,955	16,050	19,120

Sources: Statistical Abstract of the United States, 1980, p. 463; 1984, p. 447; *Federal Register 50,* no. 46 (Friday, March 8, 1985) p. 9518; *Social Security Bulletin, 53,* no. 3, (March 1990), p. 15.

Despite these problems, some official definition of poverty is needed to administer government programs. As one observer commented:

> Although the existing poverty lines are arbitrary both for statistical purposes and for operational purposes, some arbitrary lines are needed, and these serve well simply because they already exist as a convention. To reopen an argument as to whether they are 'correct' seems a fruitless exercise.[7]

As often happens, administrative efficiency rather than the needs of the poor turns out to be the underlying basis for an important policy decision—in this case, defining poverty.

IN-KIND BENEFITS: HOW MUCH ARE THEY WORTH?

Although the Social Security Administration is responsible for determining poverty levels and setting income guidelines for determining who qualifies for government welfare programs, it is the Bureau of the Census which estimates the portion of the population that lived in poverty each year. In addition to the standard definition of poverty, the bureau is now using *twelve* different calculations that consider factors such as capital gains, public assistance, and social insurance programs, both cash and in-kind.[8] There is agreement that in order to measure poverty accurately, in-kind as well as cash benefits must be considered. In 1980, the bureau began conducting research to determine the best way to calculate the value of in-kind benefits. But during the past ten years, there has been no agreement about which method to use.

Let's consider two of these approaches.[9] One is the *market-value* approach. Using this approach, the value of welfare benefits is based on what it would cost a private consumer to purchase the good or service. In some cases, this is a very easy approach to use. For example, calculating the value of food stamps is easy because the face value of the coupons used to purchase food items is equal to the amount it would cost any shopper to purchase the same item. Calculating the value of other benefits such as public housing is not as easy because there are no surveys which equate the value of comparable public and private housing.

A second method is the *recipient* or *cash-equivalent* approach. This is the cash value that recipients place on the in-kind benefits they receive. It is based on the amount of money a poor family or individual not receiving benefits uses to obtain the same goods or services. This approach is difficult to use because individual preferences vary. What is very valuable to one person is not necessarily as valuable to another. The market value of welfare benefits is considered to be higher than the recipient or cash equivalent value. For example it is believed that recipients would prefer cash to in-kind benefits and that they would trade $1,500 worth of food stamps for $1,440 in cash.

The market and recipient approaches produce similar estimates of food benefits for those in poverty (in 1987, $1,605 and $1,519, respectively). But the estimates of housing and medical benefits differ substantially. For example, in 1987 the market value was $1,786 for housing and $3,443 for medical benefits. Using the recipient method, the figures were $952 for housing and $1,010 for medical benefits. The market value approach reduced official poverty figures for all persons by 5 percent while the recipient approach reduced poverty figures by 2.5 percent. Due to the difficulties in making estimates of the value of in-kind benefits and the lack of agreement among experts about the best method to use, the government is not yet including them in official estimates of poverty.

WHO ARE THE POOR?

Poverty can occur in all kinds of families and in all areas of the country. However, the incidence of poverty varies among groups in America (see Figures 3–1 and 3–2). More whites are poor than blacks. Of the 31.9 million poor people in the nation, by government definition, approximately 20.7 million are white and 9.4 million are black. However, the likelihood that blacks will experience poverty is more than three times greater than it is for whites: *The poverty rate for the nation's black population is 31.6 percent compared to 10.1 percent for the white population.* In other words, whites outnumber blacks among the poor, but a much larger percentage of the nation's black population is poor. (This is because the total black population in the nation is only about 30 million or 12 percent of the total 245 million people.) There are nearly 5.4 million poor Americans of Hispanic origin. Hispanic-Americans are about 8 percent of the population, but their poverty rate is 26.8 percent.

*The major source of poverty today is families headed by women.** Although the poverty rate for families headed by couples is 5.6 percent, the poverty rate for female-headed households is 33.5 percent. *For families headed by white women, the rate is 26.5 percent. The rates for families headed by women who are black and of Hispanic origin are 49.0 and 49.1 percent, respectively.* There are approximately 12.6 million poor children in America, or about 19.7 percent of the total population under age eighteen. For children who are black or of Hispanic origin, the situation is especially bad; 44.2 percent of all black children and 37.9 percent of Hispanic-American children live in poverty, compared to 14.6 percent of white children.

There is some better news in the official poverty figures: Poverty rates for the elderly are lower than ever before. Poverty has been reduced from 24.6 percent in 1970 to 12 percent today. The 12 percent figure is slightly more than one percentage point below the national average for all Americans.

Poverty occurs not only in large central cities but in rural America as well. About 18.3 percent of the residents of urban cities are poor, and about 16 percent of rural residents are poor. There is some poverty in the nation's suburbs, but proportionately this figure is lower—8.3 percent. Suburban areas experience less poverty because the poor are unlikely to find low-income housing there! How persistent is poverty? Researchers conducting the University of Michigan's Panel Study of Income Dynamics (PSID) tracked 5,000 American families for over ten years

---

* Additional information on poverty among blacks, Hispanic-Americans, and women is found in Chapter 11.

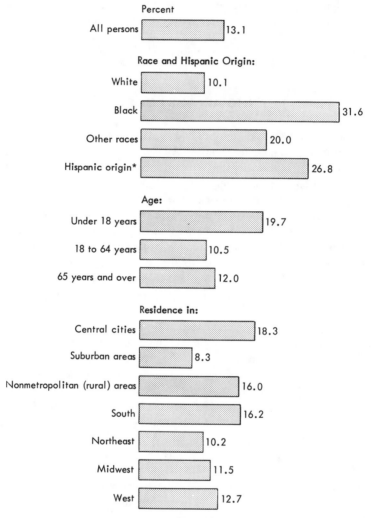

* Persons of Hispanic origin may be of any race.

FIGURE 3–1   Poverty rates for persons with selected characteristics: 1988 (*Source:* U.S. Bureau of the Census, *Money, Income and Poverty Status in the United States. 1988*, series P-60, no. 166, p. 6.)

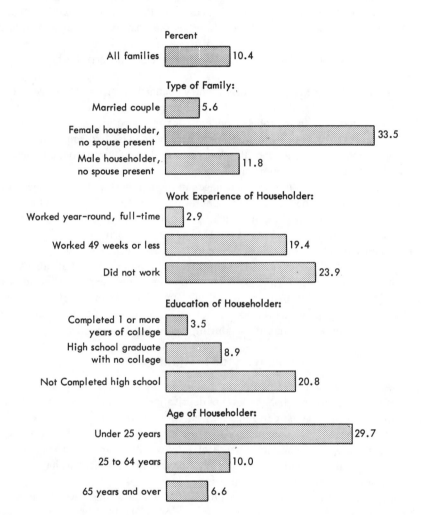

FIGURE 3–2 Poverty rates for families with selected characteristics: 1988 (*Source:* U.S. Bureau of the Census, *Money, Income and Poverty Status in the United States, 1988,* series P-60, no. 166, p. 8.)

and found that only 3 percent were persistently poor—that is, they were poor throughout this period. There is some consolation in the fact that people's circumstances change—although they may lose their jobs, separate, divorce, or become ill, later they may find work, remarry, or get well, thus improving their financial condition. But more recent and methodologically sensitive studies of *spells of poverty* indicate that persistent poverty is much more serious than once thought. While the majority still experiences poverty for a short time (one or two years), 60 percent of those classified as poor at any given time will experience poverty for eight years or longer.[10]

Has the percentage of poor in this country changed? Franklin D. Roosevelt said in his second inaugural address in 1937, "I see one-third of a nation ill-housed, ill-clad, ill-nourished." He was probably underestimating poverty; economic historians think that over 50 percent of the nation would have been classified as poor during the Great Depression. Since that time, the American political and economic system has succeeded in reducing the proportion of poor.

Figure 3–3 allows us to observe changes in the numbers and percentages of the poor since 1959. All of these figures account for the effects of inflation, so there is no question that poverty (as defined in official government statistics) declined considerably during the 1960s and reached lows of 11 to 12 percent during the 1970s. However, poverty increased in the early 1980s. It rose to 15.2 percent in 1983, but dropped back to 13.1 percent by 1988. A sluggish economy that resulted in increased unemployment, along with some cuts in government social welfare programs, explained much of the increase. The Reagan administration hailed the later decreases in poverty as evidence that its economic policies had worked, but others point to the fact that poverty continues to remain higher than it was during the 1970s.

Poverty as Inequality

Poverty can also be defined as *inequality in the distribution of income*. This definition is not tied to any absolute level of deprivation. Instead, it focuses on *relative deprivation*—some people perceive that they have less income or material possessions than most Americans, and they believe they are entitled to more. Even with a fairly substantial income, one may feel a sense of *relative deprivation* in a very affluent society where commercial advertising portrays the average American as having a high level of consumption and material well-being.

Today, the poor in America are wealthy by the standards that have prevailed over most of history and that still prevail in many areas of the world. Nonetheless, millions of American families are considered poor, by themselves and by others, because they have less income than most Americans. These people *feel* deprived—they perceive the gap between themselves and the average American family to be wide, and they do not accept the gap as legitimate. Eliminating poverty when it is defined as relative deprivation really means achieving greater *equality* of income and material possessions.

By the standards that have prevailed over most of history, and still prevail over large areas of the world, there are very few poor in the United States today. Nevertheless, there are

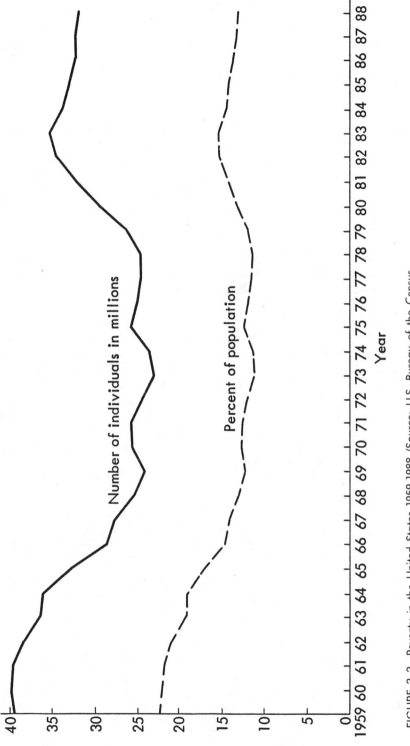

FIGURE 3-3 Poverty in the United States 1959-1988 (Source: U.S. Bureau of the Census, Money, Income and Poverty Status in the United States: 1989, Series P-60, No. 166, p. 58.)

millions of American families who, both in their own eyes and in those of others, are poor. As our nation prospers, our judgment as to what constitutes poverty will inevitably change. When we talk about poverty in America, we are talking about families and individuals who have much less income than most of us. When we talk about reducing or eliminating poverty, we are really talking about changing the distribution of income.[11]

How can we measure poverty as inequality? Economists frequently measure the distribution of total personal income across various classes of families. Since relative deprivation is a psychological as well as a social and economic concept, these classes or groups are difficult to establish, but a common method is to divide all American families into five groups—from the lowest one-fifth in personal income to the highest one-fifth. Table 3–2 shows the percentage of total personal income received by each of these groups since 1936. If perfect income equality existed, then each fifth of American families would receive 20 percent of all family personal income, and it would not even be possible to rank fifths from highest to lowest. But clearly, personal income in America is distributed unequally.

The poorest one-fifth of American families now receive less than 4 percent of all family personal income. This group's share of income, like that of the middle class, rose slowly through the years and then declined during the last decade. The opposite situation occurred for the wealthy, defined in Table 3-2 as the highest one-fifth of Americans in personal income. This group received almost 52 percent of all family personal income in 1936. Its share of income declined for many years, then rose again in the last decade; a similar situation occurred for those whose income falls in the top 5 percent of all Americans. The income gains made by the poorest families have been lost. Between 1980 and 1988, the income of those in the lowest quintile declined by 27 percent, while the highest quintile gained 12 percent. Although some of the hardships of the poor are mitigated by in-kind benefits (food stamps, public housing, Medicare, Medicaid, school lunches, and similar programs) which are not counted as income, even small reductions in their income can have serious consequences.

TABLE 3–2   The Distribution of Income in America (percent distribution of family personal income, by quintiles, and top 5 percent of consumer units, selected years)

QUINTILES	1936	1941	1950	1960	1970	1980	1988
Lowest	4.1%	4.1%	4.5%	4.8%	5.4%	5.2%	3.8%
Second	9.2	9.5	12.0	12.2	12.2	11.6	9.6
Third	14.1	15.3	17.4	17.8	17.6	17.5	16.0
Fourth	20.9	22.3	23.4	24.0	23.9	24.1	24.2
Highest	51.7	48.8	42.7	41.2	40.9	41.5	46.3
Total	100.0	100.0	100.0	100.0	100.0	100.0	100.0
Top 5 Percent	26.5	24.0	17.3	15.9	15.6	15.6	18.3

Source: Bureau of the Census, *Statistical Abstract of the United States, 1980,* p. 454; *1985,* p. 448; *Money Income and Poverty Status in the United States: 1988,* series P-60, no. 166, p. 31.

WHY ARE THE POOR POOR?

Poverty is explained in many ways. We naturally assume that illness, old age, disability, lack of job skills, family instability, discrimination, unemployment, and general economic recessions all contribute to poverty. But how do these problems *interact* to create poverty?

Perhaps the most popular explanation among economists is the *human capital theory*. This theory explains income variations in a free market economy as a result of differences in productivity. The poor are poor because their economic productivity is low. They do not have the human capital—knowledge, skills, training, or education—to sell to employers in a free market. As partial evidence for this theory, we observe that poverty among families headed by a person with less than a high school education is nearly 21 percent, while poverty among families headed by a person who completed high school is almost 9 percent (see again Figure 3–2). For those with some college education, the poverty rate is 3.5 percent.

Economists recognize that poverty may also result from inadequate demand in the economy as a whole, in a particular segment of the economy, or in a particular region of the nation. A serious recession and widespread unemployment raise the proportion of the population living below the poverty level. Full employment and a healthy economy improve opportunities for marginal workers, but these factors do not directly reduce poverty among individuals who have no marketable skills.

Absence from the labor force is the largest single source of poverty. Over two-thirds of the poor are aged persons, children, or disabled people who cannot reasonably be expected to find employment. No improvement in the national economy is likely to affect these people directly. They are outside the labor market and are largely the concern of government rather than of the private economy.

Finally, we must consider poverty that is the direct effect of discrimination against African-Americans, Hispanic-Americans, other ethnic minorities, and women. It is true that *some* of the differences in black and white incomes are a product of educational differences between blacks and whites. However, *even if we control for education,* we can see that blacks at the same educational levels earn less than whites. As shown in Table 3–3, white family income is substantially higher than black family income at every educational level. For example, blacks with high school educations do not earn much more than whites with only an eighth-grade education. White families also earn more than Hispanic-American families at every educational level, although the income differences are not as large as those between whites and blacks. If the human-capital theory operated freely—without interference in the form of discrimination—then we would not expect differences between blacks, whites, and Hispanic-Americans at the same educational levels. But, unfortunately, this is not the case.

When in 1776 Thomas Jefferson wrote on behalf of the Second Continental Congress that "all men are created equal...," he was expressing the widespread dislike for hereditary aristocracy—lords and ladies, dukes and duchesses, and queens and kings. The Founding Fathers wrote their belief in equality of law into the U.S. Constitution. But their concern was *equality of opportunity*, not *absolute equality*.

TABLE 3–3   Median Family Income by Ethnicity and Educational Level (1987)

	ALL FAMILIES	WHITE	BLACK	HISPANIC
Education				
Elementary School:				
Less than 8 years	$10,884	$15,264	$12,149	$13,540
8 years	12,999	18,718	13,210	16,319
High School:				
1–3 years	16,727	22,653	12,166	17,939
4 years	25,910	30,958	20,263	25,130
College:				
1–3 years	31,865	37,324	25,115	31,006
4 years	43,952	50,908	36,568	43,382

Source: Bureau of the Census, *Statistical Abstract of the United States, 1989,* pp. 441 and 447.

Indeed, the Founding Fathers referred to efforts to equalize income as "leveling," and they were strongly opposed to this notion. Jefferson wrote:

> To take from one, because it is thought his own industry and that of his fathers has acquired too much, in order to spare to others, who, or whose fathers have not, exercised equal industry and skill, is to violate arbitrarily the first principle of association, the guarantee to everyone the free exercise of his industry and the fruits acquired by it.[12]

Equality of opportunity requires that artificial obstacles to upward mobility be removed. Distinctions based on race, gender, ethnicity, birth, and religion have no place in a free society. But this is not to say that all people's incomes should be equalized. Andrew Jackson, one of the nation's first democrats, explained:

> Distinctions in every society will always exist under every just government. Equality of talents, education or wealth cannot be produced by human institutions. In the full enjoyment of the gifts of heaven and the fruits of superior industry, economy, and virtue, every man is entitled to protection by law; but when the laws undertake to add to these national distinctions, to grant titles, gratuities, and exclusive privileges, to make the rich richer...then the humble members of society have a right to complain of the injustice of their government.[13]

How much equality can we afford? Utopian socialists have argued for this rule of distribution: "From each according to his ability, to each according to his needs." In other words, everyone produces whatever he or she can, and wealth and income are distributed according to the needs of the people. There is no monetary reward for hard work, or skills and talent, or education and training. Since everyone's needs are roughly the same, everyone will receive roughly the same income. Collective ownership replaces private property. If such a utopian society ever existed, then near-perfect income equality would be achieved, with each fifth of the population receiving 20 percent of all personal income.

But all societies—capitalist and socialist, democratic and authoritarian, traditional and modern—distribute wealth unequally. It is not likely that income differences will ever disappear. Societies reward hard work, skill, talent, education, training, risk taking, and ingenuity. Distributing income equally throughout society threatens the work ethic. The real question we must confront is *how much* inequality is necessary and desirable for a society. We may or may not believe that the current distribution of income (as shown in Table 3–2) is fair.

If the problem of poverty is defined as *inequality,* then it is not really capable of solution. Regardless of how well off poor individuals and families may be in absolute standards of living, there will always be a lowest one-fifth of the population receiving something less than 20 percent of all income. We might reduce income inequalities, but *some* differences will remain, and even these differences might be posed as a problem.

Poverty as Culture

Some argue that poverty is a *way of life* passed on from generation to generation in a self-perpetuating cycle. This *culture of poverty* involves not just a low income but also attitudes of indifference, alienation, and apathy, along with lack of incentives and of self-respect. These attitudes make it difficult for the poor to utilize the opportunities for upward mobility that may be available to them. Increasing the income of those who are poor may not affect joblessness, lack of incentives, lack of educational opportunities, unstable family life, or the high incidence of crime, delinquency, and other social problems among the members of this group.

There are sharp differences between scholars and policy makers over the existence of a culture of poverty. The argument resembles the classic exchange between F. Scott Fitzgerald and Ernest Hemingway. When Fitzgerald observed, "The rich are different from you and me," Hemingway retorted, "Yes, they have more money." Observers who believe that they see a distinctive culture among the poor may say, "The poor are different from you and me." But opponents of the culture-of-poverty notion may reply, "Yes, they have less money." But are the poor undereducated, unskilled, poorly motivated, and "delinquent" because they are poor? Or are they poor because they are undereducated, unskilled, poorly motivated, and "delinquent"? The distinction is a serious one because it has important policy implications.

One especially controversial view of the culture of poverty is set forth by Harvard Professor Edward C. Banfield, who contends that poverty is really a product of "present-orientedness."[14] According to Banfield, individuals caught up in the culture of poverty are unable to plan for the future, to sacrifice immediate gratifications in favor of future ones, or to exercise the discipline that is required to get ahead. Banfield admits that some people experience poverty because of involuntary unemployment, prolonged illness, death of the breadwinner, or some other misfortune. But even with severe misfortune, he claims, this kind of poverty is not squalid, degrading, or self-perpetuating; it ends once the external cause of it no longer exists. According to Banfield, other people will be poor no matter what their external circumstances are. They live in a culture of poverty that continues for generations because they are psychologically unable to provide for the future. Improvements in their circumstances may affect their poverty only superficially. Even increased income is unlikely to change their way of life, for the additional money will be spent quickly on nonessential or frivolous items.

More recently, Nicolas Lemann has described reasons for the culture of poverty that he believes exists in poor inner city ghetto communities which are comprised largely of black residents.[15] He attributes hard core poverty in these areas to an anthropological cause—the rural southern heritage of many of its residents. As sharecroppers, these individuals were unable to own property, save money, maintain stable, family relationships, or obtain an education, and he contends, these patterns have carried over to the present day.

Opponents of the culture-of-poverty idea argue that these notions divert attention from the conditions of poverty that *currently foster* family instability, present-orientedness, and other ways of life of the poor. Social reformers are likely to focus on the conditions of poverty as the fundamental cause of the social pathologies that afflict the poor. They note that the idea of a culture of poverty can be applied only to groups who have lived in poverty for several generations. It is not relevant to those who have become poor during their lifetimes because of sickness, accident, or old age. The cultural explanation basically involves parental transmission of values and beliefs, which in turn determines behavior of future generations. In contrast, the situational explanation of poverty shows how present social conditions and differences in financial resources operate directly to determine behavior. Perhaps the greatest danger in the idea of a culture of poverty is that poverty in this light can be seen as an unbreakable, puncture-proof cycle. This outlook may lead to a relaxation of efforts to ameliorate the conditions of poverty. In other words, a culture of poverty may become an excuse for inaction.

If one assumes that the poor are no different from other Americans, then one is led toward policies that emphasize opportunity for individuals as well as changes in their environment. If the poor are like other Americans, it is necessary only to provide them with the ordinary means to achieve—for example, job-training programs, good schools, and counseling to make them aware of opportunities that are available to them. The intervention that is required to change their lives, therefore, is one of supplying a means to achieve a level of income that most Americans enjoy.

On the other hand, if one believes in the notion of a culture of poverty, it is necessary to devise a strategy to interrupt the transmission of lower-class cultural values from generation to generation. The strategy must try to prevent the socialization of young children into an environment of family instability, lack of motivation, crime and delinquency, and so forth. One rather drastic means to accomplish this would be simply to remove children from lower-class homes at a very early age and to raise them in a controlled environment that transmits the values of the conventional culture rather than of the culture of poverty. Such a solution is not realistic. More acceptable solutions used today are special day-care centers and preschool programs which are designed to remedy cultural deprivation and disadvantage. Theoretically, these programs would bring about change in young children through *cultural enrichment*.

Poverty as Exploitation

Both Marxist and non-Marxist writers have defined poverty as a form of *exploitation by the ruling class*. Sociologist Herbert Gans contended that poverty serves many functions for the middle and upper classes in America, such as providing a cheap source of labor.[16] Gans implication is that poverty is maintained by ruling classes in order to make their own lives more pleasant. Poverty does not have to exist; it could be eliminated with the cooperation of the middle and upper classes. But it is unlikely that these classes will ever give up anything they believe they have earned through their own hard work, useful skills, or business enterprise. Many Americans believe that they are immune from financial disaster and poverty.

Other authors have also written about the class-based nature of poverty. Two of them have called our society the "upside-down welfare state" because "the welfare state is a complicated system in which those who need help the most get the least, and those who need it least get the most."[17] They say that all Americans, rich or poor, benefit from government welfare programs. The poor receive government assistance through the Aid to Families with Dependent Children, Food Stamp, and Medicaid programs. The middle class receives government assistance in the form of home mortgage loans and educational grants. The rich receive government assistance in the form of income tax deductions, government contracts, and subsidies to business and industry. The difference is that government assistance to the poor is called *welfare,* while government assistance to the rich is called *good business.* In the final analysis, the poor receive only a pittance of all government assistance. Much government assistance goes to the middle and upper classes.

Social scientists Frances Fox Piven and Richard A. Cloward have also commented on the economic, political, and social utility that the upper classes see in maintaining poverty. In 1971, they published *Regulating the Poor: The Functions of Public Welfare* and claimed that "[t]he key to an understanding of relief-giving is in the functions it serves for the larger economic and political order, for relief is a secondary and supportive institution."[18] Piven and Clowand argued, especially with regard to the Aid to Families with Dependent Children program, that welfare had been used as a device to control the poor in order to maintain social stability. Welfare programs were expanded in times of political unrest as a means of appeasing the poor, and welfare rules and regulations were used as a means of *forcing* the poor into the labor market during times of political stability, especially when there was a need to increase the number of people in the work force. Piven and Cloward have updated their original ideas. They now believe that this cyclical pattern of contraction and expansion of welfare has been replaced by a more permanent set of welfare programs.[19] But these programs are a threat to Corporate America because they provide basic subsistence, which makes people less dependent for their survival on business and industry and fluctuations in the labor market. Piven and Cloward believe in the right to welfare. They encouraged Americans to resist the philosophies of Reaganomics and to preserve the social welfare programs.

If poverty is defined as the exploitation of the poor by a ruling class, then it might be suggested that only a restructuring of society to eliminate class differences would solve the problem of poverty. Marxists call for the revolutionary overthrow of capitalist society by workers and farmers and the emergence of a new *classless* society. Presumably, in such a society there would be no ruling class with an interest in exploiting the poor. Of course, in practice, Communist societies have produced one-party governments that dominate and exploit nearly the entire population, and recently most of these governments have given way to more democratic governance.

These perspectives help us to understand that there are indeed class differences in views on poverty. If the upper classes do not deliberately exploit the poor, they sometimes express very paternalistic attitudes toward them. By paternalistic, we mean that the upper classes have little understanding of the lives of poor people, yet they believe they "know what's best" for the poor in social welfare policy. Moreover, the upper classes frequently engage in charitable activities and support liberal welfare programs to demonstrate their idealism and *do-goodism,* whether the poor are actually helped or not.

Poverty As Structure

Poverty can also be considered by studying the *institutional* and *structural* components of society that foster its continuation. We have already mentioned that poverty can, in part, be attributed to the effects of discrimination. *Institutional discrimination* refers to practices that are deeply embedded in schools, the criminal justice system, and other organizations that serve gatekeeper functions in society. For example, poor school districts generally have fewer resources which can be used to promote adequate educational opportunities for its young citizens than schools in middle- and upper-class districts. These differences were tolerated for many years, but they have now become the bases for court challenges to the ways in which public school education is funded in a number of states. Health care institutions and other service organizations are generally not well organized in poorer communities. Lack of access to health care and other resources also contribute to circumstances that make it more difficult to avoid poverty. Another striking example of institutional discrimination occurs in jails and prisons which are overpopulated with men who are black, of Hispanic origin, and poor. Problems of this nature can only be ameliorated by changing the structure of societal institutions which perpetuate them.

Issues related to the economic structure of the country have also resulted in deep-seated poverty that arises from inadequate demand in a particular sector of the economy or in a particular region of the nation. For example, industrialization and technological development appear to have bypassed large segments of Appalachia, one of the country's poorest areas. The closing of steel mills in large eastern cities and auto plants in midwestern cities has also forced workers into poverty. Many workers are able to locate new jobs, but those with few marketable skills are least likely to secure jobs in other segments of the economy; neither are they able to relocate to other communities to find employment.

In recent years there has been a concern about a group referred to as the *underclass* which has been the most severely affected by changes in community and economic structure. Karl Marx used the term *lumpenproletariat* (the proletariat in rags) more than a hundred years ago to describe those who had, in essence, dropped out of society.[20] In the 1960s this concept reemerged. The term "underclass" was adopted to describe those who had been unable to weather changes in the country's economic structure and who were not able to obtain jobs in a market that relied increasingly on more highly skilled and educated workers.[21]

Today, the term underclass is used with particular reference to poor, black, ghetto communities characterized by long-term unemployment, long-term welfare dependency, and overall social disorganization, including high levels of street crime.[22] Use of the term underclass is controversial because of its derogatory sound and because it fails to distinguish the diversity of the types of individuals that comprise it.[23] Nonetheless, it is a group of considerable concern because these individuals are clearly outside the mainstream of the social, economic, and political institutions that are part of the lives of most citizens. Prior to the 1960s these inner city communities were not severely depressed as they are today.[24] In the 1940s and 1950s they were home to blacks of all social classes. Fair housing and other anti-discrimination laws had not yet evolved that would allow many middle- and upper-class blacks to move to more affluent city and suburban neighborhoods. Schools, businesses, and other social institutions in these neighborhoods were utilized by all residents, and the economic exchange in these communities provided jobs for many residents, including those with marginal job skills. But as professional and blue collar workers were able to find better housing in the suburbs, only the most disadvantaged were left behind. According to several authors, community leaders were no longer present to bring stability to these neighborhoods. Their departure also caused a severe decline in the economic enterprises within these communities. At the same time, the job market in the cities underwent considerable change. Industrial and manufacturing jobs were being replaced by jobs in the financial, technical, and administrative fields, and these were not the kinds of jobs for which most poor inner city residents were prepared. Jobs in the food and retail industries which inner city residents might have been able to fill more readily were increasing in numbers in the suburbs, but those who needed these jobs the most could not find housing there. It has been said that these structural changes left open a path for social disorganization. As a result, inner city neighborhoods deteriorated and problems such as unemployment, teen pregnancy, and drug dealing increased.

Recommendations to remedy this type of severe or persistent poverty have included proposals that multiple approaches be used, for example, that job training, relocation, and other types of services be coupled with efforts to bring the poor into touch with the mainstream society. These solutions sound similar to those suggested to interrupt the culture of poverty. The important distinction is that the notion of a culture of poverty is concerned with changing *personal* characteristics of the poor that prevent them from functioning in the mainstream society. Some have referred to this as a "blame the victim" mentality. Poverty viewed as a *structural* issue is quite different. It implies that the solutions to the problem lie in developing new social institutions or modifying existing ones to be more responsive to disadvantaged members of society. This is an important distinction in developing social policies. For example, rather than provide housing for the poor in ghetto communities, a structural approach would be to offer housing in non-ghetto communities to allow disadvantaged individuals to avail themselves of greater societal opportunities. Another suggestion to bring young people into the mainstream is to develop a national service requirement for *all* youth. This type of universal program for youth is quite different from those that target only those from disadvantaged backgrounds. The concept behind such a program is that it would provide for better integration of all members of society, but clearly such a requirement for national service will meet with opposition from those who feel that they would not gain by it.

POOR AND HOMELESS: NOT INVISIBLE ANYMORE

In an influential book of the 1960s, *The Other America,* the late Michael Harrington argued that most Americans were blind to the poverty of millions in their own country.[25] Harrington spoke of two nations within America, one a nation of comfortable and affluent Americans, the other a nation of the poor—those forced to suffer deprivation and humiliation because they are without access to adequate education, housing, employment, and health care. Harrington stated that most Americans are blind to poverty because the poor are "invisible"—they do not live or socialize or receive their education with the more affluent. Rural poverty can be masked by a beautiful countryside. Mass production of decent clothing also hides poverty; a poor person may be relatively well dressed but unable to afford decent housing or health care. The elderly poor are invisible because they do not venture far from home. And finally, the poor are invisible because they have no political power; in fact, they are often the victims of political action.

Poverty has recently become more visible, primarily because of the number of homeless individuals and families grew during the 1980s. Estimates of the number of homeless vary tremendously—from two-hundred fifty thousand to three million. Of course, it is difficult to get an exact count, but for the first time, the United States Bureau of the Census will try to capture the number in its 1990 census. Most of the poor have some type of permanent residence, and although the quality of this housing may vary a great deal, they do have an address to call home. But there is a group of Americans who have no permanent address at all. Some of these individuals are mentally ill. *Deinstitutionalization* of people with serious, chronic mental illnesses in the 1970s led to an increase in the numbers of these individuals who live on the streets (see also Chapter 7). Alcoholics and drug addicts are another group who comprise the homeless. Men in this group have long been a significant portion of the homeless. But today homelessness has taken on a different face—family units are included in significant numbers. Some of these families are couples without children while others are single women with children. Family violence is a primary reason that these women seek assistance from shelters. Still other families consist of two parents and children.

Unemployment among this group has contributed to its inability to afford housing. Some of the homeless do have jobs, but they do not earn enough to afford private housing, and public housing is often unavailable to them. The extent of some of the medical and social problems of shelter residents (not including unemployment) is found in Figure 3–4. The homeless tend to be young (see Figure 3–5). More than 25 percent are less than age eighteen and more than 60 percent are under age 30. A significant portion of youth who live on the streets or seek shelter care have runaway from home because they are abused or unwanted. "Unaccompanied men" are still the largest category of clients served by shelters. Forty percent of shelters are still devoted to their care, but they represent a decreasing proportion of clients than in years past. Today, these men are estimated to be 45 percent of all clients, and unaccompanied women are 14 percent. Single-parents with children comprise 30 percent of clients while couples with children are 6 percent and couples without children are 4 percent.[26]

The late Democratic Senator Hubert H. Humphrey once said, "The moral test of government is how it treats those who are in the dawn of life—the children; those who are in the twilight of life—the aged; and those who are in the shadows of life—the sick, the needy and the handicapped." There is a growing feeling that of all these groups, children, who in general have a 20 percent rate of poverty in this country, are now those least likely to be treated well by the government. The addition of families to the ranks of the homeless is perhaps the straw that motivated Congress to pass the Stewart B. McKinney Homeless Assistance Act in 1987. This act provides money for emergency shelters, nutrition assistance, health and mental health care, job training, education for homeless children, and other social services for homeless individuals and

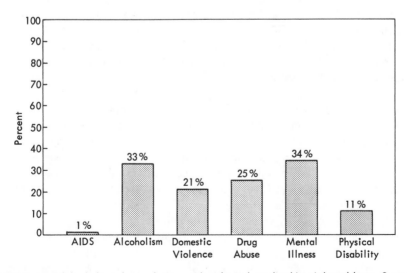

FIGURE 3–4   Adult sheltered population with selected medical/social problems. Source: *A Report on the 1988 National Survey of Shelters for the Homeless* (Washington, D.C.: U.S. Department of Housing and Urban Development, March 1988), p. 13.

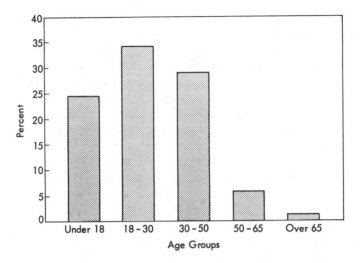

FIGURE 3–5   Sheltered homeless population by age. Source: *A Report on the 1988 National Survey of Shelters for the Homeless* (Washington, D.C.: U.S. Department of Housing and Urban Development, March 1988), p. 12.

families. There are actually several different types of shelters. The oldest are missions and similar types of facilities used by skid-row alcoholics. Many of these are run by the organizations like the Salvation Army. Shelters for battered women are another type, as are special shelters for runaway youth. More recently shelters for families have grown in number and most cities now have such facilities. According to Department of Housing and Urban Development (HUD), "[n]ine of every 10 shelters are operated by private, non-profit groups aided by many volunteers, while two-thirds of the funds to support them come from local, state and the Federal governments."[27] This humanitarian aid is welcome, but there is a fear that these shelters are becoming substitutes for permanent homes and that real solutions to homelessness are being pursued at a snail's pace. In the next pages the reader will find two excerpts from other works about homelessness, particularly among families. One is an account of homelessness among those living at the Martinique Hotel by Jonathan Kozol; the other, by Robert Ellickson, presents a view of the problem from quite a different perspective.

There are undoubtedly various views on homelessness, but there is considerable agreement that the United States is in an affordable housing crisis. The lack of affordable housing for low-income families has caused cities like New York to rent hotels (such as the Martinique) at exorbitant rates because no other alternatives are immediately available. After years of increasing rates of homeownership, it has become more difficult for many to realize what was once called the "American dream"—owning a home. It has also become increasingly difficult just to pay the rent. Communities are experimenting with new approaches to help low-income individuals and families obtain their own homes. For example, Habitat for Humanity (its most prominent volunteers are President Jimmy and Rosalyn Carter) is a not-for-profit group that rehabilitates housing for poor individuals and families. Many public housing projects are finding ways to turn ownership over to residents in the hope that they will take charge and better maintain property they own. Communities are also using other alternatives, such as low interest bond money for mortgages to low-income, first-time home buyers. But a coherent national strategy has been lacking. The Reagan administration had no plan to address this problem, and the number of affordable housing units dwindled. Congress decided to act and in 1990 it passed a new housing initiative with a $57 billion price tag, which the President is expected to approve. The funds are intended for construction of housing for low-income renters and to assist low-income individuals in purchasing homes.

ILLUSTRATION: POVERTY AT THE MARTINIQUE

It is possible to picture what a cheerful place this might have been at Christmas in the years when Woodrow Wilson was alive and Edward was the king of England and there was a tsar in Russia and fashionable musicians entertained the patrons in the ballroom of the Martinique Hotel. . . .

December 20, 1985: Heavy chains secure the doorway of the former ballroom. They are removed to let a dozen people enter at a time. The line of people waiting for their lunch goes back about 200 feet. In the semi-darkness I see adults trying to keep children at their sides. Some of the kids are acting up, yelling, racing back and forth. A few are sitting on the floor.

This is the lunch program of the Coalition for the Homeless. Meals are served to residents five days a week. The program is organized by a young man named Tom Styron. He has enlisted the help of several women living in the building. Because I have come with him today, he has enlisted my help too.

One of the women sits by the door and checks the names of those who enter. Another woman helps to serve the food. The room is so cold that both keep on their coats. One has a heavy coat. The other has an unlined army jacket. She is very thin, a Puerto Rican woman, and is trembling.

I watch the people coming to the table. The children don't avert their eyes; nor do the women. It is the men who seem most scared: grown men in shabby clothes with nervous hands. They keep their eyes fixed on the floor.

The meal is good: turkey, potatoes, raisins, milk, an orange. It would be enough if it were one of three meals to be eaten in one day. For many, however, this will be the only meal. For an adult who has had no breakfast, this is at best a pacifier to fend off the hunger pangs until late afternoon.

Many of the children have on coats and sweaters. After they eat, some of them come back to the table, timidly. They ask if there are seconds.

There are no seconds. Several families at the back of the line have to be turned away. In my pocket I have one enormous apple that I bought in Herald Square for fifty cents. I give it to a tall Italian man. He doesn't eat the apple. He polishes it against his shirt. He turns it in his hand, rubs it some more. I watch him bring it back to where he's sitting with his children: one boy, two little girls.

The coalition buys the lunches from the New York Board of Education. The program therefore does not operate when school is not in session. Christmas, for this and other reasons, may be one of the most perilous and isolated times for families in the Martinique Hotel. Christmas is a difficult time for homeless families everywhere in the United States. . . .

The Martinique is not the worst of the hotels for homeless families in New York. Because its tenants have refrigerators (a very precious item for the mother of a newborn), it is considered by some residents to be one of the better shelters in the city. In visiting the Martinique, one tries to keep this point in mind; but it is, at first, not easy to imagine something worse.

Members of the New York City Council who visited the building in July of 1986 were clearly shaken: "People passing by the hotel have no sense of the tragic dimensions of life inside. Upon entering the hotel, one is greeted by a rush of noise, made in large part by the many small children living there. These children share accommodations with a considerable cockroach and rodent population. The nearly 400 families housed at the Martinique are assisted by just seven HRA caseworkers, whose efforts to keep in touch with each family—at least once each month—often amount to no more than a note slipped under a door."

The report made by the city council offers this additional information: The average family is a mother with three children. Thirty-four percent of families became homeless after eviction by a landlord; 47 percent after being doubled

up with other families; 19 percent after living in substandard housing. Fifty percent of heads of households report that they have once held full-time jobs. Seventy percent have seen at least five vacant units they could not afford or from which they have been turned away by landlords who did not want children or welfare recipients.

The city council describes a family living here more than one year: The family was originally forced to leave a city-owned apartment when one child, a daughter, became ill from lead-paint poison. In their next apartment the family's son became ill from lead poison. "After six months of shuttling back and forth between hotels and EAUs," the city council writes, "the family found itself at the Martinique, where lead paint peels from the ceiling of their room. . . ."

It is difficult to do full justice to the sense of hopelessness one feels on entering the building. It is a haunting experience and leaves an imprint on one's memory that is not easily erased by time or cheerful company. Even the light seems dimmer here, the details harder to make out, the mere geography of twisting corridors and winding stairs and circular passageways a maze that I found indecipherable at first and still find difficult to figure out. After fifty or sixty nights within this building, I have tried but cannot make a floor plan of the place.

Note: The HRA is the New York Human Resources Administration and EAUs are Emergency Assistance Units.

Source: Copyright © 1988 by Jonathan Kozol. Reprinted from *Rachel and Her Children: Homeless Families in America* by Jonathan Kozol by permission of Crown Publishers, Inc.

ILLUSTRATION: THE HOMELESSNESS MUDDLE

During the past decade, homelessness has emerged as a major social problem; yet our attempts to combat it seem only to have worsened things. Although the number of *shelter beds* in the United

States almost tripled between 1983 and 1988 (going from 98,000 to 275,000), beggars now frequent downtown sidewalks and parks in ever-growing numbers. To understand why this has happened—in particular, why increases in government shelter programs have increased the count of homeless people as they are currently defined—one must realize that the view of homelessness proffered by activists like Robert Hayes, Jonathan Kozol, and Mitch Snyder is fundamentally flawed. Although these *advocates deserve credit for bringing* attention to the *human tragedy of homelessness,* their central policy proposal—more government-funded housing projects—is as wrong-headed as their *assessment of the current situation.* Instead of providing unconditional shelter to all who apply for it, policymakers should devise aid programs that better *reflect the diversity* of the *homeless population and that do* more to discourage dependency.

The current confusions in homelessness policy start with semantics. The term "homeless" is now used to describe people in two quite different situations on a given night. First, it applies to the street homeless—*people who* sleep in vehicles, parks, bus stations, and other *places not designed as residences.* Second, it includes the sheltered homeless— those who obtain temporary housing either in shelters that local governments or charities operate, or in rooms that can be rented with emergency housing vouchers supplied by welfare agencies. Unlike the street homeless, the sheltered homeless sleep in places designed for residential living; members of both groups, however, almost invariably lack permanent homes.

This bundled definition of homelessness leads to the paradoxical result that greater governmental spending *on shelter programs increases the reported number of homeless people.* New beds in free shelters draw not only people from the streets, but also those who are housed. Shelters are often used by poor people who have been doubled up with friends or relatives, living in cheap rented rooms, or confined in hospitals, detox centers, or other institutions.

To see how the bundled definition of homelessness misleads, suppose (not unrealistically) that a new hundred-bed shelter draws forty people from the street and sixty who would otherwise have slept in housing or institutions. The street homeless population would fall by forty, and the sheltered homeless population would rise by a hundred— which would increase the total reported homeless population by the sixty who were drawn from their previous housing. Semantic imprecision is thus a major reason why recent bursts in aid to the homeless have been widely regarded as inadequate and ineffectual. To improve the quality of public debate, policymakers and journalists should distinguish between street and sheltered homeless, and should strive to report separate tallies of each. Emphasis on this distinction would help reveal the successes (or failures) of new shelters in reducing street populations; it would also reveal that about half of homeless individuals—and the vast majority of homeless families—are in shelters, not on the streets.

Source: Reprinted with permission of the author Robert C. Ellickson from: *The Public Interest,* No. 99 (Spring, 1990), pp. 45-46. © 1990 by National Affairs, Inc.

DOES WELFARE CAUSE POVERTY?

The belief that welfare programs can actually *increase* the number of poor persons is certainly not new. Since Elizabethan times, welfare payments have been kept minimal to discourage potential recipients from choosing welfare over work. Although the Great Depression of the late 1920s and 1930s made the country realize that poverty could befall almost anyone, many have clung to the idea that welfare should be made an unattractive alternative to employment. A good deal of attention has been given to the idea that much of today's poverty is a *direct* result of the social policies and programs of the 1960s and 1970s. The argument is presented this way: From 1947 to 1965 the poverty rate was reduced by more than half without massive government social welfare intervention, but by the mid-1960s it was thought that the poverty that remained was due to lack of opportunities and bad luck.[28] The solution was government intervention to reduce poverty and create more opportunities for the disadvantaged. Welfare spending and the numbers of welfare programs increased, but the number of poor did not decrease. During the 1970s, the poverty rate remained at around 12 percent.

The first book to receive widespread attention that claimed welfare was to blame was George Gilder's *Wealth and Poverty,* published in 1981. Gilder discusses what he calls "the devastating impact of the programs of liberalism on the poor."[29] He wrote:

> What actually happened since 1964 was a vast expansion of the welfare rolls that halted in its tracks an ongoing improvement in the lives of the poor, particularly blacks, and left behind—and here I choose my words as carefully as I can—a wreckage of broken lives and families worse than the aftermath of slavery.[30]

Gilder uses many Horatio Alger-type success stories, and he points to examples of how poor Americans and immigrants to the United States were able to achieve prosperity through their hard work and the advantages that a capitalistic economic system affords to those who are willing to *sacrifice* to *succeed.* Gilder also contends that the expansion of the welfare system has led to an erosion of the work ethic and self-reliance. The book contains strong gender biases because it focuses on the importance on jobs for men over those for women. Gilder contends that as welfare benefits (AFDC, Food Stamps, Medicaid, public housing) increase, the value of a *man's* labor to this family decreases, especially if that man earns low wages at his job. The welfare system saps his dignity and makes him less necessary to his family. This in turn leads to family breakup and to further reliance on welfare. Gilder also criticizes antidiscrimination policies, which he says favor credentials over the drive to succeed.

In 1984 Charles Murray made much the same argument in his book *Losing Ground: American Social Policy, 1950–1980.*[31] Relying on a number of statistical presentations, Murray concludes that the number of poor increased following passage of the social programs of the Great Society, that the underclass has fallen further behind, and that social welfare policy is responsible. Murray compares three measures of poverty—"official poverty," "net poverty," and "latent poverty"—to make his point. *Official poverty,* as discussed earlier, is the amount of poverty measured by the U.S. government's poverty level calculations. *Net poverty* is official poverty minus the value of in-kind benefits. *Latent poverty* is the number of people who would be poor if they did not receive social insurance and public assistance payments. Murray claims that in-kind benefits have reduced the official poverty figures—but not as much as they should considering the large amounts of money spent on in-kind programs like Food Stamps and Medicaid. Even worse is the fact that latent poverty is much higher than official poverty. In 1980, official poverty stood at 13 percent. Latent poverty increased after 1968, reaching 22 percent of the population by 1980. The war on poverty was supposed to make people economically self-sufficient and get them off welfare. The unfortunate situation is that these programs failed to reduce the need for welfare.

Those critical of Murray's work contend that the statistics and the analyses he presents can be misleading; they say that poverty is a complex issue and that many factors must be presented in any discussion of the rising number of poor people.[32] For example, bad economic times result in higher unemployment, which is the lesson of the Great Depression. Lack of jobs—not the desire to be on the dole—adds to the ranks of the poor. In hard times it is not surprising that the underclass who are in marginal jobs are likely to be unemployed and will require welfare assistance.

Murray's view leads him to suggest a drastic alternative to the current welfare system. He advocates ending all existing federal social welfare programs for working-age people (AFDC, Food Stamps, Medicaid, and so on), except for Unemployment Insurance, and leaving the rest of welfare to private charities and state and local governments. While Galbraith and Harrington were the topics of discussion in the 1960s, the talk of the 1980s was Gilder and Murray. We now wonder what the turn of the century will hold to explain poverty.

SUMMARY

Defining *poverty* is a *political* activity rather than a *rational* exercise. We have discussed five approaches to defining poverty—as deprivation, as inequality, as culture, as exploitation, and as structure. Society cannot agree on one best approach for defining poverty.

If we use the official government poverty level as our arbitrary yardstick, there were about thirty-two million poor people in the United States in 1988, or about 13 percent of the population. However, if we count in-kind benefits as well as cash benefits, the number of poor persons is lower. Since the government began counting, poverty has declined dramatically. Poverty levels reached lows of 11 to 12 percent in the 1970s; however, poverty began to rise again in the early 1980s, reaching a high of about 15 percent. Poverty is most frequently found in black households and households headed by women. Children make up a large number of the poor. The growth in the number of the homeless is also a concern.

Poverty has many causes. Some people such as elderly and disabled individuals, are not able to engage in productive employment. Others are poor because they lack the resources and opportunities of the nonpoor. Discrimination is another source of poverty. Even with the same number of school years completed, African-Americans and many other ethnic minorities earn less than whites; women earn less than men. Equality of opportunity remains an obstacle to the elimination of poverty in the United States.

The way in which poverty is defined has important implications for strategies to alleviate the problem. Human-service professionals have a commitment to increasing opportunities for poor people as a means of reducing poverty. These professionals strive to maximize human potential whenever possible and believe that disadvantaged individuals will make use of opportunities to overcome poverty. They reject the idea that many of the poor do not want to work and that they use their resources unwisely. Poverty may also be the result of structural changes in social institutions such as the economy that leave people without adequate means for survival. If this is the case, solutions should not be directed at individual inadequacies but at the way educational, economic, and other social institutions can be made more responsive to those who are disadvantaged.

Some writers view poverty as a form of exploitation by the ruling classes. The dominant classes in society maintain poverty in order to produce a source of cheap labor—so that they can "use" the poor economically, socially, and politically. This definition of the problem magnifies class conflict and implies that only a radical restructuring of the social system can reduce poverty.

Recent books have blamed the worsened condition of the poor and minorities on the social welfare policies of the Great Society. They espouse the position that welfare has become a more attractive alternative than low-paying jobs and has destroyed the incentives to self-sufficiency. The topic of poverty and its causes certainly has an ability to generate debate in America.

NOTES

1. E.E. Schattschneider, *The Semi-Sovereign People* (New York: Holt, Rinehart & Winston, 1961), p. 68.
2. James L. Sundquist, *Politics and Policy* (Washington, D.C.: Brookings Institution, 1968), pp. 111–12.
3. See U.S. Bureau of the Census, *Money Income and Poverty Status in the United States, 1988,* series P-60, no. 166, for calculations of poverty using noncash benefits.
4. Sheldon Danzinger and Robert Haveman, "The Reagan Budget: A Sharp Break with the Past," *Challenge 24* (May–June 1981), pp. 5–13.
5. "Food Takes Smaller Bite of American Budgets," *Austin American-Statesman* (August 7, 1989), p. A6.
6. Sar A. Levitan, *Programs in Aid of the Poor,* 5th ed. (Baltimore: Johns Hopkins University Press, 1985), pp. 3–4.
7. Robert A. Levine, *The Poor Ye Need Not Have with You* (Cambridge, Mass.: MIT Press, 1970), p. 19.
8. U.S. Bureau of the Census, *Money Income and Poverty Status is the United States, 1988,* Appendix D.
9. The remainder of this section is based on the U.S. Bureau of the Census, *Estimates of Poverty Including the Value of Noncash Benefits, 1987,* technical paper 58 (August 1988).
10. See Martha S. Hill, "Some Dynamic Aspects of Poverty," in M.S. Hill, D.H. Hill, and J.N. Morgan, *Five Thousand American Families: Patterns of Economic Progress, Vol. 9* (Ann Arbor: Institute for Social Research, University of Michigan Press, 1981); Mary Jo Bane, "Household Composition and Poverty," in Sheldon H. Danzinger and Daniel H. Weinberg, eds., *Fighting Poverty: What Works and What Doesn't?* (Cambridge: Harvard University Press, 1986), pp. 209–31 and note 3, p. 398; Mary Jo Bane and David T. Elwood, "Slipping into and out of Poverty: The Dynamics of Spells," Working Paper 119 (Cambridge, Mass.: National Bureau of Economic Research, 1983); cited in Bane, "Household Composition," in Danzinger and Weinberg, *Fighting Poverty*; William Julius Wilson and Kathryn M. Neckerman, "Poverty and Family Structure: The Widening Gap Between Evidence and Public Policy Issues," in Danzinger and Weinberg, *Fighting Poverty*, especially p. 241; William Julius Wilson, *The Truly Disadvantaged: The Inner City, the Underclass, and Public Policy* (Chicago: The University of Chicago Press, 1987), pp. 9–10.
11. Victor R. Fuchs, "Redefining Poverty and Redistributing Income," *Public Interest,* no. 8 (Summer 1967), p. 91.
12. Cited in Richard Hofstadter, *The American Political Tradition* (New York: Knopf, 1948), p. 42.
13. Ibid., p. 45.

14. Edward C. Banfield, *The Unheavenly City* (Boston: Little, Brown, 1968).
15. Nicolas Lemann, "The Origins of the Underclass," *Atlantic Monthly* (June 1986), pp. 31–55; (July 1986), pp. 54–68.
16. Herbert J. Gans, "The Uses of Poverty: The Poor Pay All," *Social Policy 2*, no. 2 (July–August 1971), 20–24.
17. Thomas H. Walz and Gary Askerooth, *The Upside Down Welfare State* (Minneapolis: Elwood Printing, 1973), p. 5.
18. Frances Fox Piven and Richard A. Cloward, *Regulating the Poor: The Functions of Public Welfare* (New York: Random House, 1971).
19. Frances Fox Piven and Richard A. Cloward, *The New Class War* (New York: Pantheon Books, 1982).
20. Michael Harrington, The New American Poverty (New York: Penguin Books, 1984).
21. Ibid.
22. For a discussion of the term underclass see Wilson, *The Truly Disadvantaged,* especially p. 7.
23. Ibid.
24. The remainder of this section relies on Wilson, *The Truly Disadvantaged,* and Lemann, "The Origins of the Underclass."
25. Michael Harrington, *The Other America: Poverty in the United States* (New York: Macmillan, 1962).
26. These figures are from *A Report on the 1988 National Survey of Shelters for the Homeless* (Washington, D.C.: U.S. Department of Housing and Urban Development, March, 1988).
27. Ibid., see foreword.
28. See James Gwartney and Thomas S. McCaleb, "Have Antipoverty Programs Increased Poverty?" (Tallahassee: Florida State University, 1986).
29. George Gilder, *Wealth and Poverty* (New York: Bantam Books, 1981), p. ix.
30. Ibid., p. 13.
31. Charles Murray, *Losing Ground: American Social Policy, 1950–1980* (New York: Basic Books, 1984).
32. Robert Kuttner, "Declaring War on the War on Poverty," *Washington Post* (November 25, 1984), pp. 4, 11. Also see Daniel Patrick Moynihan, "Family and Nation," the Godkin Lectures, Harvard University (April 8–9, 1985).

4

PREVENTING POVERTY
The Social
Insurance Programs

PREVENTING POVERTY THROUGH
COMPULSORY SAVINGS

Why not require people to insure themselves against poverty, in much the same fashion as people insure themselves against other tragedies, such as deaths, accidents, and fires? The preventive strategy uses the concept of *social insurance*. This involves compelling individuals to purchase insurance against the possibility of their own indigency, which might result from forces over which they had no control—loss of job, death of the family breadwinner, or physical disability. Social insurance is based on the same principles as private insurance: It involves the sharing of risks and the setting aside of money for a "rainy day." Workers and employers pay *premiums* (Social Security taxes), which are held in trust by the government under each worker's name (and Social Security number). When age, death, disability, or unemployment prevents workers from continuing on the job, they or their dependents are paid out of the accumulated trust fund. Social insurance appears to offer a simple, rational approach for dealing with the causes of poverty.

There are important distinctions between *social insurance* programs and *public assistance* programs. If (1) the beneficiaries of a government program are required to make contributions to it before claiming any of its benefits (or if employers must pay into the program on behalf of their workers) and if (2) the benefits are paid out as legal entitlements regardless of the beneficiaries' personal wealth, *then* the program is called *social insurance*. On the other hand, if (1) the program is financed out of general tax revenues and if (2) the recipients are required to show that they are poor in order to claim benefits, *then* the program is called *public assistance*.

Over the years, social insurance programs have been more politically viable than public assistance programs. Perhaps people believe that social insurance is merely enforced savings and that eventually they will get back their own money (although we shall see that this is not entirely true). In other words, people feel entitled to Social Security because they have paid specific Social Security taxes. But public assistance recipients have never specifically *paid into* a public assistance fund. Their assistance checks come out of general tax funds. The fact that many public assistance recipients have at some time paid into the general revenue fund through income taxes gets overlooked. Moreover, while the vast majority of Americans expect to live to see some Social Security benefits returned to them, they do not expect to become public assistance recipients. Conservatives can support social insurance as a form of thrift; liberals can support it because it tends to redistribute income from workers to those who are aged, sick, disabled or unemployed and to dependent children. Reaching agreement on public assistance is a more formidable task (see Chapters 5, 8, and 10, and especially Chapter 6).

Government old-age insurance, the first social insurance program, was introduced in Germany in 1889 by the conservative regime of Chancellor Otto von Bismarck. The idea spread quickly, and most European nations had old-age insurance pension programs before the beginning of World War I in 1914. Private old-age pension plans were begun in the United States by many railroads, utilities, and large manufacturers at the beginning of the twentieth century. The U.S. government began its own Federal Employees Retirement program in 1920. By 1931, seventeen states had adopted some form of compulsory old-age insurance for all workers. During the Great Depression, a California physician, Francis E. Townsend, began a national crusade for rather generous old-age pensions to be paid by the government from taxes on banks. The Townsend Plan was perceived by conservative government and business leaders as radical and unworkable—as a major step toward socialism. But the combination of economic depression and larger numbers of older people in the population helped to develop pressure for some type of old-age insurance. Finally, in the presidential election of 1932, Franklin D. Roosevelt advocated a government insurance plan to protect both the unemployed and the aged. This campaign promise and party platform plank actually became law—the Social Security Act of 1935.

THE SOCIAL SECURITY ACT OF 1935

Through the Social Security Act of 1935, the federal government undertook to establish the basic framework for social welfare policies at the federal, state, and local levels. As amended, this act now provides for

1. federal Old Age, Survivors, Disability, and Health Insurance (OASDHI),
2. unemployement compensation programs in the states,
3. federal public assistance to the aged, blind, and disabled under the Supplementary Security Income (SSI) program,

4. public assistance to families with dependent children under the Aid to Families with Dependent Children (AFDC) program,
5. federal health insurance for the aged (Medicare), and
6. federal-state assistance for the poor in paying medical costs (Medicaid).

In this chapter we examine Old Age, Survivors, and Disability Insurance and unemployment compensation. In Chapter 5 we consider SSI; in Chapter 6, AFDC; and in Chapter 10 we examine the health provisions Medicare and Medicaid.

The original Social Security program, as enacted in 1935, covered only retirement benefits for workers in about half of the labor force; many farm and domestic workers and self-employed individuals were exempted, as were state and local government employees. This old-age insurance was financed by employer-employee contributions of 1 percent each on a wage base of $3,000, or a maximum contribution by workers of $30 per year. It paid for retirement benefits at age sixty-five at a rate of about $22 per month for a single worker, or $36 per month for a married couple. Benefits were paid as a matter of right, regardless of income, as long as a worker was retired. Thus, retired workers were spared the humiliation often associated with public charity. (Actually, no benefits were paid until 1940 in order to allow the trust fund to accumulate reserves.) Economist Joseph A. Pechman and his colleagues write of the original Social Security Act:

> [T]he old age-provisions in the Social Security Act were in part a first attempt to solve the long developing crisis of the aged and of economic security in general . . . in part a reaction to the short-run crisis of the depression; and in part a compromise measure to blunt the political appeal of the enormously expensive and essentially unworkable Townsend Plan.[1]

One might attribute the Roosevelt administration's political success in gaining acceptance for the Social Security Act to several factors; including

1. the weakening of ties among extended family members and the increasing inability of urban families to care for their aged members,
2. the economic insecurities generated by the Great Depression of the 1930s and the increasing fear of impoverishment even among the middle class, and
3. political movements on the left (the Townsend Plan, for example) and right which threatened the established order.

Roosevelt's skills as a national leader might be added to these factors. Social Security was presented to the Congress as a *conservative* program which would eventually abolish the need for public assistance programs, in that individuals would be compelled to protect *themselves* against poverty.

The first major amendments to the original Social Security Act came in 1939 when Congress made survivors and dependents of insured workers eligible for benefits. In 1950, farmers and self-employed individuals were added to the list, bringing the total number of covered workers to over 90 percent of the work force. In 1956, disability insurance was approved for totally and permanently disabled workers. Later, workers were permitted to retire at age sixty-two rather than sixty-five, on the condition that they would accept 80 percent of the monthly benefit otherwise available at sixty-five. In 1965, prepaid medical insurance, Medicare, was added to the program, and in 1977 an automatic cost-of-living adjustment (measured by rises in the Consumer Price Index) was adopted to help Social Security payments keep pace with inflation. In 1981, at President Reagan's request, some measures were taken to reduce program spending. A minimum benefit was retained for current beneficiaries but was eliminated for new beneficiaries, and children of deceased, disabled, and retired workers who were aged eighteen to twenty-two were no longer eligible for benefits.

OASDHI: THE NATION'S LARGEST SOCIAL PROGRAM

OASDHI is the nation's largest social welfare program.[2] It now covers approximately 95 percent of workers. Both employees and employers must pay equal amounts toward the employee's OASDHI insurance. Upon retirement, an insured worker is entitled to monthly benefit payments based upon age at retirement and the amount earned during working years. Monthly payments are generally modest—an average of $566— although some individuals receive the maximum—now nearly $1,000 a month. Insured workers may also be eligible for benefits if they become disabled. The disability may be physical or mental and must prevent work for at least one year or be expected to result in death. Benefits are also payable to the dependents of retired and disabled workers and the survivors of deceased workers. The term dependent refers to spouses and to minor and disabled children of workers who meet certain qualifications, such as age requirements and definitions of disability. A lump-sum benefit is also payable upon the death of an insured worker. And virtually *all* persons sixty-five years of age and over, whether or not they have ever paid into Social Security, are entitled to Medicare—hospital insurance, which covers hospital and related services, and voluntary supplemental medical insurance, which covers a portion of physicians' services.

OASDHI is a completely federal program administered by the Social Security Administration (SSA) in the Department of Health and Human Services. But it has an important indirect effect on federal, state, and local public assistance programs: By compelling people to insure themselves against the possibility of their own poverty, Social Security has reduced the welfare problems that governments might otherwise face.

The growth of OASDHI in numbers of recipients (beneficiaries), average monthly benefits, and as a percentage of the federal government's total budget is shown in Table 4–1. Social Security taxes are the second largest source of income for the federal government; these tax revenues are exceeded only by the federal personal income tax. Many individuals now pay more in Social Security taxes than they do in income taxes. The Social Security tax is marked on the paycheck stubs of many workers with the abbreviation FICA, which stands for the Federal Insurance Contributions Act.

Social Security is considered a regressive tax, because it takes a larger share of the income of middle- and lower-income workers than of the affluent. That is because

1. the Social Security tax is levied only against wages and not against dividends, interest,

Table 4-1   Social Security Growth

	1940	1950	1960	1970	1980	1989
Number of beneficiaries (in thousands)	222	3,477	14,845	25,312	35,900	39,000
Average monthly benefit for retired workers (in dollars)	23	44	74	100	360	566
Social insurance taxes as a percent of all federal revenue	—	—	15.9	22.5	32.0	32.0
Medicare expenditures[a] (in millions of dollars)	—	—	—	6,800	31,376	87,734

[a]The Medicare program did not begin until 1965.

Sources: Social Security Administration and Budget of the U.S. Government.

rents, and other nonwage income sources, which are more frequently sources of income for the wealthy, and

2. the wage base which is taxed stopped at $51,300 in 1990. Although this figure is likely to rise every year, it still leaves all income in excess of this amount untaxed.

None of this was a concern when Social Security taxes amounted to very little, but today the size of Social Security revenues—one-third of the federal government's income—has an important impact on the overall equity of the revenue structure. Moreover, unlike the federal income tax, Social Security taxes make no allowance for family dependents or high medical expenses. However, the regressive nature of the Social Security tax on current workers is offset at retirement, because benefits are figured more generously for those who earned less, and because retirees in higher income brackets must now pay income taxes on part of their Social Security benefits.

What began as a very modest *insurance premium*—a maximum annual tax contribution of $30—is now a major expense for both employers and employees. The combined contribution of employees and employers produces a Social Security tax rate which now stands at 15.3 percent. The maximum annual contribution for both employer and employee has grown from $30 to about $4,000, well over a 100-fold increase since the program was begun over fifty-five years ago (see Table 4–2). And even though half of the full 15.3 percent Social Security tax is paid by the employee and half by the employer, most economists agree that the full burden of these taxes falls on the workers. This is because employers must consider the Social Security tax as a cost of hiring a worker, and the wage that the employer can pay the worker is, in effect, reduced by the amount paid into the Social Security trust fund.

THE BEST LAID PLANS: UNINTENDED CONSEQUENCES OF SOCIAL SECURITY

The original strategy of the Social Security Act of 1935 was to create a trust fund with a reserve that would be built from the insurance premiums (Social Security taxes) of workers. This trust-fund reserve would earn interest, and both the interest and principal would be used in later years to pay benefits. Benefits for insured individuals

Table 4–2   Social Security Taxes for Selected Years

YEAR	TAX RATE	MAXIMUM WAGES TAXABLE[a]	MAXIMUM ANNUAL TAX[b]
1937	1.00%	$ 3,000	$ 30
1950	1.50	3,000	45
1955	2.00	4,200	84
1960	3.00	4,800	144
1966	4.20	6,600	277
1969	4.80	7,800	374
1973	5.85	10,800	632
1978	6.05	17,700	1,071
1980	6.13	25,900	1,588
1981	6.65	29,700	1,975
1982	6.70	32,400	2,171
1984	7.00	37,800	2,646
1985	7.05	39,600	2,792
1986	7.15	42,000	3,003
1988	7.51	45,000	3,380
1989	7.51	48,000	3,605
1990	7.65[c]	51,300	3,924

[a]Currently, maximum taxable wages are increased either by Congress or automatically in multiples of $300 if there is a cost-of-living increase in Social Security benefits.

[b]This amount is paid by both the employee and the employer.

[c]The tax rate is projected to remain at 7.65 into the next century.

Source: Social Security Bulletin, Annual Statistical Supplement (1988), pp. 13 and 16.

would be in proportion to their contributions. General tax revenues would not be used at all. The Social Security system was intended to resemble private, self-financing insurance. But it did not turn out that way.

By the early 1980s, everyone knew that Social Security was in trouble. Rather than a reserve system, Social Security had become a pay-as-we-go program. Income from the program (about $200 billion per year) matched the outgo in Social Security benefits. The program was on the verge of bankruptcy. Over the years, political pressure to raise the benefits while keeping taxes relatively low reduced the trust-fund reserve to a minor role in Social Security finance. Social Security taxes were lumped together with all other tax revenue in the federal government's budget. In the first years of the program, Roosevelt's planners quickly realized that building the reserve was taking money out of the depressed economy and slowing recovery. The insurance-fund idea was clearly pushed aside, and the plan to build a large self-financing reserve was abandoned in 1939 under political pressure to pump more money into the economy. Over the years, Congress encountered pressure to increase benefit levels to retirees, even though these retirees never paid enough money into their accounts to actually justify higher benefits. COLAs, adopted in 1977, proved to be a very popular protection against inflation for older Americans, but Social Security ran into trouble. It could no longer cover these regular increases, especially in times of high inflation. Moreover, benefits under Social Security are no longer proportional to contributions; benefits are figured more generously for those whose wages were low than for those whose wages were high. Today, the only remaining aspects of an insurance program are that individuals must have paid into the system to receive benefits (although even this requirement has been dropped for Medicare), and beneficiaries are not required to prove that they are needy. Americans view their Social Security benefits as a right.

To keep up with increased benefits, the Social Security tax has risen dramatically in two ways: First, the tax rate assessed against both employer and employee has risen; second, the wages subject to taxation have also risen (see again Table 4–2). Not only is the Social Security tax the second largest source of federal revenue, social insurance benefits are now the single largest expenditure of the federal government.

Crisis Intervention and Social Security

As the problems of Social Security intensified, it became clear that something would have to be done. A number of approaches to rescuing Social Security were proposed. Some were proposed by Democrats and condemned by Republicans, and for other proposals it was just the other way around. Now partisan politics would have to be put aside in favor of solutions to the ailing retirement system. In 1981, President Reagan issued an executive order establishing the National Commission on Social Security Reform. The commission, also referred to as the Greenspan Commission after its chairperson, Republican economist Alan Greenspan, was comprised of fifteen individuals with backgrounds in business and industry, politics, labor organizations, and academia. Among the members were Senator Robert Dole (R-Kan.), Senator Claude Pepper (D-Fla.), who served in Congress and championed Social Security until his death at age eighty-eight in 1989, Senator Daniel Patrick Moynihan (D-N.Y.), Martha E. Keys (former congress member from Kansas and former Assistant Secretary of Health and Human Services), Lane Kirkland (president of the AFL-CIO), and Robert Ball (former commissioner of Social Security and a social insurance scholar).

Needless to say, there were many disagreements about the best way to tackle the problems of Social Security. Some wondered if there would be a compromise at all. Finally, the commission's report was issued with the joint support of President Reagan and Speaker of the House Thomas P. ("Tip") O'Neill (D-Mass.). Numerous changes were then enacted by Congress. Among the most important were a delay of the popular cost-of-living adjustment (COLA) and a *stabilizer* that was placed on future COLAs. This stabilizer may reduce the increases that beneficiaries would have received in a given year under the old law. Although Social Security benefits continue to be indexed according to the Consumer Price Index (CPI), if trust funds fall below certain levels, future benefits will be indexed according to the CPI or the average increase in wages, whichever is lower. (The 1989 COLA was 4 percent, and the 1990 COLA 4.7 percent. This 4.7 percent raise turned out to be the largest in seven years.)

Under former provisions, no Social Security benefits were counted as taxable income. Now, half of an individual's or couple's social security benefits are taxed if taxable income plus one half of Social Security benefits exceed $25,000 for single persons and $32,000 for couples. Younger people can no longer look forward to receiving full retirement benefits on their sixty-fifth birthdays. Higher retirement ages will be phased in beginning in the year 2003. (If you were born in 1938, you will be sixty-five in 2003). By 2027, the retirement age will reach sixty-seven for those planning to collect full benefits. (If you were born in 1960, you will be sixty-seven in 2027.) Beneficiaries will still be allowed to retire earlier, at age sixty-two, but the amount of benefits will fall from 80 percent to 70 percent of full retirement by 2027. Beneficiaries who receive Social Security benefits as well as other government pensions (such as military retirement) but who paid into the Social Security system for only a short time may receive lower Social Security benefits under a new formula. This is called reducing *windfall* benefits.

Some of the good news is that by 2008, those who choose to retire after age sixty-five will receive 5 percent more in benefits than they would today. Medicare benefits will still be available at age sixty-five. Other good news is that Social Security beneficiaries will be able to earn more while losing less. Today, Social Security beneficiaries ages sixty-two to sixty-five can earn nearly $7,000 from employment before they begin to lose Social Security benefits. Additional earnings are "taxed" by 50 percent (that is, beneficiaries lose $1 in benefits for every $2 they earn). Those ages sixty-five to sixty-nine may earn about $9,000 a year without penalty; earnings over this amount are taxed by one-third. Prior to 1990, the "tax" on benefits for these individuals was also $1 for every $2 earned. This tax reduction was designed to encourage older Americans to continue working; since taxes are paid on their wages, more money is pumped back into the economy. There is no earnings limit for those age seventy and older, and there is encouragement to eliminate earning restrictions for retirees of all ages.

More workers are now covered under the Social Security system. All new federal employees must participate; also included are Congress members, the president and vice president, federal judges, and all employees of nonprofit organizations, among others. Many of these individuals were formerly included under separate systems. For example, federal employees were covered under a separate, more generous retirement system.

The commission made a few adjustments to eliminate gender discrimination in the program, but these changes did not address inequities which many of today's older women face. Some members of the commission wanted to do more to help women, but there was disagreement about whether the commission should tackle this problem; therefore, many issues related to women were not fully addressed. (See Chapter 11 for a discussion of gender inequalities under Social Security.)

Other reforms, such as the use of more efficient accounting procedures, were also intended to make the Social Security fund solvent without altering the basic structure of the program.[3] Predictions are that the system will be solvent until the middle of the twenty-first century. In fact, the 1983 amendments have created a sizable *surplus* in the Social Security trust fund. In a few short years the program went from red to black ink. Each *day* the fund is accumulating $109 million more than it is paying out in benefits![4] Of course, all this will be needed when the baby boomers reach retirement, and the portion of the population that is older grows even larger. But until the baby boomers retire, should we tamper with these funds? Shall we use them for programs to house the homeless, or should we use the surplus funds to improve programs for children as we have already done for their grandparents and great-grandparents? Many feel that the fund should only be used for programs that will insure long-term financial growth and not for those that produce only short-term gains (for example, for home mortgage loans that would be repaid with interest rather than for public housing, a form of public assistance). In what seems to be an exchange of positions by Democrats and Republicans, the surplus has caused Senator Daniel Patrick Moynihan to propose decreasing the Social Security tax while President Bush opposes the idea. While the debates about how to handle the Social Security windfall continue, the surplus has already been put to use. It is being subtracted from the national budget deficit. But this has been labeled as another ploy to avoid tackling the real problems of how to balance the budget and reduce the deficit. One strong suggestion is to put Social Security *off budget* so that it cannot be used to mask Congress's inability to balance the federal budget.

INTERGENERATIONAL EQUITY

As the twentieth century draws to a close, some wonder whether the Social Security program has become outmoded. According to a number of individuals, the current system is a bad deal because (1) today's workers and employers view the Social Security tax as overly burdensome and (2) the number of aged persons supported by the working population is increasing. Social Security taxes have continued to increase, and the *dependency ratio*—the ratio of beneficiaries to workers—is growing rapidly. In spite of assertions that the Social Security program is now on a strong footing, many young people doubt that Social Security will provide the basics needed for an adequate living in their old age—or whether it will be there at all. Some argue that Social Security was never intended to support people fully during their retirement years. It was intended to help, but not fully subsidize, elderly citizens. Up to now, however, almost all retirees have received Social Security benefits that *greatly* exceed their Social Security tax contributions over the years. This helps to explain the popularity of the Social Security program among its thirty-nine million beneficiaries.

But what about today's workers? They are not likely to get back as much as they will pay into the system during their working years. For example, if you are now twenty-seven, your contributions and those of your employer, from now until retirement at age sixty-five, will likely total over $225,000. But if these same monies were set aside in a private fund, such as an Individual Retirement Account (IRA), in your own name and allowed to accumulate tax free at an interest rate of 7.5 percent, you would wind up with a nest egg at age sixty-five of over $1 million.[5] Needless to say, Social Security benefits, even including survivors, disability, and health provisions, will never amount to $1 million for an individual. Today's young workers may be paying a high price for what they might hope to regain. (For example, a worker who is now 25 years old, is making $20,000 a year, has steady lifetime earnings, and retires at age sixty-five can expect to receive about $1,000 per month in Social Security benefits.[6] If the worker lives until age eighty, his or her Social Security benefits will total about $180,000, still less than his or her Social Security contributions over a lifetime and far less than an IRA would pay. If the worker lives to age eighty-five, benefits will amount to $240,000, nearly the same as his or her projected lifetime contributions.) In addition to paying Social Security taxes, many young workers feel they must also invest in other retirement plans to insure an adequate standard of living in the twenty-first century. These payments take another chunk out of current earnings.

An even greater problem for young workers is the increasing *dependency ratio.* This refers to the number of recipients as a percentage of the number of currently contributing workers. At present, each one hundred workers support about twenty-nine beneficiaries. But as the U.S. population grows older—because of lower birth rates and longer life spans (see Figure 4–1)—we can expect forty-four beneficiaries per one hundred workers after the year 2000. This means that every two workers must support one Social Security recipient—a very heavy burden that will place additional pressures on current workers to keep the system financially solvent. If predictions are wrong, and the Social Security system cannot finance these promised benefits, political pressures will mount to force Congress to use general tax revenues to keep the system from bankruptcy. Many people already support the use of general revenues.[7] However, in light of current budget deficits, Congress and the president would like to avoid this alternative.

Martha Ozawa believes that a key to the future of Social Security is to promote "intergenerational equity," that is, to be fair to both the old and the young.[8] Thus far,

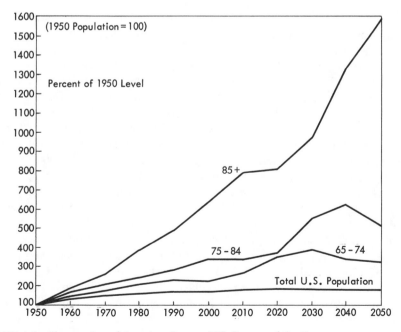

FIGURE 4–1   The graying of America. *Source:* U.S. Bureau of the Census.

she says, politicians have focused on how to increase benefits to retired persons without considering how much current workers should be expected to pay into the system. Ozawa believes that in order to establish equity between the generations, future benefits should equal past contributions in addition to interest. This approach would work to prevent retirees from receiving benefits that are much higher than what they contributed and would eliminate undue tax burdens on younger workers. However, this approach could leave many older Americans with inadequate incomes in retirement if their contributions to the Social Security system during their working years were low. In order to rectify this problem of "intragenerational equity" (fairness among members of the same generation), Ozawa advocates paying the poor elderly at higher rates. Regardless of the approach to be used in the future, Social Security may not survive unless the ratio of contributions to benefits is brought into line for future retirees. This may be a reasonable approach, especially because the financial status of many older people has improved over the years. In fact, there is a growing concern that the nation has helped raise millions of older Americans out of poverty but that it has not done the same for the greater numbers of children who now live in poverty.

Of the thirty-nine million Social Security beneficiaries, 62 percent are retirees. They represent a large bloc of voters—older people vote more often than younger people—so it has been very difficult to modify Social Security. There are also many other good reasons to proceed cautiously with major modifications in Social Security. For example, it has been suggested that people be given an *option* to participate in Social Security. Many workers might prefer to put their funds in an IRA type of account with the hopes of doing better than what Social Security will afford them during retirement. The fear is that given the option, many people would fail to set aside anything at all, and this would place an even greater strain on the welfare system when these individuals retire. If wealthier workers chose to invest in IRAs rather than Social Security, and if only lower-wage workers contributed to Social Security, there might be too little in the fund to pay adequate Social Security benefits to participants.

There are also a number of other important reasons that support maintaining a social security system similar to the current one. According to Dorcas Hardy, Commissioner of Social Security, "Those who propose to scrap the current system in favor of a privately-funded alternative [may be failing] to grasp the important social goals of the existing program."[9] The goals of a social insurance program differ from those of private pension and retirement programs. Redistribution of resources is an important goal in social welfare programs that is not found in private plans. For example, Social Security is the *major* source of retirement income for *most* older Americans.[10] It provides at least half of the income of 62 percent of current retirees and it is the *only* income of 19 percent of single retirees. It is an especially important source of income for poor Americans. As an example, for retirees with total income of less than $10,000 a year, it provides 80 percent of income, and for those with income less than $20,000 annually, it provides 67 percent of income. Social Security is the primary reason why poverty among the elderly has decreased significantly. It is certainly the government's largest social welfare program, and probably its most successful.

Other important insurance goals of the program include the benefits that accrue to disabled workers and their dependents and to the survivors of deceased workers.[11] Disability and death can occur to workers of all ages. Without Social Security, many younger persons might be left with little or no income, since they may not have private disability insurance or large life insurance policies that would guarantee them or their families adequate income.

The program can also be considered a good investment for young workers because it is *highly portable*.[12] It goes with the worker from job to job, a feature that is not true of many other pension plans that are tied to a specific job and employer. Portability is important in a mobile society where workers are likely to change jobs at least several times during their careers.

Still another critical insurance aspect of the program is that it protects younger people from having to support their own elderly or disabled parents. Most young people would find it quite difficult to provide much financial support to their parents, and older people do not want to burden their children with this responsibility. Some authors describe it this way:

> Social Security provides a rational, dignified, and stable means of protecting against certain risks to economic well-being to which individuals and family members are exposed over the course of their lives...When the program is examined from a long-term perspective, the benefits and costs...are shown to be distributed widely across all generations.[13]

Exception has also been taken with the argument that the program is unfair to members of ethnic groups (see the illustration on page 85). No one is arguing with the fact that black- and Hispanic-Americans often face more health risks and have shorter life spans than whites. What they are saying is that due to these increased risks, younger black- and Hispanic-Americans and their families benefit more frequently from the disability and survivors portions of Social Security (although this may not be much of a consolation), and they tend to receive larger benefits proportionate to their wages in all components of the program.[14]

Of course, there is little chance that the United States will abandon the Social Security program. While changes will be made periodically, Social Security is likely to remain the country's largest and most important retirement program for years to come.

ILLUSTRATION: 1983 SOCIAL SECURITY REFORMS UNFAIR
TO MINORITIES AND THE YOUNG

The sweeping 1983 reforms of the Social Security system, when fully understood, may not endure. These so-called reforms ignore the interests and contributions of young workers and minorities.

By ignoring those who will be the mainstay of the system in the twenty-first century, Congress and the president may have set in motion an angry and powerful countervailing force that could radically restructure the Social Security system before the end of this decade.

The most unfair aspects of the Social Security reforms are the increase in the retirement age to sixty-seven, the increase in the tax rate to almost 8 percent..., as well as the *reduction* in benefits to twenty-first century retirees. None of these changes would have been necessary if President Reagan had [had] the courage and foresight to impose the Social Security tax on the income of the wealthy...

An examination of the impact of the 1983 Social Security changes illustrates the potential for deep-seated dissatisfaction with the Social Security system, particularly among the young and minorities.

THE AVERAGE MALE HISPANIC WILL NEVER RECEIVE ANY SOCIAL SECURITY BENEFITS, EVEN IF HE WORKS FOR FORTY-FIVE YEARS

The average black and Hispanic, particularly the average male Hispanic, *never* retires. The median life expectancy of male Hispanics is sixty-four, while the present full retirement age for Social Security is sixty-five. As a result, approximately half of the Hispanic population in the United States never draws any retirement benefits from Social Security. In addition, the average Hispanic draws about nine years less in Social Security benefits than the typical Anglo whose life expectancy is seventy-three years of age.

As a result of this mortality disparity, the 1983 increase in the retirement age to sixty-seven is a gross injustice to Hispanics who are presently disproportionately underserved by the current system. Equally important, the proposed increase in the retirement age unfairly harms those, such as Hispanics, whose primary occupations are in demanding physical labor (such as farm work) that takes its toll long before the age of sixty-seven.

If all Americans drew from Social Security as little as the typical Hispanic retiree does, Social Security would have a substantial surplus...

SOCIAL SECURITY WOULD BE INSOLVENT WITHOUT HISPANICS

The median age of the Hispanic population is eight years younger than the white population. (The median age is twenty-three versus thirty-one for the Anglo population; and only 4 percent of the Hispanic population, compared with 11 percent of the entire population, is over sixty-five.) This unique youth factor means that over the next two generations, the work force supporting Social Security will be increasingly Hispanic and the retiree force increasingly and disproportionately Anglo.

ALL INCOME SHOULD BE TAXED FOR SOCIAL SECURITY

The Social Security tax is probably the world's most regressive tax...

...A typical chief executive of a Fortune 500 corporation, earning $400,000 per year, pays only one-half of 1 percent of his/her earnings to Social Security... *[t]he typical American's contribution to Social Security is at a rate nine times higher than that paid by most chief executives.*

On the other hand, if Social Security taxes were imposed on *all* earnings, the Social Security system would be in the black every year and have an overall surplus of $1.1 *trillion* by the beginning of the next century. (The absence of an all-inclusive tax is of special significance to minorities since their median income is only two-thirds that of other Americans...)

RECOMMENDATIONS TO PROTECT SOCIAL SECURITY AND ENSURE SUPPORT FROM MINORITIES AND YOUNG WORKERS

In recognition of these realities regarding the unfairly harsh impact of Social Security reforms on young workers and minorities, the League of United Latin American Citizens, the nation's largest Hispanic membership organization, offers four interrelated long-term recommendations to strengthen Social Security and ensure future worker support while fully protecting the rights of the elderly:

1. The inclusion of "all earnings" for purposes of Social Security tax. This would produce an estimated $178 billion in additional revenue over the next six years and, based on similar projections, an additional $1.1 *trillion* over the next generation .... It makes unnecessary all other so-called Social Security reforms.
2. A return to age 65 for retirement.
3. A moratorium on rate increases.
4. No reduction in benefits for future retirees.

The continued ignoring of legitimate worker grievances could create an atmosphere in which a majority of the workers conclude that those who contribute the most will receive the least. It was just such unfair "taxation without representation" that inspired the American Revolution and President Reagan's 1980 election.

Source: Robert Gnaizda & Mario Obledo, *Gray Panther Network* (Spring 1985), p. 12.

UNEMPLOYMENT COMPENSATION

A second major insurance program—Unemployment Compensation—was included in the original Social Security Act of 1935. Again, the underlying rationale was to compel employers to contribute to trust funds which would be held for the employees in the event of job loss. The federal government requires employers to pay into *state* administered unemployment insurance programs that meet federal standards. The federal standards are flexible, and the states have considerable freedom in shaping their own unemployment programs. In all cases, unemployed workers must report in person and show that they are willing and able to work in order to receive unemployment benefits. In practice, this means that unemployed workers must register with the U.S. Employment Service (usually located in the same building as the state unemployment compensation office) as a condition of receiving unemployment compensation. States cannot deny workers benefits for refusing to work as strikebreakers or refusing to work for less than prevailing rates. But basic decisions concerning the amount of benefits, eligibility, and length of time that benefits can be paid are largely left to the states. However, in all states, unemployment compensation is *not* a protection against *long-term* or *hard-core* unemployment.

Each state maintains an unemployment compensation trust fund of its own, which is financed from taxes on employers with an average range from 1 percent to 4.5 percent of their total payroll. The federal government also maintains an unemployment compensation trust fund to bail out any state trust fund that becomes exhausted.

Average state payments to the unemployed range from lows of about $100 per week to highs of about $170.[15] But not everyone who is unemployed receives assistance. In fact, as few as 30 to 40 percent of those who are unemployed may receive benefits at any given time.[16] Some did not work at their last job long enough to qualify. Others were fired for poor job performance or left their jobs voluntarily. These causes of unemployment are not covered by unemployment compensation. Other workers have exhausted their unemployment benefits.

What Is Unemployment and Who Is Unemployed?

Until unemployment compensation insurance was adopted in 1935, the loss of one's job was an economic catastrophe. Most families depended on the support of one worker—usually the father. If he lost his job, the family's income was immediately reduced to zero. But today, almost three-fifths of American families benefit from the earnings of more than one worker. Unemployment is still serious, but a second income provides a buffer against economic disaster. A combination of (1) short-term help from unemployment insurance, (2) food stamps, and (3) other forms of public assistance for those out-of-work for long periods of time can also help reduce the real costs of becoming unemployed for those with limited resources. The cost of unemployment can be viewed as the difference between income from unemployment insurance and public assistance programs and the wages of a potential job. The benefits now available to unemployed workers have had an important effect on their motivations and expectations. Unemployed workers may not have to jump at the first available job that comes along. They may decide to pass up, at least for a while, low-paying or undesirable jobs in the hope of finding better-paying, more satisfying employment.

The unemployment rate is a monthly estimate by the U.S. Department of Labor of the percentage of the work force that is out of work and *actively* seeking jobs. Each year the total work force grows as the population increases. This means that the total number of jobs must grow each year to keep pace with population growth. There have been considerable fluctuations in unemployment rates during this century. In the early 1980s, unemployment rates were at 10 and 11 percent. Current unemployment is hovering at about 5 percent, the lowest in fifteen years. Today's rates are far below the 20 to 30 percent unemployment rate estimated during the depression of the 1930s but slightly above the 3 to 4 percent lows achieved during the 1950s. At current levels, however, the nation is near full employment, since clearly there is some unavoidable minimum unemployment. In a large, free economy, hundreds of thousands of people move and change jobs and temporarily find themselves unemployed. This *frictional* unemployment is estimated to be about half of the total unemployment during normal (nonrecession) periods. But others find themselves unemployed because of poor job skills, poor health, low mental capacities, or because they live in areas with limited job opportunities. These *structurally* unemployed are estimated to be less than 20 percent of the total unemployed, but they represent the greatest challenge to achieving full employment.

In order to determine the unemployment rate, a survey based on about sixty-thousand household interviews is conducted each month. Those who are sixteen years of age and older are included in the survey. Some believe that the count underestimates unemployment while others believe it overestimates it. For example, the Labor Department is frequently criticized because it counts part-time workers as employed; yet many part-time workers would prefer full-time work. It is also criticized because many of the poor in America are never counted as unemployed. That is because they have become discouraged and have given up even trying to find a job. These discouraged workers are excluded from official unemployment statistics, but efforts are made to determine how many people fall into this category. Currently, there are an estimated 100,000 discouraged workers at any given moment.[17]

On the other hand, in order to qualify for public assistance, such as food stamps, able-bodied individuals must sign up with the state employment office in their area. Some argue that this drives unemployment figures up, because some of these individuals may not really intend to seek employment.[18]

Women, blacks, and teenagers suffer from higher unemployment rates than adult white males do. In good times or bad, the unemployment rate for black Americans is double the white unemployment rate. Unemployment rates for women are slightly higher than unemployment rates for men. But the teenage (sixteen to nineteen years old) unemployment rate is usually three times higher than the adult male rate. The highest unemployment rate of all is for black teenagers; a 40 percent unemployment rate for this group is not uncommon.

How much unemployment is too much? There is an old saying: "When your neighbor is unemployed, it's a recession. When you are unemployed, it's a depression." It is sometimes still argued that unemployment among women and teenagers is not as urgent a problem as unemployment among male adults, who are generally the family's primary breadwinners. Others vehemently reject this notion, contending that at least one-third of working women support their families alone and that many other women work because of low family income. It is also argued that jobs for teenagers produce long-term social benefits—teens learn work habits and the importance of holding a steady job in later life.

The unemployment picture would improve considerably if jobs and unemployed workers were better matched. This could be done in two ways. First, those unable to locate employment near their homes could be encouraged or assisted to relocate to areas where jobs are available. Relocation assistance is often provided for higher-paid workers by their employers but not for low-wage earners who may need this assistance the most. Second, more job training and retraining programs could be offered to workers with limited or outdated skills to help them learn those skills that employers are seeking. The Job Training Partnership Act (discussed in Chapter 9) is intended to help with this problem. Demographic trends may help to further reduce unemployment. During the 1970s and 1980s, a substantial number of baby boomers entered the labor market, contributing to rises in unemployment. "[B]ut the aging of America's population may reduce competition among young workers for entry-level jobs. These trends will be of special significance to blacks and Hispanics who will comprise much of the future addition to the labor force."[19] The education of these future workers will be critical because the bulk of new jobs will require post-high school education.

Reforming Unemployment Insurance

How can the unemployment insurance program be improved to better assist the unemployed? According to one task force that studied unemployment, the program should be made "...more reliable for those who depend on it, more responsive to changes in the economy, and more effective in providing relief and helping put people back to work."[20] The task force cites four major problems with unemployment insurance. First, the program is too complex. Basic benefits are provided, and then there are *triggers* which allow additional benefits to be paid during periods when unemployment is especially high. These triggers and benefit periods change frequently, adding to confusion in the program. Second, the program is too rigid. It can fail to help states and areas with the highest unemployment. Since many long-term unemployed persons are not counted when unemployment statistics are compiled, the severity of a state's unemployment can be underestimated. Unless unemployment is high, the triggers are not set off, and extended benefits are not made available in that state. In addition, if unemployment in a particular area of a state is high, but if the overall state unemployment rate is relatively low, the depressed area does not receive additional payments. Third, there are few inducements for workers to seek training that would qualify them for new jobs. Training opportunities are limited. The attitude is to take the first job available, whatever it is. As a result, short-term solutions are used in favor of longer-term gains. Fourth, program financing should be altered so that the states with the highest unemployment rates receive more federal financial assistance; otherwise, these states face additional financial burdens and potential economic depressions at a time when growth is needed most. In order to improve the program, steps should be taken to simplify triggers and other regulations, to provide more assistance to states and areas with high unemployment, to count more accurately the number of unemployed, and to provide more inducements for training and job searches that will better match jobs and workers.

WORKERS' COMPENSATION

Workers' compensation is another type of social insurance program. Each state operates a workers' compensation program. The programs vary by state, but each provides cash payments and medical benefits to workers injured on the job. "All [workers' compensation] laws include some or all diseases attributable to the worker's occupation. Most exclude injuries due to the employee's intoxication, willful misconduct, or gross negligence."[21] Dependents of workers killed in job-related mishaps are generally entitled to benefits. Some states provide benefits to widowers as well as widows. Employers participate by insuring their workers. Some use a private insurance company, other self-insure, and in some cases, the state insures employers. The types of jobs covered by workers' compensation also differ from state to state. Some state workers' compensation systems are in serious trouble and in need of reform because of increased claims, rapidly rising insurance rates, and large program deficits.

SUMMARY

One strategy for preventing poverty in the United States is through social insurance programs. The purpose of social insurance is to help workers insure themselves and their dependents against poverty, which may result from the advanced age, death, disability, or unemployment of the worker. The major social insurance program is known as the Social Security program. It is financed through premiums paid by both workers and employers and is administered by the federal government.

Social insurance programs differ from public assistance programs. Social insurance programs require that beneficiaries make contributions to the program; contributors are entitled to benefits regardless of their wealth. Public assistance recipients must be poor in order to receive benefits, and benefits are paid from general tax revenues rather than through recipients' contributions.

The Social Security Act of 1935 was the first major piece of federal welfare legislation. This act has been amended many times; today it includes a number of social insurance programs, including Old Age, Survivors, and Disability Insurance and Medicare. Its public assistance programs include Aid to Families with Dependent Children, Supplemental Security Income, and Medicaid.

Social Security was originally intended to be a self-financing program, but it developed into a *pay-as-we-go* system because life expectancy increased, and payments were continually raised to keep up with the cost of living. In order to finance the growing program, the amount of taxable wages increased over the years, and the rate at which these wages were taxed also increased. The thirty-nine million recipients of Social Security are a strong voting bloc, and any changes that would reduce benefits have met with strong resistance. Eventually, it looked as if the program would be bankrupt. In 1981, President Reagan appointed a bipartisan commission to come up with solutions to the ailing Social Security program. After many disagreements, the commission made a number of recommendations which were adopted by Congress. The changes included raising the retirement age, increasing the taxable wage base and the Social Security tax rate, taxing part of the Social Security benefits of those in upper-income categories, increasing benefits to those who retire later and decreasing benefits to those who retire early, and allowing retirees to earn more while losing less in Social Security benefits. Accounting procedures were modified to make the program more efficient, cost-of-living adjustments were delayed, and methods of computing these adjustments were altered to provide cost savings if the trust fund runs low. The Social Security program places a considerable strain on current workers, and future workers face an even greater responsibility to keep the system afloat, but there are many benefits of the program including the fact that it keeps many recipients from living in poverty and protects children from having to support their elderly or disabled parents. For the time being, it appears that the system is on a steady footing. In fact, a sizable surplus is now mounting, which will be needed to insure benefits when the baby boom generation retires. No major changes in the retirement, survivors, or disability of the program are likely to be instituted in the near future.

Unemployment compensation is another large social insurance program. While unemployment rates are about 5 percent nationally, unemployment among blacks, and teenagers is considerably higher. Unemployment insurance does not help with long-term unemployment, and a number of suggestions have been made to make the program more sensitive to unemployed workers and areas with high unemployment rates. Workers' compensation, another social insurance program, is designed to assist workers who have been injured or become ill in work-related situations. Social insurance programs are clearly a preferred political alternative to preventing poverty.

NOTES

1. Joseph A. Pechman, Henry J. Aaron, and Michael K. Taussig, *Social Security: Perspectives for Reform* (Washington, D.C.: Brookings Institution, 1968), p. 32.
2. For further background on the Social Security programs, see Robert M. Ball, *Social Security Today and Tomorrow* (New York: Columbia University Press, 1978); Alice H. Munnell, *The Future of Social Security* (Washington, D.C.: Brookings Institution, 1977); Bruno Stein, *Social Security and Provisions in Transition* (New York: Free Press, 1980); and Sar A. Levitan, *Programs in Aid of the Poor for the 1980s,* 4th ed. (Baltimore: Johns Hopkins University Press, 1980).
3. For a more detailed description of recommendations, see "Report of the National Commission on Social Security Reform," *Social Security Bulletin 46,* no. 2 (February 1983), pp. 3–38. For more on House and Senate action, see "Social Security Rescue Plan Swiftly Approved," *1983 Congressional Quarterly Almanac,* pp. 219–226. For a concise consideration of the changes adopted see Wilbur J. Cohen, "The Future Impact of the Social Security Amendments of 1983," *The Journal/The Institute of Socioeconomic Studies 8,* no. 2 (Summer 1983), pp. 1–16.
4. This paragraph relies on Christine Gorman, "The $12 Trillion Temptation," *Time* (July 4, 1988), p. 58.
5. William G. Flanagan, "Social Security—Don't Count on It," *Forbes 126,* no. 12 (December 8, 1980), pp. 161–162.
6. "Retirement" pamphlet, U.S. Department of Health and Human Services, Social Security Administration, SSA Publication No. 05–10035 (January 1989), pp. 10–11.
7. Wilbur J. Cohen, *Social Security: The Compromise and Beyond,* (Washington, D.C.: Save Our Security Education Fund, 1983), pp. 33–34.
8. Martha N. Ozawa, "Benefits and Taxes under Social Security: An Issue of Intergenerational Equity," *Social Work 29,* no. 2 (March 1984), pp. 131–137.
9. Dorcas R. Hardy, "The Future of Social Security," *Social Security Bulletin,* 50, 8 (August 1987), p. 7. Reprinted from The Connecticut College Alumni Magazine, Spring 1987.
10. Martynas A. Ycas and Susan Grad, "Income of Retirement-Aged Persons in the United States," *Social Security Bulletin,* 50, 7 (July 1987) pp. 5–14.
11. Eric R. Kingson, "Misconceptions Distort Social Security Policy Discussions," *Social Work, 34,* no. 4, (1989), pp. 357–362.
12. Ibid.
13. Eric R. Kingson, Barbara A. Hirshorn, and John M. Cornman, *Ties that Bind: The Interdependency of Generations* (Washington, D.C.: Seven Locks Press), 1986.
14. E.R. Kingson, E.D. Berkowitz, and F. Pratt, *Insuring the Social Security of American Families: A Discussion Guide to Social Insurance with Lesson Plans* (Washington, D.C.: Save Our Security Fund, in press), cited in Kingson, "Misconceptions Distort Social Security."
15. *Social Security Bulletin, Annual Statistical Supplement, 1988* (Washington, D.C.: Social Security Administration, 1988), p. 304.
16. "Study: 31% of Jobless Get Benefits," *Austin American-Statesman* (August 16, 1989), pp. 1, 6.
17. Robert D. Hershey, Jr., "Unemployment Rate Decreases to 4.9%," *Austin American-Statesman* (April 8, 1989), pp. A1, A16.
18. Kenneth W. Clarkson and Roger E. Meiners, "Government Statistics as a Guide to Economic Policy: Food Stamps and the Spurious Increase in the Unemployment Rates," *Policy Review 1,* no. 1 (Summer 1977), pp. 27–51.
19. *Management of the United States Government, Fiscal Year 1990* (Washington, D.C.: 1989), pp. 2–4.
20. Donald J. Pease and William F. Clinger, Jr., "Reform Unemployment Insurance," *The Wall Street Journal* (January 29, 1985), p. 26.
21. Department of Health and Human Services, *Social Security Handbook 1984,* 8th ed. (Washington, D.C.: Social Security Administration, SSA publication no. 05-10135, July 1984), p. 387.

5

HELPING THE "DESERVING POOR"
Aged, Blind, and Disabled

Those who are aged, blind or disabled are among the groups considered the *deserving poor*—those whom society has moral and ethical obligations to assist. Four types of provisions are available to assist these individuals:

1. Social Security disability and retirement benefits for those with work records (see Chapter 4),
2. public assistance for those with little or no income whose conditions prevent them from pursuing gainful employment,
3. social service programs, since virtually all aged, blind, and disabled individuals can benefit from a wide range of rehabilitative and social services,
4. legislation aimed at reducing discrimination in employment, education, and housing, and at providing greater access to public and private facilities.

EARLY AID FOR THE DESERVING POOR

Most states had programs to assist the elderly poor before the Social Security Act of 1935 was passed. Massachusetts was among the first states to appoint a commission to study the problems of the elderly.[1] In 1914, Arizona passed a law establishing a pension program for the aged.[2] The territory of Alaska passed a law entitling elderly persons to pensions in 1915.[3] By the time the federal government adopted the Social Security Act, thirty states already had their own old-age assistance programs.[4] Eligibility requirements for state old-age programs were very stringent. In order to qualify, recipients generally had to be at least sixty-five years old, be citizens of the United States, and meet residency requirements in the location where they applied for benefits. In cases where relatives were capable of supporting an elderly family member, benefits were often denied. Those elderly who did participate usually had to agree that any assets they had left at the time of their death would be assigned to the state.[5]

Old age was not the only condition which concerned Americans. Those who were blind were also considered deserving. In fact, terms of residence and other eligibility requirements were often more lenient in state pension laws for the blind than they were for the elderly. By 1935, twenty-seven states had pension programs for individuals with severe visual handicaps.[6] Other types of diseases, injuries, and handicaps were also considered disabling, but early in the 1900s, policies to assist poor persons who were not elderly or blind varied considerably among states,[7] and some states had no programs at all.

When the Social Security Act of 1935 was passed, its most far-reaching provision was the Social Security insurance program, which provided financial payments to retired workers. It was not until 1956 that disabled workers were also covered under the social insurance provisions. The original Social Security Act did include public assistance programs for some special target groups. Following the precedent established by many states, the public assistance programs included Aid to Dependent Children (ADC), Old Age Assistance (OAA), and Aid to the Blind (AB). In 1950, Aid to the Permanently and Totally Disabled (APTD) was added. OAA, AB, and APTD were called the *adult categorical assistance* programs. Although these programs were authorized by the federal government, each state could decide whether it wanted to participate in any or all of them. All states eventually adopted the OAA and AB programs, but several states chose not to participate in the APTD program. The federal government shared costs with the states and set minimum requirements for program participation. Elderly persons had to be at least sixty-five years old to receive federal aid. Blind and disabled recipients had to be at least eighteen years old. The states were primarily responsible for administering the programs, and they retained a great deal of discretion in determining eligibility requirements (such as residency and income and asset limitations) and the amount of payments. The states also determined the definitions of disability and blindness.

State administration of the OAA, AB, and APTD programs had serious ramifications for some beneficiaries. Individuals who moved to another state might have been denied benefits because they did not meet eligibility requirements there or because they were required to reestablish residency. Benefits also varied drastically and were often meager. In the OAA program in 1964, the state of West Virginia paid an average monthly benefit of $50, while Wisconsin paid an average of $111.[8] Beneficiaries from poorer states generally received less because their states had less money to operate the program.

SSI: "FEDERALIZING" THE AGED, BLIND, AND DISABLED PROGRAMS

When President Nixon took office in 1972, he said he wanted to clean up the "welfare mess." Nixon's proposal for welfare reform was to provide a minimum income to poor

Americans, one which would replace the AFDC, OAA, AB, and APTD programs and bring an end to the uneven treatment of welfare recipients from state to state. His *guaranteed annual income* proposal, known as the Family Assistance Plan (FAP), was the target of controversy in Congress. Liberals thought that the reforms were too stingy, while conservatives believed that the reforms provided too much in welfare benefits and would reduce the incentive to work. Senator Daniel P. Moynihan (D-N.Y.), then an advisor to President Nixon and a supporter of the FAP, wrote in his book, *The Politics of a Guaranteed Annual Income,* that most of the controversy focused on the reform of the AFDC program.[9] AFDC was not reformed, but in the midst of the controversy, the OAA, AB, and APTD programs underwent substantial revisions that were almost unnoticed.[10]

The major change Congress made in 1972 in OAA, AB, and APTD was to federalize these programs under a new program called Supplementary Security Income (SSI). *Federalizing* meant that Congress largely took the programs out of the hands of state governments. The state governments would no longer determine basic eligibility requirements or minimum payment levels, nor would they directly administer the programs. These changes represented the most sweeping reform of the adult categorical assistance programs since APTD was added in 1950. SSI replaced the OAA, AB, and APTD programs by establishing a minimum income for recipients and by standardizing basic eligibility requirements across all states; however, all but seven (mostly southern) states have some type of program which supplements SSI payments. State supplements may be administered by the federal government or the state. The federal government distributes the supplements and pays the administrative costs for states that offer them to all recipients. States that choose to set their own requirements, by including only certain beneficiaries or by disregarding additional income, administer their supplemental program at their own expense. Under the change to SSI, no state could pay beneficiaries less than they had previously received.

How SSI Works

Because SSI is administered by the Social Security Administration, and because its name resembles that of the Social Security retirement program, some people think that these programs are the same, but they are quite different. SSI is a means-tested public assistance program while Social Security is a social insurance program. SSI is funded through general revenues while Social Security is funded through a special payroll tax. However, older persons may receive SSI benefits in addition to Social Security if their income from Social Security and other sources and their assets meet the eligibility requirements of the SSI program.

Sometimes a person qualifies for benefits under two of the SSI components.[11] For example, an individual may qualify under the portions of the program for the aged and for disabled individuals. Since there are more income exclusions under the program for the disabled individuals, it may be more advantageous for that individual to receive SSI as a disabled recipient rather than as an aged recipient.

Children as well as adults may qualify for benefits under the disabled and blind portions, since age is no longer a factor in determining eligibility. In determining benefits for children, their parents' income is considered. Beneficiaries cannot receive SSI and AFDC benefits simultaneously. When an individual meets the qualifications for both programs, a determination must be made as to which program provides the greatest benefits. The disability of the largest group of children receiving SSI is mental retardation.

In most cases, residents of publicly operated facilities like rest homes or halfway houses cannot qualify for SSI payments, but there are some exceptions. For example, individuals living in public institutions may be eligible if their primary reason for residence is to acquire vocational or educational training. Others may qualify if they are living in public facilities with no more than sixteen residents or in public emergency shelters for homeless persons.

Sixty-five is still the minimum age to qualify for SSI to the aged. Under the portion of the program for blind recipients, "A person [who] can see no better than $20/200$ or who has a limited visual field of 20 degrees or less in the better eye with the use of eyeglasses" qualifies.[12] A more liberal definition of visual impairment may be used to qualify individuals under the disabled portion of the program. Adults (those at least eighteen years of age) qualify as disabled if they cannot work because of a physical or mental impairment that "is expected to [last]...for at least twelve months or...to result in death."[13] Children under the age of eighteen qualify if their disability or impairment is similar in severity to that of an adult with the same condition. Drug addicts and alcoholics who are disabled may qualify for payments but they must comply with a treatment program. In these cases, their payments are made to a responsible third party.

In order to qualify, beneficiaries can have only limited resources. As of 1989, an individual's resources cannot exceed $2,000 and a couple's resources cannot exceed $3,000. Resources include items like real estate, savings accounts, and personal belongings. However, several types of resources are not included in determining eligibility. For example, the individual's home is not counted, and the value of a car up to $4,500 is not counted.

In addition, *countable* income must be less than the maximum SSI payment. In 1990, the maximum monthly federal payment was $386 for an individual and $579 for a couple. In the case of child beneficiaries, allowances are made which take into consideration the parents' work expenses and the living expenses of the family. Income includes earnings from work, Social Security payments, other cash benefits, and interest income, and it may also include items given to the individual such as food, clothing, and shelter. Some income is disregarded (not counted) in calculating benefits. Generally, the first $20 a month from any source is disregarded, and food stamp benefits are also disregarded. The first $65 of income from work, plus half of all additional earnings are not counted. The idea of allowing beneficiaries to keep half of all earned income (up to prescribed limits) is to encourage employment. Work related expenses for blind and disabled individuals are usually also disregarded in determining payments. One-third of the SSI payment is deducted if the beneficiary resides in the home of someone who is contributing to his or her support. This provision may be considered a disincentive to families willing to care for SSI recipients. Payments are adjusted each year to keep pace with the cost of living. The illustration that follows (see pages 99–100) provides examples of how SSI payments are calculated.

Recipients' cases are generally reviewed at least every three years in order to determine if they are still eligible. For disabled beneficiaries, more frequent *continuing disability reviews* may be required, in which new medical information is submitted in order to determine if the person continues to be disabled. In most cases, Medicaid benefits are automatically provided to SSI recipients.

Costs and Recipients of SSI

The overall costs of the adult public assistance programs during the last half century are found in Table 5–1. In 1940, the costs of OAA were $473 million. In 1987, under SSI, costs for the aged amounted to about $3.2 billion. Expenditures for the AB program have been more modest because there are far fewer blind than aged and disabled recipients. In 1940, the program for the blind cost $22 million to operate; today it costs $291 million. The most dramatic growth in expenditures has been for disabled recipients. Costs have risen from $287 million in 1960 to nearly $9.5 billion in 1987.

Average payments to recipients have increased but generally remain modest. An elderly recipient now receives an *average* of $187 a month. A number of elderly SSI recipients also receive some income from Social Security retirement. Blind beneficiaries receive the highest payments, averaging $300 monthly, and disabled recipients receive an average of $288 monthly (see Table 5–2).

State participation can have an important effect on the monthly payment amount of the 44 percent of SSI recipients who receive state supplements. These additional payments range from $2 to $292 monthly. Obviously, some states are more generous than others; however, only four states offer supplements that bring payments to the poverty level.[14]

Over the years, the number of elderly recipients has decreased, especially when compared with the rate of growth in the elderly population (see Table 5–3). In 1950, about 2.8 million people received old-age assistance. Today, there are about 1.5 million recipients. The declining number of recipients can be attributed primarily to the increasing number of people who have become eligible for Social Security insurance benefits and to reductions in poverty among the elderly population. When SSI was enacted, however, it was anticipated that many more elderly would become eligible for some assistance. Indications are that more than half of eligible older individuals are still not participating.[15] One group of pollsters asked a group of elderly persons who were poor why they had not applied. "Twenty percent said they had never heard of SSI. Another 21 percent said they believed they were not eligible. Fourteen percent said they did not need SSI; 6 percent were not willing to accept welfare; and three percent said they did not want to deal with the government."[16] The federal government has stepped up outreach efforts to enroll eligible individuals who are not participating in SSI—with special emphasis on the aged. Some pilot projects have been conducted in conjunction with the American Association of Retired Persons (AARP), which have yielded positive results.

TABLE 5–1   The Costs of the Adult Public Assistance and SSI Programs for Selected
Years (in millions of dollars[a])

YEAR	AGED	BLIND	DISABLED	TOTAL
1940	$ 473	$ 22	—[b]	$ 495
1950	1,485	53	$8	1,546
1960	1,922	94	287	2,303
1970	1,866	98	1,000	2,964
1980	2,734	190	5,014	7,938
1987	3,194	291	9,458	12,943

[a]Includes federal and state costs.

[b]Program did not begin until 1950.

Sources: Bureau of the Census, *Historical Statistics of the United States, Colonial Times to 1970* (Washington, D.C.: 1975), p. 356; *Social Security Bulletin, Annual Statistical Supplement, 1988*, p. 313.

TABLE 5–2   Average Monthly Payments for the Adult Public Assistance and SSI Programs
for Selected Years[a]

YEAR	AGED	BLIND	DISABLED
1940	$20.25	$25.35	—[b]
1950	43.05	46.00	$44.10
1960	58.90	67.45	56.15
1970	77.65	104.35	97.65
1980	131.75	215.70	200.06
1987	187.24	299.74	288.29

[a]Includes federal and state payments.

[b]Program did not begin until 1950.

Sources: Bureau of the Census, *Historical Statistics of the United States, Colonial Times to 1970* (Washington, D.C.: 1975), p. 356; *Social Security Bulletin, Annual Statistical Supplement, 1988*, p. 314.

TABLE 5–3   Number of Recipients of the Adult Public Assistance and SSI Programs for
Selected Years (in thousands)

YEAR	AGED	BLIND	DISABLED	TOTAL
1940	2,070	73	—[a]	2,143
1950	2,786	97	69	2,952
1960	2,305	107	369	2,891
1970	2,082	81	935	3,098
1980	1,838	79	2,276	4,193
1987	1,483	84	2,889	4,456

[a]Program did not begin until 1950.

Sources: Bureau of the Census, *Historical Statistics of the United States, Colonial Times to 1970* (Washington, D.C.: 1975), p. 356; *Social Security Bulletin, Annual Statistical Supplement, 1988*, p. 312.

The number of blind recipients has been much smaller and more stable due to advances in the prevention and treatment of blindness, as well as to the large number of blind persons who are self-supporting.

Most of the growth in SSI is the result of large increases in the number of permanently and totally disabled recipients. Many states had strict definitions of disability. When the program was federalized, a standard definition of disability was adopted that helped many new recipients join the rolls. The number of recipients has grown from nearly 370,000 in 1960 to nearly three million today.

SSI did not fare badly under the Reagan administration because Congress resisted attempts to cut benefits and to reduce the number of disabled recipients. In spite of lower than expected enrollments, a ten-year review of the SSI program by the SSA concluded that the program had done well in meeting most of its objectives.[17] With respect to the age, ethnicity and gender of recipients, the program appeared to be reaching those most likely to be poor. In terms of future planning, the growth in the number of disabled recipients cannot be overlooked, because few disabled recipients work and most continue to remain on the rolls. Since the advent of SSI, more children have entered the program with disabilities such as mental retardation. This may mean that they will be eligible for benefits throughout their lifetimes.

ILLUSTRATION: DETERMINING SSI PAYMENTS

Methods of calculating public assistance payments often seem complex and are not well known to those outside the welfare system. The following examples provided by the Social Security Administration illustrate how benefits are calculated for some aged recipients of SSI.[a]

1

Sam Johnson is sixty-six, lives alone in a small house he owns, and his only income is his Social Security benefit of $182.00 a month. He gets $153.40 of this in his check, after his $28.60 Medicare medical insurance premium is deducted.

Income not from current earnings:		
Monthly Social Security benefit	$182.00	
Less $20	−20.00	
Remainder: Countable income not from current earnings	$162.00	$162.00
Income from current earnings:	None	+None
Total countable income for the month		$162.00
Basic SSI amount for the month	$386.00	
Less total countable income	−162.00	
Monthly SSI payment	$224.00	$224.00
His Social Security benefit is		+182.00
So his total monthly income will be		$406.00

2

Now let's say Mr. Johnson is married and lives with his wife who is sixty-five. She gets $91.00 a month from Social Security—from which a Medicare medical insurance premium is deducted. The couple's total Social Security income is $273.00 a month.

Income not from current earnings:		
Couple's monthly Social Security benefits	$273.00	
Less $20	−20.00	
Remainder: Countable income not from current earnings	$253.00	$253.00
Income from current earnings:..................... None		+None
Total countable income for the month		$253.00
Basic SSI amount for the month	$579.00	
Less total countable income	−253.00	
Monthly SSI payments................................	$326.00	$326.00
Their Social Security benefits are....................................		+273.00
Their total monthly income will be		$599.00

3

Mr. Johnson takes a weekend job which pays $100 a month gross wages. Here's how these earnings affect Mr. and Mrs. Johnson's total income.

Income not from current earnings:		
Couple's monthly Social Security benefits	$273.00	
Less $20	−20.00	
Remainder: Countable income not from current earnings	$253.00	$253.00
Income from current earnings:		
Wages for the month	$100.00	
Less $65	−65.00	
Divide remainder by 2................................	35.00/2	
Countable income from current earnings	$17.50	+17.50
Total countable income for the month		$270.00
Basic SSI amount for the month	$579.00	
Less total countable income	−270.50	
Monthly SSI payment	$308.50	$308.50
Their Social Security benefit is.......................................		+$273.00
And Mr. Johnson's monthly earnings are		+$100.00
So their total monthly income will be		$681.50

[a]*Benefits for blind and disabled recipients are calculated in a similar manner; however, other factors are considered in these portions of the SSI program, such as additional income exclusions for work-related expenses.*

Source: Department of Health and Human Services, Social Security Administration, "A Guide to Supplemental Security Income," (SSA Publication no. 05–11015, January 1984 ed.) pp. 16–19, updated to reflect 1990 SSI payment levels and current Medicare premiums.

DEFINING DISABILITY

Since considerable attention is devoted to older persons in Chapter 4 (Social Security) and Chapter 7 (Social Services), much of this chapter is devoted to an analysis of social policies and services for persons with disabilities. Most Americans agree that disabled individuals are among the *deserving* poor; however, defining *disability* presents obstacles. There are many types of disabilities and handicaps. Amputations, arthritis, blindness, bone problems, brain injuries, burns, cancer, cerebral palsy, cleft lip and palate, deafness, diabetes, disfigurement, emotional disturbances, epilepsy, heart disease, mental retardation, mongolism, multiple sclerosis, muscular atrophy, muteness, paralysis, respiratory disorders, stroke, and stuttering are just some.[18] In addition to classifying these problems as disabilities or handicaps, one might classify them in terms of degree of impairment.[19] For instance, those with visual impairments may have varying degrees of sight. Some individuals are so severely handicapped that they can perform few of life's day-to-day functions, yet other disabled persons are able to function quite well in society. *Disabilities* have traditionally been defined as *health-related problems that prevent the individual from working.*[20] A broader definition includes not only employment limitations, but also limitations in all roles and tasks a person usually performs in society, especially if these limitations exist for long periods of time.[21] It is estimated that forty-three million Americans have physical or mental disabilities.[22]

The U.S. government supports a large number of programs for those with handicapping and disabling conditions. In order to determine which individuals are eligible to participate in some of these federally funded programs, the following definition is used:

> A handicapped person is anyone with any type of physical or mental disability that substantially impairs or restricts one or more such major life activities as walking, seeing, hearing, speaking, working, or learning. Handicapping conditions include but are not limited to cancer; cerebral palsy; deafness or hearing impairment; diabetes; emotional illness; epilepsy; heart disease; mental retardation; multiple sclerosis; muscular dystrophy; orthopedic, speech, or visual impairment; perceptual handicaps such as dyslexia, minimal brain dysfunction, and developmental aphasia.
>
> The U.S. Attorney General has also ruled that alcoholism and drug addiction are physical or mental impairments that are handicapping conditions if they limit one or more of life's major activities.[23]

In the 1980s, controversy erupted over whether or not those with Acquired Immune Deficiency Syndrome (AIDS) and others who carry the Human Immunodeficiency Virus (HIV) are covered under the federal definition of disability. Several decisions support the interpretation that these conditions are included.[24] For example, in *School Board of Nassau County, Fla. v. Arline,* the U.S. Supreme Court in 1987 ruled that those with contagious diseases (in this case a schoolteacher with tuberculosis) are handicapped. This decision did not directly address the issue of those with the HIV infection who do not have symptoms of AIDS, but in 1988 the Justice Department reversed an earlier opinion it had issued and stated that both those with AIDS and HIV carriers are covered under the federal definition. In addition, under the Civil Rights Restoration Act of 1988, employers cannot be held liable for discrimination if they fail to hire or retain a person with a contagious disease if more than "reasonable accommodations" are needed to protect others from the disease. But since the HIV infection which causes AIDS is not contracted through casual contact, it rarely poses a threat that would require such accommodations.

REHABILITATIVE SERVICES FOR THE DISABLED

Financial assistance through SSI is an important resource for elderly and disabled persons who are unable to work and whose incomes are so little that they cannot maintain an adequate standard of living. However, handicapped and disabled persons often need more than financial assistance. For example, even the most severely mentally retarded person can benefit from programs of physical and mental stimulation. For those with less severe disabilities, physical therapy, artificial limbs, or other services may be needed to carry out day-to-day activities. Others need special educational programs and learning devices. Still others require vocational education and reeducation.

The Vocational Rehabilitation Program

Although the first institutions for disabled individuals in the United States were established in the early part of the nineteenth century, training and education programs to assist those who were living in the community and who showed potential for employment did not emerge until the twentieth century.[25] One of the first was developed in Massachusetts in 1916.[26] In 1920, Congress passed the Vocational Rehabilitation Act (also called the Smith-Fess Act) to assist vocationally disabled civilians and disabled veterans returning from World War I by providing funds through a federal-state matching formula. The federal and state governments shared program costs on a fifty-fifty basis. The program was appealing because it was generally less costly to rehabilitate people to work than to provide them with long-term income maintenance payments. Although originally intended for those with physical disabilities, in 1943 those with mental illness and those with mental retardation were included; and in the 1960s, those with socially handicapping conditions, including adult and juvenile offenders, were also added.[27]

Today the federal government provides the majority of funding for the Vocational Rehabilitation (VR) program. Each state operates its own program according to federal guidelines and also supplements federal funding of the program. An individual who applies for VR services is evaluated by a doctor and/or other experts to determine whether a disability exists. Only those who have a reasonable chance of becoming employed or reemployed qualify for services. For women at home, the criterion is that they have the potential to perform independent living skills.[28] Each person who qualifies for assistance is assigned a VR counselor who develops an individualized plan for the disabled client; the plan may include medical services, training, education, guidance, financial assistance, and job-placement services.

The concept of the individualized rehabilitation plan sounds like a rational way to optimize services to the disabled; however, clients may not receive all the services they need. When available funds cannot be stretched to meet the needs of all eligible participants, clients' needs must be prioritized. In addition, because each state administers its own program, individuals with the same or similar disabilities may receive different types and amounts of services depending on the state in which they live.

In recent years, the VR program has served fewer clients. In 1975, nearly 1.4 million clients were served, but in the 1980s these figures were consistently below one million.[29] The number of new applications processed also declined. While more than eight-hundred thousand were reviewed in 1975, today slightly fewer than six-hundred thousand are processed each year, and the percentage of clients accepted into the program has dropped from 64 percent in 1975 to 58 percent in 1987. The number of clients who are considered rehabilitated after participating in the program has also declined. In 1970, 77 percent of the clients were classified as rehabilitated. The figure dropped to 70 percent in 1975, and in the 1980s it was as low as 61 percent. However, total funding in current dollars has increased, tripling from about $560 million in 1970 to $1.6 billion in 1987.

In addition to the VR program, there are other provisions for employment of handicapped individuals. The state employment offices (see Chapter 4) have a legal responsibility to assist those with handicaps, and handicapped individuals may also qualify under the Job Training Partnership Act (see Chapter 9).

Creaming

In its earlier days, critics charged the VR program with a practice called *creaming*. Creaming means accepting into the program those candidates who are most likely to become rehabilitated. While the goal of the VR program is rehabilitation, it is easier for some disabled persons to be rehabilitated than others. Most of the program's early clients were young, white males whose disabilities were neither chronic nor severe.[30]

> In 1938 the federal [vocational rehabilitation] office captured the policy that lay behind the selection of the vocational rehabilitation caseload when it told the states that eligibility does not necessarily imply feasibility. Anyone over 18 was technically eligible for rehabilitation, but such factors as advanced age, extreme disability, bad attitude of mind, or low social status limited feasibility.[31]

Although this attitude has changed since the early days of the program, the fact remains that VR is not an entitlement program. Funds are limited. Not everyone in need of assistance may be served, and for those who are served, counselors may not be able to procure all the funds and services the client needs.

Deinstitutionalization and Normalization

One of the first responses of modern society to those with severe physical and mental handicaps was *indoor* relief—i.e., the *warehousing* of these individuals in large institutions. Over the years, conditions in institutions became more humane, but until recently these large facilities were the primary means of assisting those considered too severely handicapped to remain at home and in the community. The movement toward deinstitutionalization gained judicial backing when in 1972, the U.S. Supreme Court ruled in the case of *Wyatt* v. *Stickney* that "[n]o persons shall be admitted to the institution unless prior determination shall have been made that residence in the institution is the least restrictive habilitation setting."[32] Today, the goal of deinstitutionalization has been taken further to include the desire for *normalization* among disabled persons. Normalization, a concept that originated in Europe (primarily Sweden) during the 1960s, means that regardless of the severity of their disabilities, handicapped individuals should have the opportunity to live as much like other citizens as possible.[33] For example, their homes should be located in regular residential communities and should resemble other homes in the community, and they should be afforded opportunities for shopping, recreation, and other everyday life activities.[34] Advancements in educational techniques and physical therapies and other medical technologies have made it possible for many more individuals to live independently. While it seems logical from both humanistic and cost-savings perspectives, normalization of handicapped persons has met with serious problems. Despite the trend toward normalization, handicapped people continue to face obstacles such as negative attitudes and rejection by the general public, employers, and even by professionals who underestimate the abilities of persons with disabilities; architectural and other barriers also continue to prohibit or restrict the use of buildings; public transportation and other facilities and programs may continue to provide minimal assistance and foster dependence rather than promote rehabilitation.[35] The illustration entitled "Neighbors Pull in Welcome Mat" is an example of the roles that state and local politics play in the controversies over deinstitutionalization and normalization.

ILLUSTRATION: NEIGHBORS PULL IN WELCOME MATS

"FEAR OF UNKNOWN" BLAMED IN FIGHT TO KEEP OUT COMMUNITY HOMES

CORPUS CHRISTI—Mister Rogers would be upset to learn that it is not a beautiful day in the neighborhoods.

Television's preacher of friendly neighborhoods would find that the welcome mat has been replaced by fear and loathing as mentally retarded people attempt to move into ordinary neighborhood houses here and elsewhere in Texas. The state, through court orders and legislative funding, is reducing the populations of the 13 state schools for the retarded by moving the residents into community homes, if they can be opened.

The image of this self-proclaimed "Sparkling City by the Sea" has been tarnished over the past year as some attempts to open homes for retarded adults met with vehement opposition;

• One case went to court, leaving an $85,000 house vacant for months while lawyers argued over six retarded people

who wanted to live in the neighborhood. Forty neighbors cited their 1946 deed restrictions prohibiting any "noxious or offensive trades" or anything that would be an "annoyance or nuisance."

The neighbors said the value of their property would fall if the home opened on their quiet street. Lawyers for the retarded successfully fought back by publicizing another, illegal section of that same neighborhood deed covenant—one that banned any residents who are not "of the Caucasian or White Race."

• After being denied county permission to open four homes, but battling successfully to open three others, the Nueces County mental health and retardation center has decided not to open any more group homes.

"Some of the comments we received were not terribly flattering to us or to our clients," said Bob Shaw, director of mental retardation services for the center. "I think it's an honest reaction of people who have some fear of the unknown. I don't think Corpus is terribly unique in this."

• More than 150 neighbors opposed a home opened by the center in Robstown near Corpus Christi.

This kind of bitter feuding was not supposed to happen in Texas this year.

Last year, the legislature passed a law making it illegal for cities or neighborhoods to prevent small group homes for the retarded, mentally ill or other disabled people from locating in residential areas. The bill was hailed as landmark legislation by advocates for the rights of the retarded.

However, to win the support of lobbyists for Texas towns and cities, the mental retardation officials agreed to exempt existing neighborhood deed restrictions from the bill. That exemption has allowed residents of Corpus Christi, Odessa, and Temple to go to court armed with long-time property laws to try to stop group homes for the retarded and mentally ill from opening.

Laywers for the retarded won their fight in Corpus Christi, but lost in Odessa. The Temple case, which involves homes for the mentally ill, is pending.

Consequently, advocates for the retarded are seeking to eliminate the existing deed restriction exemption in the next session of the legislature.

"We need to go back and change it because people are using the existing deed restrictions to keep mentally retarded people out of residential areas," said Carmen Quesada, executive director of the Texas Association for Retarded Citizens. "We need to remove the last barriers."

Diane Shisk, attorney for Advocacy Inc., which represents disabled Texans, said that just as racial restrictions are blatantly discriminatory and no longer constitutional, restrictions discriminating against the retarded also should be thrown out because they violate public policy.

Officials of the Texas Department of Mental Health and Mental Retardation disagree.

"I see no reason to make any changes, and I would have to be convinced of the need," said Jaylon Fincannon, deputy Texas commissioner for mental retardation.

According to the American Planning Association, most state and city planners surveyed in 1985 "said that group homes of six to eight developmentally disabled persons should be allowed in any residential district."

The planners noted that the U.S. Supreme Court and lower courts have warned that neighborhood fears and opposition cannot be the basis for local zoning decisions about group homes.

"The opposition is still very strong and vocal, but the courts, state legislatures and local planning professionals are lining up in favor of change," the planners said in a January newsletter.

Marvin Maloney, attorney for the 40 Corpus Christi neighbors, said he will be working next year to change the new state law.

"I really question the constitutionality of" the legislation, Maloney said. "That thing is terribly strong. It gives the mental health-mental retardation department power to do anything they want to do anytime they want to."

He said he also will fight to protect deed restrictions because they are "almost sacred. That's one of the few rights and privileges landowners have. It's tampering with justice when you start interfering with deed restrictions which have been in effect for 40 years."

"We're not bigots," said Jim Burkhardt, one of the Corpus Christi neighbors who sued when they learned of plans to make a group home out of a one-story brick house on a large lot on Princess Drive. "Rather, it's MHMR's dishonesty and the way they come storming in here. They ran over us."

He said a television news crew "came knocking on the doors of this neighborhood one Monday night after dark, sticking microphones in our faces and asking us if we knew a group home was moving in. That's how we found out."

Burkhardt and Joyce Vogelpohl, another neighbor, said most of the residents opposed the home because they believe the value of their homes would drop sharply.

Vogelpohl, who bought her house two years ago for $95,000, said, "There's no way in the world somebody would buy it from me for that" now, she said.

"Because of public ignorance, we'll never be able to sell our house. People will say, "I don't want to live in that neighborhood with a bunch of crazy people down the street.""

Not every group home started in Corpus Christi met with resistance, however. Donald M. Taft, a former Corpus Christi State School official, bought six houses in the city and put more than 70 retarded people in them. He said his group homes have operated successfully since last summer without neighborhood friction.

Court papers filed in the Odessa case by Advocacy Inc. said "numerous studies over a 10-year period have confirmed that fears of diminished property values are without factual basis." The lawyers cited studies from Princeton University, New York State University and state governments in Ohio and Illinois. "Indeed, some studies show enhanced values in some instances," the brief said.

The proposed group home in Odessa has been vacant since August, when the Permian Basin mental retardation center began leasing the four-bedroom house for $600 a month. Neighbors sued in November, citing a 1950 deed restriction that required only single-family homes in the area. A state judge ruled in favor of the neighborhood, but Advocacy Inc. has appealed the decision to the Texas State Court of Appeals.

Court papers filed by Advocacy Inc. argued that deed restrictions "are not enforceable if they are unreasonable and against public policy.

"The strong public policy in favor of establishing family homes for mentally retarded persons in residential communities overrides the restrictive covenant," Advocacy Inc. said.

Smithie Amburgey, who has lived in the Odessa neighborhood 35 years, said the residents "were pleased that someone just can't come in and say, 'You don't have any rights anymore.'

"They don't understand we're not against the mentally retarded or any advancement for them," she said. "It's just that they tried to push this through over us, and they could have gone anywhere else. We're all for keeping our neighborhood as single-family homes."

Although the court case filed in November in Temple involves community homes for the mentally ill rather than the retarded, it is mentioned by advocates for the retarded as another example of why the recent state law should be changed.

The mental health and retardation center in Temple was sued after it opened several duplexes for mentally ill people in a neighborhood with a deed restriction that defines the area as a single-family area. It does not allow more than one person to live in a duplex unless they are related by blood, marriage or adoption.

"I had not anticipated the degree of reaction and some of the anger and prejudice that came spilling out," said Steven Schnee, executive director of the mental health center. "I guess I'm a sort of Pollyanna. I'd hoped that as a society we had moved further.

"It's a controversial area," he said. "What's happening is that we as a society are having to step back from a position of out of sight, out of mind, where we put people in large institutions and said, 'They're gone.'

"That's neither clinically appropriate nor economically feasible," he said.

Source: Denise Gamino, "Neighbors Pull in Welcome Mats," *Austin American-Statesman* (July 29, 1986), pp. A1, A4.

Mainstreaming

An important issue faced by children with handicaps and their families and communities is *mainstreaming*. Mainstreaming requires that handicapped children be placed and taught in regular public school programs whenever possible rather than in separate schools or in separate classrooms. The Education for All Handicapped Children Act of 1975 states that every disabled child is entitled to an "appropriate elementary and secondary education." If a child must be placed in a private school by the local education authority in order to obtain an appropriate education, this service must be provided at no cost. Other services, including transportation and special devices, must also be provided.

Some people hail mainstreaming as a sensible and effective way to insure that children with physical and mental handicaps are afforded full opportunities to learn and to interact with other children. In this way, children with handicaps are not made to feel more different than necessary, and nonhandicapped children learn how much they have in common with these "special" children. Children who are mainstreamed may attend some special classes, and the teachers in regular classrooms are assisted in developing educational programs to meet the needs of their handicapped pupils.

Like other social policies and programs, mainstreaming is not without conflicts. Some school systems, especially smaller and poorer ones, are likely to feel unfairly burdened by the financial costs of providing all the necessary services. An individual education program must be developed for each child, and parents have the right to participate in the development of these programs. Unfortunately, there is the possibility that these educational programs will not be carried out for students, who will be left in regular classrooms without special assistance because of lack of time and resources. Others emphasize that many regular classroom teachers want to be helpful, but they are already overburdened with large classes and heavy workloads that prevent individualized instruction. The federal government assists the states and communities with block grants to fund the act. Child advocates, however, have complained that Congress has appropriated only a fraction of the funds that could be expended under the act. In 1985 the House Education and Labor Committee reported that 633,000 additional handicapped children were receiving a public-school education as a result of the legislation.[36]

Developmental Disabilities Program

The Developmental Disabilities Assistance and Bill of Rights Act of 1978 is one piece of federal legislation that authorizes a broad range of services for those with disabling conditions. According to this act:

> A developmental disability is a severe, chronic disability attributed to a mental and/or physical impairment, manifested before the person reaches age 22, which is likely to continue indefinitely and which results in substantial functional limitations in three or more of the following areas of major life activity: self-care, receptive and expressive language, learning, mobility, self-direction, capacity for independent living, economic self-sufficiency.

In addition, it is expected that the developmentally disabled person will need services "of lifelong or extended duration." Developmentally disabled individuals and professionals in the DD field are generally pleased with this definition because it does not restrict services to only those with specific diagnoses. But there is concern that the definition omits less severely disabled persons who need services that could substantially improve the quality of their lives. In addition, an argument can be made that age twenty-two is an arbitrary cutoff point which was adopted as much for reasons of administrative expediency as for developing a rational definition.

Additional services target specific disability groups.[37] For example, every state has either a commission to serve those who are blind or a special unit in its Vocational Rehabilitation offices. Throughout the country, there are about fifty-five schools providing education and training specifically to blind children at the kindergarten through twelfth-grade levels. At the federal level, the Deafness and Communicative Disorders Branch of the Rehabilitation Services Administration provides consultation to the states in developing services for those who are deaf or have other communication disorders. It also works on developing new technological devices to assist handicapped individuals. Sixty-two schools in the U.S. provide residential programs for deaf children from infancy through high school. In 1972, the Economic Opportunity Act was amended to include a goal that 10 percent of Head Start enrollees be handicapped children.

A New Bill of Rights for Those with Handicaps

Most everyone in the United States and in many other countries is now familiar with the blue-and-white symbol of a person in a wheelchair similar to the one shown in Figure 5–1. In a parking lot it means that certain spaces are reserved for handicapped drivers; on a building door, it means that handicapped persons can move about in the building independently; on a restroom door, it means that stalls are equipped with handrails and raised toilets so that handicapped individuals can use these facilities more easily.

FIGURE 5–1   International symbol of access for the handicapped.

Persistent political efforts by handicapped individuals, their families, and other advocates have resulted in legislation requiring increased access for individuals with disabilities. For example, the Architectural Barriers Act of 1968 included specifications aimed at making buildings accessible and safe for those who are blind, deaf, using wheelchairs or who have other handicaps. It requires that all buildings constructed partly or totally with federal funds and buildings owned or leased by federal agencies have ramps, elevators, and other barrier-free access. Although it sounded as if the law might be expensive to implement, estimates were that the cost to the builder was only "one-tenth of one percent of the total cost of a new building."[38] But many buildings today continue to fall short of the standards for restrooms, doors, and warning signals. In addition, locating suitable housing is particularly difficult. For example, those in wheelchairs find that few apartments or houses are equipped with extra-wide doorways or appliances that can be easily reached.

One of the most important pieces of civil rights legislation for those with disabilities is Title V of the Rehabilitation Act of 1973. Under this act:

1. Federal agencies must have affirmative-action programs to hire and promote qualified handicapped persons.
2. The Architectural and Transportation Barriers Compliance Board was established to enforce the 1968 Architectural Barriers Act. Its activities have now been expanded to include communications barriers.
3. All businesses, universities, foundations, and other institutions holding contracts with the U.S. government must have affirmative-action programs to hire and promote qualified handicapped persons.
4. Discrimination against qualified disabled person—employees, students, and receivers of health care and other services—in all public and private institutions receiving federal assistance is prohibited.

There are offices of civil rights in the Department of Health and Human Services and in the Department of Education which have responsibility for enforcing federal laws that prohibit discrimination against people with handicaps.

But no piece of legislation, court decision, or administrative ruling holds more significance for handicapped individuals than the Americans with Disabilities Act passed with overwhelming support by Congress in 1990 with strong backing from the Bush administration. The definition of disability in this bill is the same as that now being used in parts of the Rehabilitation Act and in amendments to the Fair Housing Act. A disabled individual is defined as one who has "a physical impairment that substantially limits one or more major life activities, a record of such an impairment, or being regarded as having such an impairment." One of the bill's most important aspects is that it goes much farther in requiring that the private sector provide accommodations for handicapped individuals than any other previous legislation. For example, retail establishments such as restaurants, hotels, and theaters must be made accessible to those with disabilities. In debates over the bill, businesses argued that not only were the costs to adopt the new measures unrealistic and outrageously expensive, but that they were also potentially unsafe and unclear. For example, in testimony about the bill, a representative of the National Association of Theater Owners argued against allowing patrons in wheelchairs the freedom to sit wherever they want, because "it is not only reasonable, but it is essential from a safety standpoint that wheelchair patrons be seated near an exit."[39] Prohibitions on employment discrimination are also significantly broadened under the act. They pertain to businesses with 25 or more employees and include bans against discrimination in hiring, firing, compensation, advancement, and training; and they also require employers to make "reasonable accommodations" for those with disabilities unless this would cause "undue hardship." Reasonable accommodations may include the use of readers or interpreters, modifying buildings, adjusting work schedules, and purchasing needed devices. But just how far must employers go to insure that they have made "reasonable" efforts, and what is considered a "hardship?" According to the U.S. Chamber of Commerce, "[t]his vague language is an invitation to litigation."[40] Telecommunications provisions require that telephone companies provide relay services for hearing- and speech-impaired customers. In the area of transportation, all new buses and trains must be made accessible to wheelchairs, but old vehicles are exempt. Over the past several years, Amtrak, the federally subsidized rail system, has been taking steps to assure that all new cars have facilities for handicapped passengers. The provisions contained in the bill are to be phased in over a three year period. Senator Steny Hoyer (D-Md), the bill's chief sponsor, called the bill an "Emancipation Proclamation" for individuals with disabilities.

Airlines are not included in the Americans with Disabilities Act because they are covered under the 1986 Air Carrier Access Act which prohibits airlines from discriminating against handicapped travelers. Directives issued in 1990 by the U.S. Department of Transportation state that if an airline requires that a handicapped individual be escorted, the escort must be allowed to fly free.[41] Another directive is that many planes must have movable armrests and that wide-body planes must have an accessible lavatory. In addition, individuals with handicaps must be allowed to select any seat, except where this might be a safety hazard. The National Federation for the Blind was outraged at even this restriction. Not surprisingly, the Air Transport Association (composed of airlines) expressed its concern that the directives would be excessively costly to implement. Implementation of the many provisions contained in the new Americans with Disabilities Act will also require some carefully written directives, rules, and guidelines if the spirit of this new legislation is to be realized.

There are many more public-policy issues that involve handicapped individuals. The right to refuse treatment and to informed consent, the issue of guardianship, the right to be accorded fair treatment when accused of crimes, the issues of voting rights and of zoning restrictions on community residences are some that remain on the public agenda.[42]

Additional social welfare policy issues confront advocates of the rights of individuals with mental retardation. There has been some outcry against the Supreme Court's recent decision which allows states to execute death row inmates who are mentally retarded and against a decision by the Iowa Supreme Court which once again gives courts the power to decide whether mentally retarded persons can be sterilized. The institutionalization of mentally retarded individuals has been particularly vexing because they are often denied the same rights as mentally ill individuals to have their cases reviewed in order to determine if they should be discharged from institutions.

GENERAL ASSISTANCE:
THE STATE AND COMMUNITY RESPONSE
TO WELFARE

Most of the major social welfare programs discussed thus far are totally or partly the responsibility of the federal government. But some social welfare programs are developed, administered, and financed by state and local governments, independent of the federal government. The term used to describe many of these programs is General Assistance. General Assistance (GA) predated the New Deal, when local and state governments were the major suppliers of public assistance, but the New Deal failed to include many of the groups that were covered under the original General Assistance programs.[43]

General Assistance programs are administered differently from state to state and administration may also differ among localities in the same state. The types and amounts of services also vary, as do the types of recipients served. In some cases, the state government is entirely responsible for the General Assistance program. It determines the policies and procedures for General Assistance, and state workers accept applications and provide assistance to recipients. In other areas, although the state may set policies and determine eligibility requirements, General Assistance is administered by city and county governments. In these cases, the state may provide all the funding, or the state and local governments may share funding responsibilities. Some states have no involvement in General Assistance. Local governments are free to establish General Assistance programs if they desire; but if not, there may be no General Assistance available.

Why is General Assistance needed when there are a number of federally mandated and supported programs? General Assistance exists because the United States uses a fragmented approach to meeting welfare needs. Some poor people do not meet the criteria for any of the major federal or federal-state welfare programs. They may not be aged, blind, or disabled, at least not according to federal standards; they may not have dependent children; they may not be entitled to unemployment benefits, or they may have exhausted them. They may need immediate assistance, unable to wait for federal benefits which may take thirty days or more to begin. In other words, to qualify for welfare programs, simply being *needy* is not always enough.

While most Americans have heard of the AFDC, Food Stamp, and Medicaid programs, General Assistance is not as well known. In some places, it is referred to as *county welfare, county aid,* or *general relief.* Some programs provide cash assistance; others rely on in-kind assistance like medical care; and some use a combination of the two.

General Assistance has many uses. Historically, the program has helped individuals who receive little or nothing from other types of social welfare programs but who need aid, especially in emergencies. AFDC and SSI beneficiaries are usually not eligible for GA except while they are waiting for these payments to begin. In some areas, the emphasis is on helping those who are poor cover medical expenses. Other uses have been to assist aged and disabled individuals, especially prior to improvements in the SSI program, and also to help the unemployed and those who earn very little from employment.[44]

The most recent report on General Assistance commissioned by the federal government described these programs as

> ...an important component of the income assistance system...serving as the ultimate "safety net" for low income individuals and families who are not eligible for federally-supported assistance programs...Eligibility criteria vary from strict disability requirements...to broad income requirements with no categorical restrictions. Benefit levels vary from small one-time payments to regular payments virtually identical to AFDC or SSI. Forms of assistance vary from bus tickets or firewood to vendor payments to vouchers to cash. Some jurisdictions have one comprehensive GA program, and some have several special programs.... Some have strict work requirements or workfare programs, and some have no special work provisions.... Compounding all this variation is the fact that GA program characteristics...are unusually sensitive to budget pressures...and change much more frequently than any other part of the welfare system.[45]

Following passage of the Social Security Act, General Assistance expenditures decreased sharply from almost $1.5 million in 1935 to about $450,000 in 1936.[46] While annual expenditures have fluctuated over the years, they are currently about $2.5 billion, with about 1.2 million people served each month.[47] These broad descriptions of the General Assistance program should be interpreted cautiously. Because there are no federal regulations requiring reporting, "record keeping is notoriously lax,"[48] and information is difficult to obtain.[49] Examples of two General Assistance programs are found in the following illustration.

ILLUSTRATION: TWO GENERAL ASSISTANCE PROGRAMS

There is a great deal of diversity among General Assistance programs and a lack of understanding about how they work. Below are two illustrations of General Assistance programs. The first is a state program; the second is a county program.

GENERAL ASSISTANCE IN MASSACHUSETTS

Massachusetts operates a program called General Relief (GR), which is entirely funded by the state and operated by the Massachusetts Department of Public Welfare in all sixty-nine of its local offices. It provides cash payments and medical assistance to low-income individuals who are not eligible for federally-subsidized assistance. All who qualify are assisted. Recipients are usually single individuals, but couples and families are also eligible. Adults with mental or physical disabilities and those over the age of forty-four who worked twenty or fewer hours per week in the last six months may qualify for benefits. Families with dependent chil-dren who do not meet AFDC requirements may also qualify if 1) the parents are employed but earning little or 2) the parents are unemployed but employable and are willing to register for work and accept suitable employment. Others who qualify are SSI applicants waiting for payments (the state recovers these payments from the Social Security Administration); ex-convicts (assistance is limited to two months); halfway house residents; vocational rehabilitation program recipients; those caring full-time for incapacitated relatives eligible for medical assistance; and full-time students under the age of nineteen living with an unemployable parent. No income limits for participants are specified, but those whose current income exceeds payment levels do not qualify. Asset limits and payments are lower than in the AFDC and SSI programs. Some additional payments are made to those who need special diets and those with excess rent costs. There are some relative responsibility requirements—for example, spouses are responsible for each other, and parents are responsible for their minor children. Liens are not placed on recipients' assets (except in cases of fraud). Payments can be recovered if the recipient has insurance that pays for expenses due to illness or injury. Recipients do not have to be United States citizens, and state residents are covered regardless of how long they have lived in Massachusetts. Payments can be received as long as needed, but recertification occurs every six months. Some medical assistance is provided, and although services are less comprehensive than in the Medicaid program, physician office visits, dental care, some prescription drugs, eye care, and home health care can be provided through payments to vendors.

GENERAL ASSISTANCE IN POLK COUNTY, IOWA

Iowa has no statewide nonfederal assistance program. Provision of General Relief (GR), as it is also called in Iowa, is left to the discretion of county governments. Where available, the program is usually administered by the county Department of Social Services. Polk County, one of the state's most populous areas, has a GR program which is funded through a special property tax. It is primarily used to provide emergency and on-going assistance and some medical care to low-income individuals who are not eligible for AFDC or SSI; but AFDC and SSI recipients may be helped in emergencies. Assistance in Polk County is provided to all individuals, couples, and families who qualify and is generally more liberal than in other Iowa counties. Recipients must be unemployed as a result of medical disability or barriers to employment such as age or lack of skills and experience; or they must be in an emergency situation due to "circumstances beyond their own control," such as eviction or utility shut-off. Mothers who are no longer participating in AFDC because their youngest child is older than six may qualify; so too may high school students who are no longer eligible for AFDC because they are too old. Families with unemployed parents who do not qualify for AFDC may also receive GR. There are relative responsibility laws between parents and children and between grandparents and grandchildren. The county can file liens against property and estates to reclaim benefits, and it can sue relatives for repayment. There are no United States citizenship requirements, but assistance is usually restricted to those who have lived in the county for one year. When nonresidents are aided in emergencies, the county may try to recover costs from the recipients' legal county of residence. Recipients can receive payments as long as necessary but must reapply each month. There are no specific income and asset limitations for eligibility, but benefit levels for single individuals are equal to those in the SSI program. There are work requirements for those capable of employment, and the county provides jobs with the city government and nonprofit organizations. The number of hours of employment required generally equals the amount of assistance divided by the state minimum wage. For those who do not comply with work requirements, future applications are considered more closely.

Source: Department of Health and Human Services, *Characteristics of General Assistance, 1982* (Washington, D.C., May 1983), pp. 119–123, 155–158.

WELFARE AND FEDERALISM

American federalism—the constitutional division of power between the national government and the states—affects the administration and financing of social welfare programs. The major public assistance programs in the United States (AFDC, SSI, Medicaid, Food Stamps, and General Assistance) are administered and funded in different ways. AFDC and Medicaid are joint ventures of the federal and state governments, which share in funding the programs. The federal government sets guidelines, but the states play a major role in determining eligibility requirements and payment levels. Food Stamps and SSI are largely programs of the federal government, which finances minimum benefits and establishes basic eligibility requirements. The states may supplement basic SSI benefits, and many do. SSI checks are mailed directly to recipients by the Social Security Administration. Food stamps are generally distributed through state and local welfare offices. General Assistance is a highly discretionary type of program and is the major public assistance program funded and administered by state and/or local governments with no federal participation. Most social service programs, like mental health and child welfare, are jointly funded by the federal and state governments. The federal government sets broad guidelines, and the states have responsibility for administering the programs.

During the Reagan presidency, debate over the appropriate approach to federalism in social welfare programs took on new vigor. Prior to the Reagan years, the trend in welfare programs was toward greater centralization or federalization of welfare programs, as in Food Stamps and SSI. But Reagan was successful in returning more power to the states. He consolidated hundreds of smaller categorical grants into nine large block grants covering health, mental health, and other social services.

Block-grant proponents claim that most welfare issues are rightfully the concerns of the states and not the federal government, and they look at the cost savings of block grants as evidence that these measures work. Critics agreed that block grants resulted in cost savings, but they contended that the savings hurt those who needed services. Others believe that there is not even much evidence of savings.[50] States responded in different ways to the reduced funding. Some states used more of their own monies to fund needed social services, but others responded by replacing more expensive services with less expensive ones.[51] A case in point is Texas, which "...lowered its average daily cost for day care from $10.87 to $8.15 under the new Social Services Block Grant, when it was able to drop from its requirements proposed federal standards on staff-pupil ratios and staff training requirements."[52] In this case, the ironic result was that Texas was able to decrease total day-care spending while simultaneously increasing the number of children served![53]

As we shall see in Chapter 6, even within the major, categorical federal-state programs like AFDC, there has been considerable discussion about the role of state experimentation, and President Bush is encouraging latitude for states to pursue their own versions of work requirements. Disagreements over the role of federalism in social welfare programs and over the virtues of centralized versus decentralized welfare programs have led the United States to use many different combinations of federal, state, and local involvement to address human needs.

SUMMARY

Four types of provisions are available to those who are aged, blind, or disabled: social insurance, public assistance, social and rehabilitative services, and civil rights legislation. The major public assistance program for these groups is the Supplemental Security Income (SSI) program. In 1972, Congress passed legislation that federalized the adult categorical assistance programs—Old Age Assistance, Aid to the Blind, and Aid to the Permanently and Totally Disabled under the SSI program. SSI has been one of the major innovations in providing welfare benefits to Americans since the original Social Security Act became law in 1935. Under SSI, states no longer directly administer the adult categorical programs. The federal government now sets minimum payment levels and basic eligibility requirements for beneficiaries, but many states supplement payments. These changes helped to reduce inequitable treatment of recipients from state to state. SSI was the only portion of President Nixon's welfare-reform package that Congress passed.

One of the largest social service programs for those with disabilities is the Vocational Rehabilitation (VR) program, but it is a limited program because not everyone who is disabled is entitled to assistance. The primary criterion for participation is the individual's potential for returning to work. The VR program has been accused of creaming, of accepting clients who are most easily rehabilitated and of ignoring the more severely disabled who may have to do without services.

Individuals with physical and mental handicaps face a number of obstacles in achieving independence. Those with more severe handicaps have been housed in large institutions, often with little chance of realizing their maximum potential. In other cases, community rejection, lack of transportation, and lack of access to buildings and other facilities prevent disabled individuals from interacting in society. Laws which emerged in the 1960s and 1970s were important steps in the recognition of the rights of those with disabilities. The Architectural Barriers Act of 1968 was one important piece of legislation, but the most important achievement of this period was Title V of the Rehabilitation Act of 1973 which prevents programs and agencies that receive federal funds from discriminating against handicapped persons in employment, education, and use of services.

Another important piece of legislation passed during this period was the Developmental Disabilities Assistance and Bill of Rights Act. It provides an array of services to those whose disability was manifested before age twenty-two. The Education for All Handicapped Children Act guarantees all children, regardless of their disability, a free publicly-funded education. Under this act, children are supposed to be "mainstreamed"—placed in regular schools and classrooms whenever possible. In theory, mainstreaming is a widely accepted concept, but it has resulted in controversies when teachers with heavy workloads have not had the time to invest in these children's educations and when school systems feel they do not have the resources to provide adequately for severely handicapped children. But no piece of legislation has been more encouraging for integrating those with handicaps into society then the Americans with Disabilities Act of 1990 with its expanded provisions to prevent discrimination in public accommodations, employment, communications, and travel.

An important public assistance program for some individuals with limited financial resources is General Assistance. GA programs are solely funded and administered by state and local governments with no federal government involvement. There is considerable variation in these programs across states and communities with respect to eligibility criteria and payment levels. In some cases, GA is used as unemployment relief and as a means for assisting those who do not qualify for other welfare programs. In many cases, it is used to help the indigent with medical expenses. Aid may be limited to emergency situations. Some states and communities do offer long-term assistance, but some communities have no GA program at all.

There is a lack of consensus about the best methods for funding and administering welfare programs. While some believe that the federal government is best suited to perform these functions because of its large revenue base and its ability to treat recipients equally regardless of the state in which they live, others feel that welfare decisions should be closer to the people and are rightfully a concern of the states. Many smaller categorical grants have been consolidated into larger block grants, giving the states greater control over social welfare decisions. The Reagan and Bush administrations have given states greater encouragement to try new options in their social welfare programs. Americans use many arrangements for delivering social welfare services because they cannot agree on which are best.

NOTES

1. John G. Turnbull, C. Arthur Williams, Jr., and Earl F. Cheit, *Economic and Social Security* (New York: Ronald Press, 1967), p. 83.
2. Ibid.
3. Robert J. Myers, *Social Security* (Bryn Mawr, Penn.: McCahan Foundation, 1975), p. 400.
4. Ibid.
5. Ibid., pp. 400–401.
6. Ibid., p. 401.
7. Ibid.
8. Bureau of the Census, *Statistical Abstract of the United States, 1965* (Washington, D.C.: 1965), p. 309.
9. Daniel P. Moynihan, *The Politics of a Guaranteed Income* (New York: Random House, 1973).
10. *Future of Social Programs* (Washington, D.C.: Congressional Quarterly, 1973), p. 15.
11. The following paragraphs in this section are based on *SSI*, Department of Health and Human Services, Social Security Administration, SSA publication no. 05-11000 (January 1989 Edition).
12. Ibid., p. 4.
13. Ibid.
14. *Supplemental Security Income (SSI): Current Program Characteristics and Alternatives for Future Reform*, A Background Paper by the Subcommittee on Retirement Income and Employment of the Select Committee on Aging, House of Representatives (100th Congress, August 1988), p. 4. For a description of state supplementation programs, see Donald E. Rigby and Elsa Ponce, *The Supplemental Security Income Program for the Aged, Blind, and Disabled: Selected Characteristics of State Supplementation Programs as of January 1984* (U.S. Department of Health and Human Services, Social Security Administration, SSA publication no. 13–11975, rev. December, 1984).
15. *Supplemental Security Income (SSI): Current Program Characteristics and Alternatives for Reform*, p. 11. Also see *SSI Outreach: Is the Federal Government Doing Enough?* Joint Hearing before the Subcommittee on Human Services of the Select Committee on Aging, House of Representatives and the New York State Assembly Standing Committee on Aging (101st Congress, October 2, 1989).
16. *Supplemental Security Income (SSI): Current Program Characteristics and Alternatives for Reform*, p. 11.

17. John Trout and David R. Mattson, "A 10-Year Review of the Supplemental Security Income Program," *Social Security Bulletin 47*, no. 1 (January 1984), pp. 3–24.
18. This list was taken from Jane Mullins and Suzanne Wolfe, *Special People Behind the Eight-Ball: An Annotated Bibliography of Literature Classified by Handicapping Conditions* (Johnstown, Penn.: Mafex Associates, 1975).
19. Saad Z. Nagi, "The Concept and Measurement of Disability" in Edward D. Berkowitz, ed., *Disability Policies and Government Programs* (New York: Holt, Rinehart, & Winston, 1979), p. 2; and Shirley Cohen, *Special People: A Brighter Future for Everyone with Physical, Mental, and Emotional Disabilities* (Englewood Cliffs, N.J.: Prentice-Hall, 1977), p. 8.
20. Monroe Berkowitz, William G. Johnson, and Edward H. Murphy, *Public Policy Toward Disability* (New York: Holt, Rinehart & Winston, 1976), p. 7.
21. Edward D. Berkowitz, "The American Disability System in Historical Perspective," in Berkowitz, *Disability Policies*, p. 43.
22. Julie Rovner and Martha Angle, "Anti-Bias Measure for Disabled is Passed by Senate, 76–8," *Congressional Quarterly Weekly Report* (September 9, 1989), p. 2318.
23. "It's a New Day for Disabled People," HEW Task Force on Public Awareness and the Disabled, *American Education* (December 1977).
24. See "AIDS: Covered Indirectly," *Congressional Quarterly Weekly Report* (May 13, 1989), p. 1123.
25. For a history of programs and policies addressing disability, see Richard K. Scotch, *From Goodwill to Civil Rights: Transforming Federal Disability Policy* (Philadelphia: Temple University Press, 1984).
26. Edward D. Berkowitz, "The American Disability System," p. 43.
27. Scotch, *From Good Will to Civil Rights.*
28. Berkowitz et al., *Public Policy Toward Disability,* p. 34.
29. Figures in this paragraph rely on *Statistical Abstract of the United States, 1989* (Washington, D.C. 1989), p. 360.
30. Berkowitz, "The American Disability System," p. 45.
31. FBVE, "Administration of the Vocational Rehabilitation Program," bulletin 113, rev. under imprint of the Department of Interior, Office of Education (Washington, D.C.: U.S. Government Printing Office, 1938), cited in Berkowitz, "The American Disability System."
32. *Wyatt v. Stickney*, 3195. U.S. 3 (1972).
33. Bengt Nirje, "The Normalization Principle," R. Kugel and A. Shearer, eds., *Changing Patterns in Residential Services for the Mentally Retarded,* rev. ed. (Washington, D.C.: President's Commission on Mental Retardation, 1976), p. 231.
34. Nirje, "The Normalization Principle"; and Wolf Wolfensberger, ed., *The Principle of Normalization in Human Services* (Toronto: National Institute on Mental Retardation, 1972).
35. Roberta Nelson, *Creating Community Acceptance for Handicapped People* (Springfield, Ill.: Charles C. Thomas, 1978), pp. 12–22.
36. Barbara Coleman, "Education for Handicapped Seen as Policy Success Story," *Congressional Quarterly* (November 16, 1985), pp. 2375–78.
37. Information in this paragraph is based on Office of Information and Resources for the Handicapped, Department of Education, "A Pocket Guide to Federal Help for the Disabled Person," Publication no. E–83–22002 (September 1983).
38. See "New Day for Disabled People."
39. Testimony of Malcolm C. Green, Chairman, National Association of Theater Owners, presented on May 10, 1989 before the Senate Subcommittee on the Handicapped on S.933, the "Americans with Disabilities Act," cited in "Americans with Disabilities Act," *Congressional Digest*, December 1989, p. 309.
40. Testimony of Zachary Fasman, U.S. Chamber of Commerce, presented on May 9, 1989 before the Senate Committee on Labor and Human Resources on S.933, the "Americans with Disabilities Act," cited in "Americans with Disabilities Act," *Congressional Digest,* December, 1989, p. 299.
41. "U.S. Officials Order Changes to Aid Disabled Air Travelers," *Champaign-Urbana New-Gazette* (March 3, 1990), p. A6.
42. For an extensive consideration of these issues and others, see Bruce Dennis Sales, D. Matthew Powell, Richard Van Duizend, and associates, *Disabled Persons and the Law, State and Legislative Issues* (New York: Plenum Press, 1982).
43. James Patterson, *Congressional Conservatism and the New Deal* (Lexington, Mass.: Lexington Books, 1981), p. 63. cited in Hugh Helco, *The Political Foundations of Antipoverty Policy* in Sheldon H. Danzinger and Daniel H. Weinberg, eds., *Fighting Poverty: What Works and What Doesn't* (Cambridge: Harvard University Press, 1986), p. 315.

44. For a discussion of how General Assistance has been used, see Duncan M. MacIntyre, *Public Assistance: Too Much or Too Little?* (Ithaca, N.Y.: New York State School of Industrial and Labor Relations, Cornell University, 1964), p. 51.

45. *Department of Health and Human Services, Characteristics of General Assistance Programs 1982* (Washington, D.C., May 1983), pp. 1–2.

46. Bureau of the Census, *Statistical Abstract of the United States, 1943* (Washington, D.C.: 1943), p. 193.

47. U.S. Bureau of the Census, *Statistical Abstract of the United States, 1989* (Washington, D.C., 1989), p. 349.

48. Joel F. Handler and Michael Sosin, *Last Resorts, Emergency Assistance and Special Needs Programs in Public Welfare* (New York: Academic Press, 1983), p. 81.

49. *Characteristics of General Assistance Programs, 1982.*

50. John L. Palmer and Isabel V. Sawhill, eds., *The Reagan Record* (Cambridge, Mass.: Ballinger, 1984), p. 17.

51. Ibid.

52. George E. Peterson, "Federalism and the States," in Palmer and Sawhill, *Reagan Record*, p. 245.

53. Ibid.

6

ASSISTING POOR FAMILIES
Aid to Families
with Dependent Children

THE DEVELOPMENT OF AFDC

The family is the primary social unit, yet the United States has no broad family policy. One program that is intended to assist is Aid to Families with Dependent Children (AFDC). It provides cash assistance to poor families so that children can continue to be cared for in their own homes. Today, one-fifth of all children live in poverty. If there is any segment of society for whom people have compassion, it is children who are completely dependent on others to meet their needs. Why, then, has AFDC been mired in a sea of controversy? As we shall see, much of the conflict centers on the adult beneficiaries of the program.

Mothers' Aid

Dependent children, in terms of public assistance programs, are those whose parents or guardians lack the financial resources to provide adequately for their care. The states began formalizing laws to assist such children in the early twentieth century, with local governments often providing the financing. These laws were established to assist children whose fathers were deceased; sometimes assistance was also provided to children whose fathers were disabled or absent through divorce or desertion. These early programs were called *mothers' aid* or *mothers' pensions*.

ADC

The federal government stepped in to share responsibility for dependent children in 1935, when the Aid to Dependent Children (ADC) program was included as part of the original Social Security Act. At first, ADC was conceived of as a short-term device to assist financially needy children. The program was intended to diminish and eventually to become *outmoded* as more and more families came to qualify for assistance under the social insurance programs of the Social Security Act.[1] According to Senator Daniel P. Moynihan, "[t]he program began as one whose typical beneficiary was a West Virginia mother whose husband had been killed in a mine accident."[2] But the emphasis of the early ADC program was not on providing aid for the wives of deceased workers; it was on providing assistance to mothers on behalf of their children.

Keeping the Family Together

From 1935 until 1950, the ADC program grew slowly. Some changes were made, but they did not arouse much public notice. The needs of parents in ADC families were eventually considered when in 1950 adult heads of households were also made eligible for ADC assistance. Other improvements were made in the program. Medical services, paid in part by the federal government, were made available to recipients. In 1958, a formula was developed so that states with lower per capita incomes received more federal financial assistance for their ADC programs than wealthier states.

But other parts of the program were becoming sore spots. One of the most stinging accusations leveled against the ADC program was that it contributed to the desertion of fathers from families. While the argument has been difficult to prove empirically,[3] we can see how the concern arose. Under the ADC program, families that had an able-bodied father residing at home were not eligible for benefits. In many cases, unemployed fathers qualified for other types of assistance—unemployment compensation, disability insurance, or Aid to the Permanently and Totally Disabled. But it was also possible that the father did not qualify for any of these programs or had exhausted his benefits. In other words, some fathers fell through the cracks. The unemployed, able-bodied fathers who could not find work did not qualify for ADC and could not support his family. However, if the father deserted the home, the family became eligible for ADC assistance. It is not known how many fathers did this. Fathers (or mothers) may be absent for many reasons. They may be in institutions or separated from their spouses because of incompatibility or other reasons. But the fact remained that when an able-bodied but unemployed father was at home, the family could not receive ADC.

In order to address this problem, two changes were made in the ADC program. First, in 1961, a new component called the ADC-Unemployed Parent (UP) program was enacted. This made it possible for children to receive aid because of their parent's unemployment. Second, in 1962, the name of the program was changed to Aid to Families with Dependent Children (AFDC) to emphasize the *family* unit. A second adult was considered eligible for aid in states with AFDC-UP programs and also in cases where one of the child's parents was incapacitated.

In 1967, the AFDC-UP program was changed to the AFDC-Unemployed Father program, but in 1979 the Supreme Court ruled that it was unconstitutional to provide benefits to unemployed fathers but not to unemployed mothers. The name was changed back to the AFDC-UP program. Only half of the states voluntarily adopted unemployed parent provisions, and the number of fathers who received aid remained small. In 1988, under provisions of the Family Support Act, all states are now required to have an AFDC-UP program. The act contains some of the most significant changes made in the AFDC program since its inception. States that have not operated UP programs previously can restrict eligibility to six months per year. While this provision sounds as though it might add many new clients to the AFDC program, requirements in some states are quite stringent and favor assisting those recently unemployed while excluding the hard-core unemployed.

Interestingly, a review of studies of AFDC-UP programs does not show that they are associated with increased marital stability. In fact, evidence has pointed in the opposite direction.[4] In addition, although some evidence indicates that there is greater marital instability in states with higher AFDC payments, there is "little support" for higher payments "being a powerful destabilizer."[5] And more recently, researchers have concluded, "that the impacts of welfare on family structure are very modest. Comparisons of changes in family structure over time with changes in the welfare system and of differences in family structures across states both suggest that welfare has minimal effects on family structure."[6]

Man-in-the-House Rules

The number of able-bodied parents who receive welfare assistance continues to fuel debate in a public concerned with the morality of welfare recipients. The work ethic is firmly entrenched in American culture. According to this ethic, those capable of self-support should not be entitled to public assistance benefits. In the early days of ADC and AFDC, this concern was reflected in *man-in-the-house-rules*. It was clear that only in specific circumstances could able-bodied fathers be present while the family collected AFDC benefits. These concerns also carried over into welfare mothers' relationships with other men. The thought of welfare mothers allowing able-bodied men to spend time in their homes presented a threat to those who wanted to insure that payments went to the "right" people. The AFDC check was intended for the children and the mother, and in some cases, the children's father. It was considered immoral and illegal for the mother to allow anyone else to benefit from the welfare check. *Midnight raids*—home visits to welfare mothers late at night—were sometimes conducted to insure that no adult males resided in AFDC households, because these men might be considered *substitute fathers* responsible for the family's financial support. Today, midnight raids are considered unethical by most professional standards.

Making Parents Pay

In 1968, the Supreme Court determined that man-in-the-house rules could not be used as a method for "flatly denying" children public assistance. The emphasis today has shifted to methods of making children's *legal* fathers and mothers support their dependents. In 1974, the federal government began placing greater emphasis on enforcing child-support obligations owed by absent parents to their children by encouraging states to locate absent parents, to establish paternity, and to obtain child support.[7] Concerns regarding these measures arose because of the rising number of children receiving AFDC who were born to parents who were not married to each other. In addition, few absent parents of children receiving AFDC contributed to their children's support, regardless of whether they were ever married to the custodial parent. These concerns persist today. For example, in 40 percent of all homes in which the father is not present, a child support order has never been obtained, and fathers are paying full support in only twenty-six percent of all cases (see Figure 6–1). The Office of Child Support Enforcement in the Department of Health and Human Services was established to oversee the child support enforcement program, and each state was to insure that its enforcement program was carried out under federal guidelines. But Congress felt that state efforts were still too lax, and it passed the Child Support Enforcement Amendments of 1984 to make it tougher for parents to avoid making child-support payments. Sentiments regarding the new measures were so strong that the bill passed both houses of Congress unanimously. In addition to AFDC families, the amendments extend assistance to all families in which children are not receiving

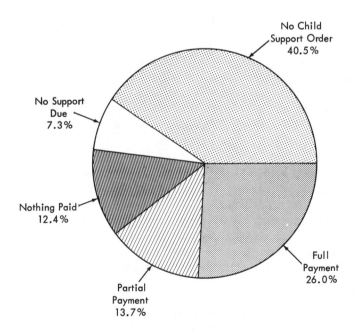

FIGURE 6–1   Percentages of female-headed households which receive and do not receive child support. Source: *Budget of the United States Government Fiscal Year 1991,* (Washington, D.C.: U.S. Government Printing Office), January 29, 1990, p. 197.

financial support from their noncustodial parent. Under these provisions, states establish procedures to (1) garnish (withhold) a parent's wages if support payments are at least thirty days overdue, (2) impose liens against the delinquent parent's income, real estate, and other property, and (3) intercept federal and state income tax refunds. Judges across the country have also taken issue with delinquent parents, and many are resorting to jailing parents who fail to comply. Some communities print the names of nonsupporting parents in local newspapers. Noncustodial fathers have begun to organize groups to focus attention on *their* rights. These fathers feel they are at a disadvantage because they must pay child support even though they may have little legal recourse if the child's mother refuses visitation privileges or spends the child support unwisely.

WHAT ARE AFDC FAMILIES LIKE?

The public has a number of images of AFDC families. The following information, collected through the National Integrated Quality Control System's monthly sample of AFDC cases, may confirm some of these ideas and challenge others.[8]

1. AFDC families are smaller than some people think. The size of the average family is three—one adult and two children. Actually, 43 percent have one child, and 31 percent have two children. Only 10 percent have four or more children.
2. Sixty percent of the families have children who are younger than six (the age when most children begin first grade), and 85 percent have children under the age of twelve.
3. Only 11 percent of AFDC families have a father in the home. (Many states never voluntarily adopted an AFDC-UP program that would have allowed more fathers to participate.) The vast majority of children live with their mothers only. Nearly half of the parents of AFDC children have never married each other. In 36 percent of the cases, the parents are separated or divorced. In only 5 percent of families is a parent deceased or considered incapacitated.
4. Although similar numbers of black and white families receive AFDC, black families are overrepresented in the program because they are more likely to be poor. Black families make up 41 percent of all caseloads, and white families make up 40 percent. Fourteen percent are Hispanic, 2 percent are Asian, and 1 percent are Native Americans.
5. Most AFDC families live in private housing which they rent. Twenty-one percent reside in public or subsidized housing. Only 5 percent live in housing they own or are buying.
6. Most AFDC parents are not employed. Over half the fathers and nearly one-third of the mothers are classified as unemployed. Many parents are excused from work requirements to care for young children at home. Nine percent of all fathers and 6 percent of all mothers in the program are employed.
7. The median age of AFDC mothers is about twenty-nine, and fathers' median age is thirty-four. Despite the numbers of children born to teenagers, teens comprise only 7 percent of AFDC parents.
8. All recipients are eligible for Medicaid, and 81 percent receive food stamps.
9. The average length of stay on AFDC at the time this information was compiled, 27 months, is not as long as some people may assume. Fifty-nine percent had received AFDC for no more than three years, and 32 percent for one year or less (although some of these families may have received AFDC prior to the current case opening), but 26 percent had received AFDC for five years or more.

The issue of long-term dependence on welfare has been particularly vexing. Researchers suggest that there are two types of AFDC recipients. The largest group receives AFDC for a relatively short period of time, while a much smaller group is on the rolls for a considerably longer time. One study indicated that "at least 50 percent leave within two years, and 58 percent leave within eight, but [t]he 15 percent of recipients who stay eight years or more on the program collect more than 50 percent of the benefits paid out."[9]

AFDC AND WORK

Historically, Americans have been unwilling to provide money and services to those who are able to work. This feeling is evident in the AFDC program where several approaches have been used to get parents off welfare and into jobs.

Rehabilitation for Work

In 1962, social service amendments were added to AFDC and other public assistance programs as a means of *rehabilitating* the poor. The rehabilitation approach was designed to reduce poverty by treating personal and social problems which stood in the way of financial independence.[10] Services included counseling, vocational training, child-management training, family-planning services, and legal services. States found a bonus in providing social services to clients—for every dollar spent by the states, the federal government matched it with three dollars, but states were criticized for claiming federal funds for many of the services they were already providing to clients.[11] To insure the success of the social service amendments, worker caseloads were to be small—no more than sixty clients—but it was difficult to find enough qualified social workers to provide services.[12] What had sounded good in theory could often not be put into practice.

Job Training and WIN

When social services were first introduced as a means of helping recipients overcome obstacles to financial independence, the AFDC caseworker was responsible for seeing that the family got its benefit check and its social services. In fact, AFDC mothers may have feared that if they did not accept the social services offered or urged by the caseworkers, benefits might be terminated. Social workers began complaining that they had to spend so much time determining eligibility that they did not have time to provide many of the social services needed.[13]

In 1967, Congress chose to separate the provision of social services to AFDC recipients from the issuance of benefit checks. A payments worker was responsible for matters related to the distribution of the welfare check, while another worker was responsible for the social services provided to recipients. This approach was based on the recognition that not all poor families necessarily need social services, since poverty may be attributable to a variety of causes. The 1967 amendments were also aimed at eliminating some AFDC families' feelings that they must accept social services from the AFDC caseworker in order to receive financial benefits. Families who wished to receive social services were still entitled and encouraged to do so, and social workers could devote more time to these cases.

But enthusiasm for the rehabilitation approach to helping welfare clients was fading rapidly. The approach had not been a booming success; welfare rolls continued to grow. A new approach was needed, and the one chosen was tougher. The 1967 amendments also emphasized work, and both "carrot" and "stick" measures were employed to achieve this purpose.[14] The "stick" included work requirements for unemployed fathers on AFDC, as well as for mothers and some teenagers. The "carrot" was the Work Incentive Now (WIN) program established by Congress to train recipients for work and to help them locate employment. The federal government threatened to deny federal matching funds to states that paid benefits to able-bodied recipients who refused to work or receive job training.

Other measures were also taken to encourage recipients to work. According to the *thirty plus one-third rule,* welfare payments were not reduced for the first $30 of earned income, and one-third of all additional income was disregarded in determining eligibility until the limit on earnings was reached. Day-care services were provided for WIN participants, but in many cases shortages of licensed facilities prevented placing children while their parents worked or trained for jobs. And the cost of working—clothes, transportation, and child care—often outweighed what the parents earned.

AFDC rolls still continued to climb. Strategies aimed at encouraging welfare recipients to work once again failed to produce the results that rational planners had intended. Perhaps the failure of these approaches had much to do with the fact that AFDC recipients may not have earned enough in marginal, low-income, or minimum-wage jobs to make employment a rational alternative for them after deducting work-related expenses. Short-term training programs generally do not enable recipients to substantially increase their earning capacities.[15] Many recipients just cannot earn enough to fully support themselves. Some find that in order to survive, they must rely on a combination of "a little work and a little welfare." The situation for one woman is found in the accompanying illustration, "Living on Welfare," and a description of the AFDC application process is found in the illustration "Applying for AFDC," (see p. 132).

Workfare

The WIN program remains in operation today along with a renewed interest in the concept of workfare—mandatory employment in return for welfare payments. Workfare is not a new idea. In its most punitive forms, the workhouses of the Elizabethan period and similar institutions in the United States fit under the rubric of workfare.[16] Some believe that after nearly four hundred years of various forms of workfare programs, both experience and empirical evidence indicate that they have failed to improve the job skills of participants; they have failed to reduce the costs of welfare; they do not discourage malingering because the number of malingerers receiving welfare is already negligible; and welfare recipients who can would gladly take jobs if decent ones were available.[17] But the concept of workfare has received increasing support. As more women with young children have joined the labor force, the argument has been that AFDC mothers should work, too. Feminist Barbara Ehrenreich calls this line of thinking illogical: Just because it is the trend, does not mean it is right. She also says that, "[w]e are being asked to believe that pushing destitute mothers into the work force (in some versions of workfare, for no other compensation than the welfare payments they would have received anyway) is consistent with women's striving toward self-determination."[18] Nonetheless, the country is moving ahead with workfare demonstrations.

One job program that received especially good press in the 1980s is the Massachusetts Employment and Training Program, which is called ET. Welfare recipients register for work, but they have options. Those who *choose* to participate in ET may decide between career counseling, education and training, on-the-job training, and job placement. Although Massachusetts has one of the highest AFDC payment levels, participation in ET has been high. Those who participate in training

---

ILLUSTRATION: LIVING ON WELFARE

The following is taken from a letter written by an AFDC mother to an AFDC Jobs Club leader. Jobs Clubs are support groups that provide links to social services in the community.

"Before I became involved with the [Jobs Clubs program], I was feeling so frustrated... I had thought about getting another job, but no enthusiasm to try. I can't make ends meet on $3.35 an hr. and no benefits... I have had quite a few of those types of jobs, only to wind up quitting because I was in a worse situation than when I started. It always seems that when I had tried to get ahead, to better myself, welfare was there to knock me back down. It was always the same—no experience, no decent paying job, no benefits, back to welfare—like being on a ferris wheel, you get yourself high on the feeling of doing better with your life, only to be pulled back down. I hate being on welfare... It makes me so angry when I hear phrases like, 'People on welfare are just too ignorant and lazy to work.' I have shed a few tears over those phrases. Not of self pity but of anger and pity for those people who put blinders on to the underlying problems—the situations that those people on welfare are trying to deal with. '*Some*' of the people who have never had to experience being poor, being on welfare, find it easy to put down those who have. Welfare recipients (I hate that phrase too) are not living a life of ease! A good percentage of us are high risk for strokes, heart attacks, ulcers, nervous conditions due to worry, worry, worry. When I get my check each month, I pay my rent and barely have money to pay on utilities. I can't go out and buy my sons clothes, take them to movies... Rich or poor, we are all human. We all have the same wants and needs. I've tried to teach my kids that what is most important, number one, is love, communication, being safe, smart, and good. I've always told them that they are just as good as anyone not on welfare. Some kids at school are made fun of when they're known to be on welfare."

Source: This letter appeared in Nancy R. Vosler and Martha N. Ozawa, "Two Approaches to Welfare-to-Work," *Links* (St. Louis, MO: Washington University, Fall 1989), p. 4. The *Links* article was adapted from Nancy R. Vosler and Martha N. Ozawa, "An Analysis of Two Approaches to Welfare-to-Work," *New England Journal of Human Services*, 8, 4, 1988, pp. 15–21.

get day-care services for a year, and their Medicaid benefits are assured for fifteen months. Employers do not know that participants are welfare recipients. Although the program is not without critics (some point out that ET began at a time when unemployment in the state was quite low and recipients could be readily placed in jobs), results are positive, saving the state millions of dollars and placing many people in jobs. ET offers flexibility to welfare recipients. It is based on the idea that welfare recipients are responsible individuals. A mandatory, more punitive approach to work programs might not produce the same success.[19]

Studies funded primarily by the Ford Foundation and conducted by the nonprofit Manpower Development Research Corporation (MDRC) have shown some positive results in several states with more mandatory approaches to workfare. One multisite study primarily involving the states of Arkansas, Virginia, and West Virginia, and the cities of Baltimore and San Diego, showed that:

1. Workfare was "successful" for AFDC mothers but not necessarily for AFDC fathers; mothers employment rates increased and so did their earnings.
2. There were welfare cost savings, but participants did not necessarily net substantially more than they would have from welfare.
3. Participants without recent work histories made greater gains than those with recent work histories.
4. Participants generally worked at entry-level jobs and did not substantially increase their work skills.
5. Participants and employers were generally pleased with the program although participants felt they were underpaid and that the employer benefited most.[20]

The researchers randomly assigned subjects to experimental and control groups, so the results are considered reliable. The outcomes are somewhat promising. The states used different models, but most relied primarily on job search assistance and temporary (thirteen weeks) mandatory employment. No one model proved to be superior, but without more intensive long-term efforts, results may remain modest.

The MDRC also did study a long-term mandatory workfare program—the Saturation Work Incentive Model (SWIM) in San Diego—and it also found higher employment rates and earnings for experimental group participants; there were also welfare savings.[21] But again, net income for experimental subjects did not change much—"[g]ains in earnings were largely offset by reductions in government transfer payments."[22] Participants spent the first two weeks in a job search workshop. Those who did not find jobs "were assigned to three months unpaid work experience as well as biweekly job club sessions"[23] that help provide links to social services in the community.

The latest work requirements in AFDC come under the Job Opportunities and Basic Skills (JOBS) program which offers job development, job placement, and community work experience services. These efforts are coordinated with the Job Training Partnership Act (discussed further in Chapter 9). Under the Family Support Act of 1988 work requirements have been made more stringent. The workfare concept is evident in that one parent in two-parent families receiving AFDC must work a minimum of sixteen hours per week in a public or private sector job. States must require single parents with children three years of age and older to work, and they can impose this requirement on parents with children as young as one year, if they wish. The federal government has also increased pressures on states to assure that specific quotas of families are meeting work requirements.

Teen parents without high school educations are not required to work, but they are now required to attend school as a condition of receiving AFDC payments. Many of the 1988 provisions are targeted at the young in the hope of preventing them from becoming structurally unemployed.

The 1988 act requires states to provide child care for parents who are employed or attending training. The federal government is supporting this requirement with unlimited matching funds. In addition, similar to ET, child care benefits will be extended to twelve months for families that leave the AFDC program due to increased earnings. Families will have to contribute to the costs of child care on a sliding scale based on their ability to pay. States may use a variety of options to provide child care including direct provision of services, prepayment vouchers, and direct reimbursement to parents, but no one expects a quick solution to the problem of securing enough qualified placements for children.

In order to make work more attractive, the amount of earnings disregarded in determining AFDC payments has been increased. Ninety dollars a month is now disregarded for work expenses, and current child care disregards are $200 a month for a child up to the age of two and $175 a month for older children. Another incentive to maintain employment is the extension of health care benefits. Many families can receive Medicaid benefits for as long as twelve months after leaving the AFDC program as a result of increased earnings if their income remains below 185 percent of the poverty line. States can charge those with higher incomes a premium, but there are several options for providing health care coverage during the last six months of eligibility, including use of the employer's health care program, a state uninsured plan, or a health maintenance organization. It remains to be seen whether these efforts will produce the same positive results that have been demonstrated in states like Massachusetts.

GROWTH OF THE AFDC PROGRAM

The growth of welfare programs is generally measured by three factors: (1) the number of program recipients, (2) the total costs of the program, and (3) the benefits received by each recipient. During the welfare rights movement of the 1960s and 1970s, the number of AFDC families rose sharply. As the rolls swelled, so did the total costs of the program. Today the number of families has stabilized. Average payments, however, have not grown as rapidly. Once inflation is taken into account, it is easy to see that payments have not begun to keep up with the cost of living.

Number of Recipients

Although AFDC was originally designed as a short-term program, it did not turn out that way. AFDC is now more than fifty-five years old, and the number of families receiving assistance has grown dramatically (see Figure 6–2). For example, in the ten year period between 1968 and 1978, the number of families doubled. Considering the number of individuals receiving AFDC as a percentage of the total U.S. population, in 1950 the group amounted to 1.5 percent; by 1970 the proportion had reached 4.7 percent; and at its peak it was 5.3 percent. In 1988, 3.7 million families (about 11 million individuals or 4.5 percent of the population) received AFDC payments. The large number of families now dependent on AFDC is directly related to the increase in the number of children who do not receive financial support from their fathers.

Increasing Costs

AFDC costs grew incrementally during the first thirty years of the program, but during the 1960s and 1970s they escalated rapidly. In 1940, the total costs were $133 million; by 1960 they were $750 million, and by 1980 they had risen to $12.5 billion (see Figure 6–2). Even after controlling for inflation, costs spiraled. Rising expenditures were primarily a consequence of the large numbers of new families who joined the rolls during the 1960s and 1970s. In 1987, the total bill for AFDC exceeded $18 billion.

Monthly Payments and the Cost of Living

Rising costs in the AFDC program might lead us to believe that payments to AFDC families have also increased, but this is not really the case. In 1963, the average monthly payment to an AFDC family was $122; by 1978 this payment had doubled to $250. But after controlling for inflation, AFDC recipients had no more purchasing power in 1978 than they had in 1963. At present, AFDC payments average about $355 monthly. More people have access to AFDC, but in the light of inflation, public assistance payments to AFDC families have not changed very much.

There is a great deal of variation among states in AFDC payments. California has one of the highest payment levels—an average of about $532 per month for a family. Alabama is among the lowest at $114. In other words, a recipient family in California is likely to receive four and a half times more than a recipient family in Alabama. Even though the cost of living is lower in Alabama than in California it is not easy to care for a family on $532 a month anywhere in the United States.

Each state determines its AFDC payment levels in a seemingly rational manner. The costs of food, shelter, and other necessities are calculated according to family size. The figure obtained is called the *standard of need,* but a number of states pay recipients less than the minimum standard of need, and the standard might remain the same for years before adjustments are made, even though the cost of living has risen. Cost-of-living increases are not automatic in the AFDC program like they are in the SSI and Food Stamp programs. State legislatures must vote each time increases in payments are considered, and most do not like to entertain this question often.

Table 6–1 shows the need standard for each state for an adult and two children and the maximum amount the family can generally expect from AFDC if it has *no* income. Note that some states have relatively high standards of need (at least in relation to other states) and pay the full amount (Alaska and California, for example).

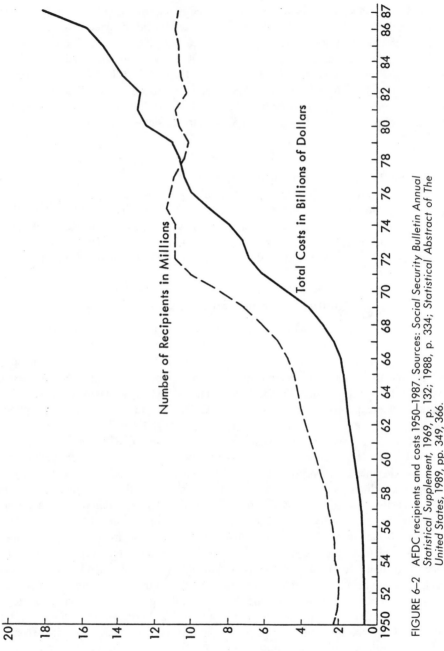

FIGURE 6–2   AFDC recipients and costs 1950–1987. Sources: *Social Security Bulletin Annual Statistical Supplement, 1969*, p. 132; 1988, p. 334; *Statistical Abstract of The United States,* 1989, pp. 349, 366.

TABLE 6–1   AFDC Need Standard by State and Maximum Payments to Families of One Adult and Two Children with No Countable Income, 1988[a]

STATE	NEED STANDARD	MAXIMUM PAYMENT	STATE	NEED STANDARD	MAXIMUM PAYMENT
Alabama	$384	$118	Missouri	$312	$282
Alaska	779	779	Montana	434	359
Arizona	621	293	Nebraska	364	364
Arkansas	705	204	Nevada	550	330
California	663	663	New Hampshire	496	496
Colorado	421	365	New Jersey	424	424
Connecticut	514	514	New Mexico	264	264
Delaware	333	333	New York	539	539
District of			North Carolina	532	266
Columbia	712	379	North Dakota	371	371
Florida	807	275	Ohio	712	309
Georgia	376	270	Oklahoma	471	306
Hawaii	929	557	Oregon	420	420
Idaho	554	304	Pennsylvania	587	384
Illinois	713	342	Rhode Island	517	517
Indiana	320	288	South Carolina	403	206
Iowa	497	394	South Dakota	366	366
Kansas	401	401	Tennessee	365	173
Kentucky	218	218	Texas	574	184
Louisiana	658	190	Utah	502	376
Maine	573	416	Vermont	930	629
Maryland	522	377	Virginia	322	291
Massachusetts	579	579	Washington	800	492
Michigan	572	462	West Virginia	497	249
Minnesota	532	532	Wisconsin	647	517
Mississippi	368	120	Wyoming	360	360

[a]Needs standards and payment figures may not reflect area differentials within some states or amounts allocated for special needs.

Source: Adapted from U.S Department of Health and Human Services, Family Support Administration, Office of Family Assistance, *Characteristics of State Plans for Aid to Families with Dependent Children under Title IV-A of the Social Security Act* (Washington, D.C., 1989), p. 375.

Other states also have a relatively high need standard but pay well below that amount (Ohio and Arizona, for example). Some have a relatively low standard and make payments commensurate with the standard (see Kentucky and New Mexico). In some cases, the standard of need is moderate and payments reflect the standard, while in other cases the moderate standard is accompanied by a low payment. In order to understand how equitable these standards and actual payments are, it is necessary to consider how accurately they reflect what it actually takes to maintain a decent standard of living. Of course, the value of other benefits the family might also receive, such as food stamps and public housing, should also be considered (see Chapter 3 on the value of in-kind benefits).

ILLUSTRATION: APPLYING FOR AFDC

Most Americans have never seen an application for welfare benefits, nor will they ever know what it is like to apply for public assistance. Application procedures and forms have been simplified over the years to make it easier to apply. For example, because AFDC recipients usually qualify for food stamps and Medicaid, many states use a combined application for all these programs (see Figure 6–3). Nevertheless, applying for welfare can be a difficult process. In addition to providing basic information like names and Social Security numbers of family members, evidence of expenses and income through rent and utility receipts, pay statements, and other documentation is also required. The family's assets are also carefully considered since there are limitations, which vary from state to state, on the amount an individual can possess while remaining eligible for AFDC. Applicants must agree to an investigation, and the welfare department is free to contact *anyone* it deems necessary to verify the information given by the applicant.

There are also a number of responsibilities borne by public assistance recipients. They must cooperate in obtaining child support from non-custodial parents. This includes cooperation in determining the paternity of any child for whom AFDC is requested unless there is good reason, such as the threat of physical harm, which makes this requirement unreasonable. Any child support payment received must be turned over to the state, and changes in the recipient's address, income, and property must be reported within five days. The application contains several warnings about the penalties for fraud (which have been criticized as attempts to intimidate applicants and prevent them from pursuing benefits).

Applicants are guaranteed certain rights in the application process, such as nondiscrimination due to color, gender, religion, national origin, handicaps, and political beliefs. They are also told that they will be informed of the decision on their application within thirty days. Those who believe they have been unjustly denied benefits may request a fair hearing to present their case.

Problems often arise during the application process. Applicants may not be aware that it may be several weeks before payments begin. They may be upset or angry when they are not able to receive on-the-spot assistance or when they are deemed ineligible. Other factors can also produce frustration. Applicants may not come prepared with the proper documentation and may have to return several times before the application is completed. Since AFDC applicants often apply at very stressful times in their lives, the atmosphere of the waiting room and the treatment by receptionists and eligibility workers are also important considerations. Eligibility workers also find their jobs stressful as is evidenced by high turnover rates in these positions. Establishing a more rational application process for both clients and workers seems to be a challenge for the welfare bureaucracy.

REFORMING WELFARE

During the past few decades, there has been widespread agreement that the public assistance system is in urgent need of reform, but there is little agreement about what this reform should be. Below we consider some of the various types of approaches.

READ AND SIGN THIS PAGE IF YOU WΛNT CASH OR MEDICAL ASSISTANCE

I UNDERSTAND THAT BY SIGNING THIS APPLICATION FORM, I CONSENT TO ANY INVESTIGATION MADE BY THE DEPARTMENT OF PUBLIC AID TO VERIFY OR CONFIRM THE INFORMATION I HAVE GIVEN OR ANY OTHER INVESTIGATION MADE BY THEM IN CONNECTION WITH MY REQUEST FOR PUBLIC ASSISTANCE.

WHEN YOU FILE AN APPLICATION FOR CASH OR MEDICAL ASSISTANCE, A DETERMINATION OF YOUR ELIGIBILITY UNDER ANY OF THE PROGRAMS ADMINISTERED BY THE DEPARTMENT WILL BE MADE UNLESS YOU DO NOT WANT TO BE CONSIDERED FOR A PARTICULAR PROGRAM(S). THE DEPARTMENT WILL NOT DETERMINE YOUR ELIGIBILITY FOR THAT PROGRAM(S).

I AGREE TO INFORM THE AGENCY WITHIN 5 DAYS OF ANY CHANGE IN MY HOUSEHOLD'S NEEDS, INCOME, PROPERTY, LIVING ARRANGEMENTS, SCHOOL ATTENDANCE OR ADDRESS.

I UNDERSTAND GIVING FALSE INFORMATION OR FAILURE TO PROVIDE THE ABOVE INFORMATION CAN RESULT IN REFERRAL FOR PROSECUTION FOR FRAUD.

I UNDERSTAND THAT IF I AM NOT SATISFIED WITH THE ACTION TAKEN ON MY APPLICATION I HAVE THE RIGHT TO A FAIR HEARING. I UNDERSTAND I CAN ASK FOR A FAIR HEARING BY GETTING IN TOUCH WITH THE OFFICE WHERE I APPLIED OR BY WRITING TO: THE DEPARTMENT OF PUBLIC AID, 100 S. GRAND AVE. E., SPRINGFIELD, ILLINOIS 62762-0001.

I UNDERSTAND THAT UNDER ILLINOIS LAW, THE ASSIGNMENT OF SUPPORT RIGHTS IS A REQUIREMENT OF MY ELIGIBILITY FOR AID TO FAMILIES WITH DEPENDENT CHILDREN (AFDC). IF I AM APPROVED FOR AFDC, I ASSIGN ALL SUCH RIGHTS TO THE ILLINOIS DEPARTMENT OF PUBLIC AID FOR AS LONG AS I RECEIVE AFDC. I ALSO UNDERSTAND THAT MY COOPERATION IN OBTAINING SUPPORT PAYMENTS FOR MEMBERS OF MY ASSISTANCE UNIT IS A REQUIREMENT OF MY PERSONAL ELIGIBILITY FOR AFDC (UNLESS DECLARED EXEMPT FOR GOOD CAUSE). I FURTHER AGREE TO FORWARD ALL CHILD SUPPORT PAYMENTS I RECEIVE TO THE ILLINOIS DEPARTMENT OF PUBLIC AID.

I UNDERSTAND AND AGREE THAT BY SIGNING THIS FORM, I GIVE THE DEPARTMENT OF PUBLIC AID THE RIGHT, WITHOUT THE NECESSITY OF ANY OTHER ASSIGNMENT OF CLAIM OR AUTHORIZATION, TO RECOVER, UNDER THE TERMS OF ANY PRIVATE OR PUBLIC HEALTH CARE COVERAGE, ANY AMOUNT FOR WHICH I OR A MEMBER OF MY HOUSEHOLD MAY BE ELIGIBLE.

BY SIGNING, I SWEAR THAT THE INFORMATION GIVEN ON THE ELIGIBILITY FORM IS TRUE AND CORRECT TO THE BEST OF MY KNOWLEDGE AND BELIEF.

THE DEPARTMENT OF PUBLIC AID SECURES AND USES INFORMATION ABOUT ALL CLIENTS THROUGH THE INCOME AND ELIGIBILITY VERIFICATION SYSTEM. THIS INCLUDES SUCH INFORMATION AS RECEIPT OF SOCIAL SECURITY BENEFITS, UNEMPLOYMENT INSURANCE, INCOME TAX REFUNDS AND WAGES FROM EMPLOYMENT, ANY INFORMATION OBTAINED WILL BE USED IN DETERMINING ELIGIBILITY FOR ASSISTANCE AND THE AMOUNT OF ASSISTANCE PROVIDED FOR ALL PROGRAMS. WHEN DISCREPANCIES ARE FOUND, VERIFICATION OF THIS INFORMATION MAY BE OBTAINED THROUGH CONTACTS WITH A THIRD PARTY SUCH AS EMPLOYERS OR CLAIMS REPRESENTATIVES. THIS INFORMATION MAY AFFECT YOUR ELIGIBILITY FOR ASSISTANCE AND THE AMOUNT OF ASSISTANCE PROVIDED.

■ SIGN YOUR NAME OR
MAKE YOUR MARK

_____
APPLICANT   DATE

_____
SPOUSE   DATE

■ IF YOU HAVE MADE YOUR MARK (X) INSTEAD OF SIGNING YOUR NAME, ONE WITNESS MUST SIGN BELOW:

_____
SIGNATURE OF WITNESS

■ APPLICATION BASED ON BLINDNESS MUST BE ATTESTED BY TWO WITNESSES:

_____   _____
SIGNATURE OF WITNESS   SIGNATURE OF WITNESS

■ IF APPLICATION IS INITIATED BY SOMEONE ELSE IN BEHALF OF THE APPLICANT, HE MUST SIGN BELOW:

_____   _____
SIGNATURE   DATE   RELATIONSHIP

_____   _____
HOME ADDRESS   APT. NO.   TELEPHONE NUMBER

IF YOU BELIEVE YOU HAVE BEEN DISCRIMINATED AGAINST BECAUSE OF RACE, COLOR, SEX, RELIGION, NATIONAL ORIGIN, HANDICAP, OR POLITICAL BELIEF, YOU HAVE THE RIGHT TO FILE A COMPLAINT WITH: THE DEPARTMENT OF PUBLIC AID, EEO COORDINATOR, 100 S. GRAND AVE. E., SPRINGFIELD, ILLINOIS 62762-0001 OR WITH: THE SECRETARY, DEPARTMENT OF HEALTH AND HUMAN SERVICES, WASHINGTON, D.C. 20201

FIGURE 6–3   Client's rights and responsibilities, part of the Illinois Department of Public Aid request for financial assistance, medical assistance, and food stamps.

Non-welfare Approaches

Early proposals called for a guaranteed annual income or a negative income tax. These may be called "non-welfare approaches"[24] because they make use of existing systems like the Internal Revenue Service (IRS) that are used by virtually all Americans—rich or poor. Milton Friedman's negative income tax plan and President Nixon's Family Assistance Plan (FAP) are among the best known proposals. They were introduced because previous plans for welfare reform had not worked. A negative income tax, it was argued, would guarantee everyone a minimum standard of living, and it would encourage recipients to work if they were allowed to keep a substantial portion of their earnings without severe reductions in benefits.

Each negative income tax or guaranteed annual income plan has its own set of procedures and requirements, but let us consider one example of how such a plan might work. Say that the guaranteed annual income for a family of four is set at $10,000, with an earnings deduction of 50 percent. A family with no income would receive $10,000. A family with earnings of $4,000 would receive a payment of $8,000 for a total income of $12,000. A family earning $16,000 would receive a payment of $2,000 for a total income of $18,000, and a family earning $20,000, the break-even point, would receive no payment. Since the program is a logical extension of the income tax system already in place in the United States, recipients would continue to file an income tax statement as they do today. Most citizens would continue to pay taxes, but those at the lower end of the income scale would receive payments or negative income taxes. Checks could be mailed through the U.S. Treasury Department as they are today when an individual receives a refund from the IRS. Since welfare applications, means tests, and other eligibility procedures would be eliminated, much of the welfare bureaucracy would be reduced.

But the United States has no practical experience with a guaranteed income or negative income tax. There is the possibility that near-poor individuals would qualify for benefits and would prefer accepting the guarantee. It is this perceived threat to the work ethic which is probably the greatest concern working against such a proposal. Planners would need to estimate how many people might qualify for payments at various levels, but policy makers might end up basing their decision about payment levels on what they believe the country can afford rather than on what seems to be a fair standard of living. Nixon introduced his FAP in 1970 in order to address many of the problems of the welfare system: disincentives to work, discouragement of family life, inequities among the states, and discrimination against the working poor. "However, the FAP failed in Congress because of the combined opposition of those who felt it was too much welfare and those who felt it was not enough."[25]

One small step that has been taken through the IRS to provide relief to low-income families is the Earned Income Tax Credit (EITC). In 1990, families with children that earned less than $20,265 qualified for the credit. The maximum payment was $953 and is due to be increased. The amount received is based on the family's income. Families expecting to receive the EITC in the next calendar year may get it in advance by requesting that it be included in the worker's regular paychecks.

The Reagan and Bush Approaches

A much different type of welfare reform was implemented during the Reagan administration. The Reagan team was committed "to determine welfare needs more accurately, improve program administration, reduce fraud and abuse, and decrease federal and state costs."[26] In order to do this, the following changes were made:

1. The income of stepparents was counted when determining a child's eligibility.
2. A cap was established for deductible child-care costs and other work-related expenses.
3. The "thirty plus one-third rule" was limited to four months.
4. The states' efforts at child-support enforcement were improved.
5. States were required to determine eligibility based on previous actual income.

Some of these changes reflected a desire to eliminate from the welfare rolls near-poor recipients, especially those with some potential to work. They clearly represent a selective and residual approach to welfare reform.

The Reagan policies were especially harsh on AFDC recipients. As many as five hundred thousand families were removed from the program.[27] Researchers at the University of Michigan's Institute for Social Research reported that the changes plunged millions of children deeper into poverty.[28] Interviews were conducted with three hundred mothers whose payments were terminated. Nearly half reported running out of all food; 42 percent were at least two months in arrears paying bills; 16 percent had their utilities shut off; and 11 percent were without telephone service. They were using various methods to survive. Almost half got old produce from grocers, and one-fifth collected bottles and cans for refunds.

President Bush's approach to AFDC reform is to encourage state innovation in work and training requirements. For example, experiments are going on which allow mothers to start businesses in their own homes. But what is considered a positive innovation to some (such as the various workfare arrangements) may sound like punishment to others. For instance, a case can be made that requirements that teen mothers attend school in order to receive AFDC may prevent those teens who do not stay in school and their babies from maintaining adequate nutrition and health care. Given the recent efforts that went into passing the Family Support Act of 1988, it is unlikely that there will be any major change in the near future in helping poor families. President Bush has not laid out any new national strategy.

Lessons from Abroad

The United States is certainly considered a welfare state, but it does far less to support young families than other industrialized countries. While the United States uses rather restrictive public assistance policies to help poor families which are primarily young and female-headed, European countries use more universal benefit systems.[29] Like the United States, Great Britain also uses a means-tested public assistance approach to help single-mother families, but there is no pressure for the mother to go to work until the youngest child is sixteen years old. Norway uses a different approach. It provides benefits to *all* families that have children younger than sixteen—whether they are one- or two-parent families and whether they are rich or poor—and it provides additional supplements for single parents. France also has a universal family allowance policy with additional benefits for young families and single-parent families. The benefits are considered generous enough so that mothers of young children can choose between work or remaining at home. Finland and the Federal Republic of Germany also have universal children's allowances. These countries all have family support policies that are more generous and comprehensive than those in the United States, and many exemplify non-welfare approaches to insuring that children and their families do not fall into poverty. Perhaps the United States should study these lessons from abroad.

SUMMARY

Perhaps the most controversial of all the welfare programs is Aid to Families with Dependent Children. Most of the criticism is directed toward the adult beneficiaries of the program who, some believe, are capable of "making it on their own." The first programs to assist dependent children were state mothers' aid programs. The federal government became involved as part of the 1935 Social Security Act. Midnight raids and man-in-the-house rules were used to insure that mothers were not "harboring" men who could support their children, but Supreme Court action has curtailed these practices.

Many Americans have an incorrect picture of the average AFDC family. AFDC families are usually small; most have only one or two children. There are about as many white AFDC recipients as black recipients, although blacks are over represented in the total. The majority of AFDC families stays on the program less than three years.

AFDC caseloads and costs rose dramatically during the 1960s. There was increased attention to the way public assistance applicants were treated, and this period became known as the *welfare-rights movement.* Much of the growth in the AFDC program has been due to the increase in single-parent families, which are headed mostly by women. Once adjustments are made to control for inflation, it is not difficult to see that the purchasing power of AFDC recipients remains meager. AFDC caseloads have remained stable in the last several years and are not expected to grow much.

Various approaches have been used to get adult AFDC recipients to work. Rehabilitating AFDC recipients so that they could overcome personal problems which prevented them from being self-supporting was one method. Another method was job training and job development. Today, there is a renewed emphasis on workfare. Reforms contained in the Family Support Act of 1988 are supposed to correct some of the disincentives to work that have been part of the AFDC—such as loss of child care and medical benefits once AFDC parents leave the rolls due to increased earnings. More dramatic alternatives to transforming AFDC, such as the universal benefits systems of some European countries, have been rejected.

NOTES

1. Laurence E. Lynn, Jr., "A Decade of Policy Developments in the Income-Maintenance System," in Robert H. Haveman, ed., *A Decade of Federal Antipoverty Programs: Achievements, Failures, and Lessons* (New York: Academic Press, 1977), p. 60; and Martin Rein, *Social Policy: Issues of Choice and Change* (New York: Random House, 1970), p. 311.
2. Lynn, "Decade of Policy Developments," p. 73.
3. Gilbert Y. Steiner, *The State of Welfare* (Washington, D.C.: Brookings Institution, 1971), p. 81.
4. John Bishop, *Jobs, Cash Transfers, and Marital Instability: A Review of the Evidence* (Madison, Wisc.: Institute for Research on Poverty, University of Wisconsin, Madison). Written testimony to the Welfare Reform Subcommittee of the Committees on Agriculture, Education and Labor, and Ways and Means of the U.S. House of Representatives (October 14, 1977), p. 9.
5. Ibid., p. 8.
6. David T. Elwood and Lawrence H. Summers, "Poverty in America: Is Welfare the Answer or the Problem?" in Sheldon H. Danzinger and Daniel H. Weinberg, eds., *Fighting Poverty: What Works and What Doesn't* (Cambridge: Harvard University Press, 1986), pp. 92–93.
7. *Paternity Determination: Techniques and Procedures to Establish the Paternity of Children Born Out of Wedlock* (Department of HEW, Office of Child Support Enforcement, April 30, 1977).
8. U.S. Department of Health and Human Services, Family Support Administration, *Characteristics and Financial Circumstances of AFDC Recipients, 1986* ((Washington, D.C.).
9. M.J. Bane and D.T. Elwood, *The Dynamics of Dependence: The Routes to Self Sufficiency* (John F. Kennedy School of Government, Harvard University, mimeo) cited in Elwood and Summers, "Fighting Poverty," p. 96. This was a report supported by U.S. Department of Health and Human Services grant contract no. HHS–100–82–0038.
10. Steiner, *State of Welfare*, p. 36; and Lynn, "Decade of Policy Developments," pp. 62–63.
11. Donald Brieland, Lela B. Costin, Charles R. Atherton, and contributors, *Contemporary Social Work: An Introduction to Social Work and Social Welfare* (New York: McGraw-Hill, 1975), p. 100; and Steiner, *State of Welfare*, p. 37.
12. Steiner, *State of Welfare*, p. 37.
13. Andrew W. Dobelstein with Ann B. Johnson, *Serving Older Adults: Policy, Programs, and Professional Activities* (Englewood Cliffs, N.J.: Prentice-Hall, 1985), p. 126.
14. Lynn, "Decade of Policy Developments," p. 74.
15. For further discussion of this point, see Sheldon H. Danzinger, Robert H. Haveman, and Robert D. Plotnick, "Antipoverty Policy: Effects on the Poor and the Nonpoor," in Danzinger and Weinberg, eds., *Fighting Poverty*, pp. 50–77.
16. Leonard Goodwin, "Can Workfare Work? *Public Welfare 39* (Fall 1981), pp. 19–25.
17. Ibid.
18. Barbara Ehrenreich, "A Step Back to the Workhouse?" *Ms.* (November 1987), p. 40.
19. Ellen Goodman, "Volunteer Workfare Program Proves Worth," *Austin American-Statesman* (March 5, 1985), p. A11.
20. Judith Gueron, *Reforming Welfare with Work* (New York: Ford Foundation, 1987).
21. Gayle Hamilton and Daniel Friedlander, *Final Report on the Saturation Work Initiative Model in San Diego* (New York: Manpower Demonstration Research Corporation, November 1989).
22. Ibid. p. x.
23. Ibid., p. vii.
24. This phrase is from William Raspberry, "The Non-welfare Approach to Aid Poor," *Austin American-Statesman* (February 26, 1988), p. A12.
25. Thomas R. Dye, *Understanding Public Policy*, 3rd ed. (Englewood Cliffs, N.J.: Prentice-Hall, 1978), p. 131.
26. Office of Management and Budget, *A Program for Economic Recovery*, February 18, 1981 (Washington, D.C.: U.S. Government Printing Office, 1981), pp. 1–11.
27. John L. Palmer and Isabel V. Sawhill, eds., *The Reagan Record* (Cambridge, Mass.: Ballinger, 1984), p. 364.
28. "AFDC Cuts Hurt," *ISR Newsletter* (University of Michigan, Spring/Summer 1984), p. 3.
29. This paragraph relies on Sheila B. Kamerman and Alfred J. Kahn, *Mothers Alone: Strategies for a Time of Change* (Dover, Mass.: Auburn House, 1988).

7

PROVIDING SOCIAL SERVICES
Helping Mentally Ill Individuals, Children, and the Elderly

Social welfare programs are often equated with programs for the poor, but there are many social services that people may need regardless of their income and social status. Developing a list of all the social services available in the United States is difficult, but it would include a number of services for individuals, families, and also communities.[1] Some services target children, like day care, after-school care, voluntary guidance programs like Big Brothers and Big Sisters of America, community youth centers, child protective services, foster-home care, and adoption assistance. Other services are directed at the family unit, such as family planning, marital and family counseling, and assessment services for courts, schools, and other agencies. Services for older Americans include special nutrition programs like Meals-on-Wheels, senior citizens centers, transportation, homemaker and chore services, adult protective services, and nursing home care. Some services are called *community organization* because they involve organizing groups such as mothers, migrant workers, newly arrived immigrants, tenants, handicapped individuals and their families, and even youth gangs. Services like education, counseling, and rehabilitation are offered in many types of settings—churches; schools; hospitals; workplaces; community mental health centers; special treatment programs for alcoholics and drug abusers; and residential facilities like juvenile detention centers, mental health hospitals, and community residences and state schools for those with mental retardation. Information, referral, advocacy, and consumer services of many types can also be added to the list, and there are many more. During their lifetimes, most Americans will use some type of social services.

WHO PROVIDES SOCIAL SERVICES?

Social services are provided by four types of organizations:

1. public agencies,
2. private not-for-profit corporations,
3. private profit-making corporations,
4. self-help groups.

Social services like day care are provided by several types of organizations. Other services, like child and adult protection, are provided by public agencies since these agencies have the legal responsibility to intervene in cases where a child or adult might be the victim of neglect or abuse.

Public agencies are established by law and are operated by federal, state, or local governments. The Department of Health and Human Services is the major federal agency responsible for providing social services. Each state has at least one major department which administers its social welfare programs, and many counties and cities also operate social welfare agencies.

Private not-for-profit agencies, also called *voluntary agencies,* are governed by boards of directors or boards of trustees that are legally responsible for these organizations. These agencies may receive funds from donations, client fees, community organizations such as the United Way, or government payments such as grants or contracts. Private not-for-profit agencies provide a multitude of services, such as day care for children, mental health services, and nursing-home care. Many of these agencies, community mental health centers, for example, charge fees to clients on a sliding scale, based on the client's ability to pay for the services. Other not-for-profit agencies, such as rape crisis centers, generally do not charge their clients. Socialization activities at senior citizen centers are also often provided at no cost. Some not-for-profit corporations act as policy advocates for their clientele by informing policy makers and the public of their clients' needs. The National Association of Retarded Citizens and its local affiliates, the Children's Home Society, and the National Council on Alcoholism are private not-for-profit agencies.

Private profit-making organizations are also called *proprietary agencies.* They too provide services like child care, nursing-home care, and mental health care, but private profit-making agencies charge their clients for services at the current market rate. Government agencies sometimes purchase services from private agencies. This occurs because the government may not directly provide a service needed by a client and cannot obtain it from a not-for-profit agency more economically. For example, specialized medical services for disabled individuals are sometimes purchased by the government from physicians engaged in private medical practices. A lack of public and not-for-profit inpatient mental health services for children and adolescents may also force states to purchase this service from private-for-profit hospitals.

Self-help groups also provide social services but generally do not rely on governmental funding at all. The structure of those groups is less formal than other social service agencies. Alcoholics Anonymous, the best known of the self-help groups, was founded in 1935 and assists persons with drinking problems. The only requirement for membership is the desire to stop drinking. The group relies only on its members for support and does not accept outside contributions. Other self-help groups are Narcotics Anonymous, Gamblers Anonymous, and Parents Anonymous. Self-help groups have proliferated in the last decade.

THE DEVELOPMENT OF SOCIAL SERVICES IN THE UNITED STATES

Before the 1900s, social services were provided by family members, neighbors, church groups, private charitable organizations, and local governments in the form of indoor and outdoor relief. The Charity Organization Society of the 1800s, which helped many of the poor, preferred to provide social services rather than financial assistance. State governments increased their involvement in social welfare services early in this century, when they began providing both cash and in-kind assistance to the destitute; however, the federal government did not become directly involved until the 1930s. Although child welfare services were part of the Social Security Act, many other forms of noncash assistance remained outside the range of federal government activities until 1956, when the Social Security Administration encouraged Congress to amend the Social Security Act to provide social services to families on relief.[2]

The rationale for federal funding of social services was to rehabilitate the poor, help them overcome their personal problems, and thereby reduce their dependence on welfare. To carry out this plan, the federal government began giving the states $3 for every $1 the states spent on social services. But this approach did not readily reduce poverty, and views on poverty began to change—being poor does not necessarily imply a need for rehabilitation. In 1967, Congress officially recognized this position by separating welfare payments from social service provisions. Although public assistance recipients are not necessarily expected to receive social services along with their checks, those services continue to be used by many clients, and the pendulum may, in fact, be swinging again. Mandatory job training requirements for many AFDC parents (if they can be called social services) may be signaling a period in which not participating in these services will mean no welfare check.

The federal government's initial willingness to subsidize social services was a boon to the states that were willing to increase the amount of social services to clients, but the costs of social services were rising so fast (from $282 million in 1967 to $1.7 billion in 1973)[3] that Congress decided to take action to curb spending. In 1976, Title XX was added to the Social Security Act to place a ceiling on expenditures and to insure that the majority of federally funded social services went to the poor. In 1981, the Reagan administration convinced Congress to replace Title XX with the Social Services Block Grant. Under this block grant, state matching requirements were eliminated, and the federal contribution to social services decreased. According to some welfare experts, many states reacted to federal spending reductions by appropriating more money for social services.[4] States can use their block grant funds as they wish, and most of them go to assist the frail elderly residing at home and children of welfare mothers needing day care.[5] The federal government contributes about $3 billion annually.

The recognition that those who are not poor can also benefit from social services has been another important development in the history of social services. The growth of public and private social service agencies which also assist middle- and upper-class families is an indication that mental health, family counseling, child guidance, and other types of social services are useful to many Americans.

Social services reach many types of people. Those who are mentally ill, alcohol and other drug abusers, abused children, and the elderly are examples of social service beneficiaries who have gained increased attention since the 1960s. We will explore social welfare policy for these groups at greater length.

SOCIAL SERVICES FOR MENTALLY ILL INDIVIDUALS AND DRUG ABUSERS

The first obstacle to rationalism in providing mental-health and drug abuse services is a lack of consensus about how to define these problems and how to determine the number in need.

Defining the Problem

Although psychiatrists, other mental-health professionals, and the public disagree about the exact definition of mental illness,[6] mental health and mental illness may be thought of as two ends of a continuum. At one extreme are people who behave in an acceptable manner in the community. At the other extreme are psychotic individuals who are unable to cope with reality and cannot function within the community. The American Psychiatric Association publishes a manual for mental-health professionals which describes dozens of different types of mental health problems. Depression is one common mental health problem that can range from mild and temporary to depression so severe that an individual may become suicidal.

Everyone experiences emotional stress at some time in his or her life. For most, professional care is not needed, and today more emphasis has been placed on preventing mental health problems and treating them before they become severe. Mental health professionals are as likely to see family members with temporary adjustment problems caused by divorce or the loss of a loved one as they are to see the severely depressed, suicidal, or schizophrenic.

Most people needing assistance seek mental health treatment voluntarily, but there are those with severe mental health problems who may not recognize their need for treatment. In these cases, state and local policies stipulate the conditions under which an individual may be judged mentally ill and in need of treatment. Involuntary admission to a mental-health hospital is generally reserved for those who in the opinion of a psychiatrist are judged to be dangerous to themselves or others and who may not perceive the need for treatment.

Defining alcoholism and other forms of drug abuse also presents obstacles, because there is no conclusive proof of the causes of these problems. The disease model of chemical dependency has been useful in reducing stigma and in helping abusers to get treatment, but there are likely many types and many causes of chemical dependency problems.

Estimating Problems

Although we cannot specifically define mental illness or alcoholism and other forms of drug abuse, estimates have been made of the numbers of people who experience these types of problems. According to the National Institute on Mental Health (NIMH), 19 percent of American adults and nearly eight million children currently have some form of mental illness.[7] Approximately 17.5 million adults experience problems of alcohol abuse and alcoholism.[8] Alcohol and other drug use among youths continue to be a serious concern. About 5 percent of all high school seniors report drinking daily, and nearly 40 percent had recently consumed five or more drinks at one time. Although daily use of marijuana by high school seniors dropped from a high of 10.7 percent of students in 1978 to 4 percent in 1986, 17 percent of high school seniors have now tried cocaine at least once.[9]

Only a small percentage of those with mental health, alcohol, and drug problems receive assistance. The NIMH reports that only one-fifth of all those experiencing mental health problems receive care.[10] The Alcohol, Drug Abuse, and Mental Health Administration (ADAMHA) reports that in 1984 about half a million people received specialized alcoholism and alcohol abuse treatment.[11] A more recent survey indicated that on October 30, 1987, more than six hundred thousand individuals were in treatment in nearly seven thousand public, voluntary, and proprietary treatment facilities across the country.[12] As large as this number receiving treatment is, these efforts do not come close to reaching the many in need.

Finding New Treatment Approaches

The mentally ill were once thought to be possessed by the devil and were hidden away from public view, but by the nineteenth century treatment of the mentally ill began to take different forms. Phillipe Pinel, a French physician, introduced *moral treatment* for those with mental illness. Moral treatment consisted of treating mentally ill individuals with kindness and consideration, providing the opportunity for discussion of personal problems and encouraging an active orientation to life; and although this approach to treating mental illness sounded good, it was not the kind of treatment offered to most mentally ill individuals.[13] For those who could not afford moral treatment, institutional treatment or incarceration were the general methods of providing mental health care. Dorothea Dix, a social reformer during the mid-1800s, sought to improve the plight of severely mistreated mental patients. Dix succeeded in improving conditions within institutions for mental-health patients, but with the increasing numbers being labeled mentally ill in the nineteenth century, institutions grew larger and less capable of helping those with mental illness.

The Industrial Revolution resulted in an increase in social problems, including mental illness.[14] People came to the cities seeking jobs and wealth and instead found overcrowding, joblessness, and misery. Those migrating to the cities were often without the support of their family and friends, and coping with urban problems was difficult. Immigrants from other countries also flocked to the cities. Those who did not acculturate or assimilate quickly into American society were often labeled as deviant or mentally ill.[15] City dwellers, overwhelmed with problems, had little tolerance for what they considered to be deviation from normal behavior. This increased the numbers who were sent to mental-health institutions.[16]

Apart from these institutions, there was little in the way of social policies and public programs for those with mental illness . Following Dix's efforts to reform mental institutions, Clifford Beers was responsible for introducing the *mental-hygiene movement*. In 1909, he founded the National Mental Health Association. Beers knew well the dehumanizing conditions of mental institutions; he himself had been a patient. Beers' efforts to expose the inhumane conditions of the institutions, like Dix's, resulted in better care, but the custodial and institutional philosophies of mental-health treatment continued.[17]

During World War II, a large number of young men were needed for military service. Part of the screening procedure for new recruits was a psychiatric examination. The number of young men who were rejected as unfit for military service or who were later discharged for psychiatric reasons was alarming. While the accuracy and methods of these psychiatric screening procedures have been criticized, the identification of so many young men with problems brought about renewed concern for mental health care.[18] This concern was reflected in the Mental Health Act of 1946 which established the National Institute of Mental Health (NIMH), with its focus on training, education, and research.

In the 1950s, another important development occurred in mental-health treatment—the discovery of improved psychotherapeutic drugs. These drugs reduced many of the *symptoms* of mental-health patients such as hallucinations. This allowed hospital staffs to eliminate many restrictions placed on patients and made patients more acceptable to the community.[19] Although the appropriate use of drug therapy has been debated,[20] it is evident that psychotherapeutic drugs have reduced the need for hospitalization for many patients. This development also helped to lay some of the groundwork for the passage of the Community Mental Health Act of 1963. As part of an emerging community mental-health movement, the act emphasized more federal involvement in community-based care, as well as coordination between community services and hospitals; improved services to chronically (now called seriously) mentally ill individuals; a reduction in state hospital treatment; an increase in community treatment, education, and prevention services; and greater utilization of paraprofessional staff.

Community Mental-Health Centers

The Community Mental Health Act of 1963 provided funds for the establishment and staffing of community mental-health centers (CMHCs) throughout the nation. Today, there are over 780 CMHCs in the United States.[21] Initially, most funding for

CMHCs came from the federal government. Today, state and local governments share costs with the federal government, and the centers collect fees from clients based on their ability to pay. Those with very low incomes pay little or no fee for service.

The Community Mental Health Act originally mandated that federally funded CMHCs provide five "essential services":

1. inpatient care,
2. outpatient care,
3. emergency care,
4. partial hospitalization,
5. consultation and education.

Inpatient care is usually provided within a psychiatric hospital or in a psychiatric unit of a general hospital within the community. Generally this care is short-term. If long-term care is needed, the patient may be transferred to a state mental health hospital or, if the patient has the financial resources, to a private hospital outside the CMHC system. Inpatient care may also include alcohol and drug detoxification and longer-term treatment for alcoholics and addicts.

Outpatient care covers a wide range of services. Among these services are individual therapy or counseling, group therapy and family therapy for those with mental-health as well as alcohol and drug abuse problems. Among the personnel who provide care are psychiatrists, nurses, psychologists, social workers, counselors, rehabilitation specialists, and paraprofessionals.

Emergency services, also known as *crisis services,* are provided on a twenty-four-hour basis. They may include the use of telephone hot lines and outreach services to clients who cannot reach a mental-health facility in times of emergency. Crisis services are often used in responding to those who are contemplating or who have attempted suicide, or who are experiencing other acute mental problems.

Partial hospitalization (often called day treatment) is the name generally given to supervised activities and mental-health services that a client receives for several hours a day. One type of partial-hospitalization service provides a structured environment for mental health clients during the day, with the clients' spending evenings at home or in a residential program in the community. Partial-hospitalization services help clients who are attempting to reintegrate themselves back into the community, perhaps following a period of psychiatric hospitalization.

The fifth service, *consultation and education* (C & E), may also be thought of as *prevention services.* C & E services are provided to many groups throughout the community: medical professionals, courts, law-enforcement agencies, schools, civic groups, religious groups, social service agencies, the elderly, and other citizens who want to learn about mental illness and substance abuse. C & E services are generally educational services that focus on the prevention of mental illness and drug abuse, the identification of these problems, and what to do if these problems occur.

In 1975, amendments to the Community Mental Health Act mandated more essential services, including special programs for children and the elderly, after-care and halfway-house services for patients discharged from mental health hospitals, and services to courts and related agencies to help screen those who may be in need of treatment. The Mental Health Systems Act of 1980 continued many of the provisions of the Community Mental Health Act and also included recommendations of the President's Commission on Mental Health which was appointed by Jimmy Carter in 1977. Provisions were added for special groups, including those with chronic mental illness, severely disturbed children and adolescents, and others who were unserved or undeserved. However, CMHCs were no longer required to provide all the essential services in order to qualify for federal funding.

Addressing the Country's Drug Problem

Concerted federal efforts to assist alcoholics and other drug abusers did not occur until the early 1970s when the National Institute on Alcohol Abuse and Alcoholism (NIAAA) was established under what is known as the Hughes Act (Senator Harold Hughes had pushed for its passage). This was soon followed by the establishment of the National Institute on Drug Abuse (NIDA).

When Ronald Reagan took office, he collapsed funding for alcoholism, drug abuse, and mental health services under the Alcohol, Drug Abuse and Mental Health Block Grant. The block grant reduced the amount of funds available to states to provide these services. Critics contend that this fiscal austerity has contributed to an increase in homelessness among mentally ill individuals and drug abusers and in the inability of others to obtain services. Today, community mental-health centers are under pressure to focus services on the needs of those with serious mental illness.

The newest component of ADAMHA is the Office of Substance Abuse Prevention (OSAP), which was established by Reagan in 1986 as a reaction to the mounting use of drugs in the United States. NIAAA, NIDA, and OSAP all address the issue of drug problems, yet the federal government has chosen to maintain the separate identities of these agencies under the ADAMHA umbrella.

In 1988 Congress passed the Anti-Drug or Omnibus Drug bill to help fight the drug war. The emphasis of this war has been on interdiction (stopping the flow of illegal drugs into as well as within the United States) and stiff legal penalties (including the possibilities of life imprisonment or the death penalty when a murder is involved in a drug-related crime). These provisions are said to strike at the *supply side* of the drug problem. Prevention, education, and treatment efforts are also included in the bill and are attempts to reduce the *demand* for drugs. There are numerous other provisions in the bill including provisions for drug-free workplaces and evicting public housing residents who engage in or permit drug use on or near the premises.

The war on drugs developed steam during the Reagan administration. The president's wife, Nancy, joined the effort. Her "Just Say No to Drugs" campaign, directed at children, was often criticized as being too simplistic to strike at the many causes of drug use and abuse. President Reagan's Commission on the Human Immunodeficiency Virus Epidemic called for "treatment on demand" for drug abusers to help prevent the spread of the virus. A sizable portion of those with AIDS have contracted the disease through needles used to inject illegal drugs, and the use of drugs can also cloud judgment and lead to unsafe sex practices. Under the Bush administration, funding for drug abuse treatment and education has increased, but social services providers are still concerned that Congress' efforts at law enforcement are draining money from needed social services.

The Rights of Patients

Sometimes treatment cannot be provided to those with mental-health problems on an outpatient basis or in community facilities. Community mental-health programs may not be equipped to assist those whose problems are severe, or specialized facilities may not exist in a community. Treatment in an inpatient mental health facility may be necessary. This type of treatment restricts an individual from participating in normal, daily activities. Until the early twentieth century, mental health patients had few rights. Today, there is a greater concern for laws and policies which protect the rights of those who are hospitalized in mental-health facilities. The federal and state governments are responsible for protecting the rights of mental health patients. Patients in mental-health hospitals and drug treatment facilities must be informed of their rights to obtain and refuse treatment, and those who are not able to read must have this information explained to them.

Some obstacles prevent patients from receiving the best treatment in these facilities. Patients should always be treated in a way that respects their individual dignity, but this manner of treatment is contingent on the quality of the treatment facility and of its staff. Facilities are often crowded and caseloads high. Some are located in remote areas where there may be an inadequate number of professionals who are trained to provide services. This makes it difficult to recruit and retain qualified staff. Yet the decisions about a patient's day-to-day activities are largely staff decisions. The patient may have little influence in choosing these activities, short of refusing to participate. Moreover, when patients refuse to participate in activities, they are often considered to be uncooperative and resistant to treatment. This may serve to prolong their stay in the hospital.

Patients have the right to know the reason for their admission and what must happen before release can be granted. They must be provided legal representation and access to mental health laws. Patients are to be afforded privacy when they have visitors, and visits should not be denied unless there is reason to believe that they might be harmful to the patient or others. Unfortunately, when hospitals are located far from the patient's home, it is more difficult for family members to visit or for the patient to visit family on short leaves of absence from the hospital. The illustration on page 147, entitled "Mental Health and Civil Rights," discusses some of the dilemmas faced in protecting the rights of individuals with mental illness.

Deinstitutionalization

Persons with mental health and drug problems frequently face social rejection. While the public generally agrees that they should be provided treatment, the public does not always agree about where this treatment should be provided. *Time* magazine recently used the acronym "NIMBY" to refer to those whose attitude is "not in my back yard."[22] This attitude persists for several reasons. Some people fear alcoholics, drug abusers, and those who are mentally ill, and they believe these individuals might change the neighborhood's character by endangering the safety of neighborhood residents. They also fear that crimes and neighborhood disturbances will increase.[23] Homeowners also believe their property will be devalued because community-based facilities will not be well maintained, thus forcing them to sell their homes at a loss. Examinations of these concerns indicate that no relationship has been found between depressed property values and the presence of residential facilities. In addition, there is some evidence that program residents are more likely to be the victims rather than the perpetrators of crimes.

The phrase "treatment in the least restrictive manner" means that the freedoms of individuals receiving treatment should be preserved whenever possible. It is not appropriate to confine someone in a state hospital when a community facility can meet the individual's needs. Hospitals may compound patients' problems by making them *institutionalized.* Patients may be forced to get up at certain times and to eat at certain times; their meals are prepared for them and their clothes are washed for them; they may be told when to bathe and when to take their medication. As a result, patients become increasingly dependent on others for survival. When and if they return to their homes and communities, they may not have the skills to live independently.

ILLUSTRATION: MENTAL HEALTH AND CIVIL RIGHTS

In October a 40-year-old former secretary named Joyce Brown was a resident of a steam grate on New York's Upper East Side. Her clothes were filthy and ragged, she used the sidewalk as a bathroom as well as a bedroom, she shouted obscenities at passersby and she often burned the money they gave her. After a year of this life, she became a constitutional test case for New York's new Homeless Emergency Liaison Project, in which city authorities pick up homeless people who appear to be mentally ill and confine them in Bellevue Hospital. The average stay is 21 days.

A judge ordered Brown freed, declaring that the woman, whose testimony was articulate and whose physical health seemed fine, was not a danger to herself on the streets; he also shook his finger at a callous society that tried to lock up the homeless instead of finding them decent housing. An appellate court reversed that ruling but denied the city permission to force medication on her. The city let her go, and a new, stylishly dressed Joyce Brown is now on the lecture circuit. She lives in a hotel and works on

and off answering the telephone for the New York Civil Liberties Union, an affiliate of the American Civil Liberties Union, which represented her in court.

The case—and perhaps the whole matter of the 300,000 homeless people (as estimated by the Agriculture Department), half of them probably clinically mentally ill, who make their homes with their shopping bags and blankets on the streets and inside office building doorways, railroad and subway stations and even airports of U.S. cities—encapsulates the paradox of what is understood these days as "civil liberties."

Legal standards for confining the mentally ill have become drastically tighter due to the efforts of civil libertarians. In 1975, the Supreme Court ruled that the mentally ill have a constitutional right to liberty and cannot be detained against their will unless they are dangerous to themselves or others or cannot survive on their own. This is a net that lets a great many with mental disorders slip through—so many that even the American Psychiatric Association, once a leading advocate of deinstitutionalizing the mentally ill, issued guidelines in 1983 advising emergency detention periods for those "likely to suffer substantial mental or physical deterioration" as well as for more dangerous cases.

But the real standoff in the Brown controversy comes from a deep conflict over what society should do about its Joyce Browns—in broader terms, to what extent concerns for moral order should prevail over notions of individual liberty. An authoritarian adherence to social order must give way in the interest of a genuinely free society, say many proponents of civil liberties. Even hardcore conservatives who get in a jam can find themselves unexpectedly grateful for the existence of the American Civil Liberties Union; there is an adage that a liberal is a conservative who has been arrested. The civil libertarians have won their major victories not in the legislature but in the courtroom—unsurprisingly, in their view, because such liberties become an issue only when majorities threaten minority rights.

To Robert Levy, the former secretary's lawyer, her life on the grate was just an alternative life-style, albeit one that some people find offensive. The street as toilet? "I've seen plenty of people doing that," he says. "Taxi drivers. It's not a pleasant sight, but it's not unusual." Burning money? "She needed only $7 to $10 per day to live on, and she knew it was dangerous to keep any more than that. . . . She would get angry when people handed her money in a way she thought was condescending."

For Levy, the case also has an aspect of political protest against municipal facilities for the homeless, the warehouselike shelters that used to be called flophouses back in the days when the homeless were known as vagrants. New York's housing stock has been declining by an estimated 30,000 units a year; rundown apartments for the poor have been first to go.

"There is a fundamental right to liberty at stake here," Levy says of his client. "There are too many circumstances in which it's hard to say whether someone really needs to be picked up."

Lawyers for the city see the situation differently. They point out that Joyce Brown was hospitalized in 1985 for an acute psychiatric episode and that her two sisters in New Jersey say she became increasingly abusive toward them before they asked her to leave their home in late 1986. To get court approval of confinement for Brown, city lawyers had to stretch the legal concept of dangerousness as far as it could go, says Paul Rephen, an assistant to the city's chief attorney. "Courts have said that self-neglect is dangerous."

And so it goes. New York's HELP, as the program is called, continues, and a denunciation of civil libertarians as "crazies" by Mayor Edward I. Koch met with wild approval from some residents. Never has the city's homeless population seemed so great; Grand Central Terminal looks like a flophouse inside. A proposal in Washington to force people living on the streets into shelters on subfreezing nights is being strongly opposed by that city's ACLU chapter. "They could take in you and me if we happened to be walking down the street at night," says chapter lawyer Elizabeth Symonds.

Source: Charlotte Low, "A Rude Awakening from Civil Liberties," *Insight* (March 21, 1988), pp. 8–9.

Note: Brown was later reported to be living on the streets again.

Deinstitutionalization, with its reliance on community facilities, may also present problems. Most communities do not have enough local treatment and residential facilities. The discharge of large numbers of patients from state institutions to their home communities has frequently resulted in added stress for both patients and communities. In addition, families are often not equipped to care for mentally ill members who may need frequent supervision or special services.

One policy approach to placing residential facilities in established neighborhoods is the use of zoning laws that require communities to incorporate provisions for these facilities. There has been some resistance from those concerned that this may have the unintended effect of creating "social service ghettos." Another approach is to educate and prepare neighbors *before* clients move in by gaining their support for the facility. But as one advocate of clients rights put it, "The purist position is that constitutionally, these people have a right to live anywhere they want; the rest of us do not need special permission to live where we choose."[24]

CHILD WELFARE POLICY

Family life in the United States has been viewed with a special reverence. Governmental interference in family life is generally thought to be an unwelcome intrusion. As a result, the United States has no official national family policy. Instead, there are many federal, state, and local laws that govern various aspects of family relations. There are more than twenty separate federal agencies that provide some types of services for children.[25] This section focuses on one area of family relations— child welfare, especially child abuse and neglect.

Discovering Child Abuse

Historically, children have been considered the possessions of their parents.[26] Parents who severely punished their children, even beat them, were not behaving deviantly; they were merely making sure that their children obeyed. In spite of early efforts to rescue children from abuse (see Figure 7–1 and the illustration entitled "Little Mary Ellen"), these practices continued to prevail in America at the same time that the Industrial Revolution brought an abundance of new social problems. Among these social problems were the conditions of urban cities, which were often overcrowded and unsanitary and where hunger and disease were not uncommon. During this period, it was thought that children from poor homes might be better raised in institutions where they could learn "proper societal values." Poverty and a poor living environment were considered to be the result of faulty values which parents transmitted to their children. Institutions such as the New York House of Refuge were established for neglected, abandoned, and delinquent youth. But the emphasis was not on protecting children from parents who harmed or neglected them, it was on placing children in institutions to help reverse the trend of poverty.

In the early twentieth century, the prevailing philosophy toward child care remained the "house of refuge" idea. Even the establishment of juvenile courts during this period did little to change this. Emphasis was on removing children from their homes, not on rehabilitating or treating parents. As the century progressed, though, more concern was expressed for children. They were removed from adult institutions, and new mothers'-aid programs provided financial security to children in their natural homes. But abusive parents were not themselves the targets of social policies or social programs; in fact, the public continued to condone parents' use of physical force on their children.

It was not the social reformers, nor the judicial personnel of the juvenile courts, nor the public at large who discovered child abuse. It was *pediatric radiologists* who identified child abuse as a problem, or *syndrome,* and it was this group which gave it legitimacy and aroused public concern. John Caffey was the first to search for a cause for the many bone fractures he was seeing in children; beginning in 1946, his work led to the identification of parents as the cause of these fractures. However, Caffey and other pediatric radiologists were not the first professionals to *see* child abuse. Emergency room staff and family physicians were the first to come into contact with these children, but at least four factors prevented them from recognizing the problem. First, child abuse was not a traditional diagnosis. Second, doctors may not have believed that parents would abuse their children. Third, if the family, rather than just the child, was the doctor's patient, reporting abuse may have constituted a violation of patient confidentiality. Fourth, physicians may have been unwilling to report criminal behavior because of the time-consuming nature of criminal cases and their reluctance to act as witnesses in those proceedings.

Pediatric radiologists, rather than other physicians, exposed child abuse because they did *not* deal directly with the child and the family. Issues regarding confidentiality—who the patient was—and court proceedings were not their primary concerns. Making public the problem of child abuse also served to elevate the status of pediatric radiologists. Radiologists were not highly regarded among members of the medical profession because they did not provide direct care to patients. *Discovering* child abuse allowed pediatric radiologists to develop closer collegial relationships with those physicians with whom they consulted.

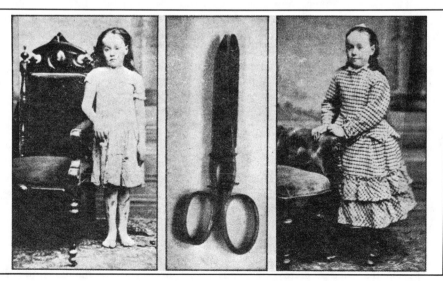

FIGURE 7–1   SPCA's Before-and-after photos of Mary Ellen, with scissors used to punish her.

ILLUSTRATION: LITTLE MARY ELLEN

Before 1875, U.S. authorities had no legal means to interfere in cases of battered children. The laws were changed with the help of the Society for the Prevention of Cruelty to Animals (SPCA).

A 9-year-old named Mary Ellen became the exemplar of the battered children's plight. Indentured to Francis and Mary Connolly (and rumored to be the daughter of Mary's ex-husband), the girl was whipped daily, stabbed with scissors and tied to a bed. Neighbors reported the situation to Etta Wheeler, a church worker, in 1874. When Wheeler found that there was no lawful way to rescue the child from her brutal guardians, she went to Henry Bergh of the SPCA for help.

Under the premise that the child was a member of the animal kingdom, the SPCA obtained a writ of habeas corpus to remove Mary Ellen from her home. On April 9, 1874, she was carried into the New York Supreme Court, where her case was tried. She was pitifully thin, with a scissor wound on her cheek. Mrs. Connolly was sentenced to a year in prison. Mary Ellen was given a new home. The following April, the New York Society for the Prevention of Cruelty to Children (NYSPCC) was incorporated.

Before-and-after photos of Mary Ellen (as a pathetic waif upon her rescue and as a healthy child a year later) still hang at the New York SPCA, framed with Mrs. Connolly's scissors.

(Reprinted with permission from Irving Wallace, David Wallachinsky, and Amy Wallace, "Significa," *Parade* magazine. Photos courtesy of ASPCA Archives.)

It was important to the medical profession that the issue of child abuse be kept under its control. Child abuse had to be called a medical rather than a social or legal problem, or else physicians would be relegated to a subordinate role in its diagnosis and treatment. In 1962, child abuse was labeled with the medical terminology "the battered-child syndrome," thus legitimizing its recognition by physicians. Magazines, newspapers, and television programs such as "Ben Casey" and "Dr. Kildare" publicized the problem.

Between 1962 and 1965, every state passed legislation on child abuse. Approaches to child abuse intervention have undergone considerable evolution. Today, child-abuse legislation is aimed more at rehabilitating parents than punishing them. Most cases are reported to welfare rather than law-enforcement agencies. The social services that neglectful or abusive parents are most likely to receive are individual and group treatment. Self-help groups, such as Parents Anonymous, are also valuable sources of support. Social services for abusive and neglectful parents are now directed at preserving the family unit.

Child Abuse and the Federal Government

The federal government's first major foray into the welfare of children began with the establishment of the Children's Bureau in 1912. The bureau was concerned with a broad range of child welfare issues—from child labor and delinquency to orphaned children. Under the Social Security Act of 1935, Title V directed the bureau to cooperate with the states to develop child welfare services. Services were expanded, primarily during the 1960s, and in 1974 Congress passed the Child Abuse Prevention and Treatment Act and established the National Center for Child Abuse and Neglect. In addition to assisting the states with programs, the center conducts child abuse and neglect research. In 1980, the Adoption Assistance and Child Welfare Act, also known as the *permanency planning law,* was enacted. Among other things, it created a new program under Title IV-E of the Social Security Act. The law was a reaction to the number of children who had become *lost* in the child welfare system; it was designed to prevent the *drift* of so many children into foster care for long periods of time. Its specific purposes were:

1. Protecting and promoting the welfare of all children, including handicapped, homeless, dependent, or neglected children;
2. Preventing or remedying, or assisting in the solution to problems that may result in the neglect, abuse, exploitation, or delinquency of children;
3. Preventing the unnecessary separation of children from their families by identifying family problems, by assisting families in resolving their problems, and by preventing breakups of the families where the prevention of child removal is desirable and possible;
4. Restoring to their families those children who have been removed, by the provision of services to the child and the family;
5. Placing children in suitable adoptive homes in cases where restoration to the biological family is not appropriate;
6. Assuring adequate care of children away from their homes in cases where the child cannot be returned home or cannot be placed for adoption.

Under this act states must do a better job of monitoring cases, including reviewing them every six months and taking additional steps to assure that within a reasonable time the child has a permanent home.

Since specific child abuse and neglect statutes remain the prerogative of the states, there is no single definition of these problems, and there is no single piece of legislation that uniformly addresses neglect and abuse throughout the nation. Although available model legislation often serves as the basis for state statutes, it is still difficult to achieve consensus on definitions of abuse and neglect. Even if agreement on definitions could be reached, the best strategies for intervention remain unclear, and funding to provide all the needed services is clearly lacking. President Bush has encouraged increased federal spending for foster care and adoptions as a means of discouraging abortions.[27]

Extent of Child Maltreatment

Child maltreatment consists of both child abuse and child neglect. Abuse occurs when severe harm is inflicted on a child—such as broken bones or burns—but it can also be emotional or sexual. Neglect occurs when a parent or caretaker fails to provide a child with the essentials needed to live adequately, including proper schooling, or it may result from psychological deprivation, such as isolating the child from others. In 1987, protective service agencies across the country received nearly 2.2 million reports of suspected child abuse or neglect.[28] The number of reports grows each year, largely due to public awareness of these problems. But this number does not include the fact that some reports cannot be substantiated, either because the report was made in error or it cannot be verified. It also does not consider that some abused and neglected children are not reported to protective services at all.

How many children are actually abused or neglected? It depends on how you count it. The federal government is now using two definitions to estimate the extent of these problems.[29] One focuses on harm that has already occurred, while the other also includes children at risk for harm. Using the more restrictive definition, it is estimated that more than one million children (about sixteen per one thousand population) were victimized in 1986 (the last year for which these estimates are available). The expanded definition would add another half million to the total. These figures are alarming. Under the restrictive definition, more children were abused than were neglected; and under the broader definition (as might be expected), more children were neglected. Using the restrictive definition, the most frequent type of abuse was physical, followed by emotional, then sexual. The most common type of neglect was educational, followed by physical and emotional. Girls were more likely to be abused than boys, and older children were more often abused than younger children; but younger children were more likely to be the victims of fatalities. Race and ethnicity were not correlated with abuse, but children from lower income families were more likely to be maltreated. Of great concern is that for every sixteen children estimated to be abused, only seven "had actually been officially reported to CPS [child protective services] and accepted for investigation."[30] Although all states mandate that anyone who suspects abuse must report it, many cases go undetected due to failure to report or failure to recognize the problem.

Problems with the System

There are what seem to be overwhelming problems in the delivery of child welfare services. With greater demands for services, state child protective service agencies cannot possibly respond to the numbers of children and parents in need of services, so they have resorted to prioritizing cases. The more serious cases get the attention while others may not get addressed unless or until they become serious. Citizens who report cases to child abuse hot lines and later find that little has been done are, not surprisingly, angry. The public is particularly outraged when a child who is not removed from the home is later severely injured or dies as a result of the abuse. On the other hand are reports of parents whose children were taken away without appropriate investigations of the situation. Social workers often take the blame in all these situations because it is they who investigate the cases, but many staff members are not professionally qualified social workers and lack the education necessary to do the job.[31] High caseloads, low pay, and highly stressful working conditions that result in increased staff turnover add to the problems in the child welfare delivery system.[32] The threat of lawsuits constantly hangs over the heads of child welfare workers. But in 1989, the United States Supreme Court ruled six to three that public employees could not be held liable for failure to protect citizens from harm caused by other private citizens. The case involved the Winnebago County, Wisconsin, Department of Social Services; the child involved was Joshua DeShaney, who suffered severe, permanent brain damage as a result of abuse by his father after the department failed to remove him from his home. Many child advocates were shocked by this decision. Although child welfare personnel might breathe a sigh of relief as a result of it, the troubling question of preventing such tragedies remains, and the threat of criminal as well as civil prosecution is still a possibility for child welfare workers and administrators.

The decision to remove children from their own homes is a difficult one. Even in cases of severe abuse, removal from the home can be traumatizing for a child, and finding an appropriate placement for the child may be difficult. Children who are removed for more than a very brief period may be placed with other relatives or friends. In many cases, however, there is no readily available alternative, but a suitable placement must be found. The number of foster homes is never sufficient, and sometimes abuse is repeated in these homes. In order to insure that as many children remain in their own homes as possible, it has become more common to remove the abuser from the home than the child. Children frequently regard their own removal from home as a punishment rather than protection.

It can also be difficult to find adoptive homes for those children who are permanently removed from their families. There are many people interested in adopting, but the preference is generally for healthy, white infants. Children in foster care often do not match this profile. Many of these children live in a number of foster homes before they reach adult status. The number of children in foster care is estimated to be five hundred thousand nationwide.[33] The number of babies born addicted to drugs and the increasing number born with the human immuno-deficiency virus have added to the problem. The term "boarder babies" has been used to describe these children who spend their young lives in institutions.

The problems of child abuse and neglect generally do not remedy themselves. Intervention and treatment are needed by all members of the family. Child protection agencies and the courts usually mandate that parents who have perpetrated abuse get help, but often there is insufficient help available. Long waiting lists for services are common at public and not-for-profit agencies, and private treatment is costly. And there are no guarantees that treatment will work. Some programs have proven to be successful; but in many cases, such as sexual abuse, intensive help by experts is lacking.

SERVICES FOR OLDER AMERICANS

In many cultures, such as among Asians, and among some subcultures in the United States, such as Native American groups, older members are respected and revered for their wisdom and knowledge. But among most groups in the United States, there continues to be a preoccupation with youth. Americans invest considerable time, money, and effort trying to remain young. However, the status of older Americans has improved considerably. While the elderly were once the age group most likely to be poor, they are now less likely to be poor than younger Americans. Longevity has certainly increased, but as people live far longer than ever before, they are also likely to become increasingly vulnerable, needing more health care services, protection, and assistance in independent living. The growing number of older Americans has also given rise to a senior citizens group that is more visible and vocal than ever before. The Social Security retirement program (discussed in Chapter 4), SSI (discussed in Chapter 5), and Medicare (discussed in Chapter 10) are important programs that help to maintain a high quality of life for older citizens. The other vital component of public response to meeting the needs of older individuals is social services. The most important legislation in this regard is the Older Americans Act of 1965.

The Older Americans Act

The goals of the Older Americans Act (OAA) read more like a wish list than a set of objectives being seriously pursued by the federal government. These symbolic goals are:

an adequate income in retirement in accordance with the American standard of living;

the best possible physical and mental health that science can make available without regard to economic status;

suitable housing that is independently selected, designed, and located, with reference to special needs and available at costs older citizens can afford;

full restorative services for those who require institutional care;

opportunity for employment with no discriminatory personnel practices because of age;

retirement in health, honor, and dignity—after years of contribution to the economy;

pursuit of meaningful activity within the widest range of civic, cultural, and recreational opportunities;

efficient community services, including access to low-cost transportation, which provide a choice in supported living arrangements and social assistance in a coordinated manner, and which are readily available when needed;

immediate benefit from proven research knowledge, which can sustain and improve health and happiness;

freedom, independence, and the free exercise of individual initiative in planning and managing one's own life.

Although the country has yet to make a real dent in meeting many of these goals, the act has provided a framework for a modest array of services to older citizens. In order to qualify for services under the OAA, a person must be at least sixty years old. Income is generally not used to determine eligibility, but the poor elderly are of special concern.

The OAA created what has become known as an *aging network* to express the concerns of older Americans.[34] The network operates at the federal, regional, state, and local levels. At the federal level is the Administration on Aging (AoA), which is part of the Department of Health and Human Services. The primary function of the AoA is to provide technical assistance to state and local governments to help them develop and implement services for the elderly; it is also supposed to conduct evaluations of programs and research on aging and act as a national clearinghouse on information about the elderly. To assist in its efforts, the AoA has ten regional offices across the United States.

At the state level, the aging network is generally found within the state's human services or welfare department. Most likely it is part of an office dedicated to programs for older citizens. The state offices assist in implementing federal policies and act as advocates for elderly citizens. They make the needs and problems of the aged known to the AoA and also to their own state legislatures, which determine how state programs for older citizens will be funded and administered.

Actually, most social services for the elderly—about 80 percent of them—are provided by family and friends.[35] But when families and friends cannot meet all these needs and when older Americans want to maintain greater independence, local agencies try to respond. At the local level there are about six hundred Area Agencies on Aging (AAAs). Each AAA is guided by an advisory council primarily composed of older individuals. The AAAs perform their advocacy function by assessing the needs of older people in their communities. AAAs also distribute funds to community agencies that deliver services directly to the aged. Among the social services they provide are nutrition programs, senior centers, information and referral, transportation, homemaker and chore services, legal counseling, escort services, home repair and renovation, home health aid, shopping assistance, friendly visitation, and telephone assurance (phone calls to the elderly for reassurance and to check on their needs).

The OAA and the aging network are important adjuncts to the major cash-assistance programs for older citizens. These social service programs provide the elderly with important links to the community by keeping them involved in the mainstream of American life. But the aging network is only as good as its reputation. Advocacy groups for older Americans are concerned that services be well publicized to insure they are utilized.

The Older Americans Act has been amended over the years, but its purposes and intent have remained the same. During the Reagan years, the AoA lost a considerable number of staff members, but President Reagan, a senior citizen himself, had little influence on the act. Provisions added in 1984 included greater emphasis on providing for the needs of ethnic minorities, assisting the elderly who have been victimized as the result of violence or abuse, and helping those with Alzheimer's disease.[36]

In addition to services for older citizens, it is becoming increasingly clear that services are also needed by the caretakers of the elderly if they are to continue to be a mainstay of support. Respite care, for example, provides relief to spouses, adult children, and others who care for the elderly, so these caretakers can go shopping, take a vacation, or have even a few hours of free time. President Bush recently vetoed a family leave bill, but private companies are experimenting with such policies. Family leave policies (which are similar to policies that permit parents to take time from work to care for a sick child) allow workers to tend to relatives such as parents or adult children who need care. Another means that might be effective in encouraging greater family involvement in elder care is tax expenditures (see Chapter 2) which would allow families to take income tax deductions if they provide for the care of their parents. This type of measure is especially helpful to lower-income families in easing the financial strain of these responsibilities. Still other public policies that could encourage family care of the elderly are expansions of Medicare and Medicaid to cover more home health care costs (see Chapter 10).

Older Americans and the Legislature

From time to time, White House conferences on aging have been conducted, with older Americans from across the United States participating as delegates. The 1981 conference focused on a number of issues that are quite similar to those found in the goals of the OAA: improvement of economic well-being; availability of quality health care; establishment of a more comprehensive social-service delivery system; expansion of housing and long-term care facilities; development of a national retirement policy; greater availability of job opportunities; the overcoming of stereotypes involving aging; and stimulation of medical research on aging. President Bush has the option of calling a 1991 conference.[37]

The House of Representatives and the Senate each have special committees to address legislation concerning the elderly. In the Senate, the committee is called the Special Committee on Aging, and in the House it is called the Permanent Select Committee on Aging. State legislatures also have committees whose functions include consideration of the needs of the elderly. About half the states also convene *Silver Haired Legislatures* comprised of older state residents who consider the needs of their peers and who report to the governors and state legislatures. In addition to these policy advisory groups, elderly people throughout the country have organized in an effort to improve their well-being. Among the best-known groups is the American Association of Retired Persons (AARP). With thirty-two million members, it might be considered the country's largest advocacy group. A smaller, but also vocal association is the Gray Panthers, which has been particularly concerned with intergenerational issues.

Older Americans and Civil Rights

There are some important civil rights issues that are unique to older persons. One of them is protection from abuse. Most states have specific statutes that prohibit various types of elder abuse, such as physical and psychological abuse as well as exploitation of resources. Abuse may occur in the older person's home, the home of a caretaker, or in an institution such as a nursing home. Sometimes the situation is termed *self-abuse*, because the older person can no longer care for him- or herself or because caretakers are unable to encourage the older person to eat or perform other self-care activities. Penalties for failing to report elder abuse vary, and in many cases, there is no real penalty. The identification of elder abuse is complicated by certain issues. For example, even those older persons capable of reporting the abuse may not do so for fear that loss of their caretaker will result in their being placed in a nursing home or other institution. In other cases, the abuser is a loved one, and the older person may not want to risk intervention by social service workers or legal action by law enforcement agencies against this individual. Elder abuse laws are newer and not as well developed as child abuse laws, but in most areas adult protective service workers and law enforcement officers are called on to intervene.

Another civil rights issue for the elderly is *guardianship,* also called *conservatorship.*[38] Guardians are appointed by courts (in most states these are probate courts that also deal with such issues as child custody and with cases involving adults who need treatment for mental illness or drug abuse) when it appears that an older person is no longer competent to manage his or her daily affairs. Once a guardian is appointed, the older person is stripped of rights and decision-making power over where to live, how to spend money, whether or not to receive treatment, and so forth. Guardianship is defined under state law, and these laws have come under increasing scrutiny as more and more older people have become the subjects of guardianship. There is a concern that many guardianship decisions are made without sufficient information. Decisions may be based on the viewpoint of the individual who believes guardianship is needed rather than on any convincing medical evidence. The older person may not be given an opportunity to have legal representation. In many cases, supervision of guardians is also lax. The elderly can be robbed of assets and treated poorly at the hands of guardians who may be relatives or someone previously unknown to the older person.

In some areas, guardianship has become a new business for entrepreneurs, since guardians may be paid a fee for their services. Some states have overhauled their guardianship programs to provide for better protection of older individuals. In many areas, guardianship is being used only as a last resort. In some cases, bill-paying or other financial management services provided by volunteers can prevent the need for guardianship; or durable power of attorney is used which can leave the older person with more rights intact by giving another individual limited powers such as in financial matters. While useful in helping the elderly maintain their civil rights, these systems can also result in inappropriate use of an individual's financial resources, because in many voluntary programs, supervision is also lacking. At a minimum, closer supervision of existing systems is needed, since good alternatives seem to be few.

Age discrimination is another concern. The Age Discrimination in Employment Act (ADEA) of 1967 protected most workers age 45 to 65 from discrimination in hiring and firing; it also addressed retention and promotion decisions made on the basis of age. In 1978 amendments were added protecting workers to age 70, and in 1987 provisions were added outlawing mandatory retirement ages for most workers. A mandatory retirement age can be used only when it can be shown to be a bona fide occupational qualification (BFOQ) for carrying out the job. A number of law enforcement and fire protection agencies have been able to retain a retirement age of fifty-five, but there have been challenges to even this age requirement. The law does not, however, cover fringe benefits. Employers can offer fringe benefit packages to older workers that differ from what is offered to the rest of the workforce. In spite of these remaining obstacles to equality in employment, the ADEA is considered the great civil rights victory of older workers.

Employers today are sometimes tempted to terminate the employment of older workers when they could hire younger workers at substantially lower salaries. Some older employees have accepted attractive retirement packages, but others believe that these are tactics used to coerce older workers to retire. The fear of being sued has led some employers to ask those who take early retirement to sign waivers stating that they accept the terms and will not sue at a later date for age discrimination.

There may be an interesting development in the employment of older people in the years ahead. As recently suggested, a new job title in the future corporate world is likely to be Administrator of Aging Affairs, because with fewer young people in the job market, recruitment and retention of older workers will be quite important.[39] Some companies are already calling back older workers.

DO SOCIAL SERVICES REALLY WORK?

Do social services really help people? Evaluating any social welfare program or policy is difficult because social-service programs are often without well-defined goals. There is also a "confusion between policy ends and policy means.... While federal and state governments are committed to 'doing something' about certain vulnerable populations, the end product of their efforts has not been specified."[40]

Even if we knew the specific goals of various social services, evaluating these services would not be easy. There are two types of major obstacles to evaluation: political and methodological. Political obstacles operate at all levels of the social service delivery system. Evaluation is threatening to federal, state, and local government, to social service administrators, to social service workers, and last but not least, to the clients themselves. Evaluation is threatening to governments because it might imply that they have developed poor policies, passed inadequate laws in response to those policies, or funded ineffective programs. Evaluation is threatening to social service administrators because it might suggest that they have done a poor job of implementing and managing the programs, laws, and policies developed by legislators. Evaluation is threatening to social service workers because it might indicate that they are not adequately skilled in delivering and providing social services to clients. Finally, evaluation may be threatening to clients because the process may invade their privacy, place additional pressure on them in times of personal crisis, and make them feel even more conspicuous about receiving social services.

A second major source of difficulty in conducting evaluations of social services is the presence of methodological problems found in the design of the evaluation. For example, there are obstacles in conducting controlled experiments. Governments generally cannot deny services to people or even assign them randomly to different types of treatment groups. This makes it difficult to generalize from special samples to the whole population. In addition, there may be a *halo effect* (sometimes referred to as the Hawthorne effect): Groups that are selected to receive services are more likely to improve because they are given attention, regardless of the effectiveness or quality of the service. Many studies that are called *evaluations* are actually little more than a tabulation of the number of people seen, or the amount of services provided, rather than an evaluation of the actual *effects* or *impacts* of programs or services on these people.

In spite of these political and methodological obstacles to evaluation, more efforts have been made to determine the effectiveness of social service programs. For example, one writer concluded that while there is very little empirical evidence on the overall effects of social service programs for the elderly, two demonstrable effects are "(1) an increase in the ability of the aged to maintain homes apart from younger relatives, and (2) an increase in proprietary nursing home beds for the sick aged."[41] In some cases, it has become more difficult to conduct broad evaluations of the effects of federal legislation because of reduced federal requirements for states to report on their activities.[42]

In the 1970s, a number of studies were conducted to evaluate the success of community mental health centers.[43] A study conducted by the United States government's General Accounting Office (GAO) spoke of the positive effects of CMHC programs. One effect cited was an increase in the availability of community care. In another report, the Senate Committee on Labor and Public Welfare also discussed the positive results that have been achieved by CMHCs through provision of community-based care in lieu of institutional care. But other reports were not as complimentary. A 1974 report by Ralph Nader stated that community mental health centers had not reduced the number of people admitted to state mental health institutions. The Nader report accused psychiatrists of benefiting unfairly from the programs and of neglecting services to the poor.

With respect to child welfare services, a 1987 review of several studies on efforts aimed at permanency planning revealed that they did produce a "somewhat higher rate of adoption from foster care."[44] While these adoptions tended to be stable, children returned to their biological parents were as likely to go back to foster care homes as they were prior to the implementation of permanency planning programs; and to date the adjustment of children in permanent placements seems no better than it is for those in temporary placement (the number of studies on this point is still scarce).

We see that attempts to evaluate the effectiveness of social services often show mixed results. While there is no doubt that the *number* of social services available to those in need has generally increased, the demonstrable *effects* of these services are often limited or ambiguous.

Should we conclude that social services are not very effective? This may be an unfair assumption to make. Each of us can think of individuals who benefit greatly from social services: an elderly person who receives adequate meals through a nutrition program such as Meals on Wheels, a friend whose depression has been relieved through services provided by a mental health center, a child whose adoption prevented transfer from foster home to foster home. In the aggregate, however, effects of social service programs cannot always be demonstrated easily, yet there is mounting pressure on human service professionals to justify that their work is useful.

Evaluation studies seem to be most useful when they contain recommendations for future service delivery. A major 1985 study of the effectiveness of mental health services conducted by National Association of Social Workers concluded with the following suggestions for providing better services:

1. Clients should be involved in defining the problems to be solved.
2. The treatment should be clearly specified.
3. Treatment expectations should be made clear to the client.
4. Paraprofessionals can play an important role in assisting mental health clients.
5. Short-term treatment tends to produce better outcomes than long-term treatment.
6. Outpatients and hospitalized and posthospitalized patients benefit from different types of services.[45]

As attempts are made to improve client services, researchers and program evaluators are also striving to develop strategies and techniques that take into account the political and methodological obstacles which they face in evaluating social service policies and programs.

SUMMARY

Social services include many types of programs, including day care, mental health care, alcohol and drug abuse services, juvenile delinquency-prevention programs, child welfare programs, and nursing home care. Not all social services are directed toward the poor. People from all walks of life may require social services. Social services are provided by both public and private agencies. The federal government chose to reimburse the states at a generous rate for providing social services, especially those to public assistance recipients. Spending increased rapidly, and the federal government exercised its option to control social service spending through Title XX of the Social Security Act, and more recently through the Social Services Block Grant.

Mental health, alcoholism, and drug abuse services are one example of social services that may be needed by an individual regardless of economic and social status. These services were first provided in large institutions where patients were often poorly treated. Better treatment methods—for instance, *moral treatment*—were regarded as too costly to provide to most patients. Dorothea Dix and other reformers helped improve institutional treatment, but it was not until the 1960s that greater emphasis was placed on community care. Two factors that paved the way for improved mental health legislation were (1) the identification of many young men with mental health problems during World War II and (2) the improvement of drugs that help the mentally ill function in society. The Community Mental Health Act of 1963 was the landmark legislation that encouraged the building and staffing of Community Mental Health Centers (CMHCs). CMHC services are available in most communities today and are financed in large part through the Alcohol, Drug Abuse and Mental Health Block Grant along with state and local funds and client fees.

One of the biggest obstacles faced by CMHCs and drug treatment programs is the fear that community residents have of clients. Residents may oppose locating treatment facilities within their community because they believe that clients may harm them, that the neighborhood will deteriorate, and that they will be forced to sell their property for less than it is worth. While these claims have not been substantiated, residents may resort to adopting zoning ordinances that prohibit the location of treatment facilities within their communities.

The United States has no official social policy for families and children, largely because of the belief that families should be relatively free from governmental intervention. In the United States, a variety of policies govern family relations; some of these laws are used to intervene in cases of child abuse and neglect. Child abuse was not *discovered* in the United States until the 1960s when pediatric radiologists began looking for the cause of bone fractures and other unexplained traumas suffered by children. Prior to that time, punishment of children was considered a parental right.

Children whose parents were incapable of caring for them were often sent to institutions to learn appropriate societal values, but parents were not the focus of services. Today, public social service agencies are largely responsible for intervening in cases of neglect and abuse and for providing services to abusive parents.

The most important legislation that recognizes the social service needs of the elderly is the Older Americans Act of 1965. The act emphasizes a variety of services for the elderly, including nutrition programs and services that increase the ability of the elderly to remain in the community. The Administration on Aging is the federal agency that is primarily responsible for administering this act and it does so by determining the needs of America's elderly and by encouraging states and communities to provide services that address these needs. In order to make sure that these services are effective, older citizens must be made aware that a network of services is available to them within their communities.

Some attempts to evaluate the effectiveness of social services have produced positive results, while others have been unclear about the benefits of social services. There are political and methodological obstacles to conducting program evaluations, but policy makers, social-service providers, and program evaluators can work together to develop better methods of assessing the effectiveness of social services.

NOTES

1. This paragraph relies on Alfred J. Kahn, *Social Policy and Social Services* (New York: Random House, 1979), pp. 12–13.
2. See Robert Morris, *Social Policy of the American Welfare State: An Introduction to Policy Analysis* (New York: Harper & Row, 1979), p. 120.
3. Department of Health, Education and Welfare, *First Annual Report to Congress on Title XX of the Social Security Act* (Washington, D.C., 1977), p. 1.
4. Ibid., p. 376.
5. John L. Palmer and Isabel V. Sawhill, eds., *The Reagan Record* (Cambridge, Mass.: Ballinger, 1984), p. 375.
6. David Mechanic, *Mental Health and Social Policy*, 3rd ed. (Englewood Cliffs, N.J.: Prentice-Hall, 1989), Chapter 2.
7. Carl A. Taube and Sally A. Barrett, *Mental Health, United States 1985* (Washington, D.C.: U.S. Department of Health and Human Services, National Institute on Mental Health, 1985).
8. Alcohol, Drug Abuse, and Mental Health Administration, *ADAMHA NEWS*, vol. XV, no. 2 (March-April 1989), p. 2.
9. Department of Health and Human Services, National Institute on Drug Abuse, *National Trends in Drug Use and Related Factors among American High School Students and Young Adults, 1975–1986* (Washington, D.C., 1987).
10. Taube and Barrett, *Mental Health, United States 1985*.
11. *ADAMHA NEWS*, vol. XV, no. 2, p. 2.
12. *ADAMHA NEWS*, vol. XV, no. 4 (June 1989), p. 7.
13. Mechanic, *Mental Health and Social Policy*, p. 83.
14. Ibid.
15. Ibid.
16. Gerald N. Grob, *The State and the Mentally Ill: A History of Worcester State Hospital in Massachusetts, 1830–1920* (Chapel Hill, N.C.: University of North Carolina Press, 1966), cited in Mechanic, *Mental Health and Social Policy*, p. 53.
17. Mechanic, *Mental Health and Social Policy*, p. 96.
18. See ibid., pp. 86–87, for a discussion of these psychiatric screenings.
19. Ibid., pp. 96–97.

20. Clara Claiborne Park with Leon N. Shapiro, *You are Not Alone: Understanding and Dealing with Mental Illness–A Guide for Patients, Doctors, and Other Professionals* (Boston: Little, Brown, 1976), pp. 93–94.
21. Department of Health and Human Services, *Report of the Administrator, Alcohol, Drug Abuse, and Mental Health Administration, 1980* (Washington, D.C., 1981).
22. Margot Hornblower, "Not in My Backyard, You Don't," *Time* (June 27, 1988), pp. 44–45.
23. The remainder of this paragraph relies on Pat Harbolt, "The Fight against Community Programs," *Access: A Human Services Magazine 4*, no. 4 (State of Florida: Department of Health and Rehabilitative Services, February '81/March '81), pp. 14–18.
24. This paragraph relies on Harbolt; quote is from p. 18.
25. For a description of these programs, see Department of Health, Education and Welfare, *Report on Federal Government Programs That Relate to Children, 1979*, prepared by the representatives of the Federal Interagency Committee on the International Year of the Child, no. (OHDS) 79–30180.
26. This section relies on Stephen J. Pfohl, "The Discovery of Child Abuse," *Social Problems 24*, no. 3 (February 1977), pp. 310–23.
27. "Bush to Request $2.4 Billion in New FY '89 Spending," *Congressional Quarterly* (February 25, 1989), p. 379.
28. *Highlights of Official Aggregate Child Neglect and Abuse Reporting, 1987* (Denver, Col.: The American Humane Association, 1989).
29. U.S. Department of Health and Human Services, National Center on Child Abuse and Neglect, *Study Findings, Study of National Incidence and Prevalence of Child Abuse and Neglect: 1988*, Washington, D.C., 1988.
30. Ibid., p. 7–1.
31. Alice A. Lieberman and Helaine Hornby, eds., *Professional Social Work Practice in Public Child Welfare, An Agenda for Action* (Portland, ME: University of Southern Maine, 1987).
32. Ibid.; also see Michel McQueen, "Family Crisis, Foster Care System is Strained as Reports of Child Abuse Mount," *The Wall Street Journal* (June 15, 1987), pp. 1, 18; and Clare Ansberry, "Desperate Straits," *The Wall Street Journal* (January 5, 1987), pp. 1 and 10.
33. Deborah Mesce, "Crisis in Child Welfare Outlined," *Austin American-Statesman* (December 12, 1989), p. A9.
34. This section relies on Linda Hubbard Getze, "Need Help? What the Aging Network Can Do for You," *Modern Maturity* (March 1981), pp. 33–36.
35. U.S. National Center for Health Statistics, *Vital Statistics of the United States: 1973 Life Tables* (Rockville, MD.: U.S. Department of Health, Education and Welfare, 1975), cited in Mario Tonti and Barbara Silverstone, "Services to Families of the Elderly," in Abraham Monk, ed., *Handbook of Gerontological Services* (New York: Van Nostrand Reinhold Co., 1985), pp. 211–39. See also Lynn Osterkamp, "Family Caregivers: America's Primary Long-Term Care Resource," *Aging*, no. 358 (1988), pp. 3–5.
36. Janet Hook, "Congress Clears $4 Billion Bill for Elderly Services, Nutrition," *Congressional Quarterly* (September 29, 1984), p. 2408.
37. See Joint hearing before the Select Committee on Aging and the Subcommittee on Human Services of the Select Committee on Aging, House of Representatives, 101st Congress, *1991 White House Conference on Aging: Options and Strategies* (June 26, 1989).
38. Paragraphs on guardianship rely on Fred Bayles and Scott McCartney, *Guardians of the Elderly, An Ailing System*, a six-part Associated Press series appearing in the *Austin American-Statesman* (September 20–25, 1987), Section A.
39. Art Garcia and Chris Barnett, " 'Strange' Titles Are Tomorrow's Reality," *Austin American-Statesman* (January 30, 1989), Business section, p. 16.
40. Morris, *Social Policy of the American Welfare State*, p. 133.
41. Ibid., p. 150.
42. See, for example, Andrew W. Dobelstein with Ann B. Johnson, *Serving Older Adults: Policy, Programs and Professional Activities* (Englewood Cliffs, N.J.: Prentice Hall, 1985), p. 125; and Sheila B. Kamerman and Alfred J. Kahn, *Privatization and the Welfare State* (Princeton, N.J.: Princeton University Press, 1989), p. 10.
43. See Lucy D. Ozarin, "Community Mental Health: Does It Work? Review of the Evaluation Literature," in Walter E. Barton and Charlotte J. Sanborn, eds., *An Assessment of the Community Mental Health Movement* (Lexington, Mass.: D.C. Heath, 1977), pp. 122–23.
44. Marsha Mailick Seltzer and Leonard M. Bloksberg, "Permanency Planning and Its Effects on Foster Children: A Review of the Literature," *Social Work* (January-February, 1987), pp. 65–68. For an

extensive review of evaluations of the various types of child welfare services, see Alfred Kadushin and Judith A. Martin, *Child Welfare Services*, 4th ed. (New York: Macmillan Publishing Co., 1988).
45. Lynn Videka-Sherman, *Harriett M. Bartlett Practice Effectiveness Project, Report to NASW Board of Directors*, National Association of Social Workers, Silver Springs, MD., July 10, 1985.

8

FIGHTING HUNGER
Nutrition Programs in the United States

The pictures of Ethiopians, their bodies reduced to flesh over bones, continue to make clear to us the dire consequences of starvation. It is frightening to know that every day thirty-five thousand people around the world die from such problems.[1] Americans shocked by media accounts of famine have responded with an outpouring of aid. Although food is abundant and starvation is rare in the United States, the poor, including the ranks of the new homeless, often face the uncertainty of not knowing where their next meal is coming from. As a result, some Americans suffer from such serious problems of undernutrition as anemia.[2] Another important term in understanding adequate health is malnutrition—"an impairment or risk of impairment to mental or physical health resulting from failure to meet the total nutrient requirements of an individual."[3] But it has been suggested that in the United States individuals "should be considered malnourished if for economic or other reasons beyond their control, they experience repetitive periods of hunger, even though their total intake of nutrients is sufficient to protect them from symptoms of deficiency disease."[4] There is as yet no acceptable definition of hunger used in public policy.[5] Some health experts have suggested that to rectify this problem, hunger should be redefined by using a policy goal of *food security*. According to this goal, all Americans should "have access to nutritionally adequate food from normal food channels."[6] Don't most people obtain their food from "normal channels"—from grocery stores, restaurants, or even directly from farmers or their own gardens? Food sources considered not normal are trash bins, soup kitchens, and food pantries.[7] Yet these sources are being used by many Americans each day.

Actually, most Americans consume about the same amount of nutrients daily, but this does not necessarily mean that their diets meet the Recommended Daily Allowances (RDAs) for the various nutrients established by the United States Department of Agriculture (USDA). For example, in one of its more recent studies, the USDA considered the nutrition of women and young children from low, medium, and high income groups, and it found that no group of children received enough zinc and iron, but they got enough of all other nutrients.[8] All groups of women were above the RDAs for six of the nutrients studied, but they were deficient in six other nutrients, and low-income women were also deficient in Vitamin E. However, *patterns* of eating are more important then counting grams of protein or other numbers on the backs of food packages.[9] For example, poor individuals may eat adequately at the beginning of the month, but when food stamps or AFDC and SSI checks run out near the end of the month, eating habits may change. Or the poor may have to decide between buying more food or paying other bills. Other patterns are also important. Children may get their main source of nutrition at school, with less to eat at home. The poor elderly may have difficulty getting to the store or may not have teeth with which to chew food. In achieving a national goal of food security, the questions faced today are not how to produce enough food, but how to see that everyone has access to an adequate diet. Issues of the organization and administration of food programs are of concern, but the more important question of who should receive benefits stands in the way of a rational nutrition policy.

EARLY POLICIES: COMMODITY FOOD DISTRIBUTION

Prior to the 1930s, states and communities used their own methods to feed their *deserving* poor, but with the advent of the Great Depression, more and more people were unable to obtain enough food to eat. They stood in bread lines or waited in soup kitchens to obtain their only means of survival. These methods of feeding the hungry were clearly inadequate for meeting the country's needs. In 1933, Congress established the Federal Surplus Relief Corporation to provide surplus commodity foods—as well as coal, mattresses, and blankets—to the poor.[10] Overproduction of food and encouragement by farmers to purchase surplus goods helped prompt the federal government to address the nutritional needs of the poor. As a result, the Federal Surplus Relief Corporation provided as much relief to the agricultural industry as it did to the hungry.[11] The early commodity distribution program was characterized by recipients waiting in long lines to receive food, an experience which some public officials believed was degrading.[12]

There were other problems with the commodity food distribution program. Perishables were difficult to preserve, and alternatives to helping the hungry were sorely needed. As a solution, the nation embarked on its first Food Stamp program in

1939. The program used two types of stamps, blue and orange. Orange stamps could be used to purchase any type of food; blue stamps could be redeemed only for surplus commodities. For every dollar spent on orange stamps, the beneficiary received fifty cents worth of blue stamps free.[13] Four years later, in 1943, the program ended. The American Enterprise Institute for Public Policy Research believes the program was terminated for three reasons:

1. Families who were poor but who were not receiving other public assistance payments were not eligible to receive assistance.
2. Widespread participation was discouraged by purchase requirements which were believed to be too high.
3. Products other than surplus foods were sometimes purchased with the free stamps.[14]

These factors contributed to the early demise of the program.

The country again turned to the commodity food distribution method. Commodity distribution was a popular method for providing food to the poor for at least two reasons. First, it insured that surplus foods would be utilized. Second, the poor were given foods which were supposed to meet minimum nutritional requirements. But the new commodity food distribution program left unsolved many problems of the original commodity program. Food preservation remained a problem; large containers of food were inconvenient for use by small families; and some foods were unappealing.

Alternatives to commodity distribution were debated until 1961 when President John F. Kennedy was able to begin a new Food Stamp program on a pilot basis. There was some early evidence that recipients purchased more and better foods under the program. This provided encouragement for passage of the Food Stamp Act of 1964.[15] The illustration on page 168 further describes America's concerns about nutrition.

THE FOOD STAMP PROGRAM

The Food Stamp program is the responsibility of the United States Department of Agriculture (USDA), but state and local welfare agencies certify eligible recipients and provide them with the stamps. Recipients are given an allotment of stamps based on their income and family size. The stamps or food coupons, like money, come in various denominations and may be exchanged for food products in regular retail stores that choose to accept the coupons, and many do. In fact, some stores display large signs that say, "We accept food coupons." Eligibility requirements and coupon allotments for the food stamp program are established at the federal level and are the same throughout the country.

The Food Stamp program was originally designed to be broader than the commodity distribution program. The states were to give food stamps to any individuals whose income prevented them from acquiring an adequate diet. This meant that those who were not welfare recipients but whose incomes were low (the near-poor) could also qualify.[16]

ILLUSTRATION: POLITICS DISCOVERS AND REDISCOVERS HUNGER

In his book, *Let Them Eat Promises: The Politics of Hunger in America,* Nick Kotz provided the following description of one Mississippi family: "Hunger in America was conceived as a national issue in April 1967 by two northern senators in an alien rural South. On a mission guided by politics, they came to study poverty programs, but in the small Delta town of Cleveland, Mississippi, they found more than they had bargained for.

"The United States Senator from New York felt his way through a dark windowless shack, fighting nausea at the strong smell of aging mildew, sickness, and urine. In the early afternoon shadows, he saw a child sitting on the floor of a tiny back room. Barely two years old, wearing only a filthy undershirt, she sat rubbing several grains of rice round and round on the floor. The senator knelt beside her.

"'Hello...Hi...Hi, baby...' he murmured, touching her cheeks and her hair as he would his own child's. As he sat on the dirty floor, he placed his hand gently on the child's swollen stomach. But the little girl sat as if in a trance, her sad eyes turned downward, and rubbed the gritty rice.

"For five minutes he tried: talking, caressing, tickling, poking—demanding that the child respond. The baby never looked up.

"The senator made his way to the front yard where Annie White, the mother of the listless girl and five other children, stood washing her family's clothes in a zinc tub. She had no money, she was saying to the other senator, couldn't afford to buy food stamps; she was feeding her family only some rice and biscuits made from leftover surplus commodities.

"For a few moments Robert F. Kennedy stood alone, controlling his feelings, which were exposed to the press entourage waiting outside the house. Then he whispered to a companion, 'I've seen bad things in West Virginia, but I've never seen anything like this anywhere in the United States.'

"Senators Kennedy of New York and Joseph Clark of Pennsylvania discovered hunger that day, raw hunger embedded in the worst poverty the black South had known since the Depression of the 1930s. Driving along muddy, forgotten roads, the two senators and their aides stopped at shack after shack to see with their own eyes hungry, diseased children; to hear with their own ears the poor describe their struggle for survival."[a]

At the same time that political figures such as Robert F. Kennedy were discovering hunger, others were also investigating the problem. The Field Foundation, supported by the Field family of Chicago's Marshall Field department store, also documented the problems of eating, or not eating, in America.[b] Ten years later, in 1977, the Field Foundation conducted a follow-up study. The findings showed that there were fewer cases of malnutrition. And the doctors who conducted the study, four of whom had conducted the original 1967 study, suggested that federal food programs were responsible for much of the difference.[c]

But social problems reappear, and the 1980s brought with them new charges of hunger in America. Increased unemployment and social program cuts were blamed. Concerned that reports of hunger were exaggerated,[d] the President's Task Force on Food Assistance was appointed, and its findings were published in 1984. It concluded that

[a]Nick Kotz, *Let Them Eat Promises: The Politics of Hunger in America* (Englewood Cliffs, N.J.: Prentice-Hall, 1969), pp. 1–2.

[b]Ibid, pp. 7–9.

[c]Nick Kotz, *Hunger in America: The Federal Response* (New York: Field Foundation, 1979), p. 9.

[d]"Hunger Reports Prompt Food Aid Expansion," *Congressional Quarterly Almanac 1983,* p. 412.

undernutrition was *not* a problem. Social-action groups lambasted the report. The president of the National Association of Social Workers called it a "political document that has not treated the problem of deprivation in this country in the objective manner that it deserves."[e] And nutrition experts said, "Despite their almost total lack of qualifications, the task force members did manage to find that hunger has reappeared in America. But because of their ineptitude, they were unable to qualify its extent, or to discern the presence of chronic malnutrition."[f]

Meanwhile, the Food Research and Action Center publicized results of its work, which indicated that infant mortality rates had increased in some areas of the country due to nutritional deficiencies; the Citizens' Commission on Hunger in New England also concluded that malnutrition and hunger again confronted America. The President's Task Force on Food Assistance recommended

block grants to the states to fund nutrition programs; it also recommended that states be penalized for failing to lower error rates in the Food Stamp program. Meanwhile, the Citizens' Commission proposed quarterly reporting to Congress on efforts to reduce hunger, as well as the formation of a bipartisan commission to develop legislation that would put hunger to rest.

Another study group, the Physicians Task Force on Hunger in America, identified 150 "hunger counties" in the U.S.—counties in which substantial numbers of poor people were not receiving food stamps. In order to reduce hunger, the physicians recommended increasing food stamp benefits, giving cash or credit cards to recipients to reduce the embarrassment of using coupons, improving outreach efforts to nonparticipants, and simplifying the entire process of obtaining food benefits.[g]

[e]"Report on Hunger Overlooks Role of Cuts," *NASW News* (February 1984), p. 19.

[f]Jean Mayer and Jeanne Goldberg, "New Report Documents Hunger in America," *Tallahassee Democrat* (March 29, 1984), p. 16E.

[g]James Pinkerton, "Overhaul of Food Stamp Program Advised to Bypass Bureaucracy," *Austin American-Statesman* (May 21, 1986), p. A9; and Physicians Task Force on Hunger in America, *Hunger in America: The Growing Epidemic* (Middletown, Conn.: Wesleyan University Press, 1985), Chap. 7.

At first, the program worked like this. The USDA determined the minimum amount individuals and families of different sizes needed to eat adequately (see the illustration entitled, "The Thrifty Food Plan"). Those who qualified for benefits paid for their food stamps on a sliding scale based on their income. Those with very little or no income received the stamps free, while those with higher incomes paid an amount that was not to exceed 30 percent of their income. It was assumed that the average family devoted 30 percent of its income to food (and as explained in greater detail in Chapter 3, the poverty level is calculated by multiplying by three the minimum amount needed by families of various sizes to acquire an adequate diet). The difference between the amount paid and the total value of the stamps was called the *bonus*.

"In theory," says one observer, "the food stamp plan *sounded* simple and workable, and should have been an enormous improvement over commodity distribution," but what really happened was "extortion."[17]

It was no accident that the stamp payment formula produced the outcries "We can't afford the stamps" and "The stamps run out after two weeks." Following their congressional leaders' twin desires of helping the farmers but not providing welfare to the poor,

Agricultural Department bureaucrats had designed a Food Stamp program so conservative that reformers called the plan "Scrooge stamps."[18]

A number of changes were made in the Food Stamp program in the 1970s that remain in place today. Benefits were increased, and eligibility and application procedures were standardized so that applicants would be treated similarly regardless of where they lived or applied for stamps. In addition, unemployed adult recipients capable of holding jobs became responsible for registering for work and accepting employment if a "suitable" job could be found.

A troublesome requirement was that recipients had to buy all the stamps to which they were entitled at one time. This requirement was modified so that a portion, rather than all the stamps, could be purchased. Efforts were made to increase program participation through advertising campaigns and outreach. Communities were not immediately forced to choose between Food Stamps and commodity distribution. They could operate both programs until 1973 when Food Stamps had to be the official program of all communities.

Eliminating the Purchase Requirement—Increasing Participation

The most significant change in the Food Stamp program came in 1977 when the purchase requirement was eliminated. Critics held that the program had not necessarily made eating better or easier for the poor. For many, the cost of the food stamps was more than they could afford. Ending the purchase requirement helped to increase participation by eliminating the need to put up cash to receive the stamps. In the Southeast, the Mountain Plains, and the Southwest, participation rose slightly more than 30 percent. These areas include many of the poorer, largely rural states. In New England, participation increases were more modest—7 percent.[19]

But participation rates continue to remain well below the number of people estimated to be eligible. It is likely that fifteen million people,[20] or between 40 to 60 percent of eligible households, do not receive the stamps.[21] The following explanations are continually cited as reasons for low participation—the stigma of "being on welfare," the lack of knowledge of the program because outreach is no longer emphasized, and the inability to get to the Food Stamp office to apply.[22] The General Accounting Office has added to the list of criticisms. Blaming low participation on "increased emphasis on determining eligibility," it cited obstacles such as "limited office hours, unnecessary screening forms, failure to help applicants obtain necessary documents...and failure to consider applicants for expedited benefits."[23] In some cases, particularly those in which the amount of benefits to be received is small, the cumbersome application process just may not be worth the hassle.

Participants and Costs

About nineteen million people, or 8 percent of all Americans, receive food stamps each month, but this is two to three million fewer than the number who received them in 1980 and 1981 when poverty rates were about the same as they are today (see Figure 8-1).[24] More whites than blacks receive assistance, but blacks are disproportionately represented among the total since their risk of being poor is greater. AFDC families are generally eligible for food stamps, and many SSI recipients are also eligible; but unlike AFDC, adults without children may qualify, and unlike SSI, disability and old age are not requirements for receiving benefits. Since Food Stamps is a public assistance program, recipients must meet a means test. *Gross* income cannot exceed 130 percent of the official poverty line ($1,376 a month for a family of four in 1990), and *net* income cannot exceed 100 percent of the poverty line. In determining payments, certain income disregards are applied. Twenty percent of earned income is disregarded along with a flat amount of $106. Allowances for housing and child-care expenses while a parent works or seeks employment are made. Medical expenses for aged and disabled individuals are also deducted. Disposable assets cannot exceed $2,000 except for those who are at least 60 years old; they may have $3,000.

Some special categories of people can receive stamps. Victims of natural disasters may qualify. Those who live in nonprofit facilities, for example, alcoholics and drug addicts in halfway houses, the homeless or battered women in shelters, and disabled and elderly individuals in group homes, may also be eligible. Students used to find it easier to qualify for stamps, but tougher work requirements have made it more difficult to do so.

In 1965, the bonus value of stamps was $32 million. By 1970, it reached $551 million, and by 1980 it had escalated to $9 billion. In 1987, these costs were approximately $10.5 billion.[25] (See Figure 8–1.) Despite its limitations, the Food Stamp program has come closer to providing for all those in need than most other welfare programs.

FIGURE 8.1   Food Stamp Program, Bonus Value of Stamps and Number of Participants, 1962–1987

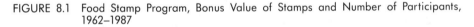

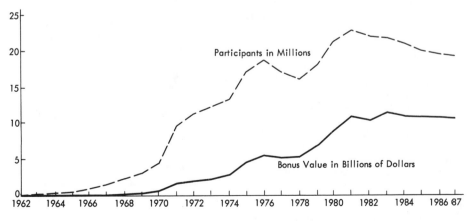

Source: U.S. Department of Agriculture, Food and Nutrition Service, *Social Security Bulletin, Annual Statistical Supplement, 1988*, p. 336.

ILLUSTRATION: THE THRIFTY FOOD PLAN—WHAT'S IT WORTH?

Periodically, the USDA calculates four different types of food plans called thrifty, low-cost, moderate-cost, and liberal-cost. As you might expect, the Thrifty Food Plan (TFP), the most economical of the four, is used to determine food stamp benefits. The TFP for a family of four is based on a prototype family of two adults, ages 20 to 54, and two children, one who is aged 6 to 8, the other aged 9 to 11. A family of four receives food stamps at this level, regardless of the age of the actual family members and regardless of any special dietary needs. The monthly food stamp allotment for a family of four with no countable income in 1990 was $331, $82.75 per week, or about 92 cents per person per meal. As countable income rises, 30 percent of it is deducted from the base payment of $331 per month. For example, a family of four whose countable income is $400 per month receives $211. Since its inception, complaints have been that the TFP is less than adequate, falling short of the RDAs for some nutrients.[a] The TFP was improved in 1983, and the House Committee on Agriculture addressed criticisms stating that "although not ideal, it theoretically provides the basis of a nutritionally adequate diet."[b] The committee did concede that the TFP falls short of providing the RDAs for some nutrients such as zinc and folacin. But it claims that this is not proof of the TFP's inadequacy since "by definition most Americans do not require daily the amounts of all nutrients listed in the RDAs"; it also reminds us that many Americans fail to eat properly even with the necessary resources.[c] The

USDA contends that it could develop even lower-cost plans, "but they would be very monotonous and less like families' food consumption practices and preferences.[d] The Physicians Task Force on Hunger believes that the TFP "was never intended to meet family nutrition requirements."[e] It stated:

> [T]he Department [of Agriculture] has *never* determined that this computerized plan represents an adequate expenditure level to achieve desirable nutrition levels.

> The thrifty food plan is an example of bureaucracy gone awry. A federal expenditure level was set, and a computer was programmed to design a food plan equal to that level—irrespective of human need.[f]

Regardless of the adequacy of the TFP, virtually everyone would agree that it takes a pretty careful shopper to feed a family of four on the plan. Many factors affect an individual's or a family's ability to use the food stamp allotment as efficiently as possible. Although benefits are indexed to reflect inflation, the adjustments in payments are made *after* the costs of food have increased. This lag has some negative effect on the amount of food that can be purchased. A number of states impose a sales tax on food purchases. Food stamp recipients are not exempt from these taxes, and this further reduces their buying power. One study found that households that followed TFP menus spent an average of 3.5 hours per day preparing meals, compared with less than 2 hours for homemakers in other studies.[g] Weekly sample

[a]Harrison Donnelly, "Congress to Decide Fate of Food Stamps," *Congressional Quarterly* (February 7, 1981), p. 278.

[b]Subcommittee on Domestic Marketing, Consumer Relations and Nutrition Committee on Agriculture, U.S. House of Representatives, *A Review of the Thrifty Food Plan and Its Use in the Food Stamp Program* (April 1985), p. viii.

[c]Ibid.

[d]Brenda Schuler, "Making Food Dollars Count," *Food and Nutrition 13,* no. 3 (July 1983), pp. 16–19.

[e]Physicians Task Force on Hunger in America, *Hunger in America: The Growing Epidemic* (Middletown, Conn.: Wesleyan University Press, 1985), p. 106.

[f]Ibid, p. 134.

[g]*A Review of the Thrifty Food Plan.*

menus (see Figure 8–2) are produced by the Department of Agriculture to guide recipients in staying within the food stamp budget.

In the late 1970s, one researcher set out to determine if food stamp shoppers differed from other shoppers in Cookeville, Tennessee.[h] He found that food stamp shoppers were less likely to prepare shopping lists. They shopped in small, nearby stores rather than in supermarkets. They seemed less concerned

[h]Gerald Underwood Skelly, "A Study of the Differential Food Purchasing Behavior of Federal Stamp Recipients and Non-Subsidized Food Purchasers" (Dissertation, Florida State University, 1978).

about price, but did buy in larger quantities. But we cannot necessarily blame these individuals for their shopping habits. They may have less access to information about sales and other shopping values. They are less likely to own automobiles, which prevents them from taking advantage of sales at stores far from their homes. The smaller convenience stores and "mom and pop" operations located in neighborhoods offer less selection at higher prices, and some large chains that once operated in inner cities have moved with the wealthier to the suburbs.[i]

[i]Rep. Mike Espy, cited in *Hunger Action Forum*, vol. 1, no. 7 (March 1988).

NUTRITION PROGRAMS FOR YOUNGER AND OLDER AMERICANS

The Food Stamp program serves people of all ages, but some nutrition programs are targeted to those in particular age groups. For example, the National School Lunch Act, which became law in 1946, allows children to obtain hot lunches at reduced prices or free if their parents are unable to pay. The program operates in the following way: The federal government, through the Food and Nutrition Service of the USDA, provides cash assistance and food commodities to state departments of education. These departments then distribute the funds and food to participating public and private not-for-profit schools. Free lunches are given to children whose family income is not more than 130 percent of the poverty line, and reduced-price lunches are available to those with family incomes between 130 and 185 percent of the poverty level. In 1987, nearly two billion free or reduced price lunches were served. Twenty-four million children (down from 26.6 million in 1980 and 25.8 million in 1981) received lunches at a cost to the federal government of $2.8 billion. In effect, because of the federal government's participation, the costs of meals for all school children, regardless of income, are subsidized.[26]

Figures on the number of children served sound impressive, but they might be more impressive if we could be certain that the bulk of benefits went to poor children. Historically, there has been concern that many of the benefits have gone to nonpoor children.[27] For example, schools had to have kitchen facilities to participate, and schools in poor neighborhoods often did not. Meals to these schools could have been catered, but school lunch administrators had been known to lobby against earmarking federal funds for free meals to poor children for fear that private caterers would take their jobs. The administrators contended that they could take care of poor children with general federal school lunch aid; yet criticisms were that they provided free lunches to only half of the children that needed them.[28] These are not just problems of yesteryear. For example, schools on Indian reservations may still not be allowed to

FIGURE 8–2 One Week's Menus for a Mother and Three Children Receiving Food Stamps

SUNDAY	MONDAY	TUESDAY	WEDNESDAY	THURSDAY	FRIDAY	SATURDAY
Grapefruit sections (1 can) Scrambled eggs (3) Cinnamon toast (6 sl)	Orange (2) quarters Ready-to-eat cereal (6 oz) Toast (5 sl)	Orange juice (2 c) Farina (3/4 c dry) Coffee cake (1/2)	Bananas (2) Ready-to-eat cereal (6 oz) Toast (5 sl) with peanut butter (4 T)	Apple (2) wedges Pancakes* Syrup (6 T) Pork sausage (1/2 lb)	Pear (1) slices Ready-to-eat cereal (6 oz) Biscuits (8)	Orange juice (2 c) Pork sausage (1/2 lb) Grits (1 c dry) Muffins (6)
Quick macaroni and cheese* Creole beans* Toast (6 sl)	Peanut butter-banana sandwiches* Celery sticks (3/4 c) Chocolate pie (1/2)	Pork and cabbage soup* Toasted cornbread (1/2) Oatmeal cookies*	Frankfurters on rolls (4) Potato salad*	Turkey noodle soup* Biscuits* (8) Pear (2) quarters	Peanut butter-vegetable sandwiches* Apples (2) Rice pudding*	Egg salad (3 eggs, 2 T celery, 1 T onion, 1 T salad dressing) sandwiches (4) Kidney bean salad*
Roast pork with gravy* Mixed vegetables Baked potatoes (1 1/3 lb) Bread (5 sl) Chocolate pie* (1/2)	Sweet-sour pork* Rice (3/4 c dry) Green beans Cornbread* (1/2)	Spinach lasagna* Garlic rolls (4) (use hot dog rolls) Orange fluff*	Braised turkey with gravy* Vegetable fried rice* Bread (5 sl) Peach cobbler*	Bean tamale pie* Toast (6 sl) Cottage cheese (1 c) with orange (2) sections Quick bread (4 sl)	Turkey-stuffing casserole with gravy* Mashed potatoes (1 lb) Mixed fruit (2 apples, 1 orange, 1/4 c raisins) Quick bread (4 sl)	Mock hamburger stroganoff with potatoes* Corn and cabbage salad* Bread (5 sl)
Ready-to-eat cereal (6 oz)	Cinnamon coffee cake* (1/2)	Crackers (24) Peanut butter (4 T)	Quick bread (4 sl)	Crackers (24) with cheese (4 1/2 oz) Lemonade (2 c)	Muffins* (6)	Popcorn (1/3 c dry) Lemonade (2 c)

*The USDA provides recipes for these items.

Notes: Amounts of foods that the family is expected to use are shown in parentheses ( ) or in recipes. Beverage is milk for everyone at least once daily. Cookies (9 oz) may be added to meals as an optional dessert.

Source: United States Department of Agriculture, "Making Food Dollars Count: Nutritious Meals at Low Cost," *Home and Garden Bulletin Number 240*, June 1983, p. 1.

participate due to lack of equipment; yet it has been claimed that the federal government has enough of the needed equipment in storage to solve the problem.[29]

During the Reagan administration, a number of attempts, some successful, were made to lower nutrition costs. Few have forgotten the well-publicized argument over whether ketchup should be considered a vegetable in school lunches. There was talk of deducting the value of school meals from families' food stamp allotments, and the president also attempted to eliminate the school lunch subsidies for children from families with incomes greater than 185 percent of the poverty level. The concern that many of the school nutrition benefits still go to middle-class children has persisted during the Bush administration.

The School Breakfast Program, begun in 1966, is much smaller than the lunch program, but it is operated in a similar fashion. Eligibility requirements are the same for free and reduced price breakfasts. In 1987, 3.6 million children received breakfasts at a federal cost of $458 million.[30] But because resources allocated are not sufficient to cover all school districts, a priority system has been established. Schools in the poorest districts and schools to which children must travel a long distance are given preference. While this may be considered a rational approach to allocating scarce resources, the breakfast program has not necessarily operated in a totally rational fashion. School districts must choose to participate. Why would schools decide *not* to participate in a program that would benefit students? First, the program means more administrative responsibilities for school personnel. Second, adoption of the program may mean that teachers and other personnel must monitor the breakfasts, forcing them to come to school earlier since the breakfasts are served before class. These factors may make the program unpopular among those who are already feeling taxed by heavy workloads and who do not want to see the school day lengthened.

There are other programs also designed to provide nutritional benefits to school and preschool children. During vacation periods, the Summer Food program offers lunches to children in especially impoverished areas, and the Child Care Food program provides breakfasts, snacks, lunches, and dinners to children in day care centers. The Special School Milk program began in 1954 when the market was full of surplus dairy products. In 1987, 162 million half-pints of milk were provided at a cost of $15 million.[31] With cutbacks, the program is now restricted to schools and child-care facilities which are not participating in other federal food programs.

The Special Supplemental Nutrition Program for Women, Infants and Children, better known as WIC, began in 1972. WIC is an especially popular social welfare program with Congress. It is intended to upgrade the nutrition of low-income women who are pregnant or breastfeeding and infants and children up to age five who are certified to be at nutritional risk. The relationship between adequate nutrition in pregnancy and lower infant mortality and morbidity rates is clear. In addition, proper nutrition in a child's early years of development is critical in preventing life-threatening illnesses and problems that may affect health throughout the life cycle. According to the Physicians Task Force on Hunger, a number of studies have specifically assessed the impact of WIC on pregnancy outcomes, and all have shown positive results.[32] For example, one researcher reports that "WIC participation is associated with improved pregnancy outcomes, in particular, a 21% decrease in low-birth-weight infants, a major decrease in neonatal mortality, and a 45% reduction in the number of women with inadequate or no prenatal care."[33] Citing another study, he added that, "Participation in WIC is associated with a statistically significant reduction in the poorer outcomes of pregnancy; in particular, with 23% fewer low-birth-weight and very-low-birth weight infants, fewer small-for-gestational-age infants, fewer premature infants, and fewer infant deaths."[34] And other researchers write that when compared with their siblings who did not receive WIC, children whose diet had been supplemented by participation in WIC "showed significant enhancement of most intellectual and behavioral measures in the current home and school setting, including IQ, attention span, visual-motor synthesis, and school grade-point average."[35] Although others have used a more qualified approach in their praise of WIC, saying that its real benefits may be getting pregnant women earlier prenatal care, virtually everyone agrees that the program is effective.[36]

The Food and Nutrition Service of the USDA operates the WIC program in conjunction with fifteen hundred local agencies, mostly health clinics and departments. Foods can be provided directly to participants, but in most cases WIC coupons are used. Participants take the coupons to local grocery stores to purchase specified foods that are high in nutrients, including iron-fortified formula and cereal, eggs, juice, cheese, and milk. The program currently serves 4.5 million women and children at a cost of $2.1 billion.[37] Funding has doubled since 1982. However, it is estimated that as many as 60 percent of those who qualify do not receive assistance because expenditures are not enough to serve all those in need.[38] In 1985, a suit by the National Anti-Hunger Coalition and others charged the federal government with failure to spend all the money appropriated for WIC. Congress resisted Reagan administration attempts to cut the program and instead increased WIC funding. The Bush administration has been supportive of WIC, but the program recently fell on hard times. Severe weather hurt crops, driving up the prices of cereal and orange juice. Faced with having to stretch their WIC dollars further, states were about to drop 280,000 women and children from the program during 1990 and to reduce the amounts given to others. Congress passed an unusual solution to the problem by allowing states to borrow against next year's WIC funding. This helped ease the immediate situation but may create an even bigger problem in the following year. The Commodity Supplemental Food Program is another, but more limited, program for low-income women and children who do not receive WIC but are receiving other welfare benefits.

The elderly have not been forgotten when it comes to nutrition. The Meals-on-Wheels program was established in 1972 as part of a general federal effort to improve the nutrition of the elderly. States receive funding for the program, some of it through the Older Americans Act (see Chapter 7), and coordinate the program through local agencies that see that meals are prepared and delivered to the homebound elderly. In some areas, the amount provided may actually be sufficient for two meals; in other areas, two meals (one hot and another cold to be eaten later) are delivered. A number of Americans volunteer their own lunch hours once or twice a week to make the deliveries. Elderly individuals who receive food stamps can pay for their meals with stamps, and a donation is suggested for those who can afford to pay in cash. Older

Americans can also use food stamps to purchase meals at participating restaurants, a benefit not available to younger food stamp recipients.

Another important type of nutrition program for older people is the congregate meal program which provides meals at sites such as senior citizen centers or churches. This is also a cooperative venture between the Departments of Agriculture and Health and Human Services. In addition to improved nutrition, there is a positive spillover effect from these programs. They provided an opportunity for older Americans, who may be isolated, to maintain contact with others in their community. A visit by the Meals-on-Wheels volunteer also provides a check, in case the elderly individual has become ill or needs other assistance. A visit to the congregate meal site provides an opportunity for socialization. Staff and volunteers may also identify other social service needs of the participants, and a variety of educational opportunities for seniors may be provided at the site.

HOW MUCH WASTE, FRAUD, AND ABUSE IN WELFARE?

Figures on the number of welfare clients who intentionally lie or withhold information in order to receive benefits are difficult to find, and they vary considerably.[39] Some indicate that only a tiny number—less than 1 percent—are reported for possibly committing fraud and that even a smaller number are prosecuted.[40] Others have gone so far as to say that "[W]hile official rates are 3 to 5 percent, professionals frequently estimate that 30 to 50 percent of AFDC cases involve some fraud."[41] Emphasis on detecting fraud has increased over the years. For example, in order to determine whether a person is not reporting or underreporting income from sources such as employment, social insurance, or other public assistance programs, welfare offices now use computer matching to check Internal Revenue Service, Social Security Administration, and other agencies' files.[42]

The increased concern with detecting abuse has even resulted in the development of a group called the United Council on Welfare Fraud which calls itself a national organization representing about 10,000 persons involved in curbing entitlement program fraud.[43] Sometimes citizens call in to report someone they believe to be wrongly receiving benefits. Occasionally, individuals have made multiple welfare applications and received several checks, but the total number of these cases has really never amounted to more than a handful at a time, in spite of media accounts that dramatize the problem. For example, the widely read *Reader's Digest* published an article entitled, "Time to Crack Down on Food-Stamp Fraud," which read, "In Kentucky undercover policemen discover that federal food stamps are being traded for automobiles, drugs and automatic weapons."[44] And a recent newspaper account began with the sentence, "Food stamps are being bartered for everything from crack to birdbaths in the poverty pockets of Dallas."[45] These stories are bound to arouse negative sentiments toward the welfare system whether or not public assistance recipients are to blame.

Other forms of cheating have gained increased attention, such as cases of the elderly transferring assets to their children in order to gain eligibility for long-term care through Medicaid without depleting their savings. Recipients are ineligible if assets have been transferred in the past thirty months.

Other accounts of waste, fraud, and abuse have focused on the vendors of welfare services. Vendors include doctors and other medical professionals who provide care to Medicaid and Medicare patients, food retailers who exchange food stamps for groceries, and landlords who receive rent payments for those who qualify for subsidized housing. It is possible that local grocers might overcharge those food stamp purchasers who are unable to take their business elsewhere, and errors might occur when items not covered by food stamps are incorrectly exchanged for the stamps. Landlords may collect the rent in subsidized housing but fail to make repairs or provide adequate heating. Some of the cases that have received the most media attention are of physicians and health clinic operators who have fraudulently charged Medicare and Medicaid for tests and other services that were never provided to patients.

The issue that has become a real concern for state welfare administrators is error rates. Errors may be attributed in part to welfare administrators and payments workers—the people who process welfare applications and who determine eligibility and the amount of payments clients receive. Some reports suggest that half of all administrative errors are made by caseworkers.[46] Errors such as overpayment and underpayment can be attributed to inadequate job training, failure by workers to understand the complicated eligibility rules, the large number of cases processed, the volume of paperwork per case, miscalculations by workers, and other unintentional or careless mistakes. Clients may misreport, or they may misinterpret questions, which also contributes to errors. But most recipients whose payments are miscalculated are hardly well off.

As a result of concerns about fraud, waste, and abuse, the federal government has applied the concept of *quality control,* which is used in business and industry, to welfare programs.[47] In industry, the term refers to a process whereby a sample of products—cars, for example—are checked or tested to insure that they perform properly. In welfare, quality control refers to the process of taking a sample of cases to insure that welfare recipients are neither receiving too much nor too little. Sampling is based on scientific techniques to assure that the cross section of cases reviewed truly represents the range of recipients.

The federal government sets the standards and procedures for quality control, and the state welfare agencies actually review and investigate the cases by interviewing clients and verifying records such as rent receipts and paycheck stubs. In any system which serves large numbers of people, some error is bound to occur. The federal government, however, believes that only a certain amount of error is acceptable or tolerable. Error-tolerance levels were set at 3 percent in the AFDC and Medicaid programs and at 5 percent in the Food Stamp program. In 1984, actual national error rates were 8.6 in the Food Stamp program, 6 percent in the AFDC program, and 2.7 in the Medicaid program.[48] When a state's error rates exceed tolerance levels, it is required to take steps to correct the problem.

The USDA's program to curb fraud and abuse is euphemistically called Operation Awareness. In 1987, only three states had met error tolerance rates in the Food Stamp program for any period of time, and state administrators bitterly complained that a 5 percent error rate in a program as complex as food stamps, in which federal directives change frequently, was unrealistic.[49] The federal government assessed the states millions of dollars for error rates considered to be too high, but only a small fraction of the money was ever collected because states contested the fines. The General Accounting Office urged the states to recoup overpayments from recipients,[50] but instead the states called for modifications in the quality control system.[51] Congress relented and forgave millions of dollars in state penalties through an AFDC *amnesty provision*. It also modified the quality control system. As of fiscal year 1991, the error tolerance rate for the AFDC program will be either 4 percent or the national average, whichever is higher.

Government officials have been criticized for focusing on overpayments and on keeping ineligibles off the rolls rather than showing more concern for those who have been unjustly denied benefits. Warnings about misreporting information on welfare applications and notices posted in some welfare offices have been called intimidation tactics designed to keep people from applying at all.[52] The government has also been criticized for paying excessive attention to sniffing out errors in public assistance at a time when deregulation of other industries has resulted in massive problems such as the collapse of many savings and loan institutions, not to mention the scandals in the securities industry. And, it is unlikely that fraud and errors in public welfare would ever match the money lost in tax avoidance and evasion by the non-poor. As one economist concluded in a major book on social welfare programs, most individuals "are simply unaware of how little waste, fraud, and abuse there is in the public welfare system."[53]

NUTRITIONAL POLITICS

The early commodity distribution programs were closely tied to federal agricultural policy. The U.S. government purchased agricultural products to guarantee a minimum income for farmers; the distribution of these products from federal stockpiles to the poor was viewed as a means of disposing of food surpluses. The federal government's commodity distribution programs had the support of the powerful farm lobby, the American Farm Bureau Federation, and the nation's farmers.

The current Food Stamp program, initiated in 1964, was also tied to agricultural policy—at least in its early years. The Food Stamp program began as a modest part of the activities of the U.S. Department of Agriculture. Initially, the program had the support of farmers and of organizations that viewed the program as a means of increasing the demand for farm goods. But by the mid-1970s, the Food Stamp program had outgrown all other farm programs and was on its way to becoming a multibillion-dollar enterprise. The Food Stamp program eventually grew much larger than all other programs of the U.S. Department of Agriculture. Agriculture interests came to believe that the Food Stamp program was not directly linked to farm prices, farmers' incomes, and farm surpluses; the stamps were used for a wide variety of packaged foods sold at retail stores. At the same time, U.S. farmers began to acquire major markets for surplus foods in foreign trade. Indeed, by 1980 nearly half of all U.S. farm products were sold in international markets. Farmers became less dependent on federal purchases of surpluses. Thus, the Food Stamp program lost an important political base—farmers and farm organizations.

The older of the major welfare programs—for example, AFDC (formerly Aid to Dependent Children) and SSI (formerly Old Age Assistance, Aid to the Blind, and Aid to the Permanently and Totally Disabled)—are *cash* assistance programs. The newer welfare programs—for example, Food Stamps and Medicaid—are *in-kind* programs. According to one poverty researcher, the bulk of welfare is now provided through in-kind rather than cash assistance programs. At the beginning of the 1960s, about 90 percent of benefits were paid in cash; only 10 percent were in-kind. Today, 70 percent of all benefits are in-kind, and only 30 percent are distributed in cash.[54] Why are the benefits of newer welfare programs administered differently from older welfare programs?

It might be argued that *cashing-out*—administering all welfare programs on a cash basis—would be more efficient. AFDC and SSI recipients who qualify for food stamps would simply have their checks increased as a more efficient means of providing nutritional benefits. While the use of food stamps does allow recipients greater choice of food products than commodity distribution, the use of stamps is still stigmatizing to recipients as they stand in grocery store checkout lines. Even the new *welfare credit cards*, which increase administrative efficiency, do little to reduce stigma. A cash allowance equal to the value of the stamps would reduce or eliminate stigma and still allow the beneficiary a choice of food products. Other savings and benefits might also result from cashing out. The costs of printing the stamps, transferring, and destroying them—more than $40 million annually—would be eliminated.[55] Concerns about underground markets for selling and trading stamps would also be eliminated.

But the choice of a cash allowance has been rejected. Part of the explanation is found in the nature of in-kind programs. Politicians who allot funds to the poor may believe that the use of stamps will insure a more adequate diet, since the stamps may be legally used only to purchase food. Proponents of the use of stamps believe that this plan reduces the chances that food allowances will be used for other purposes. Most stamps are used for basic food needs. Although we do hear reports of recipients who use stamps to buy "gourmet" food items or who sell the stamps for cash, there is really little evidence to suggest that a cash allowance would not be used to purchase food, and neither cash nor stamps can insure that recipients will purchase the most nutritious foods. In fact, many Americans, rich and poor, need guidance in obtaining a healthy diet.[56]

The Reagan administration attempted to "reform" the Food Stamp program, "to re-focus the program on its original purpose—to insure adequate nutrition for America's needy families."[57] The administration believed that the program grew too large during the 1970s by allowing many families with higher than poverty-level incomes to participate. The result was "to divert the Food Stamp program away from its original purpose toward a generalized income transfer program, regardless of nutritional need."[58] The Reagan reforms included tightening income deductions and income limitations so that only families near or below the poverty line could participate, calculating family income partly on past income rather than on current income alone, and monitoring the program more closely to reduce fraud and error.

In what might be considered one irony of federal food programs, Congress in 1983 directed the Secretary of Agriculture to give surplus foods to emergency food kitchens and similar programs in addition to schools and institutions. The surplus commodities were acquired from price support programs and from farmers who had defaulted on loans. But when surplus cheese was offered, some community-based programs had difficulty taking advantage of it because they lacked administrative funds to transport and store the products.[59] Few people ever thought the country would again resort to the widespread use of soup kitchens that were prevalent during the Great Depression, yet in the 1990s, this is the major source of nutrition for scores of people. The illustration "How People Survive on Leftovers" describes how private citizens and not-for-profit groups intervene when public measures fail to provide for those in need.

ILLUSTRATION: HOW PEOPLE SURVIVE ON LEFTOVERS

At 3 A.M. on a wet, bone-chilling night, Carol Fennelly is grubbing around in a garbage dumpster at the Maryland Wholesale Produce Market, south of Baltimore. Bundled against the cold, she quickly fills four large cardboard boxes with green peppers, then moves to the loading dock. A few words with a merchant yield three cases of blemished tomatoes and some bananas too ripe to make it to a supermarket shelf.

By 4 A.M., Fennelly and two co-workers have enough to fill their van— 15 cases each of broccoli and pears, 12 of tomatoes, four each of peppers and bananas, and a couple of boxes of grapes.

By 10 that morning, the produce has been cleaned and sorted by Fennelly and fellow members of a religious activist group called the Community for Creative Non-Violence. Some 150 needy people are lined up outside its free food pantry in Washington, D.C., soon to receive the recovered produce, along with donated day-old bread, packets of chicken giblets and U.S. government cornmeal. Later, street people may drop in for a cup of coffee and doughnuts to tide them over. Still more produce— salvaged from small truck farms, market loading docks and supermarket dumpsters—will supply an evening meal. Nearly 1,000 men and women are fed here each day.

In the war against hunger, members of small groups such as this one are shock troops on the front lines of a growing national movement to reclaim food for the poor that otherwise would be thrown away.

About a fifth of the food produced in the U.S. is wasted, a federal study revealed. Much is lost or spoiled during storage, transportation and processing, still more during meal preparation and as plate waste. Little is recoverable.

More than $6 billion worth of food at the wholesale and retail level is wasted— or used to be. Recently, the food banks have begun recovering some of this: surplus items, mislabeled goods, food whose shelflife has expired, and marred but edible items. Situated in population centers and equipped with warehouses, freezers, and coolers, the food banks ask large food companies for donations, which they then distribute to soup kitchens, emergency feeding programs and food pantries, as well as to various social welfare agencies.

By asking the agencies to contribute from 5 cents to 12 cents a pound for such goods, the food banks are largely self-supporting. The agencies, which often purchase food at wholesale or retail prices, in turn have a cheap, reliable supply of consumables. And the companies making the food donations are eligible for a tax write-off on the items.

"It's a tremendous idea, and everyone benefits," says Bill Ewing, director of marketing for Second Harvest, a network of 74 food banks. Begun as a small operation in Phoenix in 1967, Second Harvest has expanded nationwide since 1977. Last year, the organization distributed 85 million pounds of food across the U.S.

While food banks are geared to function efficiently by gathering, storing and distributing in large quantities, small neighborhood-based programs also are a vital link in the food chain. It takes little more than desire and hard work to have a significant impact.

In November 1982, Celeste McKinley of Las Vegas went to a garbage dumpster behind a supermarket, seeking waste produce to feed her pet cockatoo. "I couldn't believe what they were throwing away," she recalls. "Most of the food was still attractive and edible but no longer shelf-perfect. It was a terrible waste."

McKinley began soliciting surplus from supermarkets in the city. Today, she operates Gleaners, Inc., a free food pantry furnishing groceries to more than 15,000 needy families a month.

In New York, an organization called City Harvest operates a different type of salvage program, providing the physical link between food supplies and the agencies that need them. Six people, one office, a telephone and two vans net 2 million pounds of surplus food a year from a network of restaurants, bakeries, food suppliers and other sources.

"We have no warehouse—don't need one," says Helen Palit, the founder of City Harvest." The whole thing is done by telephone. Food suppliers have always wanted to give away their surplus, but they never knew where to send it or who would pick it up."

Manhattan is an especially rich resource. On any day, Palit may get donations of 100 pounds of pâté and 20 wheels of Brie cheese from a gourmet supplier, or thousands of pounds of lamb from a wholesaler who overbought, or surplus meals from expensive restaurants where the tab for one might run $100 or more. Food banks in other cities have similar luck.

Unfortunately, the salvage operations still claim only a fraction of the food being thrown away. Many possible donors remain untapped, while others are reluctant to contribute their surplus. Fast-food chains, for example, routinely toss out any items that sit much longer than 10 minutes under a heat lamp. The chains have resisted suggestions to freeze these foods and donate them to the hungry.

Though it is seen as a holding action to help just a few of the 35.3 million Americans living below the poverty level, the food-bank movement is growing. As Celeste McKinley says, "We help feed people, and it doesn't cost the taxpayers one cent."

Source: Michael Satchell, "How People Survive on Leftovers," *Parade Magazine*, Feb. 10, 1985, p. 9.

SUMMARY

Food is the most basic necessity of life, and fortunately, it is plentiful in the United States. Starvation is a rare occurrence. The early commodity distribution program and the current Food Stamp program have contributed to improvements in the nutrition of poorer Americans. But this does not mean that all Americans eat adequately every day. Some fail to select nutritious foods even though they can afford them. Others cannot stretch their low earnings or their food stamps to eat adequately throughout the month. The adequacy of the Thrifty Food Plan, on which food stamp allotments are based, continues to be criticized by medical professionals as inadequate, despite improvements made in 1983. Another source of controversy concerns Congress's decision to use stamps rather than cash to provide nutritional benefits. While stamps are stigmatizing, they are targeted on a specific need—nutrition. Participants must be poor or near-poor to receive foods stamps, but unlike other public assistance programs, recipients need not be disabled or aged, nor do they have to have young children to qualify for the program.

A number of other nutrition programs target children and mothers. WIC, school breakfasts and lunches, and the Special School Milk Program are the best known. The nutrition of mothers while pregnant and breast feeding and the nutrition of young children are critical in promoting normal mental and physical development. There are also special programs for the elderly, such as Meals-on-Wheels and congregate meals, that increase social contact of participants as well as encourage better nutrition.

The commodity food program had a strong base of support in farmers, but today surplus commodities are no longer the focus of nutrition programs. Controversy over nutrition programs has centered on food stamps, with some contending that the program is fraught with fraud because the stamps are sold for cash or used for illegal purchases. But it has been established that large numbers of those who would qualify for at least some benefits do not apply, either because of the stigma or the lack of information about the program, or because they do not want to bother with the welfare system. It is a troublesome fact that even with the Food Stamp and other publicly funded nutrition programs, scores of people in the United States have become more heavily dependent on food kitchens and community food pantries for meals. The abundance of food in the United States has not been sufficient to insure all an adequate diet.

NOTES

1. Richard C. H. Bell, "Action to End Plague of World Hunger Can Begin with Us," *Austin American-Statesman* (September 23, 1989), p. A15.
2. Barbara Bode, Stanley Gershoff, and Michael Latham, "Defining Hunger Among the Poor," in Catherine Lerza and Michael Jacobson, eds., *Food for People, Not for Profit* (New York: Ballantine, 1975), pp. 299–300; and Physicians Task Force on Hunger in America, *Hunger in America: The Growing Epidemic* (Middletown, Conn. Wesleyan University Press, 1985), Chapter 4.
3. See Nick Kotz, *Let Them Eat Promises: The Politics of Hunger in America* (Englewood Cliffs, N.J.: Prentice-Hall, 1969), p. 35.
4. Bode et. al., "Defining Hunger," p. 301 (quote edited slightly).
5. Hearing before the Select Committee on Hunger, House of Representatives, 101st Congress, *Food Security and Methods of Assessing Hunger in the United States* (March 23, 1989).
6. Ibid., p. 9.
7. Ibid., p. 7.
8. United States Department of Agriculture, Human Nutrition Information Service, *CSF II: Nationwide Food Consumption Survey, Continuing Survey of Food Intakes by Individuals, Women 19–50 Years and Their Children 1–5 Years, 1 Day* (August 1986); also cited in hearings before the Select Committee on Hunger, *Food Security and Methods of Assessing Hunger,* 1989.

9. The rest of this paragraph relies on Bode et. al., "Defining Hunger," pp. 300–302.
10. Lucy Komisar, *Down and Out in the U.S.A.* (New York: New Viewpoints, 1977), p. 51.
11. Ibid., p. 51; and Kotz, *Let Them Eat Promises*, p. 45.
12. Komisar, *Down and Out*, p. 51.
13. Paul A. Brinker, *Economic Insecurity and Social Security* (Englewood Cliffs, N.J.: Prentice-Hall, 1968), pp. 390–91.
14. American Enterprise Institute for Public Policy Research, Food Stamp Reform (Washington, D.C., 1977), p. 3.
15. Ibid., p. 4.
16. Laurence E. Lynn, Jr., "A Decade of Policy Developments in the Income-Maintenance System," in Robert H. Haveman, ed., *A Decade of Federal Antipoverty Programs: Achievements, Failures, and Lessons* (New York: Academic Press, 1977), pp. 55–117.
17. Kotz, *Let Them Eat Promises*, pp. 52–53.
18. Ibid., p. 53.
19. Department of Agriculture, "Food Stamp Changes Help the Rural Poor," *Food and Nutrition 10* (February 1980), p. 2.
20. Martin Tolchin, "Unclaimed Food Stamps: Millions Fail to Get Available Aid, Study Says," Austin American-Statesman (November 15, 1988), p. A6.
21. Congressional Budget Office cited in *Hunger Action Forum*, vol. 2, no. 1 (January 1989).
22. See, for example, Physicians Task Force on Hunger, *Hunger in America; Unfed America '85, A Report of Hunger Watch U.S.A. Surveys* (Washington, D.C.: Bread for the World Educational Fund), October 1985.
23. Cited in *Hunger Action Forum* (January 1989).
24. U.S. Bureau of the Census, *Social Security Bulletin, Annual Statistical Supplement, 1988* (Washington, D.C.), p. 336.
25. Ibid.
26. U.S. Bureau of the Census, *Statistical Abstract of the United States, 1989* (Washington, D.C., 1989), p. 364.
27. Dorothy James, *Poverty, Politics and Change* (Englewood Cliffs, N.J.: Prentice-Hall, 1972), pp. 58–59.
28. Kotz, *Let Them Eat Promises*, p. 59.
29. Physician's Task Force on Hunger, *Hunger in America*, p. 59.
30. *Statistical Abstract, 1989*, p. 364.
31. Ibid.
32. These studies are summarized in Physicians Task Force, *Hunger in America*.
33. Milton Kotelchuk, Testimony Concerning the Special Supplemental Food Program for Women, Infants, and Children, Subcommittee on Nutrition, U.S. Senate Committee on Agriculture, Nutrition and Forestry, April 6, 1983 cited in Physicians Task Force on Hunger, *Hunger in America*, p. 100.
34. Ibid.
35. Lou E. Hicks, Rose A. Langham, and Jean Takenaka, "Cognitive and Health Measures Following Early Nutritional Supplementation: A Sibling Study," *American Journal of Public Health*, October 1982, p. 1110. Also cited in Physicians Task Force on Hunger, *Hunger in America*, p. 118.
36. See Victor R. Fuchs, *How We Live: An Economic Perspective on Americans from Birth to Death* (Cambridge: Harvard University Press, 1983).
37. Robert Pear, "Many States Cut Food Allotments For Poor Families," *New York Times*, May 29, 1990, p. A16.
38. Statement of Bruce Vento, Joint Hearing before the Subcommittee on Domestic Marketing, Consumer Relations, and Nutrition of the Committee on Agriculture and the Domestic Task Force of the Select Committee on Hunger, House of Representatives, 100th Congress, *Hunger Emergency in America* (February 24, 1988), p. 41, and testimony of Robert Fresh, Executive Director, Food Research and Action Center, p. 370.
39. Gary W. Hutton, *Welfare Fraud Investigation* (Springfield, IL: Charles C. Thomas, 1985), pp. 21–22.
40. Department of Health, Education and Welfare, "Welfare Myths vs. Facts," pamphlet SRS-72–02009, cited in Ronald C. Federico, *The Social Welfare Institution: An Introduction*, 3rd ed. (Lexington, Mass.: Heath, 1980), p. 83.
41. Gary W. Hutton, "Welfare Fraud and the Police," *The Police Chief* (November 1979), p. 46, cited in Hutton, *Welfare Fraud Investigation*, p. 21.

42. See, for example, David Greenberg and Douglas Wolf with Jennifer Pfiester, *Using Computers to Combat Welfare Fraud, the Operation and Effectiveness of Wage Matching* (New York: Greenwood Press, 1986).
43. Letter from the United Council on Welfare Fraud, no date.
44. Randy Fitzgerald, "Time to Crack Down on Food-Stamp Fraud," *Readers' Digest* (February 1983), p. 138.
45. "Stamps for Food Traded for Drugs," *Austin American-Statesman* (June 6, 1989), p. B3.
46. National Food Stamp Information Committee, *The Facts about Food Stamps* (November/December 1975), p. 9.
47. Department of Health, Education and Welfare, *Quality Control in Aid to Families with Dependent Children*, SRS no. 74–04009, rev. 1973.
48. Joint Hearing before the Subcommittee on Domestic Marketing, Consumer Relations, and Nutrition of the Committee on Agriculture, House of Representatives and the Subcommittee on Nutrition and Investigations of the Committee on Agriculture, Nutrition, and Forestry, United States Senate, 100th Congress, 1st Session, *Quality Control and Fiscal Sanctions in the Food Stamp Program* (October 22, 1987), p. 235.
49. Ibid., pp. 6–7.
50. General Accounting Office, *Benefit Overpayments: Recoveries Could be Increased in the Foodstamp and AFDC Programs*, GAO/RCED–86–17 (Washington, D.C., 1986).
51. See, for example, Dennis P. Affhalter and Fredrica D. Kramer, eds., *Rethinking Quality Control: A New System for the Food Stamp Program* (Washington, D.C.: National Academy Press, 1987).
52. Physicians Task Force on Hunger, *Hunger in America*.
53. Edward M. Gramlich, "The Main Themes," in Sheldon H. Danzinger and Daniel H. Weinberg, eds., *Fighting Poverty; What Works and What Doesn't* (Cambridge: Harvard University Press, 1986), p. 346.
54. Gary Burtless, "Public Spending for the Poor: Trends, Prospects, and Economic Limits," in Danzinger and Weinberg, *Fighting Poverty*, pp. 23–24.
55. Fitzgerald, "Time to Crack Down," p. 141.
56. Nick Kotz, *Hunger in America: The Federal Response* (New York: Field Foundation, 1979), p. 16.
57. President of the United States, *America's New Beginning: A Program for Economic Recovery* (Washington, D.C., U.S. Government Printing Office, February 18, 1981), p. 1.
58. Ibid.
59. "Hunger Report Prompts Food Aid Expansion," *Congressional Quarterly Almanac 1983*, p. 414.

9

WARRING ON POVERTY
Victories, Defeats, and Stalemates

THE CURATIVE STRATEGY—THE "WAR ON POVERTY"

American confidence in the ability of government to solve problems was once so boundless that President Lyndon Johnson was moved to declare in 1964: "This administration today, here and now, declares unconditional war on poverty in America."[1] And later, when signing the Economic Opportunity Act of 1964 and establishing the Office of Economic Opportunity (OEO), he added: "Today for the first time in the history of the human race, a great nation is able to make and is willing to make a commitment to eradicate poverty among its people."[2] Ten years later, after the expenditure of nearly $25 billion, Congress abolished the OEO. There were still twenty-five million poor people in the country—approximately the same number of poor as when the "war on poverty" began. The government had passed a law (the Economic Opportunity Act of 1964), it had created a new bureaucracy (the Office of Economic Opportunity), and it had thrown many billions of dollars in the general direction of the problem. But according to many critics, nothing much had happened.

An especially stinging critique of the social welfare policies of the 1960s and 1970s is that they spawned *more* poverty. Rather than reduce poverty, this argument goes, the United States created additional misery through antipoverty programs that actually encouraged welfare dependency.[3] But others disagree. They believe that many programs of the Great Society were successful and that the programs that remain in place, such as Food Stamps (see Chapter 8) and Medicaid and Medicare (see Chapter 10), have continued to prevent or mitigate human suffering. But the fact remains that large numbers of Americans continue to fall below the poverty level. The failures as well as the successes of the war on poverty are important lessons in policy analysis.

Curative Attempts

The war on poverty was an attempt to apply a *curative strategy* to the problems of the poor. In contrast to the *alleviative strategy* of public assistance, which attempts only to ease the hardships of poverty, and in contrast to the *preventive strategy* of social insurance, which attempts to compel people to save money to relieve economic problems that are likely to result from old age, death, disability, sickness, and unemployment, the curative strategy stresses efforts to help the poor become self-supporting by bringing about changes in these individuals and in their environment. The curative strategy of the war on poverty was supposed to break the cycle of poverty and to allow the poor to move into America's working classes and eventually its middle classes. The strategy was "rehabilitation and not relief." The Economic Opportunity Act of 1964, the centerpiece of the war on poverty, was to "strike at the causes, not just the consequences, of poverty."

Area Poverty and Case Poverty

The first curative antipoverty policies originated in the administration of President John F. Kennedy. Kennedy was said to have read socialist Michael Harrington's *The Other America*—a sensitive description of the continuing existence of a great deal of poverty that had gone unnoticed by the majority of middle- and upper-class Americans.[4] Kennedy, the Harvard-educated son of a multimillionaire business investor, was visibly shocked when he first saw the wooden shacks of West Virginia's barren mountains during his 1960 presidential campaign. And Kennedy's economic advisor, John Kenneth Galbraith, had in 1958 written an influential book, *The Affluent Society*, which called attention to the continued existence of poverty in the midst of a generally affluent society.[5] Galbraith distinguished between *case poverty* and *area poverty*. Case poverty was largely a product of some personal characteristic of the poor—old age, illiteracy, inadequate education, lack of job skills, poor health, race—which prevented them from participating in the nation's prosperity. Area poverty was a product of economic deficiency relating to a particular sector of the nation, such as West Virginia and much of the rest of Appalachia. Pockets of poverty or depressed areas occurred because of technological change or a lack of industrialization—for instance, decline in the coal industry, the exhaustion of iron ore mines, and the squeezing out of small farmers from the agricultural market. More recently, area poverty has resulted from declines in the automobile, steel, and petroleum industries. Some of these areas have come to be called the country's "rustbelt."

Kennedy Initiatives

The initial forays in the war on poverty were begun in the Kennedy administration. The fight against area poverty began with the Area Redevelopment Act of 1961, which authorized federal grants and loans to governments and businesses in designated "depressed areas." This program was later revised in the Economic Development Act (EDA) of 1965. But over the years, the EDA has come under criticism. Most areas of the country now qualify for assistance, and some have labeled the EDA a trickle-down approach to alleviating poverty, with most benefits going to business and not the poor. Republicans have also called it a pork-barrel program to aid Democrats in getting elected. The Reagan administration tried to abolish the Economic Development Administration contending that, "There is no evidence that these programs have resulted in net job creation nationwide. EDA does not target assistance to those in need, but instead serves narrow and specialized local and regional political interests at the Nation's expense."[6] Congress has continued to support the EDA, albeit with reduced appropriations which now stand at a little more than $200 million annually.

The fight against case poverty began with the Manpower Development and Training Act (MDTA) of 1962—the first large-scale, federally funded job-training program. Eventually, MDTA was absorbed into the Comprehensive Employment and Training Act (CETA) of 1973 which was later replaced with the Job Training Partnership Act (JTPA) of 1982.

Enter LBJ

When Lyndon B. Johnson assumed the presidency in 1963, he saw an opportunity to distinguish his administration and to carry forward the traditions of Franklin D. Roosevelt. Johnson believed that government employment and training efforts, particularly those directed at youth, could break the cycle of poverty by giving young people the basic skills to improve their employability and to make them self-sufficient adults. In addition to the Economic Opportunity Act, Johnson's war on poverty included:

> *The Elementary and Secondary Education Act of 1965:* This was the first major, general federal aid-to-education program, and it provided federal funds to "poverty-impacted" school districts. Today, it remains the largest source of federal aid to education.
>
> *The Food Stamp Program:* As an important step in the development of major in-kind benefit programs, it continues today to provide relief to the poor.
>
> *Medicare:* Created by an amendment to the Social Security Act, it provides health-care insurance for the aged.
>
> *Medicaid:* It remains as the major federal state health-care program for the poor.
>
> *Job Training:* This was an expansion of the Manpower Development and Training Act, and it initiated a series of new job-training programs, including the Job Corps and the Neighborhood Youth Corps for young adults, and the Work-Study program which encourages college attendance among low-income youth.
>
> *The Economic Development Act of 1965* and *The Appalachia Regional Development Act of 1965:* These were efforts to encourage economic development in distressed areas.

THE ECONOMIC OPPORTUNITY ACT—
"COMMUNITY ACTION"

The Economic Opportunity Act created a multitude of programs that were to be coordinated in Washington by a new, independent federal bureaucracy—the Office of Economic Opportunity. OEO was given money and authority to support varied and highly experimental techniques for combating poverty at the community level. As evidence of the priority given OEO, its first director was Sargent Shriver, brother-in-law of slain President John F. Kennedy and later, the Democratic vice-presidential running mate of George McGovern in 1972. OEO was encouraged to bypass local and state governments and establish new *community action* organizations throughout the nation—semiprivate organizations, with the poor participating in their own governance. OEO was *not* given authority to make direct grants to the poor as relief or as public assistance. All of the OEO programs were aimed, whether accurately or inaccurately, at curing the causes of poverty rather than alleviating its symptoms.

Youth Programs

A number of OEO programs were oriented toward youth—an attempt to break the cycle of poverty at an early age. The Job Corps was designed to provide education, vocational training, and work experience in rural conservation camps for unemployable youths between the ages of sixteen and twenty-two. Job Corps trainees were supposed to be "hard core" unemployables who could benefit from training away from their home environment; here, it was hoped, they would break habits and associations that were obstacles to employment while learning reading, arithmetic, and self-health care, as well as auto mechanics, clerical work, and other skills. Today, the Job Corps is the most highly funded of the federal government's domestic job training programs.[7] Another program was the Neighborhood Youth Corps, designed to provide work, counseling, and on-the-job training for young people in or out of school who were living at home. The Neighborhood Youth Corps was intended for young people who were more employable than those who were expected in the Job Corps. A Work-Study program helped students from low-income families remain in high school or college by providing them with federally paid, part-time employment in conjunction with cooperating public or private agencies. The Volunteers in Service to America (VISTA) program was modeled after the popular Peace Corps idea, but volunteers were to work in domestic poverty-impacted areas rather than in foreign countries.

Community Action

The core of the Economic Opportunity Act was a grassroots community action program to be carried out at the local level by public or private nonprofit agencies, with federal financial assistance. Communities were urged to form a community action agency, which was to be composed of representatives of government, private organizations, and, most important, the poor themselves. It was originally intended that OEO would support antipoverty programs devised by the local community action agency. Projects could include (but were not limited to) literacy training, health services, homemaker services, legal aid for the poor, neighborhood service centers, vocational training, and childhood development activities. The act also envisioned that a community action agency would help organize the poor so that they could become participating members of the community and could avail themselves of the many public programs designed to serve them. Finally, the act attempted to coordinate federal and state programs for the poor in each community.

As stated in the original language of the act, community action was to be "developed, conducted, and administered with the maximum feasible participation of the residents of the areas and members of the groups served." This was one of the more controversial phrases in the act. Militants within the OEO administration frequently cited this phrase as authority to "mobilize" the poor "to have immediate and irreversible impact on their communities." This language implied that the poor were to be organized as a political force by federal antipoverty warriors using federal funds. Needless to say, neither Congress nor the Democratic administration of President Lyndon Johnson really intended to create rival political organizations that would compete for power with local governments in those communities.

The typical community action agency was governed by a board consisting of public officials (perhaps the mayor, a county commissioner, a school board member, and a public health officer), prominent public citizens (from business, labor, civil rights, religious, and civic affairs organizations), and representatives of the poor (in some cases selected in agency-sponsored elections, but more often hand-picked by ministers, social workers, civil rights leaders, and other prominent community figures). A staff was to be hired, including a full-time director, and it was to be paid from an OEO grant for administrative expenses. A target area would be defined—a low-income area of the county or the ghetto of a city. Neighborhood centers were established in the target area. Some were staffed with counselors; some offered employment assistance, and some contained a recreation hall, a child-care center, and some sort of health clinic. These centers assisted the poor in contacting the school system, the welfare department, employment agencies, the public-housing authority, and so on. Frequently, the centers and the antipoverty workers who staffed them acted as advocates for the poor and as intermediaries between the poor and public agencies. This activity was called *outreach*.

Head Start

Community action agencies also devised specific antipoverty projects for submission to the Washington offices of OEO for funding. The most popular of these projects was Operation Head Start—usually a cooperative program between the community action agency and the local school district. Preschool children from poor families were given six to eight weeks of special summer preparation before entering kindergarten or first grade. The idea was to give these disadvantaged children a *head start* on formal schooling. Congress (as well as the general public) was favorably disposed toward this program and favored it in later budget appropriations to OEO.

Legal Services

Another type of antipoverty project was the Legal Services program. Many community action agencies established free legal services to the poor to assist them with rent disputes, contracts, welfare rules, minor police actions, housing regulations, and so on. The idea behind these programs was that the poor seldom have access to legal counsel and are frequently taken advantage of because they do not know their rights. Congress amended the act in 1967 to insure that no OEO funds would be used to defend any person in a criminal case. Antipoverty lawyers using federal funds have been active in bringing suits against city welfare departments, housing authorities, public health agencies, and other government bodies.

More OEO Projects

Other kinds of antipoverty projects funded by OEO included family-planning programs (the provision of advice and devices to facilitate family planning by the poor), homemaker services (advice and services to poor families on how to stretch low family budgets), job training (special outreach efforts to bring the hard-core unemployed into established work-force programs), Follow Through (a continuation of Head Start efforts, with special educational experiences for poor children after they enter school), Upward Bound (an educational counseling program for poor children), as well as other programs.

POLITICS AND THE WAR ON POVERTY

The war on poverty, specifically OEO, became an unpopular stepchild of the Johnson administration even before LBJ left office, so the demise of the OEO programs cannot be attributed to political partisanship—that is, to the election of a Republican administration under Richard Nixon. Nor can the demise of the poverty program be attributed to the Vietnam War, since both "wars" were escalated and later deescalated at the same time. The Nixon administration began dismantling the OEO in 1973, transferring the Job Corps, the Neighborhood Youth Corps, and all job-training programs under a reorganized CETA to the Department of Labor. The administration also transferred the Work-Study program, Head Start, and Upward Bound to what was then the Department of Health, Education and Welfare. VISTA became part of a larger federal volunteer program called ACTION which continues to operate today. The Ford administration abolished OEO in 1974. It turned over a greatly reduced community action program to an independent (and now defunct) Community Services Administration, and it turned over legal services to an independent Legal Services Corporation (see illustration entitled "Legal Services Still Under Fire"). Today, considerable funding for community action agencies comes from the Community Services Block Grant (CSBG). States use the funds to support about nine hundred nonprofit community action agencies, but the CSBG has had a precarious existence due to claims that it duplicates the Social Services Block Grant and other federally funded programs. The Reagan administration tried to abolish the CSBG, saying that much of its funding goes to administrative costs and that community action agencies have been around long enough to administer programs without these funds.[8]

The reasons for the failure of the war on poverty are complex. The Office of Economic Opportunity was always the scene of great confusion. Personnel were young, middle-class, and inexperienced, and there was always a high turnover among administrators. Community action agencies throughout the country appeared directionless. Aside from Head Start, there were no clear-cut program directions for most community action agencies. Many of the poor believed that the poverty program was going to provide them with *money;* they never really understood or accepted the fact that community action agencies were mandated to provide only organization, outreach, counseling, training, and similar assistance. Many community action agencies duplicated, and even competed with, existing welfare and social-service agencies. Some community action agencies organized the poor to challenge local government agencies. As a result, more than a few local governments called upon the Johnson administration and Congress to curb community action agencies that were using federal funds to "undermine" existing programs and organizations. There were frequent charges of mismanagement and corruption, particularly at the local level. Finally, some community action agencies became entangled in the politics of race; some big city agencies were charged with excluding whites; and in some rural areas, whites believed that poverty agencies were "for blacks only."

Perhaps the failures of the war on poverty can be explained by our lack of knowledge about how to *cure* poverty. In retrospect, it seems naive to believe that passing a law, creating a new bureaucracy, and giving money to local agencies to find their own cures could have succeeded in eliminating or even reducing poverty.

Can poverty be cured? The evidence is frequently conflicting. For example, some social commentators have pointed to evaluation studies of the Job Corps program which indicate that after completing their program, enrollees have had increases in their annual income ranging from less than $200 a year to no more than about $500 a year, and they conclude that "the programs were seldom disasters; they simply failed to help many people get and hold jobs that they would not have gotten and held anyway."[9] On the other hand, government officials who reviewed the same evidence stated: "While there are always uncertainties, the size of this increment provides reasonable certainty that the Job Corps investment in human resources is profitable."[10] In a more global assessment of the job creation and training programs of the 1960s and 1970s, researchers concluded that:

[I]t is women and the economically disadvantaged who have benefited.... In most cases, the resulting employment and earnings gains...have been modest, in part because it is not easy to solve the employment difficulties of the hard-to-employ and in part because the resources devoted to any one individual are fairly modest. There is some indication that programs providing intensive (and extensive) investment in each participant, such as the Jobs Corps and Supported Work Demonstration, have, at least for some groups of the disadvantaged, more than paid for themselves from a society-wide point of view.[11]

ILLUSTRATION: LEGAL SERVICES STILL UNDER FIRE

The federal government's Legal Service Corporation (LSC) grew out of the early legal services provided as part of the OEO's community action programs in the 1960s. Today, the Legal Services Corporation is a separate nonprofit corporation which is financed by Congress from tax dollars to provide legal services to the poor. The corporation is headed by an eleven-member board appointed by the president. More than three hundred regional legal service groups around the nation are staffed by about five thousand attorneys.

According to the corporation, most of its work consists of advising the poor of their legal rights in everyday cases—rental contracts, loans, credit accounts, welfare rules, housing regulations, and other day-to-day civil law matters. The corporation is prevented by law from representing the poor in criminal cases. (The states are required by the U.S. Constitution to provide legal counsel to persons accused of felonies.) The corporation reports that only 15 percent of its cases ever reach the courtroom. Others are resolved by the parties before litigation begins.

Defenders of the Legal Services Corporation argue that the poor require legal protection as much as, or more than, the affluent. Most case work, they claim, revolves around survival issues of food, shelter, or clothing since the LSC represents the country's most powerless citizens. Government-paid poverty lawyers are prohibited from taking fees, such as a percentage of damages in accident-injury suits. Moreover, legal-service money cannot be used for political activity, public demonstrations, or strikes.

But opponents of the Legal Services Corporation complain that its primary beneficiaries and primary lobbyists are LSC attorneys themselves, and that it is irrational to establish a government agency to sue other government agencies. The Legal Services Corporation has been involved in several well-publicized class-action suits against public agencies. In these suits, lawyers from the corporation claim to represent a whole class of poor people, not just one individual or family. For example, the Bay Area Legal Services in Tampa, Florida, using federal funds, sued the state of Florida to stop it from requiring its high school graduates to pass a functional literacy test. Corporation lawyers argued that the test was discriminatory because larger proportions of black students failed it than white students. Class-action suits can also be brought against private concerns. Should the Legal Services Corporation take on such class-action cases? Even when the cause is just, it might be argued that taxpayers should not have to foot the bill for these class-action suits. Or according to one critic of the corporation: "Why should the taxpayers have to cough up $300 million a year for an elite corps of radical lawyers who want to move this country to the left?"[a]

Alternatives to the Legal Services Corporation have been proposed including *a prohibition against class-action suits* brought by lawyers who are paid through the LSC. Such suggestions are:

- *A voucher system,* similar to food stamps. Poor people would qualify for a certain number of vouchers to be redeemed at private law firms.

- *Judicare,* which, like Medicare, would be a national insurance program. Everyone would contribute a small amount, and everyone would be insured against legal expenses.

- *Pro bono (no fee) services to the poor* donated by private-practice attorneys and law-school clinics.

President Reagan tried hard to abolish the LSC, contending that much of its funding was being spent on "think tanks" rather than for direct services to the poor.[b] He endorsed replacing the LSC with pro bono services from private attorneys, law school students, and recent graduates, and for using Social Service Block Grant funds. Reagan submitted twenty-five nominations to Congress for the LSC board, but *none* were confirmed because Congress viewed these individuals as hostile to the LSC's mission. In order to get his way, Reagan made nineteen appointments to the board while the Senate was in recess, thereby avoiding the nomination and approval process. The Senate retaliated by limiting the board's power to cut funds to LSC-funded programs until such time as it confirmed the Reagan

[a]See Bill Keller, "Special Treatment No Longer Given Advocates for the Poor," *Congressional Quarterly Weekly Report* (April 18, 1981), pp. 659–664.

[b]Major Policy Initiatives, Fiscal Year 1990 (Washington D.C.: U.S. Government Printing Office, 1989), pp. 131–132.

nominees.[c] The Senate also refused to approve the board's request for *decreased* funding for the corporation. According to *Time,* "When Congress refused to... cut the corporation's budget further,... the board actually hired lobbyists to press the lawmakers for less—yes, less—money."[d] The Reagan appointed board left the corporation with an uncertain mandate for the future.

Some states have responded to cuts in legal aid funds with Interest on Lawyer Trust Accounts (IOLTA). Sometimes, private attorneys hold small amounts of money for clients for short periods of time. Since opening separate interest-bearing accounts for each client is not feasible, thirty-five states have decided to pool this money into a single account, and interest earned goes to subsidize legal services for the poor. While questions have been raised as to the propriety of the practice, a president of the New York State Bar Association explains that no one has ever successfully challenged IOLTA programs in the U.S. or other countries such as Canada and Australia. No harm is done to clients whose money is held, because their funds would not have earned interest anyway. He questions the motivations of those who claim IOLTA is unethical, suggesting that their opposition may not be to "IOLTA

itself but to provisions for legal services to the poor."[e]

President Bush has "called for a renewed national commitment to providing 'access to justice' for all Americans, and in particular for the poor, who... are often 'simply precluded from pursuing legal remedies to their grievances.'"[f] With this rhetoric, those concerned about access to legal services for the poor are waiting to see just what President Bush will do to insure his commitment. Perhaps he will take "the advice of the American Bar Association, which has urged that he select only those individuals who 'unequivocally support and demonstrate a high order of commitment to the continued existence and the effective operation of the Legal Services Corporation.'"[g] In addition, a number of lawyers have called for a return to *pro bono* services, which seem to have dropped off severely as law firms have become increasingly obsessed with income generating activities. Of the nation's 659,000 private attorneys, the American Bar Association estimates that only 18 percent provide pro bono services.[h] Perhaps what is really in order is a renewed commitment from the LSC board *combined* with the cooperation of attorneys in private practice.

[c]"Reagan's Recess Appointments Rankle Hill," *Congressional Quarterly Weekly Report* (July 14, 1984), p. 1699.

[d]Richard Lacayo, "The Sad Fate of Legal Aid," *Time* (June 20, 1988), p. 59.

[e]Letter to the editor, *The Wall Street Journal* (February 25, 1985), p. 31.

[f]Bill Whitehurst, "Bush Can Help Give Equal Access to Justice for the Poor," *Austin American-Statesman* (June 3, 1989), p. A11.

[g]Ibid.

[h]Lacayo, "The Sad Fate of Legal Aid."

In some cases, initial evidence about the effectiveness of programs has conflicted with later results. Early findings about Head Start revealed that the program was very popular among parents. But after two or three years in school, differences in educational achievement or aspiration levels of poor children who attended Head Start and poor children who did not attend seemed to vanish.[12] More recent longitudinal evidence confirms that IQ scores of former Head Start children declined after they were in school, which some think is not surprising considering the quality of a number of public schools.[13] But research also indicates that Head Start produced long-term gains that could not have been measured in earlier studies. For example, enrollees are less likely as they grow older to be dependent on welfare and less likely to be involved in crime; they are more likely to have remained in school and are more likely to hold jobs.[14]

The war on poverty has not been won, and we may be forced to conclude that social scientists simply do not know enough about social behavior to end poverty. It has also been argued that the war on poverty was never funded at a level that would make a substantial impact. OEO funds were spread over hundreds of communities. Such relatively small amounts could never offset the numerous, deep-seated causes of deprivation. The war on poverty raised the expectations of the poor, but it never tried to cope with poverty on a scale comparable to the size of the problem. Often the outcome was only to increase frustration.

In an obvious 1968 reference to public policies affecting the poor and blacks in America, Aaron Wildavsky wrote:

> A recipe for violence: Promise a lot; deliver a little. Lead people to believe they will be much better off, but let there be no dramatic improvement. Try a variety of small programs, each interesting but marginal in impact and severely underfinanced. Avoid any attempted solution remotely comparable in size to the dimensions of the problem you are trying to solve. Have middle-class civil servants hire upper-class student radicals to use lower-class Negroes as a battering ram against the existing local political systems; then complain that people are going around disrupting things and chastise local politicians for not cooperating with those out to do them in. Get some poor people involved in local decision-making, only to discover that there is not enough at stake to be worth bothering about. Feel guilty about what has happened to black people; tell them you are surprised they have not revolted before; express shock and dismay when they follow your advice. Go in for a little force, just enough to anger, not enough to discourage. Feel guilty again; say you are surprised that worse has not happened. Alternate with a little suppression. Mix well, apply a match, and run.... [15]

It would be difficult to find a better summary of the unintended consequences of the many of the public programs of the 1960s.

CAN WE "CURE" POVERTY?
MORE EVIDENCE ABOUT HEAD START

Can we "cure" poverty? Is the curative strategy effective? Recent evidence indicates that at least some strategies are more effective than we once thought. As an example, let us consider at greater length attempts to evaluate the effectiveness of one of the most popular antipoverty programs, Head Start.

When the Economic Opportunity Act of 1964 first authorized the creation of local community action agencies throughout the nation to fight the war on poverty, the responsibility for devising community antipoverty projects was placed in the hands of local participants. But within one year, the Office of Economic Opportunity in Washington and its director, Sargent Shriver, decided that Head Start programs were the most desirable antipoverty projects. OEO earmarked a substantial portion of local community action funds for Head Start programs. The typical local Head Start project was a cooperative program between the community action agency and the local school district. Preschool children from poor families were given six to eight weeks of special summer preparation before entering kindergarten or first grade. The idea of helping to prepare disadvantaged children for school was more appealing to the middle class than programs which provided free legal aid for the poor, helped them get on welfare rolls, or organized them to fight city hall. Indeed, Head Start turned out to be the most popular program in the war on poverty. Nearly all of the nation's community action agencies operated a Head Start program, and over one-half million children per year were enrolled throughout the country at the height of the program in the late 1960s. Some communities expanded Head Start into full-year programs and also provided children with health services and improved daily diets. Head Start became OEO's showcase program.

Evaluating Head Start

Head Start officials within the OEO were discomforted by the thought of a formal evaluation of their program. They argued that educational success was not the only goal of the program; that child health and nutrition and parental involvement in a community program were equally important goals. After much internal debate, Director Shriver ordered an evaluative study, and in 1968 a contract was given to Westinghouse Learning Corporation and Ohio University to perform the research.

When Richard Nixon assumed the presidency in January 1969, hints of negative findings had already filtered up to the White House. In his first comments on the poverty program, Nixon alluded to studies showing the long-term effects of Head Start as "extremely weak." This teaser prompted the press and Congress to call for the release of the Westinghouse Report. OEO claimed that the results were still "too preliminary" to be revealed. However, after a congressional committee investigation and considerable political pressure, OEO finally released the report in June 1969.[16]

The report stated that the researchers had randomly selected 104 Head Start projects across the country. Seventy percent were summer projects; and 30 percent were full-year projects. Children who had gone on from these programs to the first, second, and third grades in local schools (the experimental group) were matched according to socioeconomic background with children in the same grades who had not attended Head Start (the control group). All children were given a series of tests covering various aspects of cognitive and affective development (the Metropolitan Readiness Test, the Illinois Test of Psycholinguistic Abilities, the Stanford Achievement Test, the Children's Self-Concept Test, and others). The parents of both groups of children were matched on achievement and motivation.

The unhappy results can be summarized as follows: Summer programs did not produce improvements in cognitive and affective development that could be detected into the early elementary grades, and full-year programs produced only marginally effective gains for certain subgroups, mainly black children in central cities. However, parents of Head Start children strongly approved of the program.

Political Reaction

Head Start officials reacted predictably in condemning the report. Liberals attacked the report because they believed that President Nixon would use it to justify major cutbacks in OEO. *The New York Times* reported the findings under the headline "Head Start Report Held 'Full of Holes.'" It warned that "Congress or the Administration will seize the report's generally negative conclusions as an excuse to downgrade or discard the Head Start Program"[17] (perhaps not an unreasonable action in light of the findings, but clearly unacceptable to the liberal community). Academicians moved to the defense of the war on poverty by attacking various methodological aspects of the study. In short, scientific assessment of the impact of Head Start was drowned in a sea of political controversy.

Years Later

It is difficult for educators to believe that education, especially intensive preschool education, does *not* have a lasting effect on the lives of children. The prestigious Carnegie Foundation decided to fund research in Ypsilanti, Michigan— research which would keep tabs on disadvantaged youngsters from preschool to young adulthood. In 1980, a report was released on an eighteen-year study of the progress of 123 low-IQ children; fifty-eight of these children (the experimental group) were given special Head Start-type education at ages three and four, and they continued to have weekly visits throughout later schooling.[18] The other (the control group) received no such special educational help. Both groups came from low socioeconomic backgrounds; half of their families were headed by a single parent, and half received welfare. Because the sample was small and local, researchers were able to track the children's progress to age nineteen.

At first the results were disappointing. Most of the gains made by the children with preschool educations disappeared by the time the children had completed second grade. As children in the experimental group progressed through grade school, junior high school, and high school, their grades were not better than the children in the control group. However, throughout the school years, children with preschool educations did score slightly higher (8 percent) on reading, mathematics, and language-achievement tests than the control group. More important, only 19 percent of the preschoolers in the experimental group ended up in special classes for slow learners, compared to 39 percent for the control group. The preschoolers also showed fewer delinquent tendencies and held more after-school jobs. The key to this success appeared to be a better attitude toward school and learning among children with preschool educations. Finally, the former preschool enrollees were more likely to finish high school, more likely to find jobs, and less likely to be on welfare than those in the control group.

Positive results of this study continue to be touted, and Head Start is a good example of the need for longitudinal research. In 1990, 488,000 children were enrolled at a cost of $1.3 billion.[19] More than half of the children came from single-parent homes and half came from families with annual incomes of below $6,000. One third of the program staff are parents of current or former Head Start children. Researchers estimate that the program's benefits have exceeded per pupil costs at least seven times over.[20] Their conclusion is that a Head Start-type experience is a bargain to society in the long run because it reduces the later need for social welfare programs.[21] President Bush concurs and has proposed a substantial increase for the program, but he has stopped short of Congress's desire to increase funding to a level that would permit virtually all eligible children to enroll.[22]

JOB PROGRAMS: MAKE-WORK VERSUS THE REAL THING

The Comprehensive Employment and Training Act of 1973 (CETA) was originally proposed by the Nixon administration as a means of reforming and reorganizing the large array of job-training programs that had emerged from the Great Society programs of the 1960s. CETA was designed to accomplish two general goals:

1. *Consolidate* job programs from the Manpower Development and Training Act of 1962; the Economic Opportunity Act of 1964, including community action programs featuring job training, the Job Corps, and the Neighborhood Youth Corps; and the Job Opportunities in the Business Sector program;
2. *Decentralize* these programs, giving control and implementation to local governments.

The U.S. Department of Labor was given overall responsibility for consolidating the various job-training programs and distributing funds to city, county, and state governments, which served as prime sponsors for the programs.

Initially, CETA was directed at the *structurally* unemployed—the long-term, hard-core unemployed who possess few job skills and little experience, and who suffer from other barriers to productive employment. But later, particularly in response to the economic recession of 1974 to 1975, Congress extended the target population to include individuals affected by *cyclical* unemployment—temporary unemployment caused by depressed economic conditions. In order to increase the target group, Congress forced the Nixon and Ford administrations to accept more *public-service* jobs through CETA than either administration requested.

CETA provided job training for over 3.5 million people per year. Programs included classroom training, on-the-job experience, and public-service employment. *Prime sponsor* local governments contracted with private community-based organizations (CBOs) to help recruit poor and minority trainees, provide initial classroom training, and place individuals in public-service jobs.

As it turned out, a major share of CETA funds was used by cities to pay individuals to work in regular municipal jobs. CETA offered local governments the possibility of substantially lowering their labor costs by substituting federally paid CETA workers for regular municipal employees. In addition, CETA enabled many local governments to shift regular municipal employees (police, firefighters, refuse collectors, and others) to the CETA budget and off the city's payroll. Instead of creating new jobs, a substantial portion of CETA funds simply supported a continuation of existing jobs. Obvious substitution occurred when a government laid off employees and then rehired them in their old jobs with CETA funds. Although CETA regulations officially prohibited such substitutions, most observers agreed that the practice was widespread. Indeed, it was estimated that about half of all CETA jobs were jobs formerly paid for by local governments.

Defenders of CETA argued that substitution was not necessarily wasteful if municipal employees were going to lose their jobs without assistance from CETA. Substitution allowed cities facing financial difficulties to cut back on their own spending without laying off large numbers of their employees.

But it was clear that CETA funds were not all targeted to those who needed the assistance most—the economically disadvantaged and long-term, hard-core unemployed. One estimate was that only one-third of all CETA workers came from welfare families. Prime sponsors tended to focus on the "cream" of the labor market—skimming off the most skilled of the unemployed. Nonetheless, according to federal figures, about 40 percent of the participants were minorities, about 45 percent had less than a high school education, 39 percent were age twenty-one or less, and 73 percent were classified as "low income."[23]

The Humphrey-Hawkins Act of 1978 "guaranteed" a job to every "able and willing" adult American. The ambitious language of the act reflected the leadership of its best known sponsor, the late Senator Hubert H. Humphrey (D-Minn). The act viewed the federal government as "the employer of last resort" and pledged to create public-service jobs and put the unemployed to work on public projects. Lowering the unemployment rate to 3 percent was to be a "national goal." But the Humphrey-Hawkins Act was more symbolic of liberal concerns than a real national commitment. Of course, pressure on Congress and the president to expand funding for public-service jobs increases during recessions, but it is unlikely that the national unemployment rate will ever be reduced to 3 percent (although at current national rates of about 5 percent, we are closer than we have been in the past fifteen years). Increasingly, Congress and presidential administrations have become concerned with the creation of what has been called "real," permanent, private-sector jobs rather than with government-funded public-service jobs.

Job Training Partnership Act

In order to address criticisms of CETA and focus on private-sector employment, the Reagan administration allowed CETA legislation to expire and replaced it with the Job Training Partnership Act (JTPA) of 1982. JTPA was co-authored by the unlikely team of Senator Edward Kennedy (D-Mass) and Vice-President Dan Quayle while he was an Indiana senator.[24] Funds are provided to states in the form of block grants. The goals of the JTPA are to reduce poverty and dependency by providing the unemployed and underemployed with skill training to meet the employment needs of local communities. Under the JTPA, about six hundred Private Industry Councils have been established. These councils are composed of volunteers from the business sector who are supposed to be knowledgeable about the job skills most needed in their communities. The councils pass their advice on to job training centers established by state and local governments with federal funds.

About $3.5 billion was spent on JTPA in 1988, but is JTPA working? According to one early study funded by three private foundations in conjunction with the National Commission for Employment Policy, it is. JTPA programs have exceeded performance standards set by the federal government in several areas:

> Some 68 percent of adult enrollees obtained jobs, bettering the standard of 55 percent, as did 60 percent of welfare recipients, compared to a 39 percent standard.

> The [programs]...had an adult cost per placement of $3,410 versus the federal standard of $5,704, and had similar success with youth.

But in other areas, the results fell below expectations:

> The average wage rate per adult placement of $4.80 fell below the federal standard of $4.91.

> Youth standards (including attainment of employment competencies, entrance into training programs, return to school and completing school) were obtained by 74 percent of participants rather than the federal standard of 82 percent.[25]

While some of these results sound encouraging, they are based on federally determined performance standards; they do not compare JTPA participants with similar individuals who did not participate in JTPA. And creaming continues to be a concern.[26] Since 85 percent of JTPA funds must be used for training, little is available for support services like living allowances and child care; such services might make a substantial difference in getting some disadvantaged individuals to participate, especially "adults not on welfare and troubled youths in need of counseling."[27] One of the governments newest job program efforts is the Economic Dislocation and Worker Adjustment Assistance Act, which expands services that were available under the JTPA to assist workers dislocated due to major layoffs and plant closures. The act took effect in 1989 and is intended to provide more rapid assistance when layoffs and closures occur. Farmers, other self-employed workers and the long-term unemployed may also qualify. Services include readjustment and retraining.

THE U.S. EMPLOYMENT SERVICE: FINDING JOBS

The labor market does not always coordinate jobs with workers. This is particularly true for unskilled and semi-skilled workers. In 1933, the United States Employment Service (USES) was established under the Wagner-Peyser Act to help the millions of depression-era unemployed find jobs.[28] Today, the USES consists of twenty-four hundred state-operated employment offices throughout the nation. These offices place about five million workers in jobs each year. The poor make up about one-quarter of these placements. Employment offices are funded from federal unemployment insurance taxes paid by employers on their employees' wages. The federal government distributes funds to states using two criteria—the state's share of the labor force and its share of unemployed workers.

The USES is supposed to serve both employers and unemployed workers. It accepts job listing from private and public employers, and it accepts job applications from individuals seeking employment. For both employers and job-seekers, USES is a *free* job service. But USES sometimes has difficulty in getting employers to list jobs with the service, especially highly skilled or professional jobs. Most USES job applicants possess limited skills.

One reason for the difficulty confronting the USES in placing people may be that some individuals list themselves as job seekers in order to fulfill requirements of public assistance or unemployment insurance programs. Most state unemployment insurance programs require recipients to register with USES, to check with the service every week to see if there is a job opening in their field, and to state that they did not decline a job in their regular occupation as conditions of receiving unemployment benefits. In some cases, food stamps and other welfare benefits are being distributed to adults, whether or not there is a real likelihood that they will be employed, on the condition that they register with the USES. Employment offices also coordinate their efforts with federal and state job initiatives such as JTPA programs in their communities.

THE MINIMUM WAGE GETS A RAISE

Laws establishing minimum wages for workers have been an accepted strategy in fighting poverty since the federal Fair Labor Standards Act of 1938. The purpose of this law was to guarantee a wage that would sustain health and well-being and a decent standard of living for all workers. The minimum wage began at 25 cents per hour; by 1981 it had been increased to $3.35 where it remained until 1990. The act also established a forty-hour work week; employees can work longer, but for hourly workers, overtime usually requires additional pay. Over 90 percent of nonsupervisory personnel are covered by the law, with certain exceptions in retail trade, services, and agriculture.

Many believe that the minimum wage is the most direct and comprehensive way to increase the earnings of the working poor. Certainly, a high minimum wage helps the person who has a job, particularly an unskilled or semiskilled worker who is likely to be affected by minimum wage levels. But at the current rate if only one person in a family is employed, even if he or she works full-time, earnings still leave households with more than two members well below the official poverty level.

Some individuals argue that increases in the minimum wage increase unemployment by discouraging employers from hiring additional workers who have limited skills and whose labor may not be "worth" the minimum wage to employers. Those most likely to be excluded from jobs as a result of a higher minimum wage are teenagers. Some feel that they have not yet acquired the skills to make their labor commensurate with the minimum wage; a higher minimum wage might induce employers such as fast-food chains, movie theaters, and retail stores to cut back on their teenage help to cut costs. At a lower minimum wage, more teens might be expected to find work. The teenage unemployment rate is three times higher than the adult rate. Some economists claim that this youth unemployment is partly a result of the minimum wage, but there is no real consensus about whether a reduction or elimination of the minimum for teens would substantially reduce youth unemployment.

President Reagan proposed to address this issue of teenage unemployment with a *subminimum* or *training wage* that would allow employers to pay teenagers less during their first few months of employment. Although no such changes were made to the Fair Labor Standards Act during the Reagan administration, the minimum wage became one of the first major domestic battles of the Bush administration. Bush and Congress both favored raising the minimum wage, but they could not agree on how much of a raise was justified. Congress agreed on $4.55, but the president stood fast on $4.25. But more important than this 30 cent difference was Bush's insistence on a training wage of $3.40 for all workers in their first six months on the job. Congress vehemently opposed the training wage primarily because it would hurt those adult workers who earn the least and change jobs often in order to remain employed. President Bush vetoed Congress's version of the wage bill and the House was unable to muster enough votes (a two-thirds majority was needed) to override the president.

Finally, in November 1989, an agreement was reached, raising the minimum wage to $3.80 in April 1990 and $4.25 in 1991. Senator Edward Kennedy labeled the new wage a "disgrace," calling it "the best we could do against an anti-worker administration that refuses to do justice for America's working poor."[29] A training wage for teenage workers of $3.35 in 1990 and $3.61 in 1991 was included. Employers may pay sixteen to nineteen year-olds the training wage for the first ninety days of employment if the teenager has not worked before; this training wage can be extended for another ninety days if the employer has a training program. The training wage provision will expire in 1993, but Congress could vote to extend it. Some believe the training wage provision is virtually meaningless,[30] because eleven states already have minimum wages that exceed the federal level, and in other areas employers are already paying more than the minimum. Although it may affect rural areas, predictions are that the training wage will not have much of an impact on current wages and overall unemployment rates.

Several additional proposals for a fair wage for all workers have been proposed. They include indexing the minimum wage to inflation, setting the minimum wage at half of the national average wage (now about $9.30 an hour), and increasing the earned income tax credit (EITC) for those who earn low wages so they can take home more pay.[31]

SUMMARY

The curative strategy of the war on poverty was an attempt to eradicate many of America's social problems. But this effort to combat poverty by creating a variety of new social welfare programs failed to reduce the number of people counted as poor. The groundwork for the war on poverty was laid during the administration of President John F. Kennedy with the passage of the Area Redevelopment Act, but it was President Lyndon B. Johnson who succeeded in establishing the Office of Economic Opportunity (OEO). The purpose of the OEO was to assist the poor in establishing community action agencies to get at the causes of poverty rather than to provide direct cash grants to the poor. Job programs, literacy programs, legal-aid programs, and child-development programs were among the many services offered. Community action agencies were to be operated with the "maximum feasible participation of the poor."

The war on poverty sounded like a rational approach to remedying poverty, but the war was plagued by a number of problems that led to its demise. Many OEO staff members were inexperienced at administering social programs. The goals of the many programs were not clear, and services were often unnecessarily duplicated. Others contended that the war raised the expectations of poor Americans but provided so little funding for *each* community that it was doomed to failure. Accusations of racism toward whites and mismanagement within the programs all contributed to the demise of the OEO. The agency was abolished in 1974, when its remaining programs were transferred to other federal departments.

Case studies of Head Start programs, the Comprehensive Employment and Training Act (CETA), and the Legal Services Corporation help to illustrate how politics interferes with rational approaches to policy making. Conservatives attacked Head Start programs for having few long-term effects on participants. Liberals attacked conservatives for looking for a way to eliminate the Head Start programs. Conservatives believed that CETA paid for jobs that local governments would have funded anyway. Liberals believed that paying for these jobs was better than allowing financially troubled city governments to lay off workers. Opponents of the Legal Services Corporation reject the idea of lawyers being paid by the federal government to sue government agencies. Proponents believe that all citizens should be entitled to legal services, regardless of their financial status. Head Start and the Legal Services Corporation have survived, but CETA has been replaced with the Job Training Partnership Act. Although studies show that JTPA is producing some positive results, accusations of creaming remain, and the lack of control groups in evaluation studies makes a more objective determination of the program's effects difficult.

NOTES

1. President Lyndon B. Johnson, State of the Union Message, January, 1964.
2. Quoted in Daniel P. Moynihan, *Maximum Feasible Misunderstanding: Community Action in the War on Poverty* (New York: Free Press, 1969), pp. 3–4.
3. For an extensive elaboration of this argument, see Charles Murray, *Losing Ground: American Social Policy, 1950–1980* (New York: Basic Books, 1984).
4. Michael Harrington, *The Other America: Poverty in the United States* (New York: Macmillan, 1962).
5. John Kenneth Galbraith, *The Affluent Society* (Boston: Houghton Mifflin Co., 1958).
6. *Budget of the United States Government, Fiscal Year 1990* (Washington, D.C.: Executive Office of the President, Office of Management and Budget, 1989), pp. 2–26.
7. Ibid., p. 5–111.
8. *Major Policy Initiatives, Fiscal Year 1990* (Washington D.C.: U.S. Government Printing Office, 1989), pp. 122–23.
9. Murray, *Losing Ground*, p. 37.
10. This is a quote from Robert Taggart, Office of Youth Programs, U.S. Department of Labor, in the introduction to Charles Mallar et al., *Youth Knowledge Development Report 3.4, The Lasting Impacts of Job Corps Participation* (Washington, D.C.: U.S. Department of Labor, May 1980), p. ii.

11. Laurie J. Bassi and Orley Ashenfelter, "The Effect of Direct Job Creation and Training Programs on Low-Skilled Workers," in Sheldon H. Danzinger and Daniel H. Weinberg, eds. *Fighting Poverty: What Works and What Doesn't* (Cambridge: Harvard University Press, 1986), p. 149.
12. Westinghouse Learning Corporation, Ohio University, *The Impact of Head Start* (Washington D.C.: Office of Economic Opportunity, 1969).
13. Ann Crittenden, "A Head Start Pays Off in the End," *The Wall Street Journal* (November 29, 1984), p. 32.
14. *Newsweek* (December 22, 1980), p. 54.
15. Aaron Wildavsky, "The Empty Headed Blues: Black Rebellion and White Reactions," *Public Interest,* no. *11* (Spring 1968), pp. 3–4.
16. Westinghouse Learning Corporation, *The Impact of Head Start.*
17. For further discussion see James E. Anderson, *Public Policy-Making* (New York: Holt, Rinehart & Winston, 1975), pp. 149–151.
18. *Newsweek* (December 22, 1980), p. 54.
19. This information is cited in Julie Wurth, "Head Start still growing as others vie for attention," *The Champaign-Urbana News-Gazette,* April 29, 1990, p. A3.
20. Crittenden, "A Head Start Pays Off."
21. For additional information on evaluations of early education programs, see Nathan Glazer, "Education and Training Programs and Poverty" in Sheldon H. Danzinger and Daniel H. Weinberg, *Fighting Poverty;* pp. 153–79.
22. Julie Rovner, "Full Funding for Head Start Approved by Senate Panel," *Congressional Quarterly,* June 30, 1990, p. 2072.
23. *Budget of the United States Government, Fiscal Year 1982,* Office of Management and Budget, Washington D.C., p. 220
24. Kyle Pope, "Job-Training Programs—Awaiting Auditors' Verdict," *Austin American-Statesman* (June 12, 1989), Capital Business, pp. 1 and 8.
25. Grinker Associates, Inc., *An Independent Sector Assessment of the Job Training Partnership Act, Final Report, Program Year 1985* (New York, 1986).
26. Ibid.
27. D. Lee Bawden and John L. Palmer, "Social Policy: Challenging the Welfare State," in John L. Palmer and Isabel V. Sawhill, eds., *The Reagan Record* (Cambridge, Mass.: Ballinger, 1984), pp. 211–12.
28. Henry P. Guzda, "The U.S. Employment Service at 50: It Too Had to Wait Its Turn," *Monthly Labor Review* (June 1983), pp. 12–19.
29. Cited in "Some say minimum wage needs to be higher," *Champaign-Urbana News-Gazette,* April 1, 1990, p. A11.
30. Charles Green, "Senate Sends Minimum Wage Bill to Bush," *Austin American-Statesman* (November 9, 1989), p. A4.
31. Christine Gorman, "The Incredible Shrinking Paycheck," *Time* (August 1, 1988), p. 40.

10

IMPROVING HEALTH CARE
Treating the Nation's Ills

National health policy in America presents many examples of the problems of rational policy making. Political issues intervene at every stage of the rational decision-making process—in defining the goals of health policy, in identifying alternative courses of action, in assessing their potential costs, and in selecting policy alternatives that maximize the quality and accessibility of health care while minimizing costs.

Health care is a basic human need. Most of us would argue that nobody should suffer or die because they lack the financial resources to obtain adequate medical attention. But how much health care is enough? How much are people willing and able to pay for health care? If all of us cannot have all of the health care we want (that is, if health care is a *scarce resource*), then what means shall we use to decide who will get what care and how? As we shall see, these are largely *political* questions that do not lend themselves easily to rational planning.

Health care is an issue that affects all of us directly. For years, Congress debated the issue of subsidizing health care for the poor and the elderly and made only modest gains in covering these vulnerable populations. Then in 1965, as part of the war on poverty, major health-care programs were established for both groups. These programs were important for several reasons:

1. The poor and the aged, on the average, require more medical attention than the general population. Indeed, health problems are a contributing cause of unemployment, inadequate income, and poverty.
2. Preventive health care for many of the nation's poor is infrequent. In addition to health risks facing the poor, even minor costs can delay treatment of health problems until they develop into major crises.

3. Health-care facilities and personnel (the *delivery system* for health care) are particularly disorganized and inadequate in poor areas, both in inner cities and in poor rural communities.

We might think that providing more health-care coverage for the elderly and poor has reduced concerns about medical services in this country, but on the contrary, health care in the United States heads the list of pressing social welfare issues. The costs of health care for all citizens, rich and poor, are so astronomical that policy makers can no longer be concerned about how to provide health care for the poor and elderly alone. As we shall see, politicians, health care providers, employers, and citizens in general are concerned about the cost of health care for the entire population.

GOOD HEALTH OR MEDICAL ATTENTION?

The first obstacle to a rational approach to health policy is deciding upon our goal. Is health policy a question of *good health*—that is, whether we live at all, how well we live, and how long we live? Or are we striving for good *medical care*—that is, frequent and inexpensive visits to doctors, well-equipped and accessible hospitals, and equal access to medical attention by the rich and poor?

Good medical care does not necessarily mean good health. Good health is related to many factors over which doctors and hospitals have no control: heredity (the health of one's parents and grandparents), lifestyle (smoking, eating, drinking, exercise, worry), and the physical environment (sewage disposal, water quality, conditions of work, and so on). Of course, doctors can set broken bones, stop infections with drugs, and remove swollen appendixes. Anyone suffering from any of these or similar problems certainly wants the careful attention of a skilled physician and the best of hospital facilities. But in the long run, infant mortality, sickness and disease, and life span are affected surprisingly little by the quality of medical care.[1] If you want to live a long, healthy life, choose parents who have lived long, healthy lives, and then do all the things your mother always told you to do: Don't smoke, don't drink, get lots of exercise and rest, don't overeat, relax, and don't worry.

Historically, most of the reductions in infant mortality (deaths during the first year of life) and in adult death rates, in the United States and throughout the world, have resulted from improved public health and sanitation—including immunization against smallpox; the introduction of clean public water supplies and sanitary sewage disposal; and improvements in diets and nutrition and in standards of living. Many of today's leading causes of death (see Table 10–1, p. 208), including cancer, heart disease, stroke, cirrhosis of the liver, emphysema, accidents, and suicides, are closely linked to heredity, lifestyle, and personal habits.

Figure 10–1 shows the "crude" death rate (the number of deaths per 100,000 people) each year since 1930 and the age-adjusted death rate (which accounts for changes in the age composition of the population). As we can see, the overall death rate in the United States has continued its general decline. Considerable progress has been

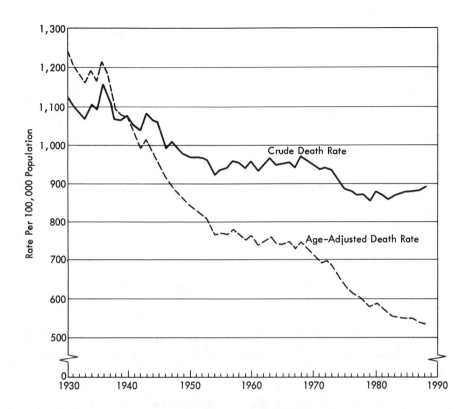

FIGURE 10-1   Crude and age-adjusted death rates: United States, 1930–1988
(*Source:* National Center for Health Statistics, "Annual Summary of Births,
Marriages, Divorces, and Deaths: United States, 1988," *Monthly Vital Statistics
Report 37,* no. 13 [July 26, 1989], p. 6.)

made in reducing death rates for many of the major killers—heart disease, stroke,
accidents, and atherosclerosis (see Table 10–1). However, the cancer death rate
continues to rise despite increased medical spending. Pulmonary diseases have also
resulted in an increased number of deaths, as have suicides and homicides and
septicemia. The number of deaths due to pneumonia and influenza, liver disease (often
associated with alcoholism), diabetes, and kidney disease have fluctuated. Heart
disease, cancer, stroke, and accidents account for nearly three-quarters of all deaths.
Infant mortality ranks as the fourteenth cause of death—at a rate of 7.5 per 100,000
population. The Human Immunodeficiency Virus (HIV) infection was first ranked as
a cause of death in 1987. Currently, it is the fifteenth leading cause of death in the
United States—at a rate of 6.6 (also see the illustration which follows on "The
Challenges of the HIV Epidemic"). Although overall adult and infant death rates for
the poor and for blacks have declined over time, they remain much higher than the
death rates for the nonpoor and for nonblacks.

Table 10–1   Leading Causes of Death (rate per 100,000 population per year)

	1960	1970	1980	1988
All causes	954.7	945.3	878.3	883.0
Heart disease	369.0	362.0	336.0	312.2
Cancer	149.2	162.8	183.9	198.6
Cerebrovascular disease (stroke)	108.0	101.9	75.1	61.1
Accidents	52.3	56.4	46.7	39.7
Pulmonary diseases[a]	9.9	15.2	24.7	33.3
Pneumonia and influenza	37.3	30.9	24.1	31.5
Diabetes	16.7	18.9	15.4	16.1
Suicide	10.6	11.6	11.9	12.3
Liver disease (including cirrohsis)	11.3	15.5	13.5	10.6
Atherosclerosis	20.0	15.6	13.0	9.6
Homicide	4.7	8.3	10.7	9.0
Kidney disease	7.6	4.4	7.4	8.9
Septicemia (blood poisoning)	1.1	1.7	4.2	8.5
Infant diseases	37.4	21.3	10.1	7.5
Human Immunodeficiency Virus (HIV) infection	--.-	--.-	--.-	6.6

[a]Figures for 1960 and 1970 include bronchitis, emphysema, and asthma.

Sources: U.S. Bureau of the Census, *Statistical Abstract of the United States, 1985* (Washington, D.C.: 1985) p. 74; *Monthly Vital Statistics Report, 37,* No. 13, (July 26, 1989), p. 7.

ILLUSTRATION: THE CHALLENGES OF THE HIV EPIDEMIC

No disease of recent times has challenged the American public like the Human Immunodeficiency Virus (HIV). In his book, *And the Band Played On,* Randy Shilts chronicled the first years of the recognition of the AIDS epidemic in America. Schilts described the situation this way: "In those early years, the federal government viewed AIDS as a budget problem, local public health officials saw it as a political problem, gay leaders considered AIDS a public relations problem, and the news media regarded it as a homosexual problem that wouldn't interest anybody else. Consequently, few confronted AIDS for what it was, a profoundly threatening medical crisis."[a] Since that time, many more specific criticisms have been leveled—the Food and Drug Administration's cumbersome requirements that prohibit prompt access to drugs that

[a]Randy Shilts, *And the Band Played On* (New York: St. Martin's Press, 1987), p. xxiii.

might have been helpful to those that were sick, lack of presidential initiative in addressing the problem, discrimination against those infected by employers, health care providers, schools, the public-at-large, and so on. Much has happened in the past few years. Some restrictions on access to drugs have been removed. Progress has been made in eliminating discrimination. Surgeon General C. Everett Koop saw to it that every household in America received objective, educational information about the virus. This and other educational campaigns have helped to ease some of the public's fears. Media accounts have dramatized the plight of persons with AIDS, both gay and straight. In 1987 Ronald Reagan appointed retired Navy Admiral James D. Watkins to chair the Presidential Commission on the Human Immunodeficiency Virus Epidemic. Watkins declared that current measures were woefully inadequate and he was praised for this forthrightness in helping to guide the work of the committee.[b] The following is the executive summary of the commission's report.

EXECUTIVE SUMMARY: REPORT OF THE PRESIDENTIAL COMMIS-SION ON THE HUMAN IMMU-NODEFICIENCY VIRUS[c]

The Human Immunodeficiency Virus (HIV) epidemic will be a challenging factor in American life for years to come and should be a concern to all Americans. Recent estimates suggest that almost 500,000 Americans will have died or progressed to later stages of the disease by 1992.

Even this incredible number, however, does not reflect the current gravity of the problem. One to 1.5 million Americans are believed to be infected with the human immunodeficiency virus but are not yet ill enough to realize it.

The recommendations of the Commission seek to strike a proper balance between our obligation as a society toward those members of society who have HIV and those members of society who do not have the virus. To slow or stop the spread of the virus, to provide proper medical care for those who have contracted the virus, and to protect the rights of both infected and non-infected persons requires a careful balancing of interests in a highly complex society.

Knowledge is a critical weapon against HIV—knowledge about the virus and how it is transmitted, knowledge of how to maintain one's health, knowledge of one's own infection status. It is critical too that knowledge lead to responsibility toward oneself and others. It is the responsibility of all Americans to become educated about HIV. It is the responsibility of those infected not to infect others. It is the responsibility of all

citizens to treat those infected with HIV with respect and compassion. All individuals should be responsible for their actions and the consequences of those actions.

Developed in the full Commission report are nearly 600 recommendations to prevent further spread of the virus, manage care of those infected with HIV, and enhance our efforts to discover a cure.

The urgency and breadth of the nation's HIV research effort is without precedent in the history of the federal government's response to an infectious disease crisis. However, we are a long way from all the answers. The directing of more resources toward managing this epidemic is critical; equally important is the judicious use of those resources.

For the reader who does not have the time to review all the material which follows, the Commission has prepared a list of its 20 most important findings and recommendations, no one of which can stand alone or be ignored. These will be detailed in the body of the report, and together comprise a comprehensive national strategy for effectively managing the HIV epidemic.

- The term "AIDS" is obsolete. "HIV infection" more correctly defines the problem. The medical, public health, political, and community leadership must focus on the full course of HIV infection rather than concentrating on later stages of the disease (ARC and AIDS). Continual focus on AIDS rather than the entire spectrum of HIV disease has left our nation unable to deal adequately with the epidemic. Federal and state data collection efforts must now be focused on early HIV reports, while still collecting data on symptomatic disease.

- Early diagnosis of HIV infection is essential, not only for proper medical treatment and counseling of the infected person but also for proper follow-up by the public health authorities. HIV infection, like other chronic conditions—heart disease,

[b]Dick Thompson, "Frank Talk About the AIDS Crisis," *Time,* June 13, 1988, p. 53.

[c] *Report of the Presidential Commission on the Human Immunodeficiency Virus* (Washington D.C.: U.S. Government Printing Office, 1988), pp. xvii–xix.

high blood pressure, diabetes, can-cer—can be treated more effectively when detected early. Therefore, HIV tests should be offered regularly by health care providers in order to in-crease the currently small percentage of those infected who are aware of the fact and under appropriate care. Since many manifestations of HIV are treatable, those infected should have ready access to treatment for the opportunistic infections which often prove fatal for those with HIV.

• Better understanding of the true inci-dence and prevalence of HIV infec-tion is critical and can be developed only through careful accumulation of data from greatly increased testing. Quality assured testing should be easily accessible, confidential, volun-tary, and associated with appropriate counseling and care services. At the present time, a relatively small per-centage of those infected with HIV are aware of their infected status. For their own protection and for the pro-tection of those not infected, strong efforts should be made to provide easily accessible voluntary testing. Many of the detailed suggestions in the report with respect to testing are directed toward increasing this percentage.

• HIV infection is a disability and should be treated as such under federal and state law in the public and private sectors. Fear has led to discrimination against persons known to be infected. This reaction is inappropriate. Infected persons should be encouraged to continue normal activities, such as work or school, and live in their own homes as long as they are able. The average time between infection and clinical symptoms is now thought to be seven to eight years—years which should be productive.

• Stronger protection is needed in federal and state law to protect the privacy of those with HIV, with sig-nificant penalties for violation of confidentiality standards, yet with a list of necessary exceptions clearly defined in the statutes. These excep-tions are listed in detail in Chapter Nine of our report, in the section on Confidentiality.

• Some preventive measures must be undertaken immediately.
  —Public health authorities across the United States must begin imme-diately to institute confidential part-ner notification, the system by which intimate contacts of persons carrying sexually transmitted diseases, includ-ing HIV, are warned of their exposure.
  —Agencies which license and certify health care facilities must move im-mediately to require every facility to notify all persons who received blood transfusions since 1977 that they may have been exposed to HIV and may need testing and counseling.

• Prevention and treatment of intra-venous drug abuse, an important fa-cilitator of the HIV epidemic, must become a top national priority. In-creased law enforcement efforts to interrupt the supply of drugs must be coupled with greatly expanded treat-ment capacity, with the goal of treat-ment on demand, to restore addicted individuals to healthful living.

• Use of other illegal drugs, as well as abuse of alcohol, are facilitators in the spread of HIV by impairing judg-ment and depressing the immune sys-tem. Federal and state efforts to limit HIV spread must contain major com-ponents in these areas. Drug and alcohol abuse education is essential for all school children, adolescents, and minorities as well as for all other Americans.

• New federal and state nursing schol-arship and loan programs need to be enacted immediately to encourage nurses to serve in areas of high HIV impact, as well as to address the nursing shortage which impedes effi-cient health care delivery in all other areas. Nurses will provide the major portion of care, both inside and out-side the hospital setting, to those with HIV. There is currently a severe nursing shortage, which is only projected to grow worse over the next decade.

- The National Health Service Corps, which places health care professionals in medically underserved areas, is currently slated for termination, but should be extended and greatly expanded. The health care industry should give special consideration to recruiting minority health professionals.

- Aggressive biomedical research is the key to unlocking the mysteries that surround finding a vaccine and cure for HIV. Greater administrative flexibility must be given to the National Institutes of Health to pursue its research goals. Liability obstacles must be removed, and clinical trials greatly expanded to include a broader spectrum of the infected population.

- More equitable and cost-effective financing of care for persons with HIV needs to be examined through a series of new or expanded demonstration programs involving federal and state government subsidy of private insurance premiums for needy patients and greater contribution to risk pools. It is important to move toward an organized system of care, with case management as a principal tool to control costs and provide quality care.

- Concerns of health care workers need to be better addressed by all levels of government as well as the private sector. All of those in the health care delivery system, ranging from the ambulance driver and other emergency "first responders," to physicians, nurses, dentists, lab technicians, social workers, chaplains, and allied health care workers, to obstetricians and surgeons performing invasive procedures, should be provided with complete information about HIV, adequate protective materials, and a safe working environment in which to provide comprehensive and compassionate care.

- Safety of the blood supply needs to be continually assured by the federal government. High priority should be placed on the Food and Drug Administration (FDA) test approval for new, less time-consuming HIV detection tests. Additionally, a restructured blood products advisory committee needs to work with FDA to continuously examine mechanisms that will protect our blood supply.

- In health care facilities, all reasonable strategies to avoid a transfusion of someone else's blood (homologous transfusion) should be implemented by substituting, whenever possible, transfusion with one's own blood (autologous transfusion). Currently available techniques of autologous transfusion include predonation of one's own blood, recirculation of one's own blood during surgery (intraoperative autologous transfusion), blood dilution techniques (hemo-dilution), and post-operative collection for retransfusion (post-operative salvage). Health care facilities should offer aggressive in-service training to their staff on these procedures, and informed consent for the transfusion of blood or its components should include an explanation of the risk involved with transfusion as well as the alternatives to homologous transfusion.

- Education programs must continue to be developed and implemented for the near term, and for the greatest possible positive impact on the next generation. Age appropriate, comprehensive health education programs in our nation's schools, in kindergarten through grade twelve, should be a national priority.

- The problem of HIV-infected "boarder babies" is one of the most heartrending the Commission has encountered. These children live their entire brief and tragic lives in hospital wards, with only doctors and nurses as family. The expected 10,000 to 20,000 HIV-infected births by 1991 also call attention to the critical need for foster homes. Unless the problems of the disadvantaged are addressed, the HIV epidemic will continue to make inroads into these populations and we will see large increases in both pediatric and drug-related HIV disease.

- The problems of teenagers, and especially run-away youth, that place them at increased risk for HIV exposure must be aggressively addressed. The spread of HIV within the heterosexual population should be better defined and accurate information communicated to the general public. Inaccurate and misleading statements suggesting that HIV cannot be spread through heterosexual activity are unwarranted.

- The HIV epidemic has highlighted several ethical considerations and responsibilities, including:

  —the responsibility of those who are HIV-infected not to infect others;
  —the responsibility of the health care community to offer comprehensive and compassionate care to all HIV-infected persons; and
  —the responsibility of all citizens to treat HIV-infected persons with respect and compassion.

- International efforts to combat the spread of HIV infection should be encouraged and assisted by the United States, through our research community and our national contribution to the World Health Organization and the Global Programme on AIDS.

The Commission believes that if the recommendations in this report are fully implemented, we will have achieved the delicate balance between the complex needs and responsibilities encountered throughout our society when responding to the HIV epidemic.

MEDICAID: HEALTH CARE FOR THE POOR

Black, Hispanic, and poor Americans have greater health problems than the white and the affluent. A case in point is the infant mortality rate, which is considered to be especially sensitive to the adequacy of health care and is therefore frequently used as a general indicator of well-being. In spite of the fact that the United States "ranks twenty-second in infant mortality among developed nations,"[2] infant deaths have declined rapidly over the last thirty years for both whites and blacks. But black infant death rates, which have been consistently higher than those for whites, remain almost twice as high as white infant death rates (see Figure 10–2). These and other health statistics clearly suggest that African-Americans and poor Americans do not enjoy the same good health as white and more affluent Americans.

Prior to 1965, medical care for the poor was primarily a responsibility of state and local governments and private charity. But interest in national health care for the poor dates back to the turn of the century, when reform groups during the Progressive Era first proposed a national health insurance plan. Opposition from the American Medical Association (AMA) forced President Franklin D. Roosevelt to abandon the idea of including health insurance in the original Social Security Act for fear that it would endanger passage of the entire act. Every year from 1935 to 1965, major health insurance bills were introduced into Congress. But all of them failed, in large part because of the opposition the AMA was able to arouse. National health insurance became a major issue in the Truman administration in the late 1940s, but the AMA

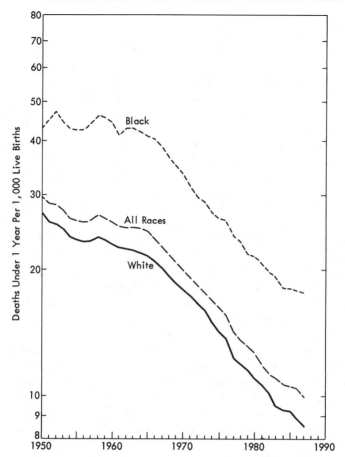

FIGURE 10–2   Infant mortality rates by race: United States, 1950–1987 (*Source:* National
Center for Health Statistics, "Advance Report of Final Mortality Statistics,
1987," *Monthly Vital Statistics Report 38,* no. 5, Supplement [September 26,
1989], p. 9.)

continually succeeded in branding national health insurance as "socialized medicine." Proposals for national health insurance generally tried to "socialize" health *insurance* but did not call for government ownership of hospitals and employment of physicians as in Great Britain. Even so, fear of government interference in medical practice and opposition from the medical community succeeded in defeating major government health programs for thirty years. In 1950, the federal government did authorize states to use federal-state public assistance funds (under the Old Age Assistance, Aid to the Blind, Aid to the Permanently and Totally Disabled, and Aid to Dependent Children programs) for medical services. In 1957, the Kerr-Mills Act began a separate federal and state matching program for hospital care for the elderly and the poor, but not all of the states participated in the program.

Then, in 1965, important changes were made in the Social Security Act to provide health care to the poor and aged. The program for poor Americans, under Title

XIX of the act, is called *Medicaid*. Medicaid rapidly grew to be the federal government's largest single public assistance program. The costs of Medicaid now exceed the costs of all other welfare programs—including SSI, AFDC, and Food Stamps. Medicaid is a combined federal and state program. It replaced earlier medical assistance under the Kerr-Mills Act. The federal government pays an average of 55 percent of Medicaid costs; in 1990 this share was about $37 billion.[3] States receive 50 to 83 percent of their Medicaid expenditures from the federal government, with poorer states receiving the most. The states carry the rest of the financial burden, about $29 billion in 1990. The states also exercise broad administrative powers. Like AFDC and Food Stamps, Medicaid is an *entitlement* program; everyone who qualifies and requests assistance must be served.

Medicaid services are provided in-kind. Patients receive services from physicians and other health-care providers, and these providers are directly reimbursed by the government. No prior contributions are required by the beneficiaries; monies come from general tax revenues. Twenty-six states use some type of program cost sharing such as requiring recipients to pay small deductibles or copayments for services, but they cannot impose these requirements for emergency and family planning services.[4] Certain recipients, primarily nursing home patients (whose income already goes to pay for their care), pregnant women, and children, are not required to share costs.

Although states differ in their eligibility requirements, they must cover certain groups, for example, all those receiving AFDC and most SSI recipients. Remember, however, that states determine who receives AFDC, and income limits for eligibility are often very low. Recipients who are eventually able to earn enough to make them ineligible for AFDC and SSI benefits must be allowed to maintain their Medicaid coverage for several additional months. Pregnant women and infants who have incomes at or below the official poverty level also qualify for Medicaid. Like other public assistance programs, assets in addition to income are considered in determining eligibility.

States can also choose to cover other groups under Medicaid, such as pregnant women and infants whose incomes are up to 185 percent of the poverty level, and other poor children as well as poor aged, blind, and disabled individuals. In addition, thirty-six states provide Medicaid to those who fall under a category that the federal government calls "medically needy." This category includes individuals and families with high medical expenses and children and pregnant women with limited incomes and assets. One of the most important improvements in Medicaid in recent years has been to broaden both required and optional Medicaid beneficiary categories to include more poor women who are pregnant and more children. But as stated in the official *Social Security Bulletin*, "Even under the broadest provisions of the Federal statute (except for emergency services for a few specific persons), the Medicaid program does not provide health services, even for very poor persons, unless they are aged, blind, disabled, pregnant, under 21, or in certain families with children who are deprived of parental support."[5] Some states do provide health care services to groups for whom they receive no federal reimbursement. For example, some provide services to those receiving unemployment compensation.

States also help set benefits under Medicaid. All states are required by the federal government to provide inpatient and outpatient hospital care; physicians' services; laboratory and X-ray services; skilled-nursing-home services and home health care for adults; family planning; rural health clinics; nurse-midwife services and prenatal care; and early, periodic screening, diagnosis, and treatment (EPSDT) services for children. States may offer other benefits if they wish, and thirty-two currently do. Most often, these involve clinic services; intermediate residential care, often provided by nursing homes; eye care; prescription drugs; prosthetic devices; dental care; and skilled nursing home care for children. Certain protections are afforded Medicaid participants. For example, they must be offered some choice in selecting health care providers.[6]

The states have a great deal of latitude in determining the extent of benefits offered, such as the number of allowable physician visits, and they determine reimbursement rates for services. When states set their reimbursement rates low, hospitals and physicians may be discouraged from providing good care or any care at all under Medicaid.

Approximately twenty-five million people per year receive Medicaid benefits. This figure is considerably less than the thirty-two million whose incomes fall below the poverty level. AFDC families comprise two-thirds of all Medicaid beneficiaries, but their medical bills account for a relatively small portion of Medicaid expenditures.[7] Two-thirds of all Medicaid funds are actually used by aged and disabled recipients, and 40 percent of Medicaid funds go to pay for long-term care for these groups. This 40 percent of Medicaid funds is used by only 7 percent of all Medicaid recipients. In 1987, the average amount of Medicaid funds spent on an AFDC child was $542, compared with $8,300 for aged nursing home patients in skilled and intermediate care facilities, and $38,000 for mentally retarded persons in intermediate care facilities.[8]

Medicaid costs have far exceeded original estimates. The rapid rise in the AFDC rolls in the late 1960s and in SSI for the disabled in the 1970s accounts for some of the increased costs of the program. Another factor has been the high rate of inflation in medical-care prices. Hospital costs and physicians' fees have raced far ahead of the inflation rates affecting all other segments of the economy. For example, in 1982 alone, health-care inflation stood at 11 percent while the general consumer price index rose by only 3.9 percent.[9] Ironically, part of this inflation has been produced by the Medicaid and Medicare programs themselves, which have created heavier demands for medical care. Finally, the large percentage of Medicaid funding spent on nursing-home care has spawned many new nursing home facilities, and it has resulted in many more aged and disabled people being placed in these facilities. The nation's governors are becoming increasingly angry about Medicaid. Congress has required the states to cover more of the poor in order to reduce sharp differences in the program across states, but states are feeling burdened by their increased Medicaid costs.[10]

Block grants are also used to provide medical care, primarily for low-income individuals. The Maternal and Child Health Block Grant provides medical care to low-income pregnant women and young children. The Health Services Block Grant provides funds for community health centers. These centers provide medical care to low-income individuals in areas with few doctors or medical facilities; treatment for those with specific health problems, such as hypertension; health programs for migrant workers; rodent-control programs; and other services. States and communities also search for creative ways to stretch health care dollars, but many people remain without a regular source of health care and without a way to pay for health-care bills.

In the past, hospitals and physicians have made up for the costs of providing services to those who could not pay their bills by shifting these costs to third-party payers (government programs and private health insurers) and to patients who could afford the bills. But today, it is becoming increasingly difficult for hospitals to do this because of cost-containment strategies in Medicare and because private insurance companies are also determined to hold down the costs of medical care. Individual consumers and employers who purchase medical benefits for their employees are also complaining about medical costs. Hospitals, public and private, are businesses. When they cannot recoup their costs, one solution is for them to provide fewer services to those who cannot pay. However, public hospitals cannot refuse to treat indigent patients; as a result, they feel that they are unfairly burdened for treating nonpaying patients when cuts in government funding to hospitals are made.

Everyone knows the old saying that "an ounce of prevention is worth a pound of cure." When the poor are denied access to health care, they may be forced to wait until their health has severely deteriorated before they seek or are able to obtain health care. This strategy does nothing to save health-care dollars but instead adds to the costs of health care. What is needed is a health-care program that will cover all medically needy persons and reimburse health-care providers at reasonable rates, but the formula for achieving this balance has eluded policy makers.

MEDICARE: HEALTH CARE FOR THE AGED

Considerable progress has been made in meeting the income and health care needs of older Americans. Older citizens have higher incomes and fewer live in poverty than ever before. But as the numbers of older Americans continue to grow, the costs of their health care raises more concerns. The aged have about two and one-half times as many restricted activity days as the general population and more than twice as many days in bed and in hospitals.[11]

Medicare, like Medicaid, began in 1965 as an amendment to the nation's Social Security Act. Under Title XVIII of the act it provides prepaid hospital insurance for the aged under Social Security and low-cost medical insurance for the aged directly under federal administration. Medicare includes

1. Hospital Insurance (HI), a compulsory basic health insurance plan covering hospital costs for the aged which is financed out of payroll taxes. (In 1990, 1.45 percent of Social Security taxable wages was used to finance HI. Beginning in 1991 this 1.45 percent will be extended from $51,300 to $125,000 of wages).
2. Supplementary Medical Insurance (SMI), a voluntary, supplemental medical insurance program that will pay doctors' bills and additional medical expenses and is financed in part by contributions from the aged and in part by general tax revenues.

The largest group of Medicare beneficiaries are those aged sixty-five or older who are eligible for Social Security retirement benefits or who would be eligible if they retired. Eligibility is not dependent on income. Long-term disabled workers and those with end-stage renal disease may also qualify, as well as some aged individuals who do not have enough earnings credits to qualify for Social Security retirement benefits. As part of the Social Security system, Medicare compels employers and employees to pay into the program during working years in order for workers to enjoy the benefits, including health insurance, after retirement. Benefits under HI include a broad range of hospital services as well as some skilled-nursing-home care and home health-care services following a hospital stay. After the beneficiary pays a deductible ($592 in 1990), Medicare pays for the remainder of the first sixty days in the hospital and a *portion* of additional days. For example, for days sixty-one through ninety, the patient must pay $148 per day; the federal government picks up the tab for the remainder.

Benefits under SMI include physicians' services, outpatient hospital care, and other medical services. The cost of SMI, $28.60 per month, in 1990 (scheduled to increase to $46.20 by 1995) has been considered reasonable enough that participation by the elderly is almost universal. SMI payments can be deducted automatically from Social Security payments. Beneficiaries of SMI must pay for the first $75 of services themselves each year (due to rise to $100 by 1995); after that, Medicare pays 80 percent of most services while the patient pays the remaining 20 percent. The home health services that are included under SMI, such as part-time skilled nursing care, do not require any deductibles or coinsurance payments. Medicare now includes benefits for hospice services.

Both the HI and SMI provisions of Medicare require patients to pay an *initial* charge. The purposes are to discourage unnecessary medical care and to recover some of the costs of the program. Medicare does *not* pay for custodial nursing-home care, most dental care (including dentures), private-duty nursing, eyeglasses and eye examinations, most prescription drugs, routine physician examinations, and hearing tests and hearing devices. The program now serves thirty-three million elderly and disabled Americans, and its costs were about $95 billion in 1990; this was a huge increase from the $3.4 billion which Medicare cost in 1965 and the $32 billion which it cost in 1980.[12] Although measures have been taken to ensure that Social Security retirement benefits are on sound footing, the problems of how to finance rapidly escalating Medicare costs have only recently begun to be addressed.[13]

The Medicare Surtax: Here Today, Gone Tomorrow

A serious problem with the current health care system in America is the inadequate coverage provided by most types of health insurance—both public and private. *Private* health insurance plans do not cover all medical needs. For example, they may: limit payments to the first thirty or sixty days of hospital care; place caps on the dollar amounts paid to hospitals and physicians for a patient during his or her lifetime; exclude the costs of various diagnostic tests, outpatient care and office visits. Moreover, private insurance often will not cover individuals who need insurance the most—those initially found to be in poor health. Perhaps the most serious concern about private insurance is that it frequently fails to cover "catastrophic" medical costs—costs that may run into the tens or hundreds of thousands of dollars for serious, long-term illnesses. Many people would lose everything they own if such a catastrophe occurred.

Public programs like Medicare also leave gaps, referred to as *medigaps,* in health care coverage. The most notable gaps are long-term custodial care and the costs of catastrophic illnesses. Congress made attempts to close some of these gaps—primarily long hospital stays as well as prescription drugs—when it passed the Medicare Catastrophic Health Care Act of 1988. Under the act, Medicare beneficiaries were entitled to unlimited hospital care after paying an annual deductible ($560 in 1989), and they received more coverage for home health, hospice, and skilled nursing care. They also would have been entitled to coverage for some of the costs of high prescription drug bills beginning in 1990. These added provisions sounded quite appealing. But the additional coverage was financed by a surtax on the incomes of Medicare recipients—$22.50 for each $150 dollars of federal income tax the individual or couple paid—and an additional $4.00 a month for SMI. The maximum surtax was set at $800. But one year after the provisions took effect, Congress repealed the law. In a nutshell, older Americans just were *not* willing to pay that much more for the increased coverage, and they successfully pressured Congress to repeal the law. What at first seemed to be a step toward more comprehensive care boomeranged. The act was of greatest benefit to poorer Americans with serious health problems. These individuals' surtax contribution was small compared to the benefits they would have received had they become seriously ill. But wealthier Medicare beneficiaries were paying a higher surtax. Many of these individuals already had supplemental Medicare policies designed to cover some of Medicare's medigaps. Of course, some supplemental policies do this better than others. Congress has had to enact legislation to regulate the sale of these policies, because some unscrupulous individuals had taken advantage of seniors' fears of impoverishment from illness by selling them policies that sounded good but did not cover the gaps. The poor often cannot afford good supplemental policies, so their medigaps are more likely to remain now that the surtax has been repealed. The surtax turned out to be a major miscalculation in health care policy.

LONG-TERM CARE

A discussion of long-term care requires clarification of the terms skilled, intermediate, and custodial nursing-home care, and home health care. Skilled care is the highest level of service and is the only type of nursing home care that is reimbursed by Medicare. It is generally needed for a short time—for example, following some surgeries. Intermediate care and custodial care are usually not covered by Medicare or by supplemental Medicare policies, yet these types of care are often needed. Medicare covers some types of care provided to people in their own homes, but it does not cover care needed on a twenty-four-hour basis.

When long-term care is needed, it is generally paid for in one of two ways. One way is for patients to pay for it themselves. The problem is that nursing home care is expensive. Even a modest facility can cost $2,000 a month. Many people enter a nursing home with some funds, but savings can easily be depleted if the stay is for a long period, and there may be a spouse at home whose living expenses must also be paid. The second way long-term care is covered is by Medicaid. In order to qualify for nursing home care under Medicaid, a person must be poor by Medicaid standards. When there was a spouse at home, both the nursing home patient and the spouse had to deplete their assets to qualify. Now, under the Medicaid Impoverishment Act of 1988, the spouse of a Medicaid nursing home patient is allowed to have considerably more assets (as much as $60,000) and income than previously. The federal government sets maximums on these amounts, and each state determines exactly how much it will allow. No only really wants to be in a nursing home or be a Medicaid patient in a nursing home. It is often easy to distinguish private-pay patients from Medicaid patients, because the rooms of Medicaid patients are not as nice, and Medicaid patients cannot have private rooms. But many more people will be spending time in a nursing home. "The Health Care Financing Administration estimates that [by the year 2035] the nursing home population will increase four times faster than the U.S. population as a whole."[14] Much of the increase will be due to the aging of the baby boom generation.

Without greater governmental participation in the costs of long-term care, the only other viable option seems to be private long-term care insurance which might cover both nursing home care and home health care. (In-home options might be more cost effective than nursing home care.) The problem is that these policies can be expensive. According to one columnist who writes extensively on the concerns of older Americans, a person at age sixty-five "might pay $675 [a year] for a typical policy, compared with $2,100 at 79."[15] The future costs of these policies is unclear because they are very new and "[i]nsurers...haven't a clue what the claims will be."[16] In addition, one health care advocacy group reported that many policies currently have "...so many restrictions that anyone entering a nursing home had only four chances in ten of collecting on their coverage."[17] But as the need becomes greater, policies are likely to improve, and the use of this option is likely to grow.

Another type of private coverage that is also not accessible to the poor is to purchase a unit like an apartment in a facility for seniors and to pay a fixed amount per month for its upkeep and maintenance. Lifetime care, including nursing home care, is then assured for the individual or couple on the condition that the dwelling becomes the property of the facility at the time of death. As usual, the wealthier one is, the more options available.

Even with these alternatives for long-term care, it is interesting to note that family members continue to be the largest source of care for the elderly.[18] Although 25 percent of older Americans can expect to spend some time in a nursing home, only 5 percent of the older population is in such a facility at any point.[19] More could be done to help families keep their elderly members at home by providing tax breaks for these caretakers and by providing more governmentally supported services for them such as respite care.

WHAT AILS MEDICINE?

Have changes in national policy made a difference in the health of the poor? There is no doubt that *access* to medical care has improved with Medicaid and Medicare. By the 1970s, it was demonstrated that the poor were actually seeing doctors about 20 percent more often than the nonpoor, and their rates of hospitalization were also greater.[20] This may not be as surprising as it seems since the poor are more likely to be ill or disabled. But there is also evidence that after controlling for health status, the poor receive less health care services.[21] Not surprisingly, the uninsured use health care less than those with some form of public or private insurance.[22]

Despite a general increase in access to health care, there has not been a concomitant improvement in the nation's health. Evidence from the early 1970s on this point was particularly bleak—there seemed to be *no* relationship between increased health care expenditures and improved health for vulnerable groups.[23] There have been general improvements in infant mortality rates, death rates due to specific causes, and average life spans for all groups, but the poor remain below the nonpoor on *all* these measures. There are many possible explanations for these general improvements, including lifestyle and environmental changes, but there are few convincing indications that Medicaid and Medicare have been mainly responsible for these improvements. Improvements in health statistics were just as great prior to the enactment of Medicaid and Medicare as they have been since these programs were enacted. Perhaps of greatest concern is that the United States spends more than any other industrialized country on health care—it is estimated that it spent more than $2,500 per person in 1990[24]—yet the United States ranks below most other industrialized countries in infant mortality rates. The effects of greater expenditures to improve the health of the country have fallen considerably short of expectations.

Also consider the contrasts posed by the states of Utah and Nevada. The residents of these states have similar incomes, education, urbanization, climate, and numbers of physicians and hospital beds. Utah enjoys one of the highest levels of health in the nation—lower death rates, fewer days lost to sickness, longer life spans. Why, on the other hand, is Nevada at the opposite end of the rankings of the states on these measures of health?

> The answer almost surely lies in the different life styles of... the two states. Utah is inhabited primarily by Mormons... who do not use tobacco or alcohol and in general lead stable, quiet lives. Nevada... has high rates of cigarette and alcohol consumption and very high indexes of marital and geographic instability.[25]

Channeling more funds to help Americans adopt healthier life styles may be one of the best uses of health-care dollars.

It has been argued that what America needs is a national health plan, but the need may *not* be for *more* health care. Indeed, some Americans may be receiving too much medicine. One point of view is that a national health plan for the United States, rather than being a step forward, might be a "giant step sideways"—and perhaps an actual health hazard.[26] Such a plan might encourage the United States to continue to put scarce resources into even more sophisticated, elaborate, and costly medical care, whether or not this care had much impact on the nation's health. The *need* is for a rational means of distributing a scarce resource—medical care—in an efficient fashion to improve the nation's health. We cannot really hope to provide *all* the health care that *everyone* wants.

HEALTH CARE AND COST CONTAINMENT

It would be much easier to offer health care benefits to cover all Americans if medical costs were not so high. Total national health care expenditures (public and private) have risen from about $30 billion in 1960 to more than $500 billion a year today.[27] Instead of spending 5 percent of the annual gross national product (the total of all goods and services the country produces) on health care, we are spending nearly 12 percent, and the figure continues to rise. Several factors have contributed to the escalation of medical costs:

1. *Third-party financing* has contributed to these rapidly increasing health costs. This includes the expansion of private insurance plans as well as the rapid growth of the Medicaid and Medicare programs.
2. The growing number of older people has also contributed. Those over sixty-five use more health care services than the rest of the population.
3. Advances in medical technology are also contributors. Amazing improvements have occurred in the diagnosis and treatment of certain illnesses—including heart disease and cancer—which not long ago were considered fatal. Equipment such as CAT scanners (which by means of a computer can take a detailed X-ray of the entire human body), the ability to transplant organs, and other extraordinary means of sustaining life are also adding to costs. The technology that continues to be developed has allowed for increased survival rates among the tiniest of infants and among persons with many types of serious ailments.
4. There has been a vast expansion of hospital facilities—an expansion which has created an excess of hospital beds that are expensive to maintain. It was the federal government, through the Hill-Burton Act, that encouraged the building of new hospitals from the late 1950s through the early 1970s. Now there are complaints that the nation is "overbedded."*
5. The threat of malpractice results in doctors ordering more tests even if their utility is questionable. There is little incentive to hold down costs when third-party financing is available. Patients generally want all the best services available, and physicians are motivated to accommodate them. As the number of malpractice suits with large awards grows, the cost of malpractice insurance increases. These costs are also passed on to consumers.

DRGs

What is being done to contain health care costs? A number of measures have been taken in the Medicare program. *Diagnosis-related groups (DRGs)* and *Medicare assignment* are two of the more prominent attempts to curb costs. In 1983, Congress enacted a controversial DRG system. Prior to this time, there were some restrictions on what Medicare would reimburse hospitals, but generally, Medicare reimbursement was based on the total amount the hospital charged for the patient's care. This was a *retrospective* (after-the-fact) method of paying for hospital care. Despite strong

---

* The reverse is true for some rural areas which may not even have a doctor, let alone a hospital. A number of rural hospitals have already closed because of rising health care costs. Problems in providing health care services in rural areas are growing.

opposition, the DRGs introduced a *prospective* method of paying for hospital costs, in which the federal government specifies in advance what it will pay hospitals for the treatment of diagnosis-related groups. (The list of DRGs consists of almost 500 different illnesses.) This plan originally pertained only to hospitals, not to physician services, and it is not used in the Medicaid program. When a hospital spends more to treat a patient than the DRG allows, it must absorb the additional costs, but when it spends less than the DRG allows, it can keep the difference. Hospitals are not allowed to change Medicare patients more than the DRG. Obviously, the purpose of DRGs is to make hospitals more cost efficient, and immediate cost savings were seen. In 1984, the average hospital stay was 7.5 days, down from 9.5 in 1983.[28] But continuing reports indicate that the DRGs may be doing more harm than good by discharging patients "sicker and quicker."[29] A report by the House Government Operations Committee indicated that more than two-hundred-thousand Medicare patients were discharged when still "medically unstable."[30] It claimed that these premature discharges had resulted in significant numbers of *readmissions,* thereby adding to the costs of treatment. The federal government's Health Care Financing Administration and the American Hospital Association have disputed these claims of inadequate care.[31]

Controlling Physician Fees

Containment of physicians' charges has been more difficult to achieve. Medicare has traditionally paid physicians what was "usual, customary, and reasonable" in their community. Opposition from physicians and the AMA to controlling fees was a formidable obstacle to overcome.[32] Cost control provisions have included freezes on the amount that "participating" physicians can charge Medicare patients. Participating physicians agree to accept Medicare approved rates as payment in full (called Medicare assignment), while "nonparticipating" physicians may charge patients in addition to the amount approved by Medicare. Incentives have been used to increase the number of participating physicians, such as prompter reimbursement by Medicare. In 1988, about two-hundred-thousand physicians, 37 percent of all physicians who benefit from Medicare, voluntarily accepted Medicare approved rates as their full fee.[33] "Medicare accounts for one-fourth of the average physician's fees."[34]

But Congress decided it was time to reckon further with the AMA, whose members now account for a smaller percentage of the nation's doctors than ever before.[35] Three major changes, largely borrowed from the Canadian national health care system, will be in effect by 1992 to control physician's fees. The first change is *expenditure targets* which set a goal for total Medicare payments to physicians each year in order to control the amount of services provided. If the total amount that physicians bill Medicare is within the year's target, the increase in physicians' fees for the next year will be larger than if the target is not met. If the target is not met, the excess costs will be taken from the next year's budget. The second change is to limit *balance billing,* which occurs when physicians charge the patient for the difference between their usual charge and what Medicare pays. Physicians will be prohibited from charging poor patients more than the amount Medicare reimburses, and there will be restrictions on how much more physicians can charge other patients. The third change is to pay physicians according to a fee schedule for about seven-thousand different services. Fees are determined by factors such as the amount of work the service involves, the costs required to perform the service, the training required to perform the service, and differences in service costs due to geographical area. The AMA has been especially critical of the expenditure targets, saying that the targets might reduce the amount and quality of medical care to the elderly. But the AMA has been criticized for its economic self-interest.[36]

Since the Medicare system is so large, the way Medicare goes, so goes the rest of health care. For example, when the DRGs were adopted in Medicare, private insurance companies adopted similar procedures. These companies are likely to adopt Medicare's new physician reimbursement strategies as well.

Cost control measures in the Medicaid program have been of a different nature—reimbursement rates in many states are very low, so low that many physicians do not participate, and private hospitals also are not required to treat Medicaid patients except in emergencies. Still, Medicaid remains the country's largest public assistance program.

PRIVATE HEALTH CARE OPTIONS—FROM HMO TO PPO

It used to be simple. When you needed health care, you went to a doctor, paid the fee on the spot, or negotiated payment arrangements with the physician. Doctors even came to the home when a family member was ill. Now, consumers complain that a glossary is needed just to figure out what type of arrangement they should select to obtain health care, even before they see a physician. Until the 1940s, few people had private health insurance. Care was paid for out of the individual's pocket as the need arose. Then companies like Blue Cross and Blue Shield developed, offering the public health insurance; a monthly premium entitles the consumer to reimbursement for many health care services. Workers generally obtain their health insurance through their employer's group plan, because these plans are less expensive than individual plans. As health care grew to be an exceedingly big business, the country's entrepreneurial spirit led to the development of other ways of offering health care benefits.

In the 1980s, health maintenance organizations (HMOs) sprung up across the country. The concept has been supported by the federal government which, in 1973, passed a Health Maintenance Organization Act that provided federal assistance for the development of HMOs. HMOs are membership organizations. Some hire doctors and other health professionals at fixed salaries to serve dues-paying members in a clinic-type setting. Others contract with physicians who treat patients in their private offices; this arrangement can provide patients with a greater choice of physicians than a clinic setting. Both types of HMOs typically provide comprehensive health care for enrollees. The members pay a regular fee (the fee may be somewhat higher than the premium for traditional, private health insurance), but they are usually entitled to hospital care and physicians' services at little or no extra costs (unlike traditional insurance which pays only a percentage of the bills after a deductible is met). HMOs do vary in the services they offer. Some cover alcoholism and drug abuse treatment, prescription drugs, and eyeglasses; others do not. Some have small copayments to defer a portion of costs and deter unnecessary visits.

Advocates say that HMOs are less costly than fee-for-service medical care, because physicians have no incentive to overtreat patients. Moreover, HMOs are supposed to emphasize preventive medicine; and, therefore, they attempt to treat medical problems *before* they become serious illnesses. Another attractive feature is that HMOs do away with the need to pay for services and then to file claims for reimbursement. Despite their growth, a number of people remain skeptical of HMOs. One complaint was that patients may see different doctors depending on when they came in for care. HMOs responded by assigning *primary care* physicians to patients. Patients can usually select from among the doctors available. HMO clinic physicians often choose to work in this type of setting because they can have better control of their work schedules, but some believe that these physicians do not work as hard as other physicians. Another complaint is that patients who wish to see specialists must be referred by their HMO physician unless they are willing to pay for these services out of their own pockets. The rising costs of health care have also led to charges that HMO physicians may be limiting care in order to cut costs. Some HMOs offer bonuses to physicians who keep costs down.[37] This sounds like a bad practice, but it has been defended by those who believe it is designed to reduce *unnecessary* rather than *necessary* care. Currently, about thirty-one million Americans are enrolled in the approximately 650 HMOs around the country.[38]

The HMO concept has not resulted in a financial cure for obtaining health care. Many HMOs are operating (no pun intended) in the red. Employees who are covered by one HMO today may find out tomorrow that the HMO has been sold to another company not of their choosing. Older Americans in many areas can use their Medicare premiums to pay for HMO participation. However, some HMOs are not anxious to accept older patients because they are more likely than others to use large amounts of expensive care.[39]

The HMO concept was soon followed by the development of preferred provider organizations (PPOs). Once again the motive is health care cost containment. Under the PPO concept, employers or their designated insurance companies will reimburse a higher percentage of services—for example, hospital care—if employees use specified hospitals (providers). Employees can use other services, but their reimbursement level is lower (for example, 80 percent as opposed to 90 percent reimbursement for using PPOs). The PPO concept resulted from competition among hospitals and other health care providers who were willing to accept a reduced fee is order to keep their patient counts high.

Some large employers offer their employees several health care options from which they can choose, but the concept of self-insurance by employers is also gaining popularity; in other words, companies directly cover the health care costs of their own employees rather than contract with an insurance company. Under this option, companies may place more limits on the type and amount of services available to employees. To keep costs down, these companies generally hire staff who shop for the best health care buys and monitor employees' utilization of services.

Regardless of the option selected, in almost all cases now, hospital stays and other treatment, unless they are of an emergency nature, must be preapproved by the health carrier. The Employee Benefit Research Center reported that in 1987 alone, businesses spent $115 billion to provide health care coverage to workers.[40] As a result of rapidly escalating health care costs, employers are asking employees to pay a greater share of premiums. Health benefits are a major cost of doing business.

So, which alternative should *you* choose? To make the best decision, employees and others must study the options available and decide what is best for them. If greater choice in selecting a family physician and specialists is important, then traditional insurance may be the best option. If an individual has high prescription drug costs, it is important to compare whether an HMO or private insurance will provide better coverage. Families with young children generally need a series of routine care services, and HMOs will usually cover this without a deductible. If you hate paperwork, the HMO might also be the best bet. Becoming an informed consumer seems to be the best defense in obtaining health care services.

THE POLITICS OF HEALTH CARE FOR ALL

Today there is a growing concern that something must be done to insure those who do not have coverage. The urgency of this position is really not due to a consensus that increased access will drastically improve health; it is due to concern that the use of available resources by the medically indigent has become a severe drain on the health care system. It is estimated that between thirty-one and thirty-eight million Americans have no health insurance at all.[41] Ironically, many of these individuals are employed. Others, perhaps fifty million, are "underinsured";[42] they have coverage, but it covers only a small fraction of actual health care costs. In addition, it has become clear that the methods used to provide health care to Americans are the most expensive of the industrialized nations (see Figure 10–3). Countries which cover virtually all their citizens have lower health care expenditures than the United States. The United Kingdom, with socialized medicine, spent about 6 percent of its total GNP on health care in 1987. Canada, which covers everyone, but where physicians and hospitals are part of the private sector, spent less than 9 percent. Sweden, known for its generous and universal social welfare benefits, spent 9 percent. But the United States spent about 11 percent. This figure will reach 12 percent in the near future.

In the 1930s, President Franklin D. Roosevelt backed off from the idea of national health insurance when he feared it might endanger passage of the original Social Security Act. AMA representatives, already an important political force, contended the plan would not work without the support of the nation's physicians. President Harry S. Truman pushed hard for a national health insurance program, but it was again branded as socialized medicine by the medical community and defeated. President Lyndon Johnson chose a narrower approach—health care for the poor and for the aged, and he succeeded in adding Medicare and Medicaid to the Social Security Act in 1965. Then, Senator Edward M. "Ted" Kennedy introduced a national health insurance plan under a bill called Health Care for All Americans. Under the plan, all Americans would have been required to have health insurance coverage. A National

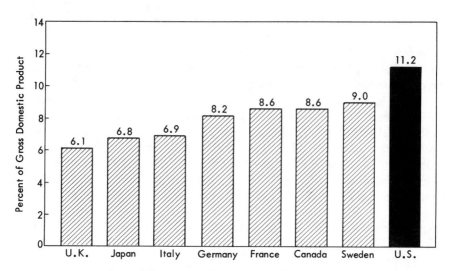

FIGURE 10–3:   Percent of gross domestic (national) product spent by eight industrialized nations. *(Source:* Data are from the Organization for Economic Co-operation and Development. *Budget of the United States Government, Fiscal Year 1991,* p. 185.)

Health Board would have overseen the program. Taxes would have been collected from workers and employers and allocated to private insurance companies to process claims. Those without jobs would have been insured through a special federal insurance fund. Everyone would have been entitled to comprehensive health care services. The government would have set physicians' fees and hospital charges, and Congress would have determined the annual national health insurance budget each year. A plan such as this would have eliminated the need for separate Medicare and Medicaid programs. Many other suggestions have been offered, but all attempts at national health care have failed. Even much more limited plans have been rejected. For example, Theodore Marmor, a national health care expert, proposed *Kiddie Care,* a plan to provide basic health care at reasonable costs to the nation's children, one that would protect against future long-term and debilitating illnesses.[43] It never got serious consideration. Lack of attention to the health care needs of children has raised serious questions of intergenerational equity. The seesaw has tilted in favor of health care to older Americans while poor, young children whose routine health care would be far less costly are often shut out.[44]

When the term national health insurance is used, most people think of the type of socialized medicine practiced in Great Britain. In that country physicians and other health care providers are employees of the national government which also owns the hospitals and other medical facilities. The Kennedy plan described above looks more like the system in Canada, in which physicians and hospitals are part of the private sector even though the government sees that all citizens have health care coverage. Canada adopted universal hospital insurance in 1958 and universal physician insurance in 1968. Physicians maintain very substantial incomes under the plan. Under the

British and Canadian arrangements, health care is rationed, in part by time rather than money. For example, in Great Britain, patients may have to wait hours to see a doctor and months to undergo nonemergency surgeries. It is those who are willing and able to *wait* rather than to *pay* who are served. There is some dissatisfaction with the current system in Great Britain, and patients who are willing and able to pay can now obtain services from physicians who are allowed to engage in limited private practice. But it is *very* doubtful that a country used to universal health care coverage would opt for a system like that in the United States. It is equally doubtful that the United States will ever adopt a system that looks like Great Britain's, because the vast majority of physicians will just not agree to become government employees. Currently, the United States and South Africa are the only industrialized countries that do not have some form of national health insurance.

Some states have moved ahead to address health care needs. Most notably, Massachusetts and Hawaii are the only states which require employers to insure most of their workforce. In addition, Massachusetts uses a fund supported by payroll taxes to help the unemployed obtain health insurance.

New proposals for national health coverage are now being considered by virtually all groups concerned about health care. Senator Ted Kennedy and Representative Henry Waxman (D-Cal.) have reintroduced plans first proposed in 1988. They are a blend of alternatives offered by President George Bush and Governor Michael Dukakis during the 1988 presidential campaign.[45] The plans combine the Massachusetts provision of requiring employers to provide health insurance with Bush's campaign suggestion of allowing the unemployed to "buy into" the existing Medicaid program according to their ability to pay or of setting up a new federal-state program for this purpose. Of course, the proposals have already been branded as a move toward "socialized medicine." Other criticisms are that requiring employers to buy insurance will contribute to unemployment and that poor people may still not have the money to buy into Medicaid. Kennedy defends the proposal by saying that the costs of his plan are about equal to what the government will spend to help the ailing savings and loan industry, and that costs to business would be no more than the alcohol and tobacco industries' bills for advertising.[46] The health care lobby—labor unions, religious and social welfare groups, senior citizen groups—generally back such a plan, while the Bush administration and business groups, especially small business groups, have reacted negatively. Businesses might respond more favorably to a national health plan that is more sensitive to the soaring costs they face in providing adequate coverage to their employees. Even the AMA has endorsed mandatory employer supported health care coverage for the population along with an expanded Medicaid program, and the development of "risk pools" for those considered uninsurable. *The New England Journal of Medicine* also recently printed articles outlining possible national health schemes.

The U.S. Bipartisan Commission on Comprehensive Health Care, (known as the Pepper Commission, after its first chairperson, the late U.S. Representative Claude Pepper) was appointed to make recommendations for providing health care coverage, including provisions for long-term care, for all those who are currently uninsured. The commission developed a sweeping package of reforms which was issued in 1990. It, too, included requirements for employer sponsored health coverage for employees and their dependents while the government would cover others and pay for a large portion of long-term care costs. The Commission failed to reach a consensus on many of its recommendations and it did not provide any clear methods of financing costs estimated to be at $66 billion annually.

The Bush administration is taking a somewhat different tack.[47] Pointing to the fact that "more care is not necessarily better care" and to studies that show that HMOs provide care as good as "fee-for-service" care provided through private insurers, the president has called for greater emphasis on *managed care*. For example, the administration is giving close scrutiny to options "bubbling up from the states," such as a proposal in Oregon to cover more people under Medicaid but to offer only *basic* services. State experimentation with the use of HMOs for Medicaid recipients is also growing. The many broad proposals being offered by a diverse group of individuals and organizations may mean that some form of universal health care coverage in the United States just might be adopted by the turn of the century.

HEALTH CARE—SOME ETHICAL DILEMMAS

In addition to direct benefit programs to insure the prevention and treatment of medical problems, bioethical dilemmas in the health care field are also a social welfare concern. Rationing health care is one of these dilemmas. Since there are limits to the amount of health care that can be provided, what factors should be considered in rationing? For example, should we forego the use of life support systems for the very old in favor of more preventive health care for young children? This is an extremely difficult question, and there is really no consensus on how health care should be prioritized or rationed. In fact, some people believe that spending 12 percent or more of the country's GNP should not be an issue at all, and that the United States should *avoid* rationing services. But health care *is* rationed by a number of factors—including whether an individual has third party coverage or can otherwise afford care; whether those who are ill present themselves for treatment; whether the medical community responds to the need rather than refusing to treat or "dumping" indigent patients. Desperate parents have attempted to influence rationing decisions by using TV to plead for a transplant donor for their terminally ill child when they felt that existing networks were not moving fast enough. In many cases, without a substantial amount of money up-front, transplants are out of reach for many patients who need them. Some state Medicaid programs will no longer pay for transplants.

Other dilemmas include the *right to die*—who should be able to make such decisions and under what circumstances? Patients have asked the courts to permit them to remove life-sustaining devices such as respirators, but there is no consistent response to this issue, and state laws on the subject are not clear. Penultimate or *living wills* can help to clarify an individual's wishes. For example, terminally ill individuals may request that they *not be* resuscitated (another term for this practice is *passive euthanasia*), or they may request that certain methods *be used* to sustain their life. But this does not necessarily mean that the patient's wishes will be carried out, because family members, medical professionals, or the state might see the situation differently. For example, in 1990, the Supreme Court reviewed the case of the Cruzans, a Missouri couple that wanted to stop feeding their unresponsive adult daughter, who was severely injured in a car crash. The couple believed it was their daughter's wish not to live in a vegetative state. The state of Missouri had refused to comply with the parents' wishes on the grounds that it has no such instructions from the patient and that her treatment was not causing pain. The Supreme Court upheld the state's position stating there was not "clear and convincing" proof of the patient's wishes. The decision is considered important because it is the first time the Supreme Court has ruled in a *right-to-die* case. The implications of the decision are that patients *do* have a constitutional right to reject medical treatment if their desires are made clear, but that the states have considerable authority in determining how this right will be upheld. Most states allow family members more authority in making decisions on behalf of patients who are in vegetative states than is permitted in Missouri.

Another reason that the question of the proper limits of life are being debated is because of the growing number of older persons. One governor gained national attention when he suggested that the elderly have a "duty to die." Medical technology may be able to sustain people, regardless of the quality of life, and the capabilities of medical technology continue to increase, making it even more difficult to decide between sustaining life and allowing death to occur. Newly identified diseases also present challenges. In one case, an elderly Florida man was found guilty of murder and imprisoned after he shot to death his wife, who was afflicted with Alzheimer's disease. He said he could no longer bear to see her suffer.

It is not difficult to empathize with the families in these situations, but medical personnel must uphold their own codes of ethics and obey state laws. Those who believe in the individual's right to determine when life should end point to the Netherlands. In that country, passive euthanasia, such as "no resuscitation orders," is not considered at all unusual. Physicians are also allowed greater latitude in helping patients with voluntary, active euthanasia (in these cases the physician administers or prescribes drugs to promote death).[48] Although active euthanasia is technically illegal, it is practiced and seldom results in serious legal repercussions if the physician follows guidelines developed as a result of judicial decisions made in the 1970s. The guidelines include stipulations that the patient must make the request, the physician must have known the patient previously, and the physician is not compelled to honor the request. The Dutch parliament is deeply divided on the morality of the issue, and therefore, has not passed legislation to support the judicial guidelines. Those opposed to active euthanasia believe that condoning the practice promotes the idea of Social Darwinism (survival of the fittest), by ridding society of those who are frail and unproductive, and that endorsing it will open the door to greater use in cases where it is not appropriate.

SUMMARY

Health care for aged and poor Americans has been on the social policy agenda since the early twentieth century. Major federal health care programs were introduced for fifty years before Medicaid and Medicare were adopted. The American Medical Association worked to delay large-scale federal government involvement in medical assistance.

Medicaid is the single most expensive public assistance program. It is operated jointly by the federal and state governments. All AFDC and most SSI recipients are automatically eligible for Medicaid. Other poor or medically indigent individuals may also qualify. Twenty-five million Americans are Medicaid recipients.

Medicare is a social insurance program financed by the government through payroll taxes. It serves the nation's aged population. The elderly are more susceptible to illness and disease than other segments of the population and require more health services. Nearly all those aged sixty-five and over are eligible for Medicare, regardless of their income. Attempts to curb Medicare spending include diagnosis-related groups, a plan that pays fixed fees to hospitals for treating medical problems. Several steps have also been taken to control physicians' fees, including expenditure targets and limits on the fees that doctors may charge patients. An attempt to increase the services covered by Medicare by charging older Americans a surtax met with opposition and was quickly repealed by Congress.

Health care expenditures make up a continually increasing portion of the federal budget and the GNP. Rising medical costs can be attributed to the expansion of private insurance coverage, the introduction of the Medicaid and Medicare programs, the growing population of elderly persons, advances in medical technology, and the expansion of hospital facilities.

The access of the poor to medical care has increased, but the health of poor Americans has not improved in proportion to expenditures. African-Americans tend to be poorer than white Americans and they have higher mortality rates than whites. Providing health care does not necessarily counteract the negative effects of the disadvantaged environments in which poor persons live. In addition, many of the leading causes of death for those in all income brackets are related to heredity and lifestyle issues such as smoking, lack of exercise, poor diet, and increased stress rather than lack of medical care. The United States spends more for health care than other industrialized nations which have more universal coverage, yet our infant mortality rate exceeds that of most of these countries.

The goals of a rational, national health care policy are to provide adequate health care for Americans while containing health care costs. Health maintenance organizations (HMOs) represent one attempt at keeping medical costs under control. Members pay fixed fees that are supposed to discourage doctors from providing too much care. Preferred provider organizations (PPOs) are another attempt to make use of care that is provided at more economical rates. These plans are generally available through employers, but HMOs are also being used in the Medicare and Medicaid programs. *Socialized medicine* such as in Great Britain is not a viable option in the United States, but a plan like Canada's, where virtually everyone has access to health insurance but where physicians and hospitals remain under private auspices, may be a reasonable option. Support for broader health care coverage of some form is growing among all segments of the population, even the AMA.

NOTES

1. Although this point may seem arguable, the research literature is extensive. See, for example, Victor R. Fuchs, *Who Shall Live?* (New York: Basic Books, 1974); Nathan Glazer, "Paradoxes of Health Care," *Public Interest,* no. 22 (Winter 1971), pp. 62–77; and Leon R. Kass, "Regarding the End of Medicine and the Pursuit of Health," *Public Interest,* no. 40 (Summer 1975), pp. 11–42.
2. *Budget of the United States Government, Fiscal Year 1991,* p. 184.
3. *Budget of the United States Government, Fiscal Year 1990,* pp. 5–115.
4. Requirements of the Medicaid program are taken from *Social Security Bulletin, Annual Statistical Supplement, 1988,* p. 55.
5. Ibid., p. 56.
6. Paul Starr, "Health Care for the Poor: The Past Twenty Years," in Sheldon H. Danzinger and Daniel H. Weinberg, *Fighting Poverty: What Works and What Doesn't?* (Cambridge: Harvard University Press, 1986), pp. 106–137.
7. *Social Security Bulletin, 1988,* p. 57; Janet Hook, "Growing Demand for Long-Term Care Drains Medicaid Coffers Nationwide," *Congressional Quarterly* (May 11, 1985), p. 892; and Starr, "Health Care for the Poor," p. 109.
8. *Social Security Bulletin, 1988,* p. 57.
9. "Major Changes Made in Medicare Program," *Congressional Quarterly Almanac 1983,* p. 391.
10. Julie Rovner, "Governors' Medicaid Protests Likely to be Swept Aside," *Congressional Quarterly* (August 12, 1989), p. 2121.
11. National Center for Health Statistics, figures cited in John L. McCoy and David L. Brown, "Health Status among Low-Income Elderly Persons: Rural-Urban Differences," *Social Security Bulletin 41,* no. 6 (June 1978), p. 14.
12. "Medicare Eyed for More Cuts as Congress Seeks Savings," *Congressional Quarterly* (March 30, 1985), p. 577; and Julie Rovner, "Reconciliation Dominates Policy-Making Process," *Congressional Quarterly* (April 29, 1989), p. 964.
13. See *Budget of the United States Government, Fiscal Year 1991,* p. 186.
14. Hook, "Growing Demand for Long-Term Care," p. 892.
15. Jane Bryant Quinn, "Footing the Bill for Old Age Health Care," *Austin American-Statesman* (January 31, 1989), p. C8.
16. Ibid.
17. Ibid.
18. U. S. National Center for Health Statistics, *Vital Statistics of the United States: 1973 Life Tables* (Rockville, MD.: U. S. Department of Health, Education, and Welfare, 1975); cited in Mario Tonti and Barbara Silverstone, "Services to Families of the Elderly," in Abraham Monk, ed., *Handbook of Gerontological Services* (New York: Van Nostrand Reinhold Co., 1985), pp. 211–39. Also see Lynn Osterkamp, "Family Caregivers: America's Primary Long-Term Care Resource," *Aging,* no. 358 (1988), pp. 3–5.
19. Robert Kastenbaum and Sandra E. Candy, "The 4% Fallacy: A Methodological and Empirical Critique of Extended Care Facility Population Statistics," *International Journal of Aging and Human Development 4,* no. 1 (1973), pp. 15–21.
20. See Ronald W. Wilson and Elijah L. White, "Changes in Morbidity, Disability and Utilization Differentials Between the Poor and the Nonpoor; Data from the Health Interview Survey: 1964 and 1973" Paper presented at the 102d Annual Meeting of the American Public Health Association (October 21, 1974), cited in Dorothy P. Rice and Douglas Wilson, "The American Medical Economy: Problems and Perspectives," *Journal of Health Politics, Policy and Law 1* (Summer 1976), pp. 151–72; and Theodore R. Marmor, "Rethinking National Health Insurance," *Public Interest,* no. 46 (Winter 1977), pp. 73–95. For a critique of the argument that access to health care is greater for the poor than the nonpoor, see Catherine Kohler Riessman, "The Use of Health Services by the Poor: Are There Any Promising Models?" *Social Policy,* no. 14 (Spring 1984), pp. 30–40.
21. Starr, "Health Care for the Poor."
22. Ibid.
23. See ibid.
24. See Michele Kay, "National Health Plan May Be Just What the Doctor Ordered," *Austin American-Statesman* (December 11, 1989), Business Section, p. 1; also see *Budget of the United States Government, Fiscal Year 1991,* p. 184.
25. Fuchs, *Who Shall Live?,* p. 53.

26. This phrase is courtesy of Peter Steinfels, "National Health Insurance: Its Politics and Problems," *Dissent 24* (Winter 1977), pp. 61–71.
27. "Health Status and Medical Care," *Economic Report of the President, House* document no. 99–19, 99th Cong., 1st Sess., February 1985, p. 137.
28. Ibid., p. 581.
29. "Hill Panels Find DRGs Leave Patients 'Sicker,'" *NASW News* (April 1985), p. 10.
30. Charles Green, "Medicare Cuts Force Elderly out of Hospitals Too Fast, Panel Says," *Austin American-Statesman* (December 1, 1989), p. A23; and Los Angeles Times News Service, "Poor Care for Some Medicare Patients is Cited," *The Miami Herald* (August 11, 1988), p. 7A.
31. Ibid.
32. Starr, "Health Care for the Poor," pp. 109–10.
33. "Medicare lists 200,000 MDs," *The Miami Herald* (August 6, 1988), p. 5A.
34. Chuck Alston, "Belt-Tightening in Medicare Pits Doctor vs. Doctor," *Congressional Quarterly* (October 7, 1989), p. 2608.
35. Chuck Alston, "A Decline in Clout for the AMA?," *Congressional Quarterly* (October 7, 1989), p. 2608.
36. "Physicians' Lobbying Machine Showing Some Signs of Wear," *Congressional Quarterly Weekly Report* (January 7, 1984), p. 77; and Alston, "Belt Tightening in Medicare," p. 2605.
37. Donald Robinson, "How Well Do You Know Your HMO?," *Parade Magazine* (February 5, 1989), pp. 12–13.
38. Ibid.
39. Ibid.
40. Julie Rovner, "Kennedy, Waxman Introduce Insurance-for-All Proposal," *Congressional Quarterly* (April 15, 1989), p. 826.
41. See, for example, "The Doctor Is In . . . But Not for Everybody," *Highlights*, The Newsletter of the American Association of Retired Persons Volunteers (July-August 1989), p. 7; Ted Gup, "Health Care: Beyond Bromides," *Time* (October 31, 1988), p. 21; and Rovner, "Kennedy, Waxman Introduce."
42. "The Doctor Is In."
43. Theodore R. Marmor, "The Politics of National Health Insurance: Analysis and Prescription," *Policy Analysis 3,* no. 1, 1977 pp. 25–48. Reprinted in John E. Tropman, Milan J. Dluhy and Roger M. Lind, eds., *New Strategic Perspectives on Social Policy* (New York: Pergamon Press, 1981), pp. 30–50.
44. See Karen Davis and Roger Reynolds, "The Impact of Medicare and Medicaid on Access to Medical Care" (Washington D.C.: Brookings Institution, n.d.), p. 3; published also in Richard Rosett, ed., *The Role of Insurance in the Health Services Sector* (New York: National Bureau of Economic Research, 1976), cited in Marmor, "The Politics of National Health Insurance," p. 38.
45. Rovner, "Kennedy, Waxman Introduce."
46. Ibid.
47. This paragraph relies on *Budget of the United States Government, Fiscal Year 1991,* p. 177.
48. Alan L. Otten, "Fateful Decision, In the Netherlands, The Very Ill Have Option of Euthanasia," *The Wall Street Journal* (August 21, 1987), pp. 1, 6.

11

CHALLENGING SOCIAL WELFARE
Racism and Sexism

Can it be that more than seventy years after women won the right to vote and more than twenty-five years after passage of the Civil Rights Act of 1964, the country is still struggling with the issues of racism and sexism? Perhaps Rip Van Winkle would be surprised at the progress that ethnic minorities and women have made during the twentieth century, but there is still considerable frustration at the inequalities that exist in the United States. Poverty and other social problems are not random events; these problems are concentrated among particular subgroups—primarily women, blacks, Hispanic-Americans, American Indians, and other ethnic groups.* This chapter explores the history of discrimination in America and the quest for gender and ethnic equality.

THE INEQUALITIES OF GENDER

There are many issues that can be discussed under the heading of gender inequities, and this section covers several of them. One of the most important is the *feminization of poverty*, which is affected both by the earnings of women in the labor market and social welfare programs. Also important are laws and policies designed to protect the rights of women, including the ill-fated Equal Rights Amendment. It is impossible to avoid the subject of abortion even though many think it should be a private rather than

---

* The terms black and African-American are used interchangeably as are the terms Hispanic-American and Hispanic origin, and the terms American Indian and Native American.

a public matter. Child care policy is addressed in an article by syndicated columnist Ellen Goodman. The section ends with a consideration of marital violence against women.

The Feminization of Poverty

During the 1980s, "the feminization of poverty,"[1] became a catch phrase, but this concept should not have come as a surprise. The majority of adult public assistance recipients have always been women. State and local mothers' aid and mothers' pension laws of the early 1900s were followed by the ADC and AFDC programs. These programs were primarily intended to assist mothers, not fathers. Even recent federal reforms extending AFDC to two-parent families in all states will not change this emphasis appreciably (see Chapter 6). Women "went on welfare" because they were expected to remain at home to care for their young children when their husbands were unable to support them (due to death, disability, or unemployment), or were unwilling to support them following divorce or desertion. When women did go to work to support themselves and their families, they were usually forced into low-paying jobs; many of them still are. These factors contributed to a pattern in which women were more likely to be poor and more likely to receive welfare payments. The pattern became further exacerbated in the 1970s and 1980s with the rapid increase in the number of female-headed households. The discussion of poverty rates for families headed by women, men, and couples in Chapter 3 clearly shows that female-headed households are most vulnerable to poverty and that women who are members of ethnic-minority groups are extremely vulnerable. To state it another way, in 1987

[a]bout 53.0 percent...of poor families were maintained by women with no spouse present. For poor Black families, 75.6...percent were maintained by women with no spouse present, for White families the comparable figure was 43.5...percent, and for Hispanic-origin families 47.9...percent.[2]

Women are also overrepresented in the SSI program. Nearly two-thirds of SSI recipients are women.[3] There are two reasons for this. Women live longer than men, and as they grow older, they are increasingly likely to suffer from infirmities due to old age or disability. They are also likely to be poorer than men, since their Social Security retirement benefits are less than men's and they are less likely to have other sources of income like pensions. The median income of males aged sixty-five and older in 1988 was about $12,500; this compared to $7,100 for women.[4] The percentage of women aged sixty-five and older who are alone and in poverty is 26 compared with 20 for men.[5] For older, white women, the figure is 22 percent; the men's rate is 17 percent. For Hispanic women, the rate is 54 percent, and for black women, 57. This is more than 20 points higher than their male counterparts (although poverty is quite high for members of ethnic minority groups of both genders).

Inequities in the Social Security retirement system have also been blamed for the lower incomes of older women. When the Social Security system was first adopted, the roles of men and women were different from those that exist today. Women were less likely to work outside the home, and divorce was less common. The Social

Security system reflected the social conditions of the 1930s, when most women were considered "dependents" of their working husbands. Since women are poorer than men, they rely more heavily on transfer payments such as Social Security, but their benefits are often minimal. Social Security provides more than half of the income for all older women in the United States.[6]

The Social Security system has not kept pace with the changing roles of men and women. Women have been inadequately treated by the Social Security system for a number of reasons:[7]

1. Women's wages remain lower than men's wages, resulting in lower benefits paid to women when they retire.
2. Women are still likely to spend less time in the work force than men because they also carry the major responsibilities for home and child care. This also results in lower benefits paid to women.
3. Divorced women are entitled to only one-half of their former husbands' benefits. If this is the woman's only income, it is generally not adequate, and she cannot collect at all if the couple was married less than ten years.
4. Widows generally do not qualify for benefits unless they are sixty years old or unless there are children under age eighteen in the home.
5. Homemakers are not covered on their own unless they have held jobs in the paid labor force.
6. Social Security benefits are often based on the earnings of the primary worker, generally the husband. The wages of a second earner may not raise the couple's combined Social Security benefits.
7. Couples in which one worker earned most of the wages may receive higher benefits than those in which the husband and wife earned equal wages.
8. Married workers benefit from Social Security more than single workers. An individual who has never worked can benefit from Social Security payments based on the work of a spouse. Single workers do not receive additional benefits, even though they have made Social Security payments at the same rate as married workers.

Two major options have been suggested for remedying inequities in the Social Security system.[8] The *earnings-sharing* option would divide a couple's earnings equally between the husband and wife for each year they are married. This option would allow benefits to be calculated separately for the husband and the wife and would eliminate the ideas of the *primary wage earner* and the *dependent spouse*. This option would also recognize that the spouse who takes care of the home is an equal partner in the marriage. A second option is the *double-decker plan*. Under this option, everyone would be eligible for a basic benefit, whether or not they had worked. Individuals who have also contributed to the paid labor force would receive a payment in addition to the basic benefit.

As a result of the Social Security Amendments of 1983, some disqualifications for benefits based on sex were eliminated, but most brought only a limited number of new recipients to the rolls. One provision allows divorced spouses to qualify for benefits at age sixty-two, and these benefits are based on a former spouse's earnings even if the ex-spouse has not claimed benefits. Another measure allows divorced husbands to claim benefits based on the earning records of their former wives.

As we would expect, couples receive the highest Social Security retirement benefits.[9] Widowed or divorced men receive more than widowed or divorced women, but it is interesting to note that never-married women now average more than their male counterparts. One improvement in the Social Security retirement system is that *average* benefits for all groups now exceed the poverty level. In the early 1970s, average benefits for unmarried men and women were only two-thirds of the poverty level.

The number of women who qualify for benefits based on their own work records has increased considerably. In 1960, about three million women were receiving Social Security benefits on their own records. By the 1980s, this figure exceeded ten million. Although many women still receive higher payments based on their husband's earnings rather than on their own, this is expected to change in the future.

The Wage Gap and Uncomparable Worth

In 1955, the Bureau of Labor Statistics calculated that women earned only 64 cents for every dollar earned by men; in 1961 the figure dropped to 59 cents (see Table 11–1). It hovered there, and "59 cents" became a well-known refrain of the Equal Rights Movement. Three decades later, the latest figures put women's earnings at 70 cents of each dollar earned by men. Many reasons have been offered to explain the difference in earning power, including the following:

1. Traditionally, women have not been the family's major wage earner, nor did they earn salaries comparable to their husbands if they did work.
2. Women's wages were considered secondary to that of their spouses.
3. Women were considered to be temporary employees who would leave their jobs to marry and have children; they were not serious about careers.
4. Women's work outside the home was considered an extracurricular activity to fill free time.
5. Women had fewer opportunities than men to obtain education that would lead to better-paying jobs.
6. Women had limited job choices because they were forced to accept employment that did not conflict with the routines of their husbands and children.
7. "Women's work"—cleaning and child rearing in their own homes—have not been wage-earning jobs.
8. Some thought that women "preferred" lower-level employment because these jobs were more compatible with characteristics they associated with women, such as nurturing qualities and lack of aggressiveness.

Today, there are elements of truth in some of these statements. Some women do terminate their employment, on a temporary or long-term basis, to raise families. The unfortunate term "mommy track" has been used to describe women who interrupt their careers or try to "juggle" both career and children. The term implies that women pay the price because their multiple responsibilities diminish chances of rising to the top of their professions. Some women do prefer to select jobs that are compatible with family routines and place family over career; however, we also know that many of the

Table 11-1   Ratio of Women's to Men's Earnings Based on Full-time Employment, Selected Years

Year	Ratio	Year	Ratio
1955	64	1975	59
1960	61	1980	60
1961	59	1984	64
1965	60	1987	70
1970	59	1989	70

Sources: Bureau of Labor Statistics and Bureau of the Census.

arguments used to rationalize women's lower pay border on the ridiculous. Most women do not work just for the fun of it. Many must work to support their families. A growing number of U.S. families are headed by women, and the salaries of many married women who work are essential to their families' economic well-being. In addition, many women find their work satisfying, challenging, and an integral component of their lives.

Women comprise nearly half of the work force. A growing number have earned advanced degrees, and many hold higher-level jobs. But women continue to earn less than men even when they hold the *same* jobs. In 1979, about 10 percent of all attorneys were women. They earned 55 percent of what men earned. Today, they comprise 15 percent of all attorneys and earn 63 percent of men's earnings. During this same period, women went from occupying 10 to 13 percent of sales representative positions, and their earnings increased from 62 to 72 cents for each dollar earned by their male counterparts. Female computer programmers do better. They make up 40 percent of their profession and earn 81 cents for each man's dollar, but in 1979 they were already earning 80 cents. In no profession do women out earn men—not even in traditional female occupations—but secretaries and nurses are close to achieving equality since they earn about 99 cents for every dollar paid to their male counterparts. Female elementary school teachers are at 95 cents. Female social workers now earn 73 cents for each dollar earned by men, but this is 10 cents less than the 83 cent figure reported for them in 1979![10] A RAND report indicates that the gap is not expected to close anytime soon. By the year 2000, it is predicted that women will earn between 74 and 80 percent of men's wages.[11]

One approach to narrowing the wage gap has been to press for equal pay for equal work. For example, it is difficult to justify paying a male accountant more than a female accountant if their job responsibilities are the same. By law, men and women who do the *same* work are supposed to be paid equally. Those who are not may use legal channels to settle their grievances. A more recent effort to reduce the gap in earnings between women and men is based on the argument of "comparable worth."[12] According to this argument, workers should be paid equally when they do *different* types of work that require the same level of responsibility, effort, knowledge, and skill. Many jobs done by men are weighed more heavily in terms of monetary compensation because the idea of the *dual labor market* creates a situation in which "women's professions"—secretarial, teaching, nursing, social work—tend to be regarded less highly than professions dominated by men. To phrase the argument another way, are the jobs in question of equal value or comparable worth to society?

While some high ranking White House officials have been known to call compensation based on comparable worth a "truly crazy proposal,"[13] others argue that comparable worth is a truly rational proposal. Twenty states have passed laws or resolutions which make comparable worth a requirement or a goal of state employment, but the rub occurs when officials attempt to actually implement such a proposal. In theory, most people can agree on the principle of equal pay for work of equal value, but how do we determine what constitutes work of equal value? How can we determine if the work of a secretary is comparable to the work of an automobile mechanic? Some contend that even if the value of jobs could be calculated in a way agreeable to everyone, the cost of implementing far-reaching comparable-worth plans would be so tremendous as to be unfeasible; but others feel just as strongly that it is time that women are paid equitable salaries.

The U.S. Commission on Civil Rights has failed to support comparable worth saying it would wreak havoc on the marketplace. Thus far the courts have responded to the issue of comparable worth by supporting salary differentials that appear to arise from labor-force competition.[14] In a case against Brown University, a male faculty member accused the university of paying an equally qualified female faculty member a higher salary. The First Circuit Court ruled in favor of the university, which argued that the female professor was paid more because she had planned to take a position at another school that had offered her a higher salary. Brown wanted to retain her. The university contended that she had greater market value than the male professor, and the court agreed. In another case in higher education, nursing faculty at the University of Washington filed suit stating that they were paid less than male faculty in other university departments. The Ninth Circuit Court ruled that under Title VII of the Civil Rights Act, suits cannot be brought before the court if salary inequities are due to labor-market conditions.

Equal Rights for Women

Women have been organizing to gain equality through political participation since the Suffragette Movement. This movement culminated in 1920 in the Nineteenth Amendment to the United States Constitution, which gave women the right to vote. Even with this right, the percentage of women who hold political office has remained small, though it is growing. For example, in 1988, women held 16 percent of the seats in state legislatures, up from 8 percent in 1975.[15] In 1989, only two of the 100 U.S. senators and twenty-five of the 435 U.S. representatives were women.[16]

Since the 1960s, the federal government has attempted to address the inequities women face in employment, education, and the marketplace with the following measures:

1. The Equal Pay Act of 1963 requires employers to compensate male and female workers equally for performing the same jobs under similar conditions. The law does not cover all groups, but amendments to the act have added to the types of jobs which are covered and to the kinds of employers who must comply.

2. Title VII of the Civil Rights Act of 1964 prohibits gender discrimination in employment practices and provides the right to court redress. The Equal Employment Opportunity Commission is the agency charged with interpreting and enforcing Title VII.

3. Executive Order 11246, as amended by Executive Order 11375, prohibits employers who practice gender discrimination from receiving federal contracts. Employers are also required to develop "affirmative action" plans (steps taken to recruit and promote women to remedy inequities). The order also established the Office of Federal Contract Compliance Programs under the Department of Labor as an enforcement agency.

4. Title IX of the Education Amendments of 1972 prohibits gender discrimination by elementary, secondary, vocational, and professional schools and colleges and universities that receive federal funds,

5. The Equal Credit Act of 1975 prohibits discrimination by lending institutions based on gender or marital status.

The Equal Rights Amendment (ERA) attempted to guarantee women equal rights through the U.S. Constitution. It stated:

> *Section 1.* Equality of rights under the law shall not be denied or abridged by the United States or by any state on account of sex.
>
> *Section 2.* Congress shall have the power to enforce by appropriate legislation the provisions of this Article.
>
> *Section 3.* This amendment shall take effect two years after the date of ratification.

Proponents of the ERA argued that this guarantee of equality under the law should be part of the Constitution—"the supreme law of the land." It is true that a number of existing federal and state laws prohibit gender discrimination, but there were concerns that these laws are inadequate to fully address the problem. ERA proponents contend that like many other social policy issues, gender discrimination is best addressed by a national policy rather than by a multitude of federal, state, and local laws that are subject to change, modification, and repeal. Proponents continue to believe that the ERA can only contribute to more equitable treatment for women.

However, opponents of the ERA were successful in halting this proposed constitutional amendment just three states short of the thirty-eight states (three-quarters) needed for ratification. In 1972, the United States Congress passed the ERA and set a 1979 deadline for state ratification. But by 1978, the amendment had not been ratified. Congress granted an extension of the deadline until June 30, 1982. Despite the endorsement of 450 organizations with fifty million members—unions, churches, civil rights groups, legal associations, educational groups, and medical organizations[17]—the ERA failed.

The "stop ERA Movement" was based on fears about what *might* happen if the ERA passed. It was argued that the ERA would lead to an extension of military registration and perhaps even to a military draft and combat duty for women, but the ERA did not specifically address the role of women in the armed services. Other issues—marriage, divorce, child custody, inheritance—were also not specifically mentioned in the ERA. It was thus difficult to predict the long-range consequences of the proposed amendment. Some feared that its passage would cause laws governing relationships between men and women to change in ways that might disadvantage women. Others claimed that the ERA would not have much of an impact at all. "Stop ERA" Chairperson Phyllis Schlafly announced to women:

ERA won't do anything for you. It won't make your husband do half the dirty diapers and dishes. It won't make your ex-husband pay support. I think the defeat of ERA is a tremendous victory for women's rights.[18]

Do Americans want the ERA? Some national polls report that majorities of Americans—both men and women—support equal rights. Support for the ERA was reported at 71 percent by the NBC-Associated Press poll in 1980; at 64 percent by Gallup in 1980; at 61 percent by *Time* magazine in 1981; and at 61 percent by the *Washington Post*-ABC Poll in 1981.[19] Although it has faded from the limelight, supporters, especially the National Organization for Women, have not given up efforts to see the ERA returned to the national agenda.

In February 1984, the Supreme Court threw a new monkey wrench into the equal rights and affirmative action arena. In the case of *Grove City v. Bell,* it delivered a ruling affecting the interpretation of Title IX of the Civil Rights Act which prohibits gender discrimination in federally funded education programs. The Court declared in a 6–3 vote that Title IX applies only to those individual programs receiving federal aid and *not* to all programs of an institution. This interpretation was in sharp contrast to the spirit with which Title IX had been applied since its enactment. Those opposed to the Court's decision feared that it would also affect application of Title VI of the Civil Rights Act of 1964 (barring discrimination based on race, color, or national origin in federally sponsored programs), as well as application of the Rehabilitation Act of 1973 (barring discrimination against handicapped individuals), and the Age Discrimination in Employment Act of 1975 (barring discrimination against older persons). In 1988, Congress passed the Civil Rights Restoration Act to return Title IX to its original intent. President Reagan thought that this new bill would go too far in regulating churches and private business and vetoed the measure, but Congress overrode him.

The Supreme Court: A Close Call on Abortion Rights

Before the 1960s, abortions were rarely permitted in any states, except in cases where the mother's life was in danger. Then about a quarter of the states made some modifications in their abortion laws, extending them to cases of rape, incest, or when the physical or mental health of the mother was in jeopardy. Obtaining an abortion was still difficult because each case had to be reviewed individually by physicians and by the hospital where the abortion was to be performed.

Then, in 1970, four states (New York, Alaska, Hawaii, and Washington) further liberalized their abortion laws, permitting women to obtain an abortion upon the woman's request with her physician's agreement. In 1973, the Supreme Court made decisions which fundamentally changed abortion policy. In the cases of *Roe v. Wade* and *Doe v. Bolton,* the Supreme Court ruled that the Fifth and Fourteenth Amendments to the Constitution, which guarantee all persons, "life, liberty and property," did not include the life of the unborn fetus. In addition, the First and Fourteenth Amendments guaranteeing personal liberties were said to extend to child-bearing decisions. The Supreme Court did stipulate some conditions under which abortions could and could not be restricted by the states:

1. During the first three months of pregnancy, the states cannot restrict the mother's decision for an abortion;
2. From the fourth to six months of pregnancy, the states cannot restrict abortions, but they can protect the health of the mother by setting standards for how and when abortions can be performed;
3. During the last three months of pregnancy, the states can prohibit all abortions except those that are performed to protect the mother's life and health.

Under the Medicaid program, poor pregnant women used to be able to obtain federally funded abortions. But in 1976, antiabortion groups were successful in pushing through the Hyde Amendment which prohibits the federal government from paying for abortions except in cases where the mother's life is endangered. The amendment does not restrict women from obtaining privately funded abortions, but it limits their ability to do so if they are unable to arrange to cover the costs. The National Abortion Rights Action League lost a Supreme Court battle to change Congress's decision. The Supreme Court upheld the Hyde Amendment, declaring that the poor do not have the right to abortions financed by the federal government except in cases endangering the mother's life. In 1977, the federal funding ban was lifted for promptly reported cases of rape and incest and in cases where "severe and long-lasting" harm would be caused to the woman. But in 1981, the law was again restricted to permit federal funding of abortions only to save the mother's life. In 1989, Congress again approved legislation to add cases to rape and incest, but President Bush vetoed it, and Congress could not muster the two-thirds vote needed in both chambers to override the veto. Six states permit the use of their own funds for abortions for poor women with certain restrictions, and thirteen others provide state-funded abortions for poor women upon request.

In 1983, the Supreme Court reaffirmed its 1973 decisions concerning the right to abortion and also extended some provisions. Abortions early in the second trimester do not have to be performed in hospitals since medical advances now make it possible to conduct these procedures safely on an outpatient basis. The court also struck down regulations adopted in Akron, Ohio, which made it more difficult to obtain an abortion, such as requiring minors to get *parental consent* and imposing a twenty-four hour waiting period between the time a woman signed an informed consent form and the time the abortion was actually performed. In 1986, the Court struck down a Pennsylvania law also aimed at discouraging women from obtaining abortions. The Supreme Court has upheld state laws that require *notification* of one or both parents of minors as long as these laws have a *judicial bypass* provision which also allows minors to ask the courts for permission to obtain an abortion.

The next major challenge to abortion was a case which led to the Supreme Court's 1989 decision in *Webster* v. *Reproductive Health Services*. The decision upheld a Missouri law which (1) prohibits the involvement of public hospitals and public employees in performing abortions and in counseling a woman to obtain an abortion unless her life is in danger; (2) requires physicians to determine whether a woman who is at least twenty weeks pregnant is carrying a fetus that is viable (able to survive outside the womb); (3) declares that life begins at conception. The ruling has lead several states to consider even more restrictive abortion laws. More restrictive legislation has been rebuffed in several states, but Pennsylvania again passed several regulations, including notification of husbands, twenty-four-hour waiting periods, and parental consent for minors. A federal judge declared these provisions unconstitutional, but an appeal is likely to be heard by the Supreme Court in another challenge to *Roe* v. *Wade*. Idaho and Louisiana have entertained bills that would permit abortion only in a few circumstances, but the wording of these bills has raised technical and constitutional questions that may make them unenforceable if they were passed. Connecticut, on the other hand, has passed a statute making abortion legal in an attempt to protect access to abortions if *Roe* v. *Wade* is further threatened.

Opponents of abortion, usually referred to as "Right to Life" groups, were generally pleased with the *Webster* ruling and believe that it is a major step in reversing *Roe* v. *Wade*. They oppose the freedom to obtain an abortion and generally base their arguments on religious, moral, and biological grounds, contending that abortion is tantamount to taking a human life. Prolifers demonstrate annually in Washington on the anniversary of the *Roe* v. *Wade* decision. Hundreds of members of antiabortion groups such as Operation Rescue have recently been arrested for blocking entrances to abortion clinics.

Proponents of abortion, who often call themselves the Prochoice movement, believe that a woman has the right to make decisions about her own body, including the decision to terminate an unwanted pregnancy. Without recourse to legal abortions, they fear that women may turn to illegal abortions that can result in health risks or even death for the mother. Proponents believe that misery and suffering may be avoided when a pregnant woman can make a decision about an unwanted child. Prochoice groups, including the National Abortion Rights Action League and Planned Parenthood (a family-planning organization), have held speakouts across the country to counteract the antiabortion movement.

Since *Roe* v. *Wade,* the number of abortions performed annually has increased from 750,000 in 1973 to about 1.5 million in 1980, and it has remained at that level.[20] Although the Court's decisions have continued to permit abortion, there is serious concern from prochoice groups about the future of abortion policy. The 1973 decision was supported 7–2, the 1983 decision 6–3, and the 1986 decision 5–4. The Missouri law was also upheld 5–4. President Reagan made three appointments to the Court during his two terms—Sandra Day O'Connor, the first woman ever to serve on the Supreme Court, and Anthony Kennedy and Antonin Scalia. All voted to uphold the Missouri law in 1989. It is the older members of the Court who have upheld abortion rights. The 1990 resignation of liberal justice William Brennan at age 84, allowed President Bush to make a Supreme Court appointment. Bush chose a conservative, David Souter. During Senate confirmation hearings, however, the new justice did not make his position on abortion clear, leaving pro-choice forces wary of the future.

While in office, President Reagan tried hard to ban federal funding to family planning clinics that so much as discussed abortion with patients. In 1990 a federal regulation adopted for this purpose was struck down by the First U.S. Circuit Court of

Appeals as a violation of free speech since abortion is a legally sanctioned activity. The decision is binding only in the First Circuit but will likely influence other jurisdictions. President Bush and his appointees to high-level administrative posts have also taken a strong anti-abortion stance. But prochoice forces are encouraged by the fact that Republicans seem worried that an antiabortion position may hurt them at the polls.

ILLUSTRATION: THE ROADS TO FAMILY POLICY

In recent sessions Congress gave serious consideration to are child-care and family-leave policies. The House and Senate agreed on a bill called the Family and Medical Leave Act. requiring that employers in about half of the workforce grant twelve weeks leave without pay to workers with a new baby or with an ill a family member. President Bush said he strongly favored family leave, but he vetoed the measure because he felt it was too restrictive on businesses and might result in reducing available jobs. The fact that Congress had agreed on the matter made the president's veto especially difficult for the bill's proponents to swallow. In the last hours of its 101st session, Congress did pass a major Child-care bill signed by the president. It takes effect in 1991 and includes a block grant plus tax credits to help low-income working families pay for Childcare. The following article by syndicated columnist Ellen Goodman describes the road to a more rational child-care policy befor this legislation passed.

CHILD-CARE LEGISLATION CHUG-GING ALONG

BOSTON—One of Marian Wright Edelman's favorite books is the classic children's story about a train that learns to run on willpower. "The Little Engine That Could" puffs to a happy ending by telling itself, "I think I can, I think I can."

Indeed the woman who thinks and speaks with the speed of a locomotive admits, "I read it all the time." More than once in the past year she's wanted to send copies of the story from her office to the folks who work a few blocks away in the House of Representatives. Anything to get them rolling again.

Edelman herself has been the engine behind The Children's Defense Fund for so many years that it may be time to rename it The Grandchildren's Defense Fund. But after a decade that put children's interests at the caboose end of the public agenda, she sees people changing direction.

The good news is that Americans are talking about children and families. "Some people say we've won because the issue is in the media," says Edelman. But the bad news, as she relays it, is that "We haven't yet won one single thing."

So as the Congress comes back to work, Edelman will begin the '90s the way she ended the '80s, chugging back up the Hill. On her agenda, No. 1 is child care, more and better care. "We see child care as a litmus-test issue on whether Congress is serious about kids." If they can't agree on this, she says, they probably can't do anything for kids.

Indeed, there is more of a national consensus about the need for child care than about nearly any other issue affecting families. Child care has been an apple-pie issue since the summer of 1988 when both presidential candidates had photo-ops at day-care centers. It's been an American flag issue since the summer of 1989 when the Act for Better Child Care was passed as an amendment to a Senate bill banning desecration of the flag.

With that backing, many expected the first serious child-care bill would get through the Capitol under full steam. Virtually every player was on board the

$1.75 billion compromise bill that was passed by the Senate. The plan set aside money for Head Start to go all day. It set aside money for public schools to provide care for 3- and 4-year-olds and after-school care for older kids. And it allotted $1 billion to help families pay for the child care of their choice.

But it was derailed at the last minute in a battle between two congressional committees over turf and money: who would distribute how much money which way? This prompted an unusually angry response from Edelman, who still smarts from the recognition that "We HAD the money for 1990. We could have served 400,000 families this year. And it went down because the men on the Hill just don't get it."

The two congressional committees, headed by men who are ostensibly child-care supporters, are still deadlocked. Says Edelman, "They don't see child care as a power issue." The question is how to find enough power, beyond the power of positive thinking, to get the issue resolved and to get some serious money out of the Congress.

There are more than 11 million pre-schoolers with working parents, and that figure is expected to hit 15 million by 1995. But parents, unlike the elderly, don't have a strong enough political base. They haven't forced child care to the top of the agenda.

Why not? In part it's because every year there's a turnover in the day-care constituency as one group of kids grows out of the need and another is born into it. Child care is an issue that parents care about deeply until they find it for their own kids. Parents retain just enough ambivalence about this care-taking to mute their voices. And parents are busy.

Children need a constituency that's larger and longer-range. We have to redefine self-interest to include a national interest in raising the next generation.

In the jargon of the '90s, child care is now listed as an answer to everything from productivity to education woes to welfare. That may finally become a common ground for everyone from grandparents to teachers to employers.

"We've got to start off the '90s taking care of home, family, kids, the future," says Edelman. "The money in this bill, $1.75 billion, is about one cent for every dollar going to the savings-and-loan bailout. This is not a budget issue, but a values and will issue."

So the supporters of child-care legislation are back on track in pursuit of enough dollars to begin. Will they get them? They think they can, they think they can, they think they can. [And they did.]

Source: Ellen Goodman, "Child-care Legislation Chugging Along," *The Champaign-Urbana News-Gazette* (January 23, 1990) (C) 1990, The Boston Globe Newspaper Company/Washington Post Writers Group.

Spouse Abuse

Like many other issues related to the family, domestic violence has remained largely outside the public policy arena until recently. Domestic violence may occur among any family members. Generally, we think of this as violence against children, spouses, and elderly parents. In this section, our primary concern is spouse abuse. Although physical abuse of husbands does occur, most victims are women. In the late 1970s, some states officially recognized that battered women were not receiving adequate legal protection. In effect, this amounted to a form of gender discrimination toward women who were victimized by their partners.[21] All states have now enacted some type of legislation to protect abused women. Battered spouses have two types of legal recourse: civil and criminal. Civil laws are used to "settle disputes between individuals and to compensate for injuries," while criminal laws are used to "punish acts which are disruptive of social order and to deter other similar acts."[22] In 1979, the federal government established the Office on Domestic Violence under the Department of Health and Human Services. The office was responsible for administrative activities including planning, policy development, technical assistance, and demonstration activities. It was abolished in 1981, and its functions were turned over to the National Center on Child Abuse and Neglect. Although federal legislation to assist victims of domestic violence has been introduced, there is no federal law which substantially addresses the problem. Instead, states and communities have responded with their own laws and services. Duluth, Minnesota introduced one of the most promising strategies for preventing additional incidents of domestic violence and other cities followed suit. According to this strategy:

> If a police officer has probable cause to believe that a person has, within the preceding four hours, assaulted a spouse, former spouse, or other person with whom he or she resides or has formerly resided, arrest is *mandatory*. The police officer still has the discretion in determining whether or not probable cause exists, but when there is visible sign of injury the officer has no choice but to arrest. A 1984 study conducted by the Minneapolis Police Department and the Police Foundation concluded that arrest was the most significant deterrent to repeat violence when compared to police use of mediation and separation.[23]

Law enforcement agencies are realizing that mandatory arrest policies are one approach to interrupting the cycle of family violence.

Most prominent among the services offered to victims are battered women's shelters. These are local service programs, and many operate with limited resources. They are able to assist only a small portion of those who need help. Domestic violence is another issue in the broad area known as family policy.

GAY RIGHTS

In 1969, a New York City police raid on a gay bar in Greenwich Village called Stonewall set off riots that culminated in the birth of the gay rights movement. For many people, gay rights is more than a legal or political issue. Debate is frequently colored by religious interpretations, moral judgments, and emotionalism. Various cities have taken up the issue of gay rights, with cities like San Francisco forbidding discrimination in city employment based on sexual orientation and voters in Houston failing to outlaw such discrimination. In the late 1980s, a handful of cities decided to extend bereavement leave to domestic partners not in traditional marriages, including gay and lesbian partners, and a few also extended health care benefits to these partners.

For almost twenty years, the Supreme Court refused to hear gay rights cases, but in 1985 the Court broke its silence and heard the case of *Oklahoma City Board of Education* v. *National Gay Task Force*. In its evenly divided 4–4 decision (Justice Powell was ill), the Supreme Court upheld a lower-court ruling that public school teachers cannot be forbidden to advocate homosexuality but that homosexuals can be prohibited from engaging in homosexual acts in public. The Oklahoma law had permitted school boards to bar from employment teachers who publicly advocated homosexuality. The Gay Rights Task Force criticized the law as a First Amendment violation of free speech while the Board of Education contended that the law was only concerned with those who publicly endorsed certain sexual acts between homosexuals.

In 1988, the Supreme Court told the Central Intelligence Agency that it could not dismiss a homosexual without justifying the reason for its action, but the Court has avoided the issue of whether homosexuals have employment rights under the "equal protection clause" (Fourteenth Amendment) of the U.S. Constitution, including the right to serve in the military. The various branches of the military are facing increased pressure to stop discriminating against homosexuals.

Members of the gay rights movement are still fighting many of the obstacles to equality. In a serious setback to the rights of homosexuals, the Supreme Court in its 1986 decision in *Bowers* v. *Hardwick* refused to strike down laws in Georgia and Texas forbidding individuals from engaging in certain types of sexual activity.

AIDS has further complicated the political controversy over gay rights. Since the majority of those with AIDS in the United States have been gay and bisexual men, fear of AIDS and ignorance about the disease have resulted in the introduction of state legislation that could result in increased discrimination against homosexuals. For example, because homosexual acts in many states are illegal, attempts have been made to deny state funds for AIDS prevention to organizations that support the rights of homosexuals. At the federal level the Helms Amendment, introduced by strident conservative Jesse Helms (R-N.C.), already prevents the National Center for Disease Control from using AIDS education funds in ways that might "encourage homosexuality." Homophobia coupled with fears about AIDS has also been blamed for increased violence against homosexuals. Many other public policy issues are also of concern to gay men and lesbians, such as discrimination in obtaining housing based on sexual orientation, the right to child custody, the right to name a lover as next of kin in case of medical emergencies, and the right of health insurance companies to ask lifestyle questions that may cause "suspected" homosexuals to be denied coverage. It has been suggested that the gay rights movement has failed because twenty years after Stonewall, gay men and lesbians have not been accorded the same civil rights protection as other minority groups.

ETHNIC MINORITIES AND POVERTY

The living conditions of whites and ethnic minorities in America continue to differ. On the average, blacks do not live as long as whites; they are in poorer health; they earn less; and they are overrepresented in public assistance programs. The effects of poverty also contribute to a less adequate lifestyle for many Hispanic-Americans. Table 11–2 compares the incomes of these three groups. Thirty-four percent of black families earn less than $10,000 annually, compared with 24 percent of those of Hispanic origin and 15 percent of white families. Whites are more than twice as likely as blacks to earn over $50,000 annually. Hispanic origin families have somewhat better

Table 11–2   Income Levels for White, Black, and Hispanic origin Families (1988)

INCOME	% OF TOTAL WHITE	% OF TOTAL BLACK	% OF TOTAL HISPANIC[a]
Under $5,000	5.0	15.4	9.9
$5,000 to $9,999	9.8	18.4	13.6
$10,000 to $14,999	9.8	13.1	13.7
$15,000 to $24,999	18.6	19.4	22.1
$25,000 to $34,999	16.5	12.5	15.5
$35,000 to $49,999	18.1	11.4	14.3
$50,000 and over	22.1	9.9	10.8
Median Income	$28,781	$16,407	$20,359

[a]May be of any race.

Source: Bureau of the Census, Money Income and Poverty Status in the United States: 1988, Current Population Reports, Series P-60, no. 168, pp. 23–24.

earning records than black Americans. In 1988, the median income of black families was $16,407, compared with a Hispanic median income of $20,359 and a white median income of $28,781.

Since black Americans earn less that white Americans and those of Hispanic origin, they are also more likely to be poor. Table 11–3 compares poverty rates for these three groups from 1959 to 1988. For each year, blacks were at least three times as likely to be poor as whites. Poverty rates are now 10 percent for whites, 32 percent for blacks, and 27 percent for those of Hispanic origin. Hispanic-Americans have been particularly concerned that poverty among their ranks increased faster during the 1980s than for other groups.

Even after controlling for education, differences in poverty levels for blacks, Hispanics, and whites are apparent. While educational attainment is closely related to income for all groups, the income of African-and Hispanic-Americans is less likely than that of whites to increase with education (see Table 11–4). For example, almost 13 percent of whites with an eighth-grade education are in poverty, compared with 35 percent of blacks and 30 percent of those of Hispanic origin. These differences persist at the high school and college levels. There are more than three times as many poor black as poor white high school graduates, and more than four times as many poor blacks with some college education as whites. Hispanic-Americans with high school educations are more than twice as likely as whites to be poor and those with some college education are three times as likely to be poor. Given the depressed economic situations of black and Hispanic-Americans, they are overrepresented in public assistance programs. Although blacks comprise about 12 percent of the total U.S. population, they comprise 41 percent of all AFDC recipients, 25 percent of SSI recipients, and 31 percent of Medicaid recipients.[24] Hispanic-Americans are 8 percent of the population and 14 percent of AFDC families. The proportion of these groups in public assistance programs has served to reinforce ethnic stereotypes, despite recognition of the effects of discrimination. In fact, patterns of racial discrimination

Table 11-3   Poverty Rates for White, Black, and Hispanic Origin Individuals for Selected Years (1959 to 1988)

INCOME	%OF TOTAL	% OF TOTAL WHITE	% OF TOTAL BLACK	% OF TOTAL HISPANIC[a]
1959	22.4	18.1	55.1	[b]
1966	14.7	11.3	41.8	[b]
1970	12.6	9.9	33.5	[b]
1975	12.3	9.7	31.3	26.9
1980	13.0	10.2	32.5	25.7
1985	14.0	11.4	31.3	29.0
1988	13.1	10.1	31.6	26.8

[a]May be of any race.
[b]Not available.
Source: U.S. Bureau of the Census, *Money Income and Poverty Status in the United States: 1988*, Current Population Reports, Series P-60, no. 168, pp. 58–59.

Table 11-4   Percent of White, Black, and Hispanic origin Families in Poverty by Educational Level, 1988

Education	% of White	% of Black	% of Hispanic Origin[a]
None	35.9	[b]	39.0
Elementary:			
Less than 8 years	22.2	35.1	31.9
8 years	12.9	34.9	30.0
High School:			
1 to 3 years	14.9	40.7	31.7
4 years	6.8	24.7	16.0
College:			
1 year or more	2.7	11.5	8.4

[a]May be of any race.
[b]Not available.
Source: U.S. Bureau of the Census, *Money Income and Poverty Status in the United States: 1988*, Current Population Reports, Series P-60, no. 168, p. 68.

are so firmly entrenched in American society that the term *institutional racism* has been used to refer to them.

However, we should not obscure the progress made by African-and Hispanic-Americans. While their income in relation to whites remains substantially lower, the proportion of those who live in poverty has decreased substantially; the quality of housing occupied by ethnic minorities has improved; and members of these groups are also more likely to hold professional jobs and to graduate from college. In the next sections we explore political reasons for the progress and setbacks in achieving equality.

ETHNIC MINORITIES, CONGRESS, AND THE COURTS

The Fourteenth Amendment to the U.S. Constitution guarantees all citizens equal protection under the law, but this amendment is also an example of how ideas that sound rational can be used to maintain and perpetuate racial and ethnic discrimination. Until 1954, the Fourteenth Amendment served as legal grounds for *equal* but *separate* protection under the law. Segregation of blacks and whites in public schools, on public buses, and in other public (and private) places was condoned. Public facilities for blacks were supposed to be equal to facilities for whites (see *Plessy* v. *Ferguson,* 1896), but this was generally not the case. It was not until the middle of the twentieth century that the Supreme Court exercised its power in overturning the separate but equal doctrine set forth in the case of *Plessy* v. *Ferguson;* the civil rights movement had begun.

Separate but Not Equal

In 1954, a growing dissatisfaction among blacks with the separate but equal doctrine resulted in a Supreme Court ruling that marked the official recognition of racial inequality in America. Schools in Topeka, Kansas, were segregated but essentially equal in terms of physical conditions and quality of education. However, in the case of *Brown* v. *Board of Education of Topeka, Kansas,* the Supreme Court ruled that separate was not equal. In its decision, the Court took the position that "the policy of separating the races is usually interpreted as denoting the inferiority of the Negro Group." The Court also stated that "segregation with the sanction of law, therefore, has a tendency to retard the education and mental development of Negro children." The *Brown* decision remains a landmark case in the history of equal rights.

However, de facto segregation of schools due to neighborhood segregation continues to exist. For example, when children from inner-city black neighborhoods attend their neighborhood schools, the schools are almost totally composed of black students. One solution to de facto school segregation is busing. In 1971, in the case of *Swann* v. *Charlotte-Mecklenburg Board of Education,* the Supreme Court approved court-ordered busing of children to achieve integration in school districts that had a *history* of discrimination. However, in 1974 in *Milliken* v. *Bradley,* the Supreme Court ruled that mandatory busing across city-suburban boundaries to achieve integration is not required unless segregation has resulted from an *official* action. This decision means that de facto segregation is likely to remain in racially segregated areas.

Busing has been one of the most bitter controversies surrounding public school education in the United States. Parents often reject the idea of sending a child to a school several miles away when a neighborhood school is nearby. Parents—generally white parents—who purposely purchased homes in certain school districts are often angered when their child must be bused to a school that they feel is inferior. Critics point to the irony of forced busing. They believe busing has contributed to *white flight*—white families moving to avoid busing. Furthermore, they point to the trend toward private-school enrollments, which also thwarts efforts to integrate public schools. However, concern remains that without school integration, poor children will continue to receive their education in disadvantaged situations.

Educational inequality also results from the way public education is financed. The major source of school funding is the local property tax. Schools in middle- and upper-class areas have larger financial bases than schools in poor areas. These financial inequities have led to a call for equal educational expenditures for all school children, regardless of their communities' economic status. Several states now face court battles over the constitutionality of the mechanisms they use to fund public elementary and secondary school education. Unequal educational opportunities continue to prevent African- and Hispanic-Americans and those of other ethnic backgrounds from obtaining jobs that might increase their earning capacity and reduce their dependence on welfare programs. Social researchers have also noted that even less progress has been made in integrating institutions of higher education. Colleges and universities which have traditionally served white students and those which have traditionally served black students continue to do so. They have failed to become well integrated.[25] Declines in the number of black males attending college is also a serious concern.

The state of public school education in general is alarming. Drop-out rates are extremely high in many areas, especially for African-and Hispanic-American students, although Asian-American students continue to excel. For example, only half of adults of Hispanic origin have completed high school compared to 80 percent of the rest of the population. President Bush has said he would like to be known as the "education president," and as an indication of this, he called an "education summit" during his first year in office. The president has been particularly supportive of preschool programs like Head Start, which is supported with federal funds. He has also met with the states' governors to discuss educational goals in basic subjects, but since the role of the federal government in school financing and policy setting remains limited, educational issues are mostly left to local and state governments. There is no indication that the federal government will significantly increase its role in this arena.

The Civil Rights Act

Since the 1954 *Brown* decision, the single most important reform with regard to racial equality has been the Civil Rights Act of 1964. The act states:

1. It is unlawful to apply unequal standards in voter registration procedures, or to deny registration for irrelevant errors or omissions on records or applications.
2. It is unlawful to discriminate or segregate persons on the grounds of race, color, religion, or national origin in any public accommodation, including hotels, motels, restaurants, movies, theaters, sports arenas, entertainment houses, and other places that offer to serve the public. This prohibition extends to all establishments whose operations affect interstate commerce or whose discriminatory practices are supported by state action.
3. The attorney general shall undertake civil action on behalf of any person denied equal access to a public accommodation to obtain a federal district court order to secure compliance with the act. If the owner or manager of a public accommodation should continue to discriminate, he would be in contempt of court and subject to preemptory fines and imprisonment without trial by jury.

4. The attorney general shall undertake civil actions on behalf of a person attempting orderly desegregation of public schools.

5. The Commission on Civil Rights, first established in the Civil Rights Act of 1957, shall be empowered to investigate deprivations of the right to vote, study, and collect information regarding discrimination in America, and to make reports to the president and Congress.

6. Each federal department and agency shall take action to end discrimination in all programs or activities receiving federal financial assistance in any form. This action shall include termination of financial assistance.

7. It shall be unlawful for any employer or labor union with twenty-five or more persons after 1965 to discriminate against any individual in any fashion in employment, because of his race, color, religion, sex, or national origin, and an Equal Employment Opportunity Commission shall be established to enforce this provision by investigation, conference, conciliation, persuasion, and if need be, civil action in federal court.

Amendments to the act in 1968 prohibit housing discrimination. It has been more than twenty years since passage of the original Civil Rights Act, yet the balance of racial power has not shifted as dramatically as many African-Americans would like. As we shall see, actions of the Reagan and Bush administrations and some Supreme Court decisions have made civil rights activists wary of the future. Interestingly, Congress exempted itself from complying with the Civil Rights Act until 1988!

HOUSING: THE INTERFACE OF RACIAL AND CLASS DISCRIMINATION

The largest item in most household budgets is housing. Whether payments come in the form of the monthly rent or mortgage, housing has consumed an increasing portion of the personal budget. As far back as the Housing Act of 1949, Congress acknowledged the need for a "decent home and a suitable living environment for every American family." Yet the poor and ethnic minorities often have little choice in where they live, and the numbers of homeless have grown.

Housing policy in the United States—public and private, formal and informal—is perhaps the most pervasive remaining tool of racial discrimination. Segregation and discrimination have been evident in government housing programs. Section 235 of the 1968 Fair Housing Act became "the largest single subsidized housing program and the most controversial."[26] According to the U.S. Civil Rights Commission, the Federal Housing Administration (FHA) contributed to the sale of inferior homes to ethnic minorities under section 235 by delegating too much authority to private industry, which had failed to comply with the spirit of the Fair Housing Act and other civil rights legislation.[27]

Redlining has also contributed to inferior living arrangements for blacks, other ethnic minorities, and the poor. Redlining occurs when a bank, mortgage company, home insurance company, or other enterprise refuses to finance or insure property in certain areas. Redlined areas are generally those occupied by poor and minority groups. Inability to obtain financing and insurance further depresses the community. It is not only the private sector that has been accused of redlining. During the 1960s, the National Commission on Urban Problems charged the FHA with neglecting loans to poor and black applicants and with condoning policies that "aided, abetted, and encouraged" neighborhood deterioration.[28] And even as the 1990s approached, studies showed that equally qualified blacks were twice as likely as whites to be denied home mortgage loans.[29] African-Americans face more segregation barriers in obtaining housing than any other ethnic group; Hispanics, and especially Asians, have fared considerably better in this regard.[30]

Although Congress has taken measures to stop discrimination, neighborhood segregation remains a fact of life in most communities. Integration, required by law in schools and work places, has not been realized to an equal extent in the area of housing. The city of Yonkers, New York, gained national notoriety in 1988 when it refused to implement a housing desegregation order. The integration of neighborhoods could eliminate the need for busing and other aids, such as magnet schools (which offer special programs and courses of study to attract students), to encourage integration in public schools.

Unhappy with the federal government's resistance to expand the amount of affordable housing and faced with the growing number of homeless people in their communities, not-for-profit and church organizations have stepped in to rehabilitate existing housing and build new housing. They have made this housing available to poor and near-poor individuals of many ethnic groups. In order to battle continuing housing discrimination, Congress in 1988 toughened the Department of Housing and Urban Development's enforcement provision under the Fair Housing Act and added protection against discrimination for handicapped individuals and families with children. But recent scandals at HUD have included accusations that prominent Republicans and former HUD officials raked in millions of dollars in consulting fees in order to steer HUD contracts to particular firms and that private escrow agents siphoned off millions from the sale of foreclosed homes. There is hope, however, that the housing situation for low-income individuals will improve. A new housing bill passed by Congress in 1990 and expected to be signed by the President, is intended to reverse a ten year pattern of retrenchment by providing billions of dollars to communities to expand housing opportunities for those with limited opportunities. The illustration that follows provides a hopeful look at what is happening in some public housing projects whose residents are primarily poor families, many headed by women and ethnic minorities.

AFFIRMATIVE ACTION

There are many aspects of equal rights that continue to engender political concern. Affirmative action, for example, refers to policies that attempt to achieve equality in admissions and employment for women and members of ethnic minority groups. Affirmative-action programs are based on the belief that women and minorities should be admitted, hired, and promoted in proportion to their representation in the population. But to what extent should affirmative-action policies be pursued? Why is it not enough to pursue policies which do not discriminate against individuals because of gender and racial and ethnic background? Should policies go much further in order to reduce inequities in employment? Originally, the federal government pursued an approach of nondiscrimination. Examples of nondiscrimination are found in President Truman's decision to desegregate the military in 1946 and in Titles VI and VII of the 1964 Civil Rights Act. Nondiscrimination simply means that preferential treatment will not be given to selected groups.

ILLUSTRATION: CHANGING THE IMAGE OF PUBLIC HOUSING

On a sunny day in October, Kimi Gray was handed a gold key in a celebration marking the first time in U.S. history that public-housing residents could become the owners of their homes. To her, it was an occasion rich with meaning. "Poor people," she says, "are allowed the same dreams as everyone else." The event was a significant step in a revolution that has been moving through more than a dozen public-housing projects across America for 15 years. In these complexes, tenants have balked at the notion that poverty means helplessness and are taking over the management of their housing.

Getting the poor and mostly undereducated residents of public housing to assume responsibility for their dwellings has been hard, but not nearly so difficult as convincing politicians that it can be done. Gray, chairwoman of the Kenilworth-Parkside Resident Management Corp. in Washington, has been leading this fight since 1972. The decision to take control of the project was forced on Gray and her neighbors, she says. Plumbing was broken and heating was, at best, intermittent. So in 1981, deciding "things couldn't get much worse and we had to do something," Gray petitioned the District government to let residents take control. The mayor eventually agreed, and in January 1982 Gray's tenant management corporation began collecting rents, making repairs and running things for itself. What the corporation got was a run-down facility with bursting pipes, flooding basements and no one trained in physical-plant management. "It was crisis that brought us together," Gray says. Welfare mothers learned plumbing skills, children were pressed into clean-up patrols. The residents thrived, and Gray became a national spokeswoman for the movement.

This success led Gray to lobby Congress for changes in housing laws giving tenants the right to buy their homes from the government. The law went into effect in 1987. Prominent Republicans, including Ronald Reagan, flocked to her cause, but Kimi Gray is no conservative ideologue. Her success depends on Great Society programs such as Job Training to drive home traditional conservative values. "We want to bring families back together, restore our pride and respect," she says. Congressman Jack Kemp another fan of Gray's who co-sponsored the 1987 legislation, calls tenant management a "synthesis of New Deal programs and conservative thinking." Selling public-housing tenants their homes, he says, "gives the poor dignity and a stake in the American dream." The management association paid $1 for the title to Kenilworth-Parkside. In 1990 residents will be able to buy shares in their units.

Kenilworth-Parkside is a hub of activity. The grounds are clean and graffiti-free, and more than 100 residents work in businesses created by Gray's management corporation. These include the day-care center, a barber and beauty shop, a moving company and a construction-management firm. Gray's plans are boundless: She has started negotiations with the Department of Transportation to establish a "reverse commute" system for driving residents in vans to unfilled jobs in nearby suburbs.

At first glance, Gray seems an

unlikely leader of a growing national movement. She spent many of her 42 years living on welfare. Raised in a public-housing complex in Washington, Gray at 19 was the mother of five children with no husband. Self-pity, however, rarely troubled her. "My grandmother taught me I had to lie in my own bed and be responsible for my life."

The lesson was well learned, and since moving to Kenilworth-Parkside 22 years ago, Gray has rarely stopped pushing for her dreams. Soon after she arrived, she became president of the local day-care center. Later she organized "College Here We Come," a program that has helped send nearly 600 academically gifted youngsters from public housing to colleges throughout the U.S. Since 1981 Gray has helped create a wide range of programs for the 3,500 residents of the project that have paid off in myriad ways: in the past six years dependence on welfare has dwindled from 85% to 2%, administrative costs of the project have dropped by nearly two-thirds, and teenage pregnancies have been cut in half. Along the way, Gray's brand of tenant management has saved the District and Federal Government about $5.7 million in operating expenses. Says Kemp: "She is inspirational, and her mind is breathtaking. She might have been born poor, but there is no poverty in her."

Such praise has been hard won. In the early years, Gray was considered a radical and troublemaker. "I'd go to meetings and get so mad I'd yell and turn the place out," she says. Politicians tried to block her plans, so Gray used a tool no politician can ignore: votes. In 1976 she organized and registered to vote 12,000 public-housing tenants. As chairman of the city-wide public-housing board, Gray is now a local political power of the first order. The success at Kenilworth-Parkside hasn't come without struggle. Poverty can drive out hope, and Gray admits that at the start of the tenant-management struggle, "there were nights I cried myself to sleep because people wouldn't listen, didn't trust me or themselves."

Slowly, attitudes began to change,

aided by new tenant rules that Gray admits are neither gentle nor subtle. Example: residents must take turns serving as hall and building captains. "People don't throw trash on the ground when they know it soon will be their turn to pick it up," she says. Tenants can use the day-care center, but only if they are working or looking for work. Residents are expected to take care of their property, which means fixing broken toilets and sinks themselves. One member of each family must take six weeks of training in such subjects as personal budgeting, pest control and basic home repairs. A system of fines is imposed on residents who break the rules. "Being poor doesn't give you the right to be dirty or lazy," she says. Though the bylaws seem downright harsh, in six years only five families have been evicted for breaking them.

Conservative black scholar Robert Woodson argues that "people change their behavior in order to stay in Kenilworth-Parkside. It's a class-specific solution in which poor people help themselves." Woodson, whose National Center for Neighborhood Enterprise helps promote tenant management throughout the U.S., says that "the federal and state governments have spent nearly $1 trillion over the past 20 years in a largely failed effort to fight poverty. Now Kimi and others are taking it out of the hands of professionals and giving jobs to tenants."

Gray is the first to admit that tenant management and ownership are not the only antidotes to public housing and welfare, but she insists that her efforts can be duplicated elsewhere. "There are thousands of Kimi Grays in America who are willing to try," she says. Woodson agrees: "Kimi and other leaders are the last best hope for many of these public-housing projects. Tenant managers can't offer guarantees, but they hold great promise. The only thing worse than poverty is accepting the status quo."

Source: Jerome Cramer, "Turning Public Housing over to Resident Owners," *Time*, (December 12, 1988), pp. 15-16. Copyright 1988 Time Inc. Reprinted by Permission.

The quest for civil rights among blacks brought dissatisfaction with this method of achieving racial equality. There was concern that a more aggressive approach should be taken to promote equality in college admissions and in employment. One aspect of this concern spurred a debate as to whether quotas rather than goals should be used to achieve racial equality. Quotas are defined as "imposing a fixed, mandatory number or percentage of persons to be hired or promoted, regardless of the number of potential applicants who meet the qualifications,"[31] while a goal is a

> numerical objective, fixed realistically in terms of number of vacancies expected, and the number of qualified applicants available...If...the employer...has demonstrated every good faith effort to include persons from the group which was the object of discrimination...but has been unable to do so in sufficient numbers to meet his goal, he is not subject to sanction.[32]

In addition, the employer is not obligated to hire an unqualified or less qualified person in preference to a prospective employee with better qualifications.

The Philadelphia Plan of 1967, issued by the U.S. Office of Federal Contract Compliance, was one of the first examples of an affirmative-action plan. The plan required that those bidding on federal contracts submit plans to employ specific percentages of minority groups. Another quota-type plan was adopted in 1971 by the Federal Aviation Administration. This plan essentially placed a freeze on hiring any additional employees if every fifth vacant position was not filled by a minority member.

Opponents of quota setting generally believe that giving preferential treatment to minorities constitutes a violation of equal protection of the laws provided in the Fourteenth Amendment to the U.S. Constitution. In 1974, a federal court upheld this belief in its decision that the University of Washington Law School should admit Marco DeFunis, Jr. DeFunis had protested the university's decision to reject his application while admitting blacks with lower grades and test scores. Other cases charging *reverse discrimination* have also been heard by the courts. The Supreme Court ruled on the issue of admitting less qualified minority applicants over white applicants in the case of Alan Bakke. The Court determined that Bakke had been unfairly denied admission to the University of California Davis Medical School because his qualifications were stronger than those of some minority candidates admitted to the school. Proponents of the decision hoped the Bakke case would help change what they perceived to be a trend of reverse discrimination against whites. Opponents feared that the *Bakke* decision threatened the future of affirmative action. There are more recent reverse discrimination charges in California. The University of California at Berkeley has been accused of discriminating against whites by favoring black, Hispanic, and Filipino applicants. Complaints have also been leveled against the University of California system for using *more stringent* admissions requirements for Asian-Americans than other applicants. Asian-Americans generally have higher scores than other groups, and they have been admitted at rates higher than their representation in the population.

Concerns about threats to affirmative action mounted during the Reagan administration. The administration was accused of reversing a pattern of improvement in civil rights that began in the 1960s and had been supported under both Democratic and Republican administrations. Reagan's recommendations for appointments to the U.S. Civil Rights Commission and his attempts to get rid of some members raised the ire of most civil rights groups. Controversy also brewed in the Justice Department. During the Carter presidency the Justice Department had taken a strong role as a proponent of civil rights. It had, for example, helped to implement a court decree requiring the police and fire departments of Indianapolis to establish quotas for hiring and promoting women and blacks. But in 1984, the Supreme Court ruled in the case of *Firefighters Local Union No. 1784* v. *Stotts* that the jobs of blacks with less seniority cannot be protected at the expense of jobs of whites with more seniority. The Justice Department used this Supreme Court decision to get Indianapolis and forty-nine other jurisdictions to abandon the use of quotas. Lower federal courts have supported quota systems established under affirmative-action plans. The National Association for the Advancement of Colored People (NAACP) and others called the Justice Department action illegal.

Another aspect of affirmative action challenged by the Reagan administration was the use of class action suits to benefit *groups* of people rather than *individuals*. During Reagan's administration, the Equal Employment Opportunity Commission expressed its desire to address cases of discrimination against particular individuals rather than assisting classes of people who have been treated unfairly. William Bradford Reynolds, then head of the Justice Department, declared that what was needed was a color- and sex-blind society rather than a color- and sex-conscious one. He also contended that quotas are a form of discrimination.

The Supreme Court did deal a victory for affirmative action with two 1986 decisions (one involved Cleveland firefighters, the other a New York sheet metal workers union). According to these decisions, " ... federal judges may set goals and timetables requiring employers guilty of past discrimination to hire or promote specific numbers of minorities, even if the jobs go to people who are not themselves the proven victims of bias."[33] But Supreme Court rulings in 1989 again put affirmative action on shaky ground. In *City of Richmond* v. *J. A. Croson Co.*, it struck down a "set-aside" program that gave preference to minority-owned firms in awarding government construction contracts. However, the court later said that Congress could pass laws ordering affirmative action in awarding federal contracts. Other Supreme Court decisions have made it easier for white males to challenge affirmative action programs for women and minorities and more difficult for employees to bring discrimination suits because the burden of proof is shifted from employers to employees.

President Bush had difficulty finding an acceptable nominee to head the Civil Rights Commission, and he angered civil rights leaders when he vetoed a major civil rights bill that would have challenged recent Supreme Court rulings because he did not believe these rulings were "significant."[34] During the Reagan years, the NAACP, NOW, and other groups were outraged by the president's position on civil rights and the reductions in the number of discrimination cases pursued by the federal government in education, employment, and housing.[35] They hoped that Bush's position would be both "kinder" and "gentler" to them. Now their feeling is that given the Supreme Court's recent rulings and lack of a Bush civil rights agenda, the only recourse is for Congress to respond again, as it did with the Civil Rights Restoration Act.

Self-Help

Some black scholars have taken the position that affirmative action is no longer helping blacks. For example, Glenn Loury, a Harvard political economist, credits the civil rights movement and affirmative action for doing much to help some blacks, but he is concerned about solutions to the problems of other blacks who remain poor.[36] Loury believes the current problems of black communities—high unemployment, crime, teen pregnancy rates—must be attacked through mutual *self-help* among blacks whether or not government continues to help.

One way groups can help themselves is to exercise their right to vote. Since the 1940s, a number of major steps have been taken to insure that minorities are provided the same opportunities to vote as whites. In 1965, President Lyndon B. Johnson signed the Voting Rights Act. The act was designed to further insure, protect, and encourage the right to a voice in the electoral process. The act is periodically reviewed by Congress. At times, concern has been expressed that support for the act may be waning, but Congress has constantly made improvements in it to promote and protect voting rights.

To date, few blacks have served in Congress. Black mayors have been elected in some of America's larger cities—Los Angeles, Detroit, and Cleveland, Washington, D.C., and most recently, New York. The nation's first black governor, Douglas Wilder, was elected by Virginia voters in 1989. Among members of the 101st Congress, there were twenty-four black U.S. representatives but no black senators. The country recently had one Hispanic governor (elected in Florida), and there are eleven Hispanic representatives in Congress. Several large cities—Miami, San Antonio, and Denver, have had Hispanic mayors. Hispanics are the fastest growing ethnic group in the country. Their growth rate is five times higher than the rest of the U.S. population. This may result in Hispanic Americans being elected more frequently and exerting greater influence in elections at all levels of government. Although the 1980s was called by some "the decade of the Hispanic," the real political impact of this segment of the population will be felt in the years ahead.

NATIVE AMERICANS AND SOCIAL WELFARE

Native Americans are probably the ethnic group most seriously affected by social welfare problems. "Indians have the lowest income, worst health and the largest indice [sic] of social problems in the U.S."[37] Currently, only one Native American is serving in Congress, and congressional members from states with the largest Native American populations find it difficult to represent these constituents because Indians' needs often conflict with those of larger, more powerful constituent groups.[38] Many federal policy decisions have wrought especially unusual hardships for the large number of American Indian tribes in the United States (there are 504 federally recognized tribes and many more without federal recognition).[39] Today, it seems astonishing that American Indians were not accorded citizenship until 1924, that some remained slaves until 1935, and that New Mexico did not allow them to vote until 1940.[40] They have been robbed of land and mineral rights, which has deprived them of a livelihood. Many of the hardships have been attributed to attempts to force them to assimilate into the majority culture, despite substantial differences between their cultures—family structure, religion, and communication patterns—and that of whites. Native Americans have also faced displacement from their own reservations and have encountered problems in adapting to urban life.

In recognition of the abuses experienced by Native Americans, the Indian Self-Determination and Education Assistance Act of 1975 emphasized tribal self-government and the establishment of independent health, education, and welfare services, but more than fifteen years later, it is clear that such legislation has not lead to many improvements in the lives of Indian people. One of the worst degradations has been the removal of Indian children from their families to be raised by others. This practice was rationalized by welfare professionals who viewed Native American child-rearing practices as overly harsh.[41] The Indian Child Welfare Act of 1978 was designed to remedy problems in the placement of Native American children by restoring greater control over these decisions to Indian tribes. Priority for placement is now given to members of the child's own tribe rather than to nonIndian families.

The Bureau of Indian Affairs (BIA) is the primary federal agency responsible for assisting Native Americans in meeting their social welfare needs. Eighty-seven percent of its employees are Native Americans,[42] but the agency has long been criticized for its paternalistic and authoritarian attitude toward its clientele. Some critics have said, "The BIA takes care of Indians' money, land, children, water, roads, etc., with authority complete as that of a prison."[43] While criticism of the BIA has not been a secret, it was only in October 1987 that official action to investigate practices of the BIA began. Senator Daniel Inouye (D-Hawaii), chairperson of the Senate Select Committee on Indian Affairs, called for full investigative hearings after an astonishing series of articles appeared in *The Arizona Republic* claiming "widespread fraud, mismanagement and waste in the almost $3 billion-a-year federal Indian programs."[44] Other accusations were that oil companies with government assistance have bilked Indians of billions of dollars from oil and gas reserves.[45] The agency responsible for many of the health care needs of Native Americans is the Indian Health Service (IHS), formerly part of the BIA and now part of the federal Department of Health and Human Services. The IHS has also been the target of criticism, including charges of inadequate and incompetent treatment of patients.[46]

In 1980, Edward Carpenter assessed the status of American Indians in a social welfare journal article by stating "that a part of the problem is related to the Indian's cultural diversification and a history of limited tribal cooperation is probably true. However, the impact of the Indian's legal status, the failure of the Congress, and the concomitant administrative morass created by the BIA appear to be the critical variables."[47] Carpenter called for a clarification of the legal status of American Indians, greater accountability on the part of the BIA, and great use of educational programs by Native Americans, but most important, he called for a hands-off policy by nonIndians and a return of responsibility for planning to Native Americans. Ten years later, a special senate committee has recommended abolishing the BIA and replacing it with a program of direct financial grants to Indian tribes. But such major changes have been met with skepticism by Indians and nonIndians alike, and no one really thinks that massive changes will take place anytime soon.[48]

CONTROLLING IMMIGRATION

Except for American Indians, all other Americans are immigrants or the descendants of immigrants. More than one hundred years after the Statue of Liberty—a symbol of freedom for many immigrants—was erected, we are still debating immigration reform. The United States is composed of people from virtually every country and every cultural, ethnic, racial, and religious group, but laws to control immigration have existed since the 1800s. For example, as large numbers of Asians entered the U.S. and as they prospered, Americans felt threatened by their successes. The Chinese Exclusion Act of 1833 and the Oriental Exclusion Law of 1924 severely restricted the entrance of these groups, as did the Quota System Law of 1981 and the Immigration Act of 1924. Immigration policies have been much more favorable to others, such as northern Europeans, perhaps because of the similarity of their physical characteristics to many Americans.

The treatment of Japanese-Americans, after Japan attacked Pearl Harbor in 1941 and World War II erupted, serves as an especially disturbing example of discrimination against Americans of foreign backgrounds. Following the attack, Japanese-Americans were interned in ten relocation camps by President Franklin D. Roosevelt for fear that they might threaten U.S. security. Another reason given for their relocation was to protect Japanese-Americans from potential harm by Americans angered by Japan's attack.[49] However, interned Japanese-Americans did not believe this action was either necessary or benevolent. They were forced to give up their jobs and their possessions. To prove they were indeed Americans, many volunteered for the armed services. Internment ended in 1943 with the recognition that citizenship and loyalty to one's country, not racial characteristics, make one an American. But it was not until 1983 that the U.S. government actually acknowledged wrongdoing. The statement came as a result of the work of the Commission on Wartime Relocation and Internment of Civilians. In 1988, reparation payments were approved for the remaining sixty-thousand survivors of internment, but they were delayed due to opposition from some congressional members who said that the U.S. could not afford the payments.

In 1965, stringent national-origin quotas limiting the number of entrants from various countries were abolished. But new issues sprang to the forefront of immigration policy. The Vietnam War displaced and impoverished many Vietnamese who later sought refuge in the United States. Of special concern are *Amerasian* children, children born to American servicemen and Vietnamese women. Several thousand of these children still live in poverty in Vietnam since they were not brought to the United States by their fathers or charitable organizations.[50] Considered half-breeds in their place of birth, these children have found themselves ostracized. Establishing their fathers' identities is difficult; thus, many have been unable to come to the U.S. In other cases, fathers have been unable to locate their children, or they have faced bureaucratic problems in trying to get their children out of Vietnam. Squalid living conditions in Vietnam had left these children and their mothers with little hope for a brighter future, but under the Orderly Departure Program and the Amerasian Homecoming Act, the United States is attempting to bring all these Amerasians (many now young adults) and their families to America.

The issue of immigration to the United States, especially immigration involving Hispanics from Mexico and Central America, has gained increased attention. The Border Patrol of the U.S. Immigration and Naturalization Service (INS) has arrested as many as one million illegal aliens at the expansive Mexican-American border each year, and at least as many probably go undetected.[51] Is this type of immigration helpful or harmful to the United States? Illegal aliens are considered useful by farmers who hire them as cheap labor at critical times when others may not be willing to do the work. But some believe that in other sectors of the economy, illegal aliens take jobs away from legal aliens and Americans who need work.[52] Some object to the high costs of providing social services to illegal immigrants and of educating their children. Others believe that these costs are offset by income and Social Security taxes paid on wages, because illegal aliens who work do not receive benefits from these taxes. Since we do not know how many illegal aliens reside in the United States (estimates have ranged from two to six million[53]), it is difficult to weigh these costs and benefits.

In addition to those fleeing from Mexico and Central America, Haitian and Cuban refugees have also been of concern. The arrival of large numbers of illegal entrants from all these countries has also been unplanned. Since Cuba and Haiti are close to the tip of Florida, many have come en masse in boats, some losing their lives in the process. Cubans originally began immigrating to the United States in the 1960s seeking political asylum from the communistic Castro regime. In 1980 and 1981, a new influx of Cuban refugees prompted President Carter to institute an airlift program and to open three refugee processing centers in the United States. Some refugees came to join their families in the United States, but the convicted criminals and undesirables who were also sent caused criticism that Castro had used the U.S. as a dumping ground.

Immigration from Haiti was spurred by the overwhelming poverty on the small island. In addition, the now overthrown Duvalier government was considered especially repressive, and attempts to institute elections and an acceptable governing structure have resulted in continuing turmoil and violence. Under the Refugee Act of 1980, the definition of *refugee* does not include those leaving their country for economic reasons. Those who want to leave because of poverty are considered to be requesting *asylum*. The issue is critical because refugees have been entitled to the same welfare benefits (AFDC, food stamps, Medicaid) as U.S. citizens, but the provision of welfare benefits to those requesting asylum is open to question.[54] President Reagan called for an immigration policy that would "integrate refugees into our society without nurturing their dependence on welfare."[55] The recent Republican administrations have viewed Central American refugees as coming for *economic* reasons, but others believe they should be accorded *political* refugee status. Many blamed the U.S. for adopting foreign policies which added to the political strife in

Central America and increased the desire of Central Americans to immigrate to the U.S.

The *sanctuary* movement is another aspect of the immigration issue. Americans involved in the movement provide food, clothing, shelter, and jobs to immigrants. Most of those helped have been Salvadorans, Nicaraguans, and other Central Americans. Sanctuary workers feel their actions are justified even if they are helping people who entered the country illegally, because these individuals face grave political oppression and persecution in their homeland. But the INS and other officials have disagreed. They point to laws that make certain actions, such as transporting illegal aliens into the country, crimes. Several sanctuary workers have been convicted and jailed for assisting refugees. The changing political climate in Central America may serve to reduce the flow of illegal aliens, but poverty remains an important factor in the desire of individuals from countries like Mexico to live in the United States.

In an effort to stem illegal immigration, two types of approaches have been used—internal and external. Internal approaches occur *within* the U.S., such as punishing employers who hire illegal aliens and enforcing provisions such as deportation of those who entered illegally. External solutions focus on better enforcement at the *border* to prevent illegals from entering the country in the first place. In a *Wall Street Journal* article, a professor of international economics argued for greater emphasis on external solutions.[56] According to his perspective, internal controls would increase the number of illegal aliens because INS resources would be used to police employers rather than to stop more illegal aliens from crossing the border. With fewer border patrols it is easier for illegal aliens to cross into the United States. Furthermore, he claims that employer sanctions would increase, not reduce, the underclass status of aliens by making it more undesirable for employers to hire them. Experience in other countries suggests that employer sanctions have not been effective in reducing illegal employment. It may also be more effective to keep people out in the first place, because once they enter, the United States hesitates to deport them.

After years of debate, Congress passed the Immigration Reform and Control Act of 1986 incorporating both internal and external approaches. The main features of the law were amnesty for certain illegals, increased enforcement at the border, employer sanctions, and a temporary worker program. Amnesty was the most controversial provision. Under this provision, aliens who had illegally resided in the U.S. prior to 1982 and could prove this were allowed to remain and obtain citizenship. The irony of this stipulation was that "illegals" had previously had to hide their residence and had likely destroyed rent receipts and other records that could have been used to verify their residence. In order to qualify for amnesty, applicants could not have received welfare (such as AFDC and food stamps) previously and were prohibited from doing so for five years after legalization. The number of people who met the deadline for amnesty fell considerably short of official estimates. This may have been due to fear that families and friends residing illegally with those who qualified for amnesty might be found out and deported. There was also a substantial fee to apply for amnesty that might have served as a deterrent. A number of people balked at amnesty, contending that it unfairly penalized those who had been waiting to enter the U.S. through legal channels and that it might encourage even more individuals to enter illegally. However, the U.S. has been giving a clear message of intolerance for new illegals. Those accused of entering without permission are now being placed in detention rather than being allowed to remain free until a decision on their status is made.

The 1986 law also requires employers to verify that employees are eligible to work in the United States. Penalties for violation of this provision include fines and possible prison terms if the employer has a pattern of hiring illegal workers. Provisions in the law do prohibit employment discrimination against otherwise qualified and eligible applicants. As a concession to certain employers, primarily farmers, the law permits hiring foreign workers when domestic workers are not available. The law also contains more liberal rules for agricultural workers who wanted to remain in the country.

A new bill passed by Congress may put immigration policy in a new light by 1992 by *increasing* the number of persons allowed to enter the United States. This would make it easier for the relatives of new immigrants to join them in the United States, and it would make it easier for Central American refugees to remain in the country. The legislation would also reduce the favoritism shown to immigrants from certain countries, and it would increase the abilities of employers to bring in immigrants with needed skills such as in science and engineering. The legislation would also strike down past provisions which have banned individuals from entering the country because of their ideological beliefs or because they are homosexual. The President is expected to sign this bill.

Illegal aliens will be counted in the 1990 census. This is a controversial measure because it is likely to mean that states with large numbers of illegal aliens will gain more seats in Congress while other states will lose representation. Census counts also are used to determine the amount of federal funds received by states and communities for various purposes. The United States has begun to reckon with the issue of how much more immigration to allow, because as the population grows older, more younger workers of all types will be needed to support the economy and the Social Security retirement system. The large influx of Hispanics has already resulted in calls for better education, health care, employment, and other social services to ease their transition into the country and to bring them into the social, economic, and political mainstream.

SUMMARY

Sexism and racism manifest themselves in many areas of American life—education, employment, income, and political participation. The disadvantages that blacks, other ethnic groups, and women have endured place them in a position of being poorer than the rest of the population. Poverty, in turn, results in greater dependence on social welfare programs for these groups.

Ever since women won the right to vote, there have been movements to enact an equal rights bill for women. Opposition to equal rights centers on concerns that women may be forced into combat or may lose other privileges. Other arguments suggest that there are already a number of laws which prohibit discrimination in hiring and payment of wages to women workers. However, since women continue to encounter discrimination, supporters of an Equal Rights Amendment believe that a guarantee of equality should be a part of the U.S. Constitution. They have vowed to continue to press the issue.

Another welfare issue that concerns women—and also men—is abortion. The Supreme Court has upheld the right of women to abortions, but prochoice groups are concerned that recent Supreme Court decisions brought by a new conservative majority on the bench will erode abortion rights. Right-to-life groups have continued to oppose abortions on moral, religious, and biological grounds, while prochoice groups have defended the need for women to maintain the right to safe, legal abortions on demand. Congress finally passed a major child-care bill for low-income families in 1990 which President Bush signed into law, but the president vetoed family leave legislation.

The rights of gay men and lesbians have made their way onto the public policy agenda. Homosexuals have begun to make progress on the local level in gaining equal treatment, primarily in employment. The Supreme Court, however, has refused to overturn state laws that prohibit certain sexual acts between members of the same sex, and other issues, such as whether homosexuals can be barred from military service, have not been resolved.

Black Americans have faced a number of struggles in their fight for civil rights. A 1954 Supreme Court decision struck down the "separate but equal" doctrine by stating that separate public facilities are not equal facilities. This decision increased public school integration, but in many communities, neighborhood segregation continues to contribute to segregation in public schools. The Civil Rights Act of 1964 addressed a number of black Americans' concerns, including equal treatment in employment and access to public facilities. However, discrimination remains an issue. Even after controlling for education, African-Americans earn less than whites, and they continue to be disproportionately represented in public assistance programs. The vigorous support of civil rights given by presidents during the 1960s and 1970s waned during the Reagan administration. Civil rights advocates decried the lack of support. Late in the 1980s, the Supreme Court also dealt some setbacks to affirmative action policies. President Bush has voiced strong support for the rights of women and ethnic minorities but his veto of a 1990 civil rights bill made civil rights advocates skeptical of his position. Hispanic-Americans have fared better in a number of ways than blacks and are the fastest growing ethnic group in the United States.

Other minority groups also face discrimination. Native Americans are among the most severely affected. The Indian Self-Determination and Education Assistance Act of 1975 was an attempt to restore to Native Americans planning power over their social welfare programs. The Bureau of Indian Affairs has been criticized for its treatment of Native Americans and has been the target of a congressional investigation.

The current refugee situation also poses problems. Refugees from Vietnam, Cuba, Haiti, Mexico, Central America, and other countries have sought to live in the United States. America has been a haven for many seeking freedom from oppression, but the large numbers of people entering this country illegally has resulted in debate over what appropriate immigration policy should be. Legislation in 1986 granted amnesty to many persons residing illegally in the United States, and beginning in 1992 Congress will permit an increased number of individuals from many countries to enter the United States.

NOTES

1. Diana Pearce and Harriette McAdoo, *Women and Children: Alone and in Poverty* (Washington, D.C.: National Advisory Council on Economic Opportunity, 1981).
2. United States Bureau of the Census, *Money Income and Poverty Status in the United States 1988*, Current Population Reports, series P–60, no. 168 (Washington, D.C., 1988), p. 2.
3. United States Bureau of the Census, *Statistical Abstract of the United States, 1988* (Washington, D.C., 1988), p. 353.
4. United States Bureau of the Census, *Money Income and Poverty Status 1988* (Washington, D.C., 1989), pp. 42–43.
5. Ibid., p. 76.
6. Martynas A. Ycas and Susan Grad, "Income of Retirement-Aged Persons in the United States," *Social Security Bulletin, 50*, 7, July 1987, p. 12.
7. This section relies on Department of Health, Education and Welfare, *Social Security and the Changing Roles of Men and Women* (Washington, D.C.: U.S. Government Printing Office, February 1979), Chaps. 1 and 2.
8. Ibid.
9. The remainder of this section relies on "Women and Social Security," *Social Security Bulletin 48*, no. 2 (February 1985), pp. 17–26.
10. Figures are from the U.S. Bureau of the Census and are found in Paul Clancy, "Women's Pay Gap Narrows," *USA Today* (September 4, 1987) p. 1.
11. "Women Narrow the Salary Gap," *Austin American-Statesman* (February 8, 1989), p. C9.
12. See M. Anne Hill and Mark R. Killingsworth, eds., *Comparable Worth: Analyses and Evidence* (Ithaca: New York State School of Industrial and Labor Relations, Cornell University, 1989).
13. This paragraph relies on Jill Johnson Keeney, "Not a Crazy Proposal," *Louisville Times*, 1984, reprinted in *The Office Professional 5*, no. 2 (February 15, 1985), p. 7.
14. "Job Description Limits," *The Wall Street Journal* (January 7, 1985), p. 18.
15. U.S. Bureau of the Census, *Statistical Abstract of the United States, 1989*, (Washington, D.C., 1989), p. 256.
16. Ibid., p. 252.
17. "ERA Ratification Status Summary," *ERA Countdown Campaign* (Washington, D.C.: National Organization for Women, 1981), p. A.
18. Quoted in David Klein, "The ERA is Wanted Dead or Alive in Florida," *Tallahassee Democrat* (January 21, 1982).
19. These polls are summarized in "Strong Public Support for ERA," in *ERA Countdown Campaign* (Washington, D.C.: National Organization for Women, 1981), p. C.
20. U.S. Bureau of the Census, *Statistical Abstract of the United States, 1984*, (Washington, D.C., 1984), p. 68.
21. United States Commission on Civil Rights, *The Federal Response to Domestic Violence* (Washington, D.C.: U.S. Government Printing Office, January 1982), pp. iv–v.
22. Lisa G. Lerman, "Legal Help for Battered Women," in Joseph J. Costa, ed., *Abuse of Women: Legislation, Reporting, and Prevention* (Lexington, Mass.: Lexington Books, 1983), p. 29.
23. *Family Violence: The Battered Woman* (Austin, Tex: League of Women Voters of Texas Education Fund, 1987), p. 33.
24. U.S. Department of Health and Human Services, *Characteristics and Financial Circumstances of AFDC Recipients, 1986*, p. 1; U.S. Bureau of the Census, *Statistical Abstract of the United States, 1988*, (Washington, D.C.) p. 353; *1989*, p. 363.
25. "Racial Progress Assessed," *Tallahassee Democrat* (April 9, 1984), p. 3A.
26. Chester W. Hartman, *Housing and Social Policy* (Englewood Cliffs, N.J.: Prentice-Hall, 1975), p. 136.
27. Ibid., p. 139.

28. Ibid.
29. Bill Dedman, "Study Finds Racial Lending Gap," *Austin American-Statesman* (January 22, 1989), pp. A1, 16; and Constance L. Hays, "Boston Banks to Fight Race Gap in Mortgages," *The Champaign-Urbana News-Gazette* (January 29, 1990), p. B5.
30. Douglas S. Massey and Nancy A. Denton, "Suburbanization and Segregation in U.S. Metropolitan Areas," *American Journal of Sociology, 94,* 3 (November 1988), pp. 592–626.
31. *Federal Policies on Remedies Concerning Equal Employment Opportunity in State and Local Government Personnel Systems* (March 23, 1973), cited in Felix A. Nigro and Lloyd G. Nigro, *The New Public Personnel Administration* (Itasca, Ill: F.E. Peacock, 1976), p. 21.
32. Ibid.
33. See Frank Trippet, "A Solid Yes to Affirmative Action," *Time* (July 14, 1986), p. 22.
34. Joan Biskiysic, "Old Rights Commission Fight Seems Ready to Erupt," *Congressional Quarterly* (November 11, 1989), p. 3060.
35. For a summary of reductions in litigation see D. Lee Bawden and John L. Palmer, "Social Policy: Challenging the Welfare State," in John L. Palmer and Isabel V. Sawhill, eds., *The Reagan Record* (Cambridge: Ballinger, 1984), pp. 204–206.
36. Glenn C. Loury, "The Moral Quandry of the Black Community," *Public Interest,* no. 79 (Spring 1985), pp. 9–22.
37. Thomas H. Walz and Gary Askerooth, *The Upside Down Welfare State* (Minneapolis: Elwood Printing, 1973), p. 25.
38. Michael P. Shea, "Indians Skeptical of Report Urging Program Overhaul," *Congressional Quarterly* (January 13, 1990), p. 98.
39. Bureau of Indian Affairs, *American Indians Today.*
40. Gerald Thomas Wilkinson, "On Assisting Indian People," *Social Casework 61,* no. 8 (1980), pp. 451–54.
41. Joseph J. Westermeyer, "Indian Powerlessness in Minnesota," *Society,* no. 10 (March/April 1973), p. 50, cited in Walz and Askerooth, *Upside Down Welfare State,* p. 31.
42. Shea, "Indians Skeptical."
43. Walz and Askerooth, *The Upside Down Welfare State,* p. 25.
44. Chuck Cook, "BIA Ordered to Prepare for Inquiry," *The Arizona Republic* (October 16, 1987), pp. A1, 5.
45. Chuck Cook, Mike Masterson, and M. N. Trahant, "Indians Are Sold out by the U.S.," *The Arizona Republic* (October 4, 1987), pp. A1, 18, 20.
46. Chuck Cook, Mike Masterson, and M. N. Trahant, "Child's Suffering is Cry for Reform," *The Arizona Republic* (October 7, 1987), p. A18.
47. Edward M. Carpenter, "Social Services, Policies, and Issues," *Social Casework 61,* no. 8 (1980), pp. 455–61.
48. Shea, "Indians Skeptical."
49. Donald Brieland, Lela B. Costin, and Charles R. Atherton, *Contemporary Social Work: An Introduction to Social Work and Social Welfare,* 2nd ed. (New York: McGraw-Hill, 1980), p. 404.
50. Walter W. Miller, "Vietnamese Society Rife with U.S. 'Footprints,'" *Austin American-Statesman* (April 2, 1985), p. A16.
51. Cheryl Arvidson, "Phantom Barrier," *Austin American-Statesman* (November 11, 1984), p. A8.
52. Ibid.
53. R. A. Zaldivar, "Independent Study Casts Doubt on U.S. Illegal Alien Estimate," *Austin American-Statesman* (June 25, 1985), p. A4.
54. Nadine Cohadas, "Cuban Refugee Crisis May Prompt Introduction of Special Legislation," *Congressional Quarterly Weekly Report* (May 31, 1980), p. 1496.
55. Statement issued by President Reagan on July 30, 1980 cited in *Congressional Quarterly Weekly Report* (August 22, 1981), p. 1577.
56. This argument is based on Jagdish N. Bhagwati, "Control Immigration at the Border," *The Wall Street Journal* (February 1, 1985), p. 22.

12

IMPLEMENTING AND EVALUATING SOCIAL WELFARE POLICY
What Happens after a Law Is Passed

Americans once thought that social problems could be solved by passing laws, creating bureaucracies, and spending money. The general belief was that if Congress adopted a policy and appropriated money for it, and if the executive branch organized a program, hired peopled, spent money, and carried out the activities designed to implement the policy, then the effects of the policy felt by society would be those intended by Congress. But today, there is a growing uneasiness among both policy makers and the general public about the effectiveness and costs of many government programs. Americans have lost their innocence about government and public policy.

IMPLEMENTING PUBLIC POLICY

Many problems in social welfare policy arise *after a law is passed*—in the implementation process. Policy implementation includes all of the following activities designed to carry out the intention of the law:

1. Creating, organizing, and staffing agencies to carry out the new policy, or assigning new responsibilities to existing agencies and personnel;
2. Issuing directives, rules, regulations, and guidelines to translate policies into specific courses of action;
3. Directing and coordinating both personnel and expenditures toward the achievement of policy objectives.

There is always a gap—sometimes small, sometimes very large—between a policy decision and its implementation. Some scholars of implementation take an almost cynical view of the process. One such scholar writes:

> Our normal expectation should be that new programs will fail to get off the ground and that, at best, they will take considerable time to get started. The cards in this world are stacked against things happening, as so much effort is required to make them move. The remarkable thing is that new programs work at all.[1]

THE POLITICS OF IMPLEMENTATION

What are the obstacles to implementation? Why isn't implementation a *rational* activity? Why can't policies be directly implemented in decisions about organization, staffing, spending, regulation, direction, and coordination? The obstacles to successful implementation are many, but we might categorize them in terms of (1) communications, (2) resources, (3) attitudes, and (4) bureaucratic structure.[2]

Communications

The first requirement for effective policy implementation is that the people who are running the program must know what they are supposed to do. Directives must not only be received but must also be clear. Vague, inconsistent, and contradictory directives confuse administrators. Directives give meanings to policies—meanings which may not be consistent with the original intent of the law. Moreover, poor directives enable people who disagree with the policy to read their own biases into programs. The Department of Health and Human Services (DHHS), the largest department of the federal government, is divided into many offices that are responsible for administering numerous programs (see Figure 12–1). These programs affect every community in the United States. The DHHS must constantly struggle with the problem of maintaining accurate communications.

Generally, the more decentralized the administration of a program, the more layers of administration through which directives must flow, and the less likely that policies will be transmitted accurately and consistently. Whatever the advantages of decentralization, prompt, consistent, and uniform policy implementation is *not* usually found in a decentralized structure.

Frequently, Congress (and state legislatures) is deliberately vague about public policy. Congress and the president may pass vague and ambiguous laws largely for *symbolic* reasons—to reassure people that "something" is being done to help with a problem. Yet is these cases, Congress and the president do not really know exactly what to do about the problem. They therefore delegate wide discretion to administrators, who act under the authority of broad laws to determine what, if anything, actually will be done. Often Congress and the president want to claim credit for the high-sounding principles enacted into law but do not want to accept responsibility for any unpopular actions that administrators must take to implement these principles. It is much easier

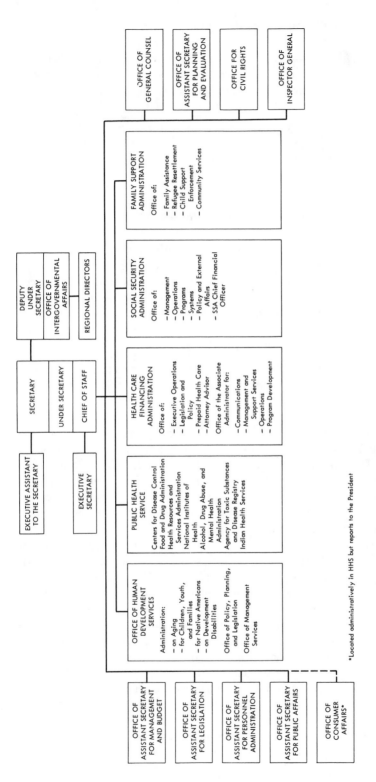

FIGURE 12-1 Organization chart of the Department of Health and Human Services (*The United States Government Manual*, 1988/1989, Office of the Federal Register, revised June 1, 1988, p. 291)

for political leaders to blame the "bureaucrats" and pretend that government regulations are a product of an "ungovernable" Washington bureaucracy.

One of the best examples of this problem occurred during the War on Poverty. In the Economic Opportunity Act of 1964, Congress and President Johnson wrote into the law a provision calling for "maximum feasible participation of the poor" in community action agencies and other programs supported by the Office of Economic Opportunity. But no one knew exactly what that phrase meant. How were the poor to help plan and run the programs? Did this phrase authorize poverty workers to organize the poor politically? Did this phrase mean that social activists paid by the government should help organize the poor to pressure welfare and housing agencies for better services? The policy was not clear, and its implementation was confusing and frustrating. Eventually, of course, the Office of Economic Opportunity was abolished, in part because of its problems in administering an unclear mandate from Congress.

Resources

Policy directives may be clear, accurate, and consistent, but if administrators lack the resources to carry out these policies, implementation fails. A critical resource is *funds*—the money needed to implement new policies. Sometimes new policies require only limited funds to implement, but many new policies and programs seem doomed to fail because insufficient resources are allocated for start-up and mainte-nance functions. Implementation studies can be useful in determining whether modifications in rules, regulations, and procedures are needed to successfully launch new policies and programs, but it has become increasingly difficult to acquire the funds needed to conduct these studies.

Resources also include *staff* with the proper *skills* to carry out their assignments, and with the *authority* and *facilities* necessary to translate a paper proposal into a functioning public service. It is common for government agencies to claim that problems with implementation arise from undersized staffs. And many of the claims are true. Indeed, one tactic of opponents of a particular policy, even after they lose the fight over the actual policy in Congress, is to try to reduce the size of the budget and staff that is to implement the policy. The political battle does not end with the passing of a law. It continues each year in fights over resources to implement the law.

It is not enough that there be adequate funds to hire personnel to carry out a policy. In addition, the personnel must have the skills necessary for the job. Staffing is especially difficult in new types of programs, especially those few that are highly innovative and experimental. There are frequently no ready-made reserves of people who are trained for the program and who know what to do. Yet there is always pressure to show results as quickly as possible to insure the continuation of the program the next year.

Sometimes agencies lack the authority, even on paper, to implement policy. Agencies may not be authorized to issue checks to citizens, or to purchase goods or services, or to provide funds to other government agencies, or to withdraw funds in the case of noncompliance, or to go to court to force compliance. Some agencies may have the necessary authority (for example, to withhold federal funds from a local government agency or a nonprofit corporation), but they may be reluctant to exercise this authority because of the adverse political repercussions that might ensue. Agencies that do not have the necessary authority to carry out policy (or agencies that fear that exercising that authority may be politically risky) must rely on *persuasion* and *cooperation*. Rather than order local agencies, private corporations, or individual citizens to do something, higher level officials may consult with them, ask for their cooperation, or appeal to their sense of public service. Successful implementation generally requires goodwill on the part of everyone involved. Agencies or administrators who must continually resort to sanctions will probably be unsuccessful in the long run.

Physical facilities may also be critical resources in implementation. Programs generally need offices, equipment, and supplies. It is difficult to run an agency without telephones. Yet many government agencies (especially new agencies) find it difficult to acquire the necessary facilities to carry out their programs. Once again, government administrators must rely on persuasion and cooperation to get other government agencies to provide them with offices, desks, telephones, travel approvals, and so on.

Attitudes

If administrators and program personnel sympathize with a particular policy, it is likely to be carried out as the original policy makers intended. But when the attitudes of agency administrators and staff personnel differ from those of the policy makers, the implementation process becomes very complex. Because administrators always have some discretion (and occasionally a great deal) in implementation, their attitudes toward policies have much to do with how a program is implemented. When people are told to do things with which they do not agree, inevitable slippage will occur between a policy and its implementation.

Generally, social service personnel enter the field because they want to "help people"—especially aged, poor, and handicapped individuals, and others less fortunate in society. There is seldom any attitudinal problem in social agencies in implementing policies to *expand* social services. But highly committed social service personnel may find it very difficult to implement policies to *cut back* or eliminate social services.

Conservative policy makers are aware of the social service orientation of the *welfare bureaucracy*. They do not believe, for example, that welfare administrators really try to enforce work provisions of welfare laws.[3] They believe that the welfare bureaucracy has been partially responsible for the growth in numbers of recipients over the years; eligibility requirements, these conservatives say, have been given liberal interpretation by sympathetic administrators. They believe that welfare administrators are a major obstacle to policies designed to tighten eligibility, reduce overlapping benefits, and encourage work.

In government agencies, it is generally impossible to remove people simply because they disagree with a policy. Direct pressures are generally unavailable: Pay increases are primarily across-the-board; promotions are infrequent and often based on seniority. Again, *selling* a policy—winning support through persuasion—is more effective in overcoming opposition than threatening sanctions is. If those who implement policy cannot be convinced that the policy is good for their clients or themselves, perhaps they can be convinced that it is less offensive than other alternatives which might be imposed by policy makers.

Bureaucratic Structure

Previously established organizations and procedures in bureaucracies may hinder implementation of new policies and programs. Bureaucratic *inertia* slows changes in policy. Administrators become accustomed to ways of doing things (standard operating procedures, or SOPs), and become resistant to change.

Standard operating procedures are routines that enable officials to perform numerous tasks every day; SOPs save time. If every worker had to invent a new way of doing things in every new case, there would not be enough time to help very many people. SOPs bring consistency to the handling of cases; rules are applied more uniformly.

However, SOPs can also obstruct policy implementation. "Once requirements and practices are instituted, they tend to remain in force long after the conditions that spawned them have disappeared."[4] Routines are not regularly reexamined; they tend to persist even when policy changes. If SOPs are not revised to reflect policy changes, these changes are not implemented. Moreover, many people prefer the stability and familiarity of existing routines, and they are reluctant to revise their patterns. Organizations have spent time, effort, and money in developing these routines. These *sunk costs* (so called because they are not recoupable) commit organizations to limit change as much as possible.

SOPs can make it difficult to handle nonconforming cases in an individual fashion. Even though particular cases may not conform to prewritten SOPs, many administrators and staff try to force these cases into one or another of the established classifications. Frustrations arise for social service personnel when they attempt to obtain services for those in need who do not meet specific eligibility criteria. Over a period of time these frustrations may contribute to staff *burnout.*

The organization of bureaucracies also affects implementation, especially when responsibility for a policy is dispersed among many governmental units. There are more than 80,000 governments in the United States: a national government, 50 state governments, about 3,000 county governments, over 19,000 city governments and nearly 17,000 township governments, not to mention 15,000 school districts and 30,000 special districts.[5] Even within the national government, many departments have responsibility for social welfare programs—for example, the Department of Health and Human Services has responsibility for AFDC and Medicaid; the Department of Agriculture administers the Food Stamp and WIC programs; the Department of Labor administers the JTPA and Job Corps programs. The story of Ernie in the accompanying illustration indicates some of the red tape that clients often face in dealing with bureaucracies. Consider how much more frustrating this type of situation must be for those who are ill, disabled, or have less formal education.

The more governments and agencies involved with a particular policy, and the more independent their decisions, the greater the problems of implementation. Separate agencies become concerned with their own turf—areas they believe should be their exclusive responsibility. Agencies may fight each other to hold on to their traditional areas of responsibility. Proponents of particular programs may insist to Congress that their programs be administered by separate agencies that are largely independent of traditional executive departments. They fear that consolidating program responsibilities will downgrade the emphasis that a separate department will give to their particular program.

ILLUSTRATION: BUREAUCRACY AND SOCIAL SERVICES

A CLIENT'S VIEW OF THE FOOD STAMP PROGRAM

Ernie* applied for food stamps in a Rustbelt state a month after one of the local factories had laid off two-thousand employees. The administration of the program in this state was handled through county welfare offices. Even though the county paid for none of the direct costs of the food stamps, the county commission had been grumbling about not receiving adequate reimbursement from the state for its administrative costs. One organization of welfare clients had charged that county officials were engaged in a purposeful "slow down" of the eligibility process, hoping to deter prospective clients from applying for food stamps.

The day before, Ernie had called the county welfare office and inquired about the procedures for applying for food stamps. The first dozen or so times he had gotten a busy signal. Finally, a secretary answered and told him in a matter-of-fact voice that he should come to the welfare office the next morning as early as possible in order to complete an application. Ernie asked whether he would need to bring any type of documentation with him, and he was told only that the procedures would be fully explained by the social worker when he completed the application.

*Ernie is a pseudonym; nevertheless, he was a real client.

The next morning, Ernie arrived at the county welfare office at 7:45 A.M. to find that there was no available parking within at least six blocks and that there was already a line stretching out the door and around three sides of the block. (The day was December 8, the temperature was just about freezing, and a light drizzle was falling.) Most of the other people in line were women with small children. One woman had four preschool children with her. She spent most of her time holding them, changing diapers and feeding the two smaller children, and trying to keep the two older ones from wandering into the street.

Around 10:00 A.M., Ernie finally made it into the building. He really didn't mind waiting the next forty-five minutes; after all, it was warmer inside. Just before 11:00 A.M., he completed his application and handed it to the secretary. She studied it for a moment and then asked, "Where are our supporting documents?" When Ernie asked for an explanation, she said, "You know, rent receipts, medical bills, stuff like that."

Ernie was very puzzled (and very angry) about not being given this information on the phone the previous day, but there was nothing he could do except go home and gather this documentation. He returned again the next morning, and the line was somewhat shorter. By 10:30 A.M., he had reached the secretary's desk and handed her his application and a fistful of documents. She indicated that this would, indeed, be adequate and invited him to sit in the waiting room to see the social worker.

At 1:30 P.M., Ernie had his first meeting with the social worker who reviewed his application and documents and informed him that he did not meet the eligibility requirements because he had refused employment the week before. (Ernie had turned down a job offer that would have required him to relocate to a community approximately sixty miles away. His reason was simple: He didn't have the money to move his family.) Unlike many food stamp applicants, Ernie didn't take this social worker's opinion as the final word. He asked to see her supervisor and was given an appointment the following week.

Ernie brought xeroxed copies of the legislation governing the Food Stamp program to the next meeting, as well as copies of the state's and county's administrative guidelines for program operation and eligibility determination. He had done this on the advice of one of his friends, a union shop steward who had helped several others denied benefits by county welfare officials. He also let the supervisor know that he knew thoroughly the procedures for appeal and that he intended to take this case "all the way to the county commission." After a five minute meeting, she approved Ernie's application.

The secretary issued Ernie a card certifying his eligibility, and then he received his next surprise. He happened to live in a state where food stamp distribution was handled by private banks. Applicants were certified by the county welfare office and then sent across the street to the bank to pick up their stamps.

The first thing that Ernie noticed upon entering the bank was a sign with large red lettering stating: "All Food Stamp Clients Must See Cashier No. 3." He could tell from the size of the lines which cashier was distributing food stamps. He also noticed that the bank's other customers seemed to resent the presence of food stamp clients. Some cast sidelong glances; others openly verbalized their hostility.

Ernie's next surprise came when he and his wife went to the supermarket to purchase groceries with their food stamps, but that's a completely different story....

Source: Reprinted from Diana M. DiNitto and C. Aaron McNeece, *Social Work: Issues and Opportunities in a Challenging Profession* (Englewood Cliffs, N.J.: Prentice Hall, 1990), pp. 229–30.

Some fragmentation of programs may be desirable. The argument for federalism—the division of governmental responsibilities between the national government and the fifty state governments—is that it allows each state to deal more directly with conditions confronting that state. Government "closer to home" is sometimes thought to be more flexible and manageable than a distant bureaucracy in Washington.

However, when programs and services are fragmented, coordination of policy is difficult. This is true whether we are talking about the fragmentation of responsibilities among different agencies of the national government or the division of responsibilities between the national government and the fifty states. Uniformity is lost. Consider, for example, the nation's fifty separate AFDC programs. These are *state-administered* programs with federal financial assistance. The federal government pays over half of the costs of AFDC. Yet actual average benefits given to AFDC families range from less than $200 per month in a number of southern states to over $400 per month in several northern and western states.[6]

EVALUATING SOCIAL POLICY

In recent years, there has been a growing interest in *policy evaluation*—in learning about the consequences of public policy. Government agencies regularly report how much money they spend, how many individuals ("clients") are given various services, and how much these services cost. Congressional committees regularly receive testimony from influential individuals and groups about how popular or unpopular various programs and services are. But *even if* programs and policies are well-organized, financially possible, efficiently operated, widely utilized, and politically popular, the questions still arise: "So what?" "Do they work?" "Do these programs have any beneficial effects on society?" "What about people *not* receiving the benefits or services?" "What is the relationship between the costs of the program and the benefits to society?" "Could we be doing something else of more benefit to society with the money and human resources devoted to these programs?"

Can the federal government answer these questions? Can it say, for example, that AFDC, SSI, Food Stamps, and Medicaid are accomplishing their objectives; that their benefits to society exceed their costs; that they are not overly burdensome to taxpayers; that there are no better or less costly means of achieving the same ends? In 1970, one surprisingly candid report by the liberal-oriented think tank, the Urban Institute, argued convincingly that the federal government *did not know* whether most of the things it was doing were worthwhile. This report stated:

> The most impressive finding about the evaluation of social programs in the federal government is that substantial work in this field has been almost nonexistent.
>
> Few significant studies have been undertaken. Most of those carried out have been poorly conceived. Many small studies around the country have been carried out with such lack of uniformity of design and objective that the results rarely are comparable or responsive to the questions facing policy makers....
>
> The impact of activities that cost the public millions, sometimes billions, of dollars has not been measured. One cannot point with confidence to the difference, if any, that most social programs cause in the lives of Americans.[7]

Now, one would surely think that since these words were written, great improvements would have been made in evaluating social welfare policies. However, two authors writing about job programs indicate that barriers to progress in policy evaluation persist. They said:

> Despite nearly twenty years of continuous federal involvement [in job creation and training programs], we still have to do a good deal of guesswork about what will work and for whom. We have had substantial and ongoing difficulties in identifying what works, for whom, and why. This has been, in large part, because of an unwillingness on the part of Congress and policy makers to allow for adequate experimentation in the delivery of employment and training services.[8]

POLICY EVALUATION AS A RATIONAL ACTIVITY

From a rational perspective, policy evaluation involves more than just learning about the consequences of public policy. Consider the following definitions by scholars in the field:

> *Policy evaluation* is the objective, systematic, empirical examination of the effects [which] ongoing policies and programs have on their target in terms of the goals they are meant to achieve.[9]

> *Evaluation research* is viewed by its partisans as a way to increase the rationality of policy making. With objective information on the outcomes of programs, wise decisions can be made on budget allocations and program planning. Programs that yield good results will be expanded; those that make poor showings will be abandoned or drastically modified.[10]

> *Formal evaluation* is an approach which uses scientific methods to produce reliable and valid information about policy outcomes but evaluates such outcomes on the basis of policy-program objectives that have been formally announced by policy makers and program administrators. The major assumption of formal evaluation is that formally announced goals and objectives are appropriate measures of the worth or value of policies and programs.[11]

These definitions of policy evaluation assume that the goals and objectives of programs and policies are clear, that we know how to measure progress toward these goals, that we know how to measure costs, and that we can impartially weigh benefits against costs in evaluating a public program. In short, these definitions view policy evaluation as a *rational* activity (see also the illustration entitled "A Rational Model of Program Evaluation").

Ideally, the evaluation of a program would include all of its effects on real world conditions. Evaluators would want to (1) identify and rank all of the goals of a program; (2) devise measures to describe progress toward these goals; (3) identify the *target* situation or group for which the program was designed; (4) identify nontarget groups who might be affected indirectly by the program (*spillover* effects), and nontarget groups who are similar to the target groups but did not participate in the program or receive its direct benefits (*control group*); (5) measure program effects on target and nontarget groups over as long a period of time as possible; (6) identify and measure the costs of the program in terms of all the resources allocated to it; and (7) identify and measure the indirect costs of the program, including the loss of opportunities to pursue other activities.

Identifying target groups in social welfare programs means defining the part of the population for whom the program is intended—poor, sick, or homeless persons, and so on. Then, the desired effect of the program on the members of the target population must be determined. Is it to change their physical or economic conditions in life—their income, their health, their housing? Or is it to change their behavior—put them to work in the private or public sector or increase their physical and social activity? Is it to change their knowledge, attitudes, awareness, or interest—to organize poor neighborhoods, to pressure slum landlords into improving housing conditions, to increase voter turnout among the poor and ethnic minorities, to discourage unrest, riots, and violence? If multiple effects are intended, what are the priorities (rankings) among different effects? What are the possible *un*intended effects (side effects) on target groups—for example, does public housing achieve better physical environments for the urban poor at the cost of increasing their segregation and isolation from the mainstream of the community?

In making these identifications and measurements, the evaluators must not confuse *policy outputs* (what governments do) with *policy impacts* (what consequences these government actions have). It is important *not* to measure benefits in terms of government activity alone. For example, the number of dollars spent per member of a target group (per pupil educational expenditures; per capita welfare expenditures; per capita health expenditures) is not really a measure of the *impact* of government activity. We cannot be content with counting how many times a bird flaps its wings; we must learn how far the bird has flown. In assessing the *impact* of public policy, we cannot simply count the number of dollars spent or clients served, but rather we must identify the changes in individuals, groups, and society brought about by public policies.

Identifying the effects of a program on *nontarget* groups is equally important. For example, what effects will proposed welfare reforms have on social workers, social welfare bureaucracies, working families who are not receiving public assistance, taxpayers, and others? Nontarget effects are often negative effects or costs (such as the displacement of poor residents as a result of urban renewal), but they sometimes turn out to be benefits (such as the boon to grocers who accept food stamps).

Evaluators must also determine whether the program's goals are long-range or immediate. When will the benefits and costs be felt? Is the program designed for a short-term, emergency situation or is it a long-term, developmental effort? Many impact studies show that new or innovative programs have short-term positive effects—for example, Head Start and other educational programs. The newness of the program, or the realization by the target group that it is being given special treatment and is being watched closely (the *Hawthorne* or *halo effect*) may create measurable changes. But these positive effects may disappear as the novelty and enthusiasm of the new program wear off. Another problem is that longitudinal studies that assess the far-reaching impacts of social welfare programs are rarely conducted owing to constraints of time and money. This leaves us with little information with which to assess the long-term consequences of most social welfare programs.

Perhaps the most difficult problem confronting evaluators is weighing costs against benefits. Benefits may be measured in terms of bettering human conditions—improved education, improved medical care for the poor, better nutrition, steady employment, and so on. Costs are usually measured in dollars. But we cannot measure many of the values of education, health, or self-esteem in dollars alone. Cost savings are not the only goals that society wants to achieve.

THE MANY FACES OF PROGRAM EVALUATION

Most governments make some attempt to assess the utility of their programs. These efforts usually take one or more of the following forms.

Public Hearings

Public hearings are the most common type of program review. Frequently, legislative committees ask agency heads to give formal or informal testimony regarding the accomplishments of their programs. This usually occurs near budget time. In addition, written *program reports* or *annual reports* may be provided to legislators and interested citizens by agencies as a *public information* activity. However, testimonials and reports of program administrators are not very objective means of program evaluation. They frequently magnify the benefits and minimize the costs of programs.

Site Visits

Occasionally, teams of legislators, high-ranking federal or state officials, or expert consultants (or some combination of all of these people) will descend upon agencies to conduct investigations "in the field." These teams can interview workers and clients and directly observe the operation of the agency. They can accumulate impressions about how programs are being run, whether they have competent staffs, whether the programs seem to be having beneficial effects, and perhaps even whether or not the clients (target groups) are pleased with the services.

ILLUSTRATION: A RATIONAL MODEL OF PROGRAM EVALUATION

Several ideal, rational models of program evaluation have been proposed. Social scientists Peter Rossi and Howard Freeman suggest that evaluation research should include three important types of questions:

1. *Program Conceptualization and Design Questions*
   Is a social problem appropriately conceptualized?
   What is the extent of the problem and the distribution of the target population?
   Is the program designed to meet its intended objectives?
   Is there a coherent rationale underlying it?

Have chances of successful delivery been maximized?
What are the projected or existing costs?
What is the relationship between costs and benefits?

2. *Program Monitoring Questions*
   Is the program reaching the specified target population?
   Are the intervention efforts being conducted as specified in the program design?

3. *Program Utility Questions*
   Is the program effective in achieving its intended goals?
   Can the results of the program be explained by some alternative

process that does not include the program?

What are the costs to deliver services and benefits to program participants?

Is the program an efficient use of resources, compared with alternative uses of resources?[a]

[a]Peter H. Rossi and Howard E. Freeman, *Evaluation: A Systematic Approach,* 4th ed. (Newbury Park, Cal.: Sage Publications, 1989), pp. 45, 46, 52. Reprinted by permission of Sage Publications, Inc.

It is also possible to identify a "Theoretical Model of Program Development" to assist in understanding exactly what stage of the policy process is being evaluated. One such model is shown here:

Evaluative research might be directed at any of the linkages suggested in the diagram. For example, one might want to inquire whether the program's administrative structure is effective in meeting program objectives or whether the program's activities have any impact on society.

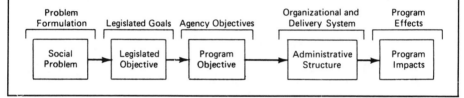

Program Measures

The data developed by the agencies themselves generally describe program or *output* measures—for example, the number of recipients of various welfare programs; the number of individuals in work-training programs; the number of hospital beds available. But these output measures rarely indicate the *impact* these numbers have on society—for example, improvements in the living conditions of poor families; the success of work trainees in later finding and holding useful employment in the nation's work force; the actual health gains of the nation in terms of sickness, life spans, death rates, and so on.

Comparison with Professional Standards

In some areas of social welfare activity, professional associations have developed their own *standards* of benefits and services. These standards may be expressed in terms of the maximum number of cases that a child protective service worker can handle effectively; or in the minimum number of hospital beds required by a population of one hundred thousand people; or in other ways. Actual governmental outputs can be compared with these "ideal" outputs. While this kind of study can be helpful, it still focuses on the *outputs* and not on the *impacts* that government activities have on the conditions of target and nontarget groups. Moreover, the standards are usually developed by professionals who themselves may be unsure about what the *ideal* levels of benefits and services should be. There is very little hard evidence that ideal levels of government outputs have any significant impact on society.

Formal Designs: Experimental Research

The "classic" research design for evaluating policies and programs employs two comparable groups—an *experimental group* and a *control group*—that are equivalent in every way *except* that the policy has been applied only to the experimental group.[12] After the application of the policy for a given length of time, its impact is measured by comparing changes in the experimental group with changes, if any, in the control group. Initially, control and experimental groups must be identical in every possible way. Research subjects are assigned randomly to the two groups and the program must be applied only to the experimental group. Postprogram differences between the two groups must be carefully measured. Also, every effort must be made to make certain that any observed postprogram differences between the two groups can be attributed to the program and not to some other intervening cause that affected one of the groups as the program was administered. This classic research design is preferred by social scientists because it provides the best opportunity for estimating changes that can be directly attributed to policies and programs (see Figure 12–2 for a model of the classic research design).

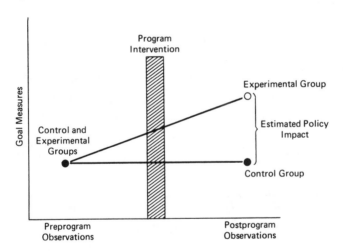

FIGURE 12–2:   "Classic" research design.

Formal Designs: Quasi-Experiments

It is frequently impossible to conduct controlled experiments in public policy, because sometimes the human beings involved cannot be placed arbitrarily in experimental or control groups just for the sake of program evaluation. Indeed, if experimental and control groups are really identical, the application of *public* policy to one group of citizens and not the other may violate the "equal protection of the laws" clause of the Fourteenth Amendment of the U.S. Constitution. Differential treatment of people with the same social problems also raises *ethical* concerns. Social workers and other professionals may find it unacceptable to deny what *may* be a promising treatment to those in need regardless of the need for better program evaluation. Frequently, it is only possible to compare individuals and groups who have participated in programs with those who have not, or to compare cities, states, and nations that have programs with those that do not. Comparisons are made to detremine whether the group that *did* participate in the program is better off than the group that did *not* participate in the program. The problem is to try to eliminate the possibility that any difference between the two groups in goal achievement may really be caused by some factor *other than* experience with the program. For example, we may compare the job records of people who have participated in JTPA programs with those who have not. The former JTPA participants may or may not have better post program job records than other groups. If they do not, it may be because JTPA trainees were less skilled to begin with; if they do, it may be because JTPA officials *creamed off* the local unemployed and gave service only to those who already possessed skills and job experience. Thus, quasi-experimental research designs, like most social science research, still leave room for discussion and disagreement. (See Figure 12–3 for a model of the quasi-experimental research design.)

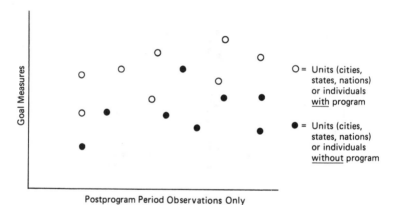

Postprogram Period Observations Only

FIGURE 12–3:   Quasi-experimental research design.

Formal Designs: Time Series

Another research design is the before-and-after study—a comparison of conditions before and after a policy or program has been adopted. Usually only the target group is examined. This design may be the only choice in jurisdictions where no control or comparison groups can be identified. When several observations are made of conditions *before* the program is adopted, and then when several observations are made *after* the program is adopted, this is generally referred to as a *time series*. These observations are designed to show program *impacts; but* it is very difficult to know whether the changes, if any, have come about as a result of the program itself or as a result of other changes which were occurring in society at the same time. (See Figure 12–4 for a model of the time-series research design.) For example, a program evaluator may be faced with the problem of determining whether a high school drug education program reduced the frequency of students' drug use or whether a decrease in the supply of drugs in the community was responsible for producing this effect.

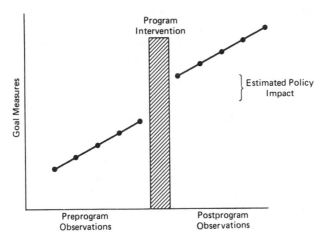

FIGURE 12–4: Time-series research design.

POLICY EVALUATION AS A POLITICAL ACTIVITY

Program evaluation may resemble scientific and rational inquiry, but it can never really be separated from politics. Let us consider just a few of the political problems that make rational policy evaluation difficult, if not impossible.

Unclear, Ambiguous Program Goals

Evaluators are often told to evaluate a program and yet are not informed of its goals or purposes. Reading the language of the original legislation that established the program may not be very helpful; legislative language frequently uses fuzzy words— "improve the conditions of life of the poor," "improve the health of society," "enhance the quality of life." Even interviews with the original legislative sponsors (congressional members, state legislators, county commissioners, or city council members) may produce ambiguous, or even contradictory, goals. Often the evaluators, at the risk of offending someone, must define the goals or purposes themselves. In this way, evaluation itself becomes a political activity.

Symbolic Goals

Many programs and policies have primarily symbolic value. They do not actually change the conditions of target groups but rather make these groups feel that their government "cares." Of course, a government agency does not welcome a study that reveals that its efforts have no tangible effects. Indeed, such a finding, if widely publicized, might reduce the symbolic impact of the program by telling target groups of its uselessness.

Unhappy Findings

Agencies and administrators usually have a heavy investment—organizational, financial, psychological—in current programs and policies. They are predisposed against findings that these programs do not work, involve excessive costs, or have unexpected negative consequences. If a negative report is issued, the agency may adopt a variety of strategies to offset its recommendations. (See the illustration, "What To Do If Your Agency's Program Receives a Negative Evaluation.")

Program Interference

Most serious studies of public programs involve some burdens on ongoing program activities. Accomplishing the day-to-day business of an agency is generally a higher priority in the mind of an administrator than making special arrangements for evaluation. Program evaluation also requires funds, facilities, time, and personnel, and administrators may not want to sacrifice these resources from regular program activities.

Usefulness of Evaluations

Program administrators are clearly dissatisfied with evaluative studies that conclude that "The program is not achieving the desired results." Not only is such a finding a threat to the agency, but standing alone, it fails to tell administrators *why* the program is failing. Evaluative studies are better received at the agency level when they include some action recommendations that might conceivably rescue the program. But even when evaluative studies show programs to be failures, the usual reaction is to patch things up and try again.

Evaluation by Whom?

One of the central political questions in evaluation is the determination of who will do the evaluation. From the perspective of the agency and its clients, the evaluation should be done by the agency or by an organizational representative of its clients. This type of *in-house* evaluation is most likely to produce favorable results. The next best thing, from the agency's perspective, is to allow the agency to contract with a private firm for an *outside* evaluation. A private firm that wants to win future contracts from the agency, or from any other agency, is very hesitant about producing totally negative evaluations. The worst evaluation arrangement, from the agency's perspective is to have an outside evaluation conducted by an independent office (the Congressional Budget Office, the General Accounting Office, or a state comptroller's office, for example). Agency staff members fear that outsiders do not understand clearly the nature of their work or the problems faced by the clients they serve and that this will hurt the program's evaluation.

ILLUSTRATION: WHAT TO DO IF YOUR AGENCY'S PROGRAM RECEIVES A NEGA-TIVE EVALUATION

Even in the face of clear evidence that your favorite program is useless, or even counterproductive, there are still a variety of administrative strategies to save it:

1. Claim that the effects of the program are long-range and cannot be adequately measured for many years.

2. Argue that the effects of the program are general and intangible, and that these effects cannot be identified with the crude methodology, including statistical measures, used in the evaluation.

3. If an experimental research design was used, claim that withholding services or benefits from the control group was unfair; and claim that there were no differences between the control and experimental groups because of a knowledge of the experiment by both groups.

4. If a time series research design was used, claim that there were no differences between the "before" and "after" observations because of other coinciding variables that hid the effects of the program. That is to say, claim that the "after" group would be even *worse* without the program.

5. Argue that the lack of differences between those receiving the program services and those not receiving them only means that the program is not sufficiently intensive, and that this indicates the need to spend *more* resources on the program.

6. Argue that the failure to identify any positive effects of the program is a result of the inadequacy of the evaluation research design and/or bias on the part of the evaluators.

THE GUARANTEED ANNUAL INCOME EXPERIMENTS

Many social scientists argue that *policy experimentation* offers the best opportunity to determine the impact of public policies. Such experimentation includes selection of equivalent experimental and control groups, the application of the policy to the experimental group only, and careful comparisons of differences between the experimental and the control groups after the application of the policy. The argument for experimental social research is that it can save money in the long run. The opposite approach is taken when giant public programs are created without any prior knowledge about whether they will work. One economist writes:

> The fact is that there have been few effective ways for determining the effectiveness of a social program before it is started; indeed, in most cases it is impossible even to forecast the cost of a new program until it has been in operation for a long time.
> Clearly this situation is not conducive to sound and effective decision making.[13]

Perhaps the most well-known example of an attempt by the federal government to experiment with public policy is the New Jersey Graduated Work Incentive Experiment funded by the Office of Economic Opportunity. The experiment was designed to resolve some serious questions about the effect of welfare payments on the incentives for poor people to work.[14] In order to learn more about the effects of the present welfare system on human behavior and, more important, to learn more about the possible effects of proposed programs for guaranteed family incomes, the OEO funded a three-year social experiment involving 1,350 families in New Jersey and Pennsylvania. The research was conducted by the Institute for Research on Poverty of the University of Wisconsin.

Debates over welfare reform had generated certain questions that social science could presumably answer with careful, controlled experimentation. Would a guaranteed family income reduce the incentive to work? If payments were made to poor families with employable male heads, would the men drop out of the labor force? Would the level of the income guarantee or the steepness of the reductions in payments due to increases in earnings make any difference in work behavior? Because the United States does not provide a guaranteed minimum income to families, because welfare payments to families are generally not tapered off gradually in relation to earnings, and because at the time of the study many states did not make welfare payments to two-parent families in which the primary breadwinner was unemployed, these questions could only be directly answered through *policy experimentation.*

But policy experimentation created some serious initial problems for the OEO. First of all, any experiment involving substantial payments to a fair sampling of families would be expensive. For example, if payments averaged $1,000 per year per family, and if each family had to be observed for three years, and if one thousand families were to be involved, a minimum of $3 million would be spent even *before* any consideration of the costs of administration, data collection, analysis and study, and reporting. Ideally, a *national* sample should have been used, but it would have been more expensive to monitor than a local sample, and differing employment conditions in different parts of the country would have made it difficult to sort out the effects of income payments from variations in local job availability. By concentrating the sample in one region, it was hoped that local conditions would be held constant. Also ideally, *all* types of low-income families should have been tested, but that procedure would have necessitated a large sample and greater expense. So only poor families with an able-bodied male between the ages of eighteen and fifty-eight were selected; the work behavior of these men in the face of a guaranteed income was of special interest.

To ascertain the effects of different levels of guaranteed income, four guarantee levels were established. Some families were chosen to receive 50 percent of the Social Security Administration's poverty-level income, others 75 percent, others 100 percent, and still others 125 percent. In order to ascertain the effects of graduated payments in relation to earnings, some families had their payments reduced by 30 percent of their outside earnings, others 50 percent, and still others 70 percent. Finally, a control sample was observed—low-income families who received no payments at all.

The experiment was initiated in August 1968 and continued until September 1972. But political events moved swiftly and soon engulfed the study. In 1969, President Nixon proposed to Congress the Family Assistance Plan (FAP), which would have guaranteed all families a minimum income of 50 percent of the poverty level and a payment reduction of 50 percent for outside earnings. The Nixon administration had not waited to learn the results of the OEO experiment before introducing the FAP. Nixon wanted welfare reform to be his priority domestic legislation, and the bill was symbolically numbered HR 1 (House of Representatives Bill 1).

After the FAP bill had been introduced, the Nixon administration pressured the OEO to produce favorable supporting evidence in behalf of the guaranteed income—specifically, evidence that a guaranteed income at the levels and graduated sublevels proposed in the FAP would not reduce incentives to work among the poor. The OEO obliged by hastily publishing a short report, "Preliminary Results of the New Jersey Graduated Work Incentive Experiment," that purported to show that there were no differences in the outside earnings of families receiving guaranteed incomes (experimental group) and those not (control group).[15]

The director of the research, economics professor Harold Watts of the University of Wisconsin, warned that "the evidence from this preliminary and crude analysis of the results is less than ideal." But he concluded that "no evidence has been found in the urban experiment to support the belief that negative-tax type income maintenance programs will produce large disincentives and consequent reductions in earnings."[16] Moreover, the early results indicated that families in all experimental groups, with different guaranteed minimums and different graduated payment schedules, behaved in a similar fashion to each other and to the control group receiving no payments at all. Predictably, later results confirmed the preliminary results, which were used to assist the FAP bill in Congress.[17]

However, when the results of the Graduated Work Incentive Experiment were later *reanalyzed* by the RAND Corporation (which was not responsible for the design of the original study), markedly different results were produced.[18] The RAND Corporation reported that the Wisconsin researchers working for OEO had originally chosen New Jersey because it had no state welfare programs for "intact" families—families headed by an able-bodied, working age male. The guaranteed incomes were offered to these intact families to compare their work behavior with control-group families. But six months after the experiment began, New Jersey changed its state law and offered all poor families rather substantial welfare benefits—benefits equal to those offered to participants in the experiment. This meant that for most of the period of the experiment, the control group was offered benefits equivalent to those given the experimental group—an obvious violation of the experimental research design. The OEO-funded University of Wisconsin researchers had not considered this factor in their research. Thus, they concluded that there were no significant differences between the work behaviors of experimental and control groups, and they implied that a national guaranteed income would not be a disincentive to work. The RAND Corporation researchers, on the other hand, considered the New Jersey state welfare program in their estimates of work behavior. RAND concluded that a guaranteed annual income program would cause recipients to work six and one-half fewer hours per week than in the absence of such a program. In short, the RAND study suggests that a guaranteed annual income *would* produce a substantial disincentive to work.

The RAND study was published in 1978 after enthusiasm in Washington for a guaranteed annual income program—or *welfare reform*—had already cooled. The

RAND study conflicted with the earlier OEO study and confirmed the intuition of many congressional members that a guaranteed annual income would reduce willingness to work. The RAND study also suggested that a *national* program might be very costly and involve some payments to nearly half the nation's families! Finally, RAND noted that its own estimates of high costs and work disincentives may "seriously understate the expected cost of an economy-wide...program." In spite of the conflicting evidence, one conclusion can be drawn from the analyses of the New Jersey Graduated Work Incentive Experiment. Policy makers are still unable to agree on the types of social welfare programs needed to reduce poverty and the conditions that might produce serious disincentives to work.

SUMMARY

Implementing public policy can be a difficult task for administrators of social welfare programs. Implementation involves a number of activities, including organizing and staffing agencies, translating policies into specific courses of action, and spending funds to operate programs. One major obstacle to successful implementation is determining the intent of social policies, because this is not always clearly defined in legislation. Other problems include obtaining sufficient resources, overcoming negative attitudes toward a program, and seeing that bureaucratic structures do not prevent the program from operating smoothly.

Americans no longer believe that social problems can be eliminated by merely passing laws and spending money for new welfare programs. We are increasingly concerned with obtaining evidence about whether social programs actually work. A rational approach to social policy evaluation includes identifying and ranking program goals and objectives, developing ways to measure these goals, identifying target and nontarget groups that might be affected, measuring tangible and intangible program effects, and measuring direct and indirect program costs. Several types of research designs lend themselves to evaluative studies of social welfare policies and programs. These are experimental designs, quasi-experimental designs, and time-series designs.

But policy evaluation is no less political than other aspects of the policy process. Evaluation is political for a number of reasons. Program goals and objectives are not always clear, but evaluators must evaluate something, even if everyone does not agree. Some program goals are more symbolic than tangible, and the symbolic goals are even more difficult to evaluate than the tangible. No administrator wants to receive a negative program evaluation. Administrators generally criticize unfavorable evaluations and take steps to counteract negative findings. Evaluations are disruptive to the day-to-day work of the agency and take time and resources from other activities. Also, an evaluation may not provide useful information about how to improve the program. In-house evaluations tend to be positive, and outside evaluations are more likely to be critical or ambivalent about the program. The well-publicized evaluations of the New Jersey Graduated Work Incentive Experiment are an example of the politics of policy evaluation.

NOTES

1. Jeffrey Pressman and Aaron Wildavsky, *Implementation* (Berkeley: University of California Press, 1973), p. 109.
2. This discussion relies on George C. Edwards, *Implementing Public Policy* (Washington, D.C.: Congressional Quarterly, 1980).
3. See Daniel P. Moynihan, *The Politics of a Guaranteed Income* (New York: Vintage Books, 1973), p. 220.
4. Herbert Kaufman, *Red Tape* (Washington, D.C.: Brookings Institution, 1977), p. 13.
5. U.S. Bureau of the Census, *Statistical Abstract of the United States, 1989* (Washington, D.C.: 1989), p. 266.
6. Ibid., p. 367.
7. Joseph S. Wholey and Associates, *Federal Evaluation Policy* (Washington, D.C.: Urban Institute, 1970), p. 15.
8. Laurie J. Bassi and Orley Ashenfelter, "The Effect of Direct Job Creation and Training Programs on Low-Skilled Workers," in Sheldon H. Danzinger and Daniel H. Weinberg, eds., *Fighting Poverty: What Works and What Doesn't* (Cambridge: Harvard University Press, 1986), p. 150.
9. David Nachmias, *Policy Evaluation* (New York: St. Martin's, 1979), p. 4.
10. Carol H. Weiss, *Evaluation Research: Methods of Assessing Program Effectiveness* (Englewood Cliffs, N.J.: Prentice-Hall, 1972), p. 2.
11. William N. Dunn, *Public Policy Analysis: An Introduction* (Englewood Cliffs, N.J.: Prentice-Hall, 1981), p. 345.
12. For further discussion of classic experimental research, see Fred N. Kerlinger, *Foundations of Behavioral Research, 3rd ed.* (New York: Holt, Rinehart & Winston, 1986), especially Chapter 19. For a discussion of the need for this type of research in the area of public policy, see Bassie and Ashenfelter, "The Effect of Direct Job Creation."
13. David N. Kershaw, "A Negative Income Tax Experiment," in David Nachmias, ed., *The Practice of Policy Evaluation* (New York: St. Martin's, 1980), pp. 27–28.
14. See Harold M. Watts, "Graduated Work Incentives: An Experiment in Negative Taxation," *American Economic Review 59* (May 1969), pp. 463–72.
15. U.S. Office of Economic Opportunity, *Preliminary Results of the New Jersey Graduated Work Incentive Experiment* (February 18, 1970). Also cited in Alice M. Rivlin, *Systematic Thinking for Social Action* (Washington, D.C.: Brookings Institution, 1971).
16. Harold M. Watts, "Adjusted and Extended Preliminary Results from the Urban Graduated Work Incentive Experiment" (University of Wisconsin, Institute for Research on Poverty, rev. June 10, 1970), p. 40. Also cited in Rivlin, *Systematic Thinking*, p. 101.
17. David Kershaw and Jerelyn Fair, eds., *Final Report of the New Jersey Graduated Work Incentive Experiment* (University of Wisconsin, Institute for Research on Poverty, 1974).
18. John F. Cogan, *Negative Income Taxation and Labor Supply: New Evidence from the New Jersey-Pennsylvania Experiment* (Santa Monica, Cal.: RAND Corporation, 1978).

NAME INDEX

288

SUBJECT INDEX